RAWAS

THE ART OF RAWAS

Conversations with Nazik Yared

Edited by Heather Reyes

SAQI

Cover painting: THE AMUSEMENT PARK, *2000 (detail)*

British Library Cataloguing-in-Publication Data
A catalogue record of this book is available from the British Library

ISBN 0 86356 909 9
EAN 9-780863-569098

Design Carla Salem and Hatem Imam
Photographs of paintings Gerard & Co, Albert Saikali and Baha'a Rifai
Photographs of the Artist Gilbert Hage
Color Separation Leogravure
Printing Calligraph Printing and Trading, Beirut, Lebanon
Paper Euro Art Silk 150 g.
Binding Baayno Bookbinders

This edition first published 2004

SAQI
26 Westbourne Grove
London W2 5RH
www.saqibooks.com

Contents

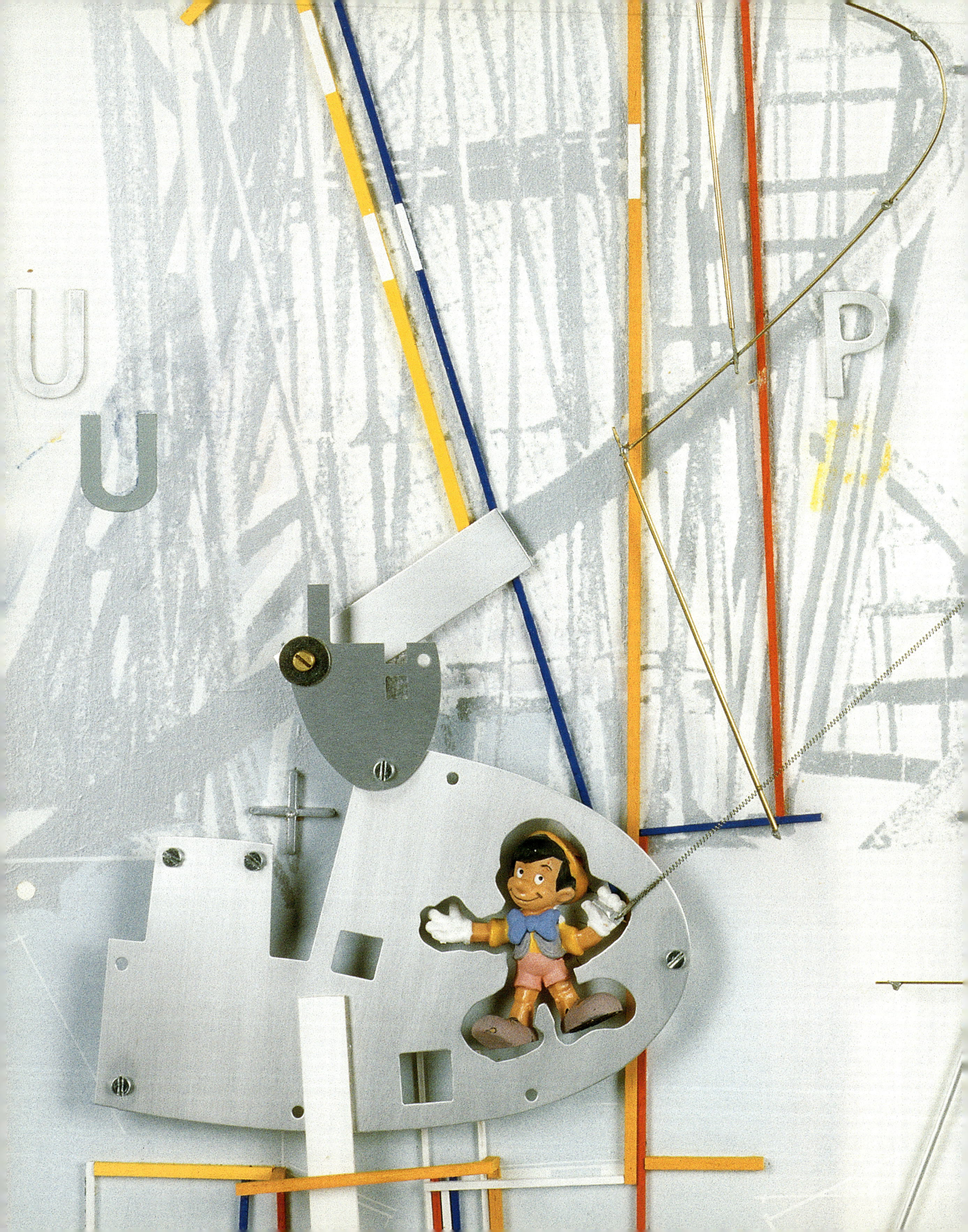
U
U
P

Foreword

Mohammad Rawas (signs M. El Rawas) is one of the most innovative Lebanese artists on the contemporary scene. His art is multifaceted and dynamic, using symbols and references from different categories of art and from human experience to create ambiguous worlds that seem to stand outside a particular place or time. His paintings take on an intriguing life of their own, nourished by inner tensions and a powerful sense of alienation from specific cultural contexts. He is dedicated to the endless quest of manipulating paint and mixed media, and to breaking the boundaries of conventional pictorial techniques.

The text which follows is based on a number of interviews with Rawas, conducted by Nazik Saba Yared, and on additional material contributed directly by the artist. It is hoped that the reader will enjoy hearing Rawas's own voice as he gives a fascinating insight into his life, his working techniques and the many influences that have shaped his powerful and unique artistic vision – as well as providing detailed comments on many of the works reproduced in this volume.

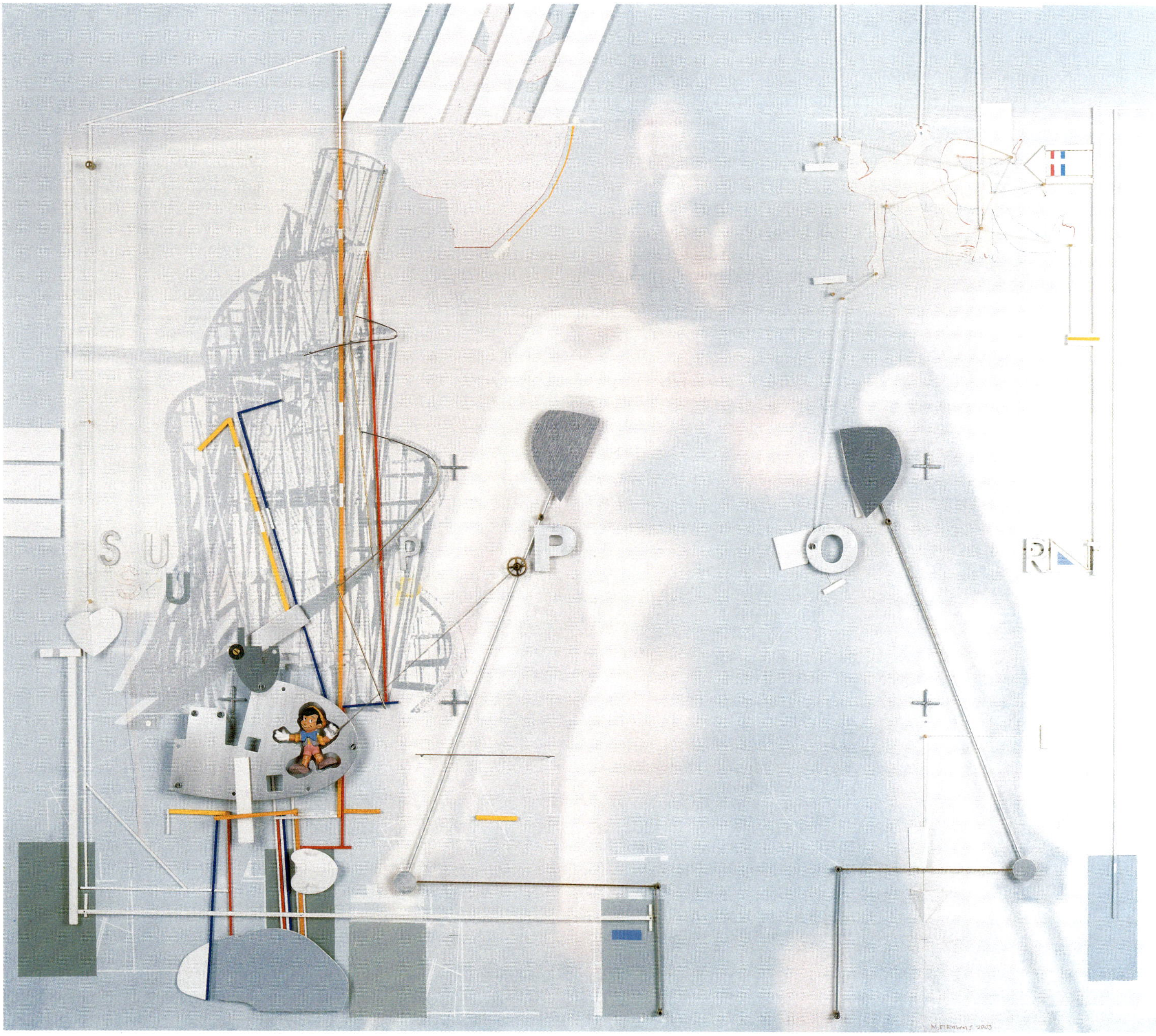

SUPPORT, 2003
Silkscreen, oil and assemblage on plywood panel
88 x 98 x 3 cm
Collection Mr. & Mrs. O. Hamza

Exhibited at Sursock Museum Salon d'Automne, Beirut, 2003

Page 5
SUPPORT, 2003 (detail)

Beginnings

I was born on 26 May 1951, on Beirut's Tariq al-Jadida (New Road). It was so named because it lay in an unbuilt area on the city's western outskirts – at that time just dunes of clean sand and reeds with only one other building apart from the one we lived in. We occupied the ground floor of the two-storey building belonging to my uncle. It was a small apartment with a big window from which you could see the distant seashore. The house had a garden with lots of flowers and fruit trees tended by my grandmother. Over time, buildings mushroomed around us and, with the rapid spread of these concrete constructions, the garden disappeared and the once two-storey building was transformed into a six-floor apartment block. I was angry and sad to lose the horizon of the seashore, to lose the garden and watch the unplanned construction of tall buildings as they rose, suffocatingly, all around us. Our flat became dark and lost the sunlight that had once brightened it. Even now I hate to live in a building's lower storeys not lit by the sun's rays. Sadly, Beirut tends to suffer from a lack of urban planning: its cityscape is a mess and became even worse during the 17 years of civil war, when public and civil rules were broken on all fronts, including planning and design.

As far back as I can remember I would copy pictures from comic magazines like *Sameer*, which I read weekly. I would also trace or copy floral patterns onto the bedsheets for my mother to embroider, since back then many people would buy fabric and make the sheets themselves. I still remember the brand of DMC threads she used for this embroidery – threads that came in graduated shades of every color. Besides that, I would draw on ordinary paper with colored crayons or pencils and stack all my drawings in a box which I put on a small bedside table.

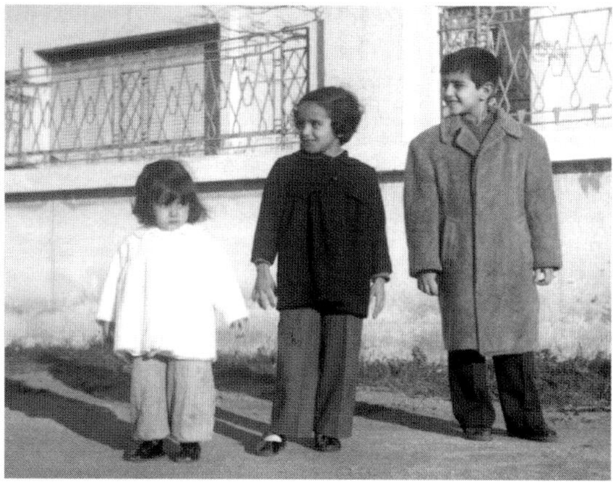

In front of the family home, with sisters Faten and Ghada, Beirut, 1957.

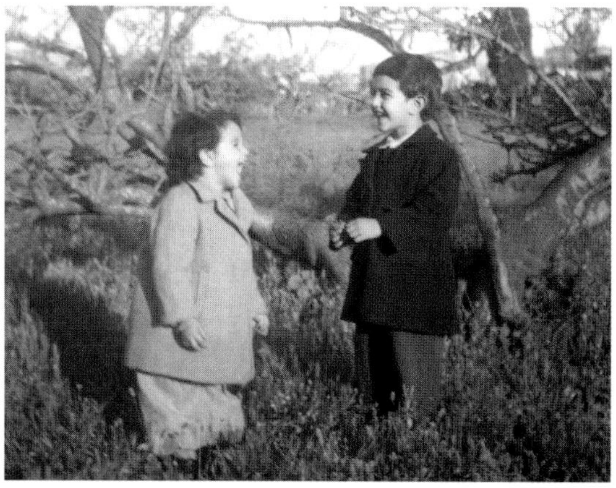

The artist and his sister Faten, in the suburbs of Beirut, 1954.

From time to time I would take them out (believing they were suffocating in their box), look at them and put them back again. I would sometimes spray them with water then spread them out on a couch to dry in front of our big window through which the sun shone, as if they were in need of water and air. I did not really look at the drawings themselves; what I cared for more was the sense of them as living things. I am still a little puzzled by this strange behavior of mine, so long ago, and cannot explain it. This is the most striking incident I remember from my early childhood. (Possibly this could have been an inkling of my later fascination with and practice of growing Bonsai trees, which are living works of art combining horticulture and design.) Years later, I do not remember why or when I destroyed all those drawings – a foolish act that I greatly regret even now.

We were five children – three boys and two girls. My mother was a modest, traditional housewife who had never attended school but, unlike most Arab women, she never differentiated between us boys and the girls: we all had to help equally with the housework, were all shown the same affection and love and were all given a university education.

My father, Bahaeddine Rawas, was an employee of the Lebanese Broadcasting Station, but also a freelance composer and writer of lyrics – a great admirer of Mohammed Abdulwahab, the Egyptian singer and composer who became famous during the first half of the twentieth century. (Abdulwahab died in 1991, but his fame has continued right up to the present time.) My father kept playing his songs, almost never listened to anything else, never to any kind of Western music, and recorded Abdulwahab's music onto open-reel tapes. I remember in the early sixties having bragged at school about possessing a Phillips open-reel tape recorder and a Garrard turntable at home. A classmate lent me a 45 rpm record of the Beatles, and this triggered my enthusiasm for Western music. Even now I only listen to Western music, mainly classical, jazz and blues. I cannot paint without music playing through a high-quality audio system: it's not only the music itself but the sound quality, too, that creates the total listening experience.

My father also loved photography and constantly took pictures of us. As far back as I can remember we always had a

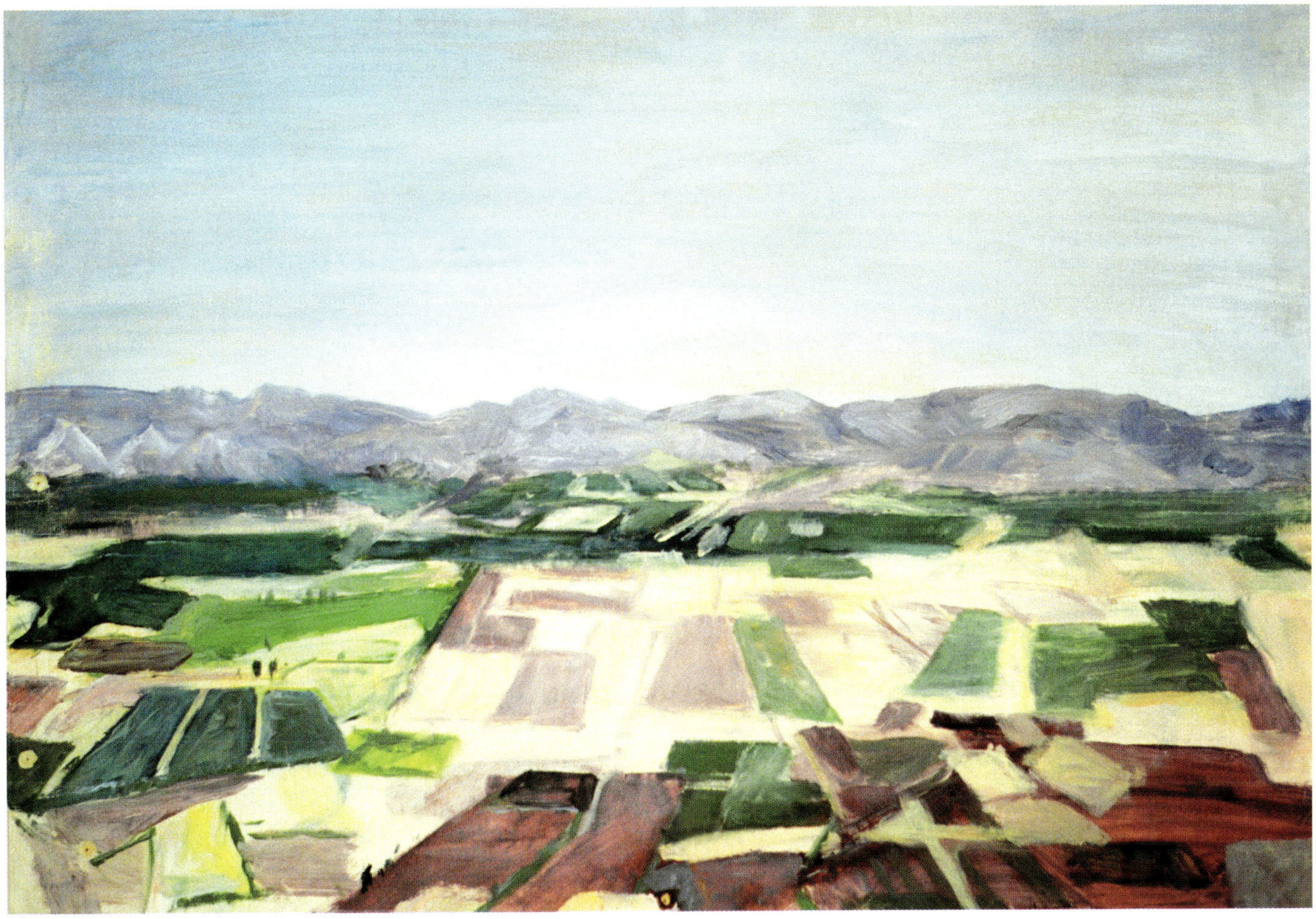

THE BEKAA VALLEY, 1967
Oil on paper
50 x 70 cm
Lost

camera at home – an 'Argus' twin-lens reflex. Perhaps my later enthusiasm for photographs springs partly from this.

When my father was nine, his father died, and he and his seven-year-old brother had to leave school and work as street vendors. He only knew how to read and write Arabic and, as he knew no foreign language, we never had foreign books at home. His mother never remarried, and had to go out to work to help support her small family. I am sure that the hardships and difficulties experienced at that tender age are what made my father bitter, suspicious, anxious and unable to trust anybody. Yet he remained a very emotional and affectionate man, caring for us a lot and constantly worrying about us. As a result, my sister and I (we were the eldest) spent the first two school years studying at home with private teachers because my father did not want us to mix with other children for fear of exposing us

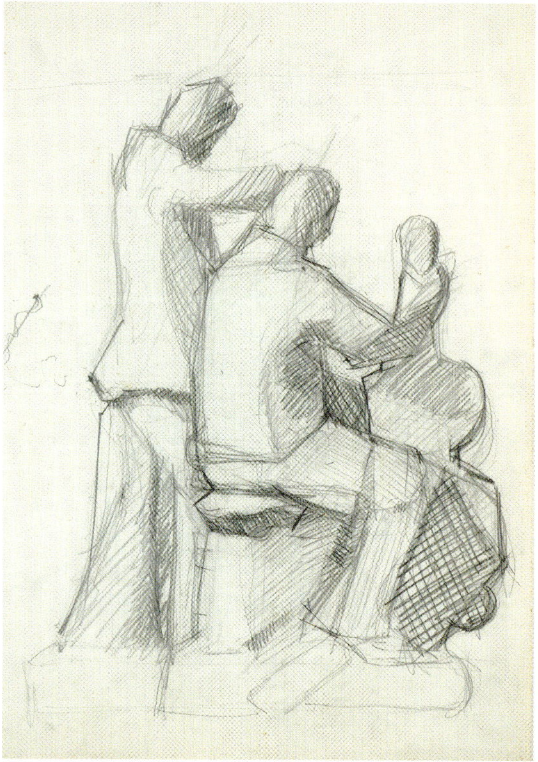

A STUDY FROM A CLAY STATUE, 1967
Pencil on paper
45 x 33 cm
Artist's collection

to disease. We were never allowed to go out and play with the neighbours' children and it was only on entering third grade that I had the perplexing experience of encountering children of my own age. Even then, my father would come to the school to check on me. I do not remember having any friends during my school days. Outside school I had no activities, was never allowed to go to the movies or anything else. My strict upbringing certainly affected my personality and may account for the fact that I enjoy my privacy and do not like crowded gatherings. I avoid most social parties because I feel they are artificial, and I hate all ceremonies, too: for me they are nothing more than a boring circus.

However, it was my father's fears and his constant worry about us that played a role in his encouraging me to paint, since this activity kept me at home. He bought me all the necessary materials and equipment; at thirteen I already had picture stretchers, canvases, paints and brushes. He would help me stretch the canvas and mix my own paints from raw pigment. My greatest reward was to have him sit and admire my finished work. My paintings then were mere copies of postcard-type European land- and seascapes and the like. Yet I learned a lot from copying and even now I still believe that beginners can greatly develop their painting skills by doing this.

At school my favorite subjects were those that called for illustrations: physics, biology, geography and, of course, drawing. I hated algebra and chemistry (which I could not understand), but I loved geometry, especially descriptive geometry, where I could enjoy imagining the planes and lines in three-dimensional space.

However, I did not like to read novels. One teacher at the Farouq branch of the Maqassed school I attended forced us to read them. He brought some novels to class, gave each of us one which we had to read and then pass on. Although I hated this authoritarian practice, I now realize that it was my only chance to read a few books of this kind. I remember particularly Ernest Hemingway's *The Old Man and the Sea*, which I loved. Yet this was not enough to instill in me a liking for novels. Right up to the present time, I only read books related to art, design and thought. What annoys me about reading novels is having to

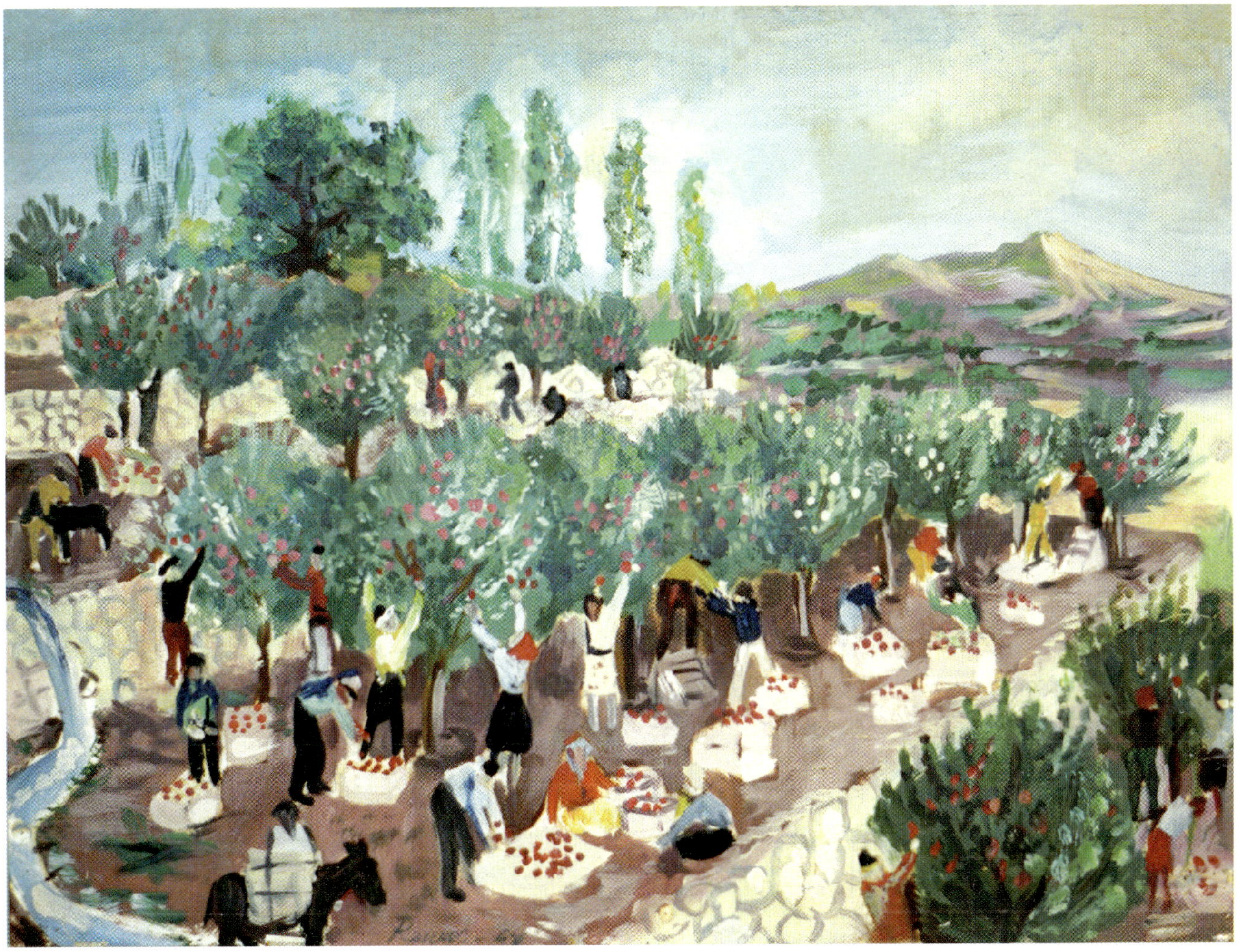

APPLE HARVEST, 1967
Oil on paper
50 x 70 cm
Lost

remember who is who in the story: one often has to turn back to remind oneself who a certain character is. I suppose another reason for my lack of enthusiasm for novels is that I see in them a certain interest in gossiping about people's personal lives, something I dislike.

When I transferred to the Raml al-Zarif public high school, I encountered philosophy as a subject for the first time – which triggered my interest in the existential question of life and its purpose. In addition, I became involved at this time with a particular kind of spirituality which led me to consider art both distracting and trivial. This caused me to stop painting altogether, until I reached a point where I could no longer bear to follow that path and deliberately decided to stop, to change, and to shift back to art. Although art is generally considered to be very different

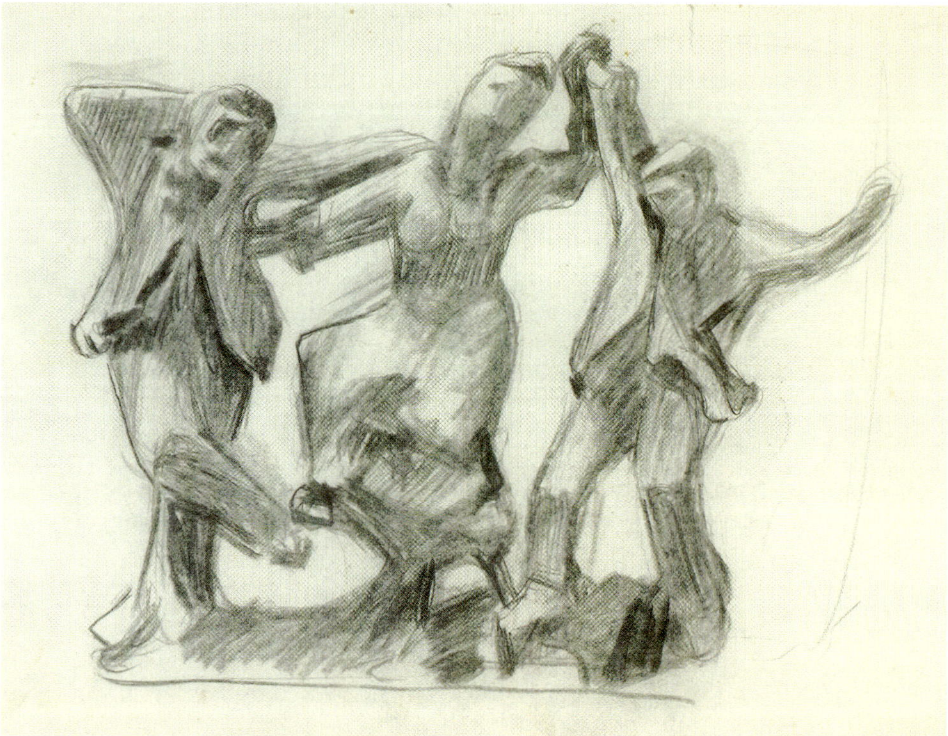

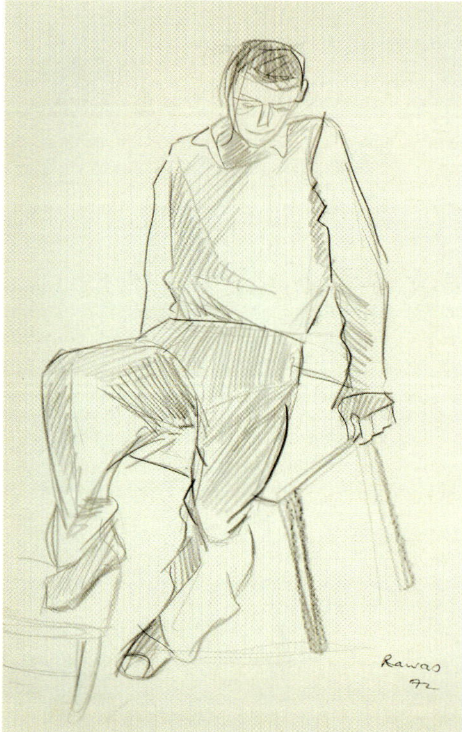

Top left
A STUDY FROM A CLAY STATUE, 1967
Charcoal on paper
32 x 39 cm
Artist's collection

Top right
A FIGURE SEATED ON A LOW TABLE, 1972
Charcoal on paper
35 x 26 cm
Artist's collection

from religion, they are alike in being 'extreme' activities. By this I mean art – for me, at least – is something that can absorb one as a human being just as much as religion can, even though their aims may be at variance. My return to art, however, did not negate my spirituality, and I have since tried to find a certain balance between the two. I recently came across an article by Paul Tillich, in *Christianity and the Existentialists* (Scribners, New York, 1956), asserting the close connection between religion and art, both being ultimately concerned with one's own being. Sometimes I recall my past spiritual training in order to calm myself and overcome my nervousness and anxiety. But another result of that period of intense spirituality is that feeling happy can make me anxious: I know I should not be fooled by the kind of happiness that is trivial and transient. And I still believe in a certain continuity of life after death. What shape or form this life takes, I do not know, but I cannot believe that we simply cease to exist.

Probably the most lasting impact on my life, however, was that left by Munir Eido, the art teacher at the Maqassed school, whom I was very lucky to have had. He was both an excellent artist and an inspiring teacher. He was very strict at school

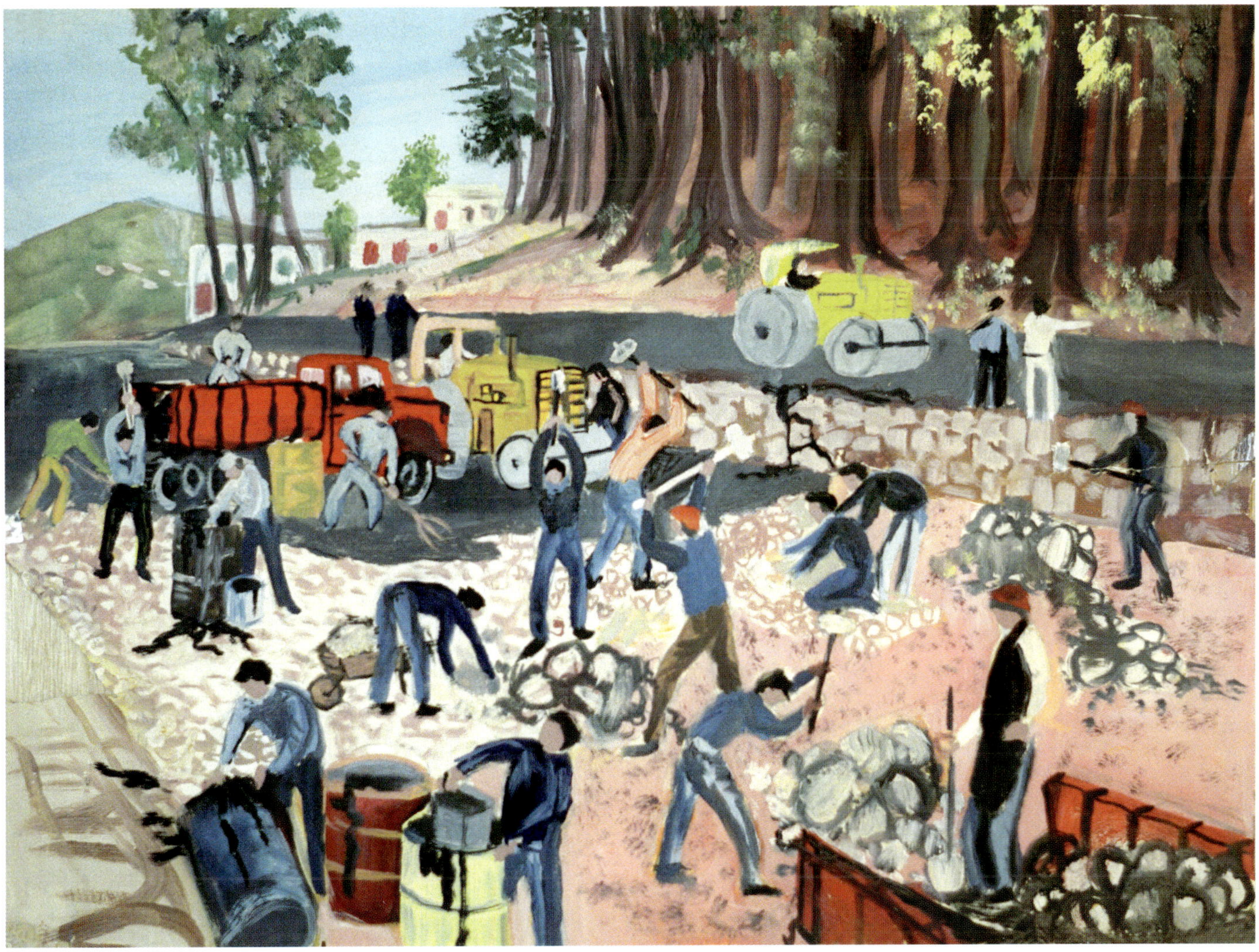

ASPHALTING THE STREET, 1967
Oil on paper
50 x 70 cm
Lost

because it was the only way to discipline the bunch of rowdy boys that we were, but he introduced us to drawing from still life by observing proportions and ratios and by taking measurements. He was the one who gave me the basic stepping-stones for drawing correctly, yet also taught me how to be free, spontaneous and original in my artistic expression. He introduced me to working with clay, too. He believed that art starts and ends with the process of creating it; exhibiting and selling is irrelevant, and it is enough to share the joy of your art with your friends. It was when I later joined the Institute of Fine Arts at the Lebanese University that I fully realized how much he had taught me and how much I owed him.

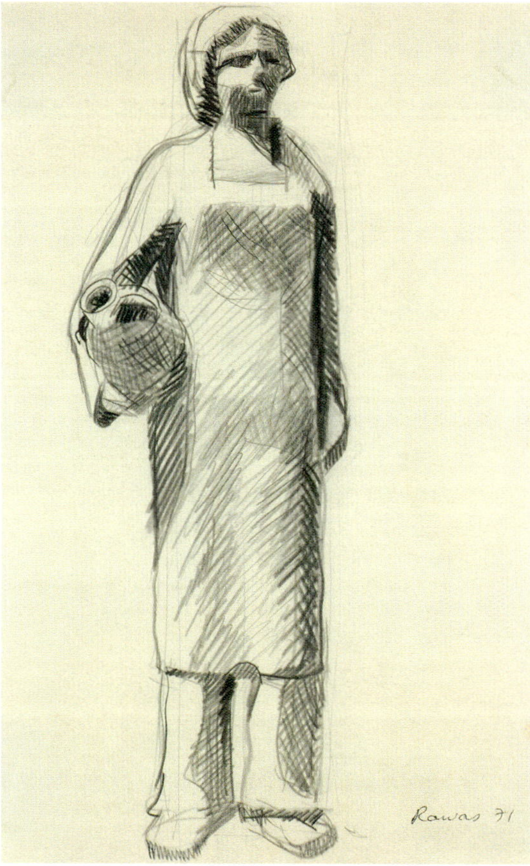

A STUDY FROM A CLAY STATUE, 1971
Charcoal on paper
35 x 26 cm
Artist's collection

Opposite page

Top left
A STUDY FROM A CLAY STATUE *(by the artist)*, 1971
Charcoal on paper
35 x 26 cm
Artist's collection

Top center
A STUDY FROM A CLAY STATUE, 1967
Charcoal on paper
35 x 24 cm
Artist's collection

Top right
A STUDY FROM A CLAY STATUE, 1967
Charcoal on paper
48 x 33 cm
Artist's collection

Bottom
A FAMILY WATCHING TV, *1971*
Ballpoint pen on paper
24 x 33 cm
Artist's collection

I participated in the Maqassed school exhibitions of 1965 and 1966 and won first prize in both. However, my first participation in a public art event was a competition organized by the Lebanese television company Lubnan wal-Mashriq (Lebanon and the East) in 1968. Winning the first prize among 145 participants greatly boosted my morale. I was 17 years old, and Munir Eido (who had selected my entries for that competition), noticing my elation, told me not to let this victory go to my head, and that now I had to work even harder. I felt rather shame-faced to have been so overjoyed with my success, and his words have remained with me ever since.

Among various factors that affected my personality in childhood, I would mention in particular my father's negative attitude towards people and friendship and his strong belief in close family relationships – to which I reacted by taking an opposite stand. I do not believe in family structures and cannot tolerate the fact that our society is modelled on them: our whole political system and our political parties are based on family relationships. Even business is carried out according to family ties and interests. My one attempt to follow a more conventional 'family' pattern was not a great success. At the age of 45 I married – but divorced seven years later. (My relationship with my ex-wife, however, remains one of deep friendship and respect – perhaps the most important qualities of a healthy human relationship.) But even when married I never wanted children because I would have had to bring them up to the very best of my ability, not leaving anything to chance. Having a child is a lifetime's project, a worry, a huge and demanding challenge. I could guide the child, but what would guarantee that the child would be receptive to my guidance? A child would be something I was responsible for without being able to control. Besides, I would have to take care of the child, nurture it in illness, devote all my time and attention to it until it got well. This time would be taken from painting. I admit that I am selfish, but my priorities are not the usual scenario: get a job, a car, a wife, kids to look after until they will have to look after me. I never felt the need for parental emotions. For me, friendship could be just as fulfilling. Family ties are of no importance to me because I believe that we go

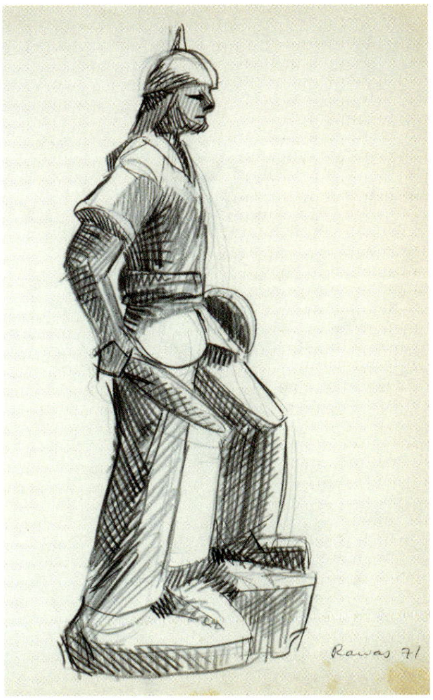
Rawas 71

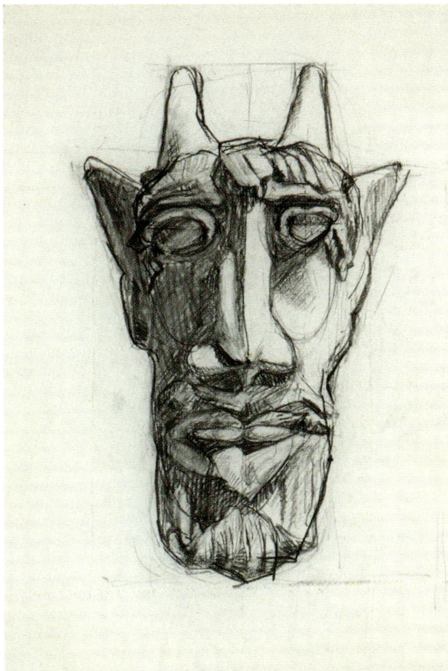

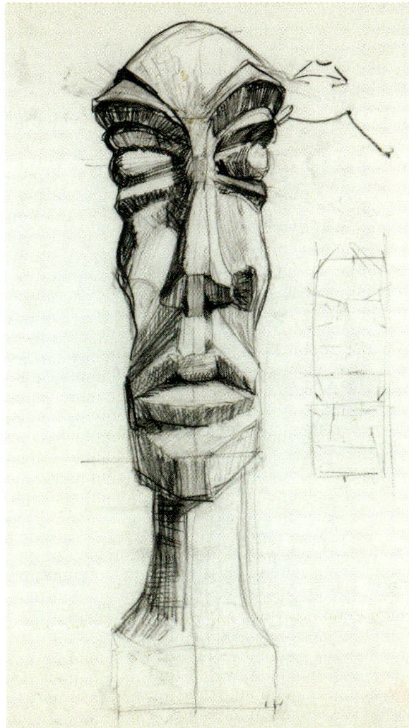

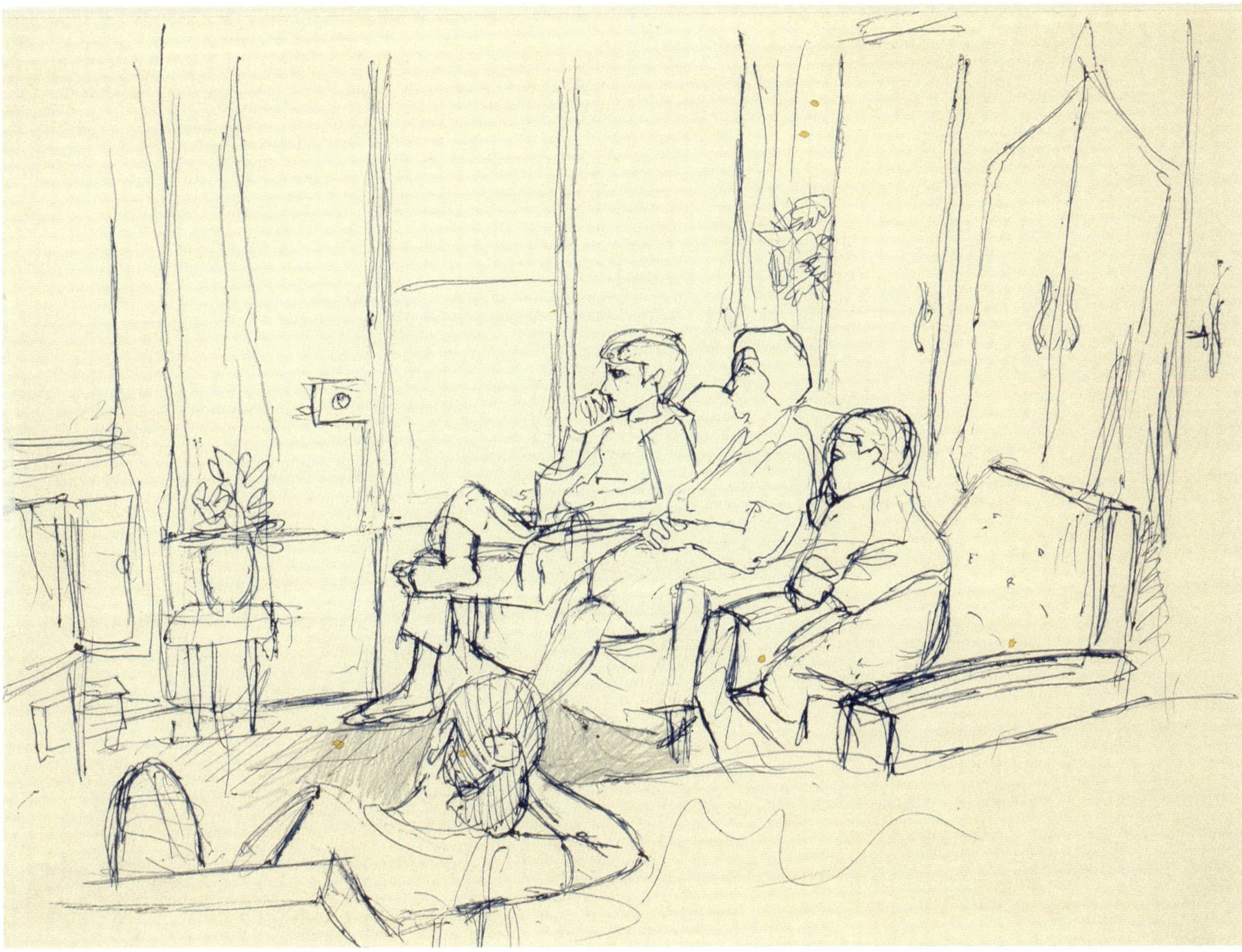

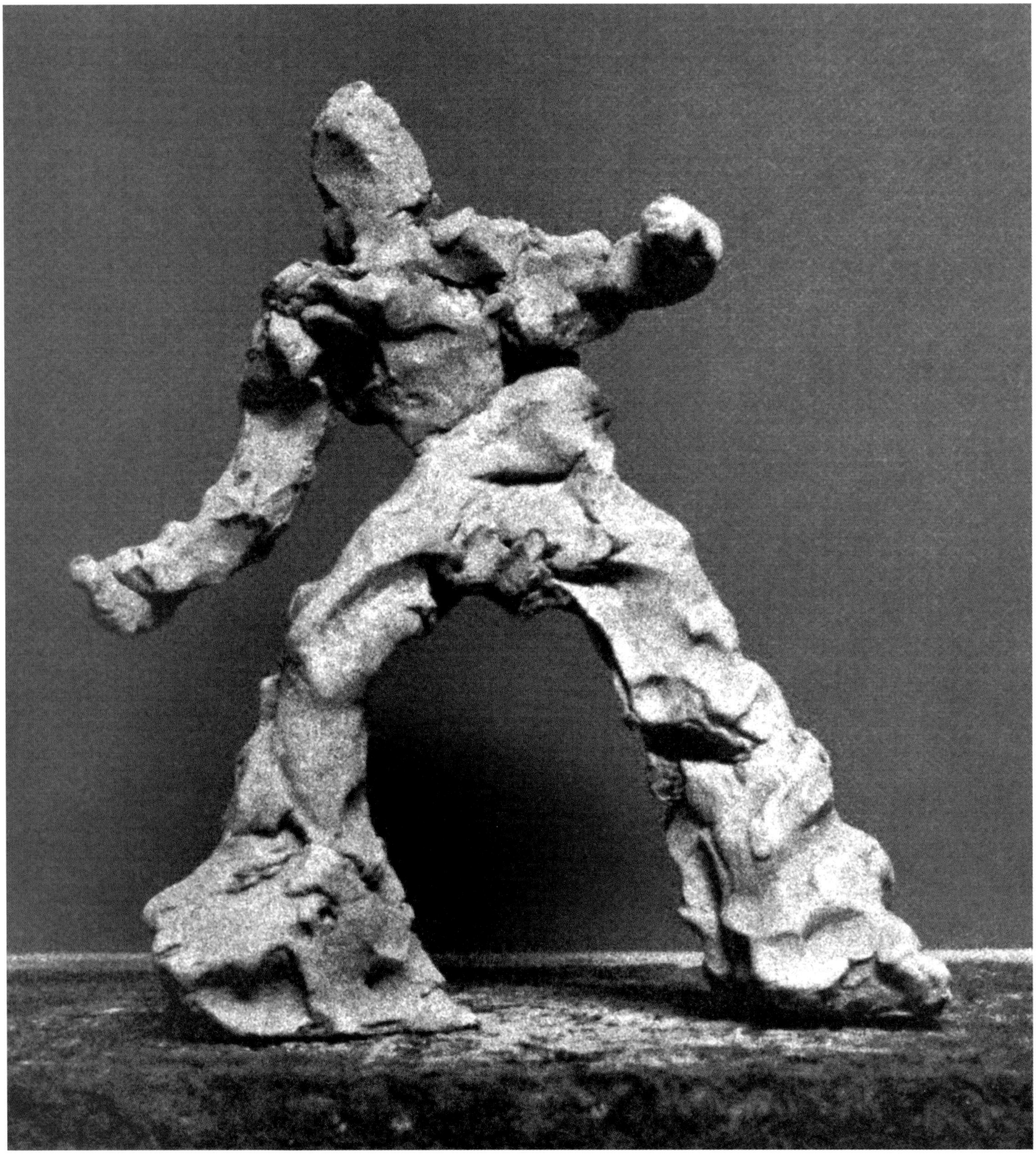

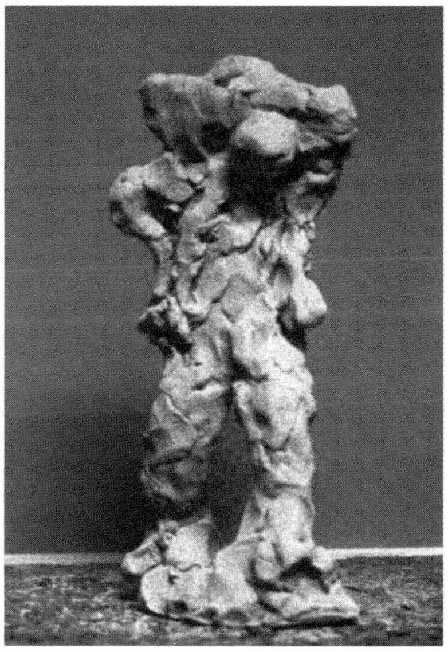

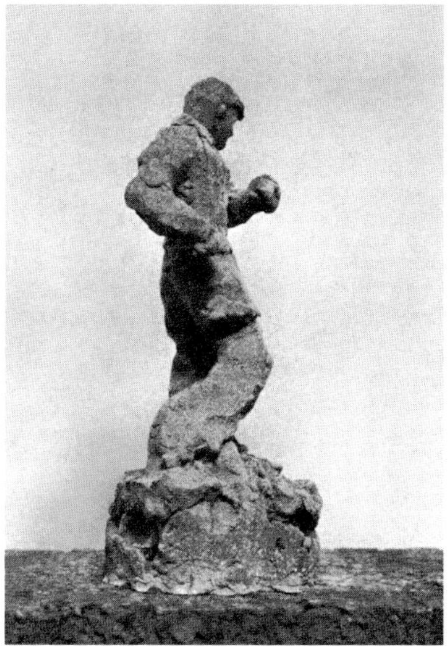

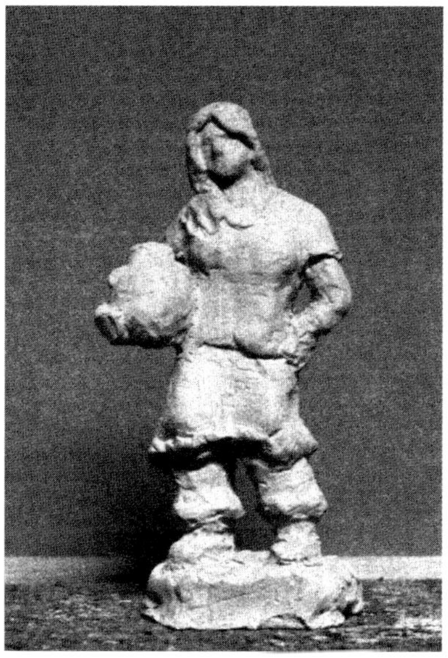

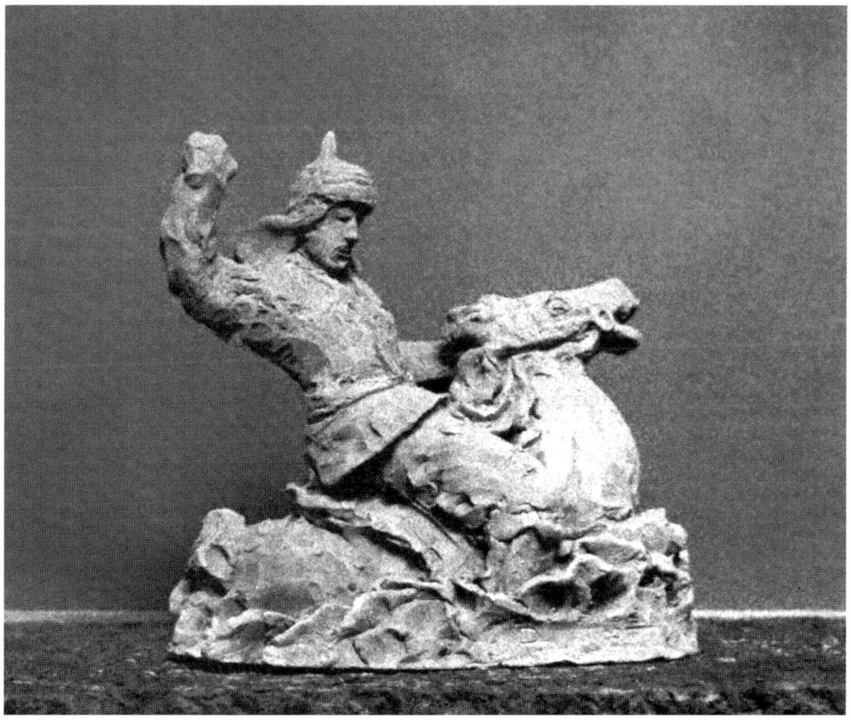

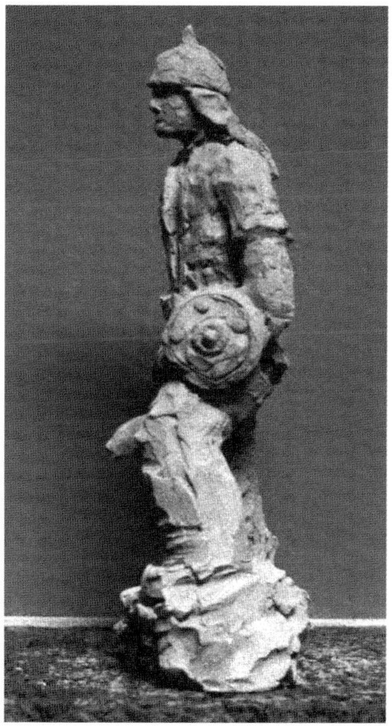

This page and opposite page

CLAY SCULPTURES, 1967-68
Dimensions vary between 15 to 30 cm

Done during the art classes of Munir Eido at the Maqassed School.
Destroyed during the war in 1982.

alone through life, just as we end up alone in the grave. We are alone as individuals, therefore it does not bring me any satisfaction to know that I could exist, after death, in my relatives' thoughts or memories.

My attitude towards family might be another reason for my disinclination to read novels and for the choice of films I see. Most novels and films involve family relationships, and I am simply not very interested in such stories and scenarios, nor can I identify with the characters as many people do.

Yet what made me fully realize how fragile and fleeting even friendship is was my losing a dear friend during the Lebanese civil war. She was killed by the explosion of the booby-trapped car that blew up the American embassy in Beirut in 1983. She simply happened to be driving past at the time. I will never forget the traumatic experience of having to identify her body in the hospital morgue. Three of my works attempt to deal with this event, with the profound pain of that loss and with coming face-to-face, for the first time, with the tragic death of a loved one: *The April the Lilies Died* (1983), *The Cruising* (1984) and *Blue in Between* (1985).

As for 'love', for me it means being entirely absorbed in the other, to feel that every aspect of myself is shared, exchanged, completed in every single moment of my life. Anything less I do not consider 'love'. In this sense, love is an impossibility. I guess this shows that I am an unreasonable perfectionist – besides being moody. (And it would be unfair of me to expect the other to tolerate the moodiness that overcomes me periodically.) I do enjoy the friendship and the company of female friends at certain times, but marriage is a different matter altogether.

Opposite page
THE APRIL THE LILIES DIED, 1983
Etching, relief and stencil
68 x 49 cm

Exhibited at:
- Seventh Norwegian International Print Biennale, Fredrikstad, 1984
- Eighth British International Print Biennale, Bradford, 1984
- Second Cabo Frio International Print Biennale, Brazil, 1985 'Honorary Award'
- Arab Contemporary Art, The Mall Galleries, London, 1986

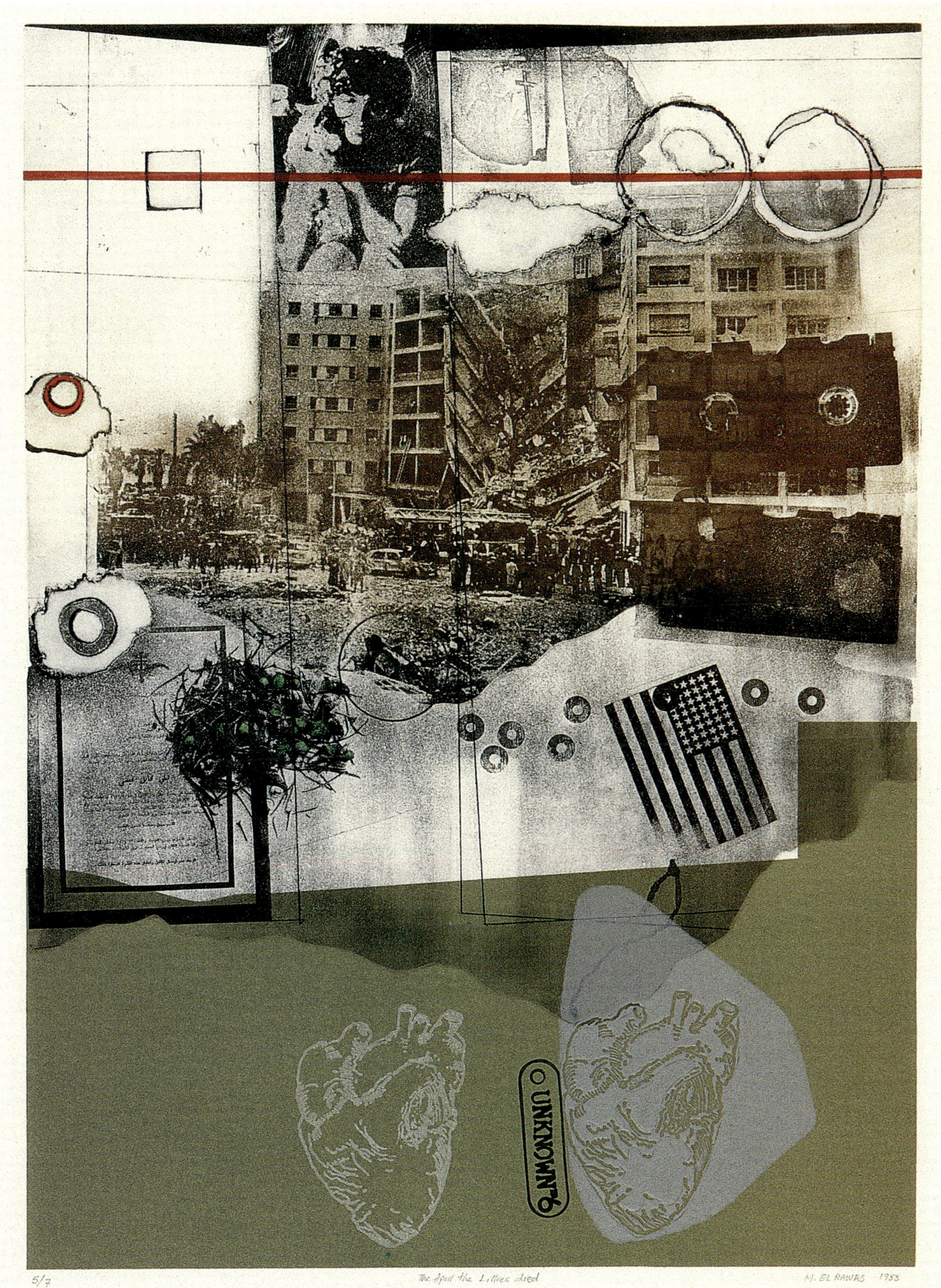
UNKNOWN
5/7
The April the Lilies died
M. EL RAWAS 1983

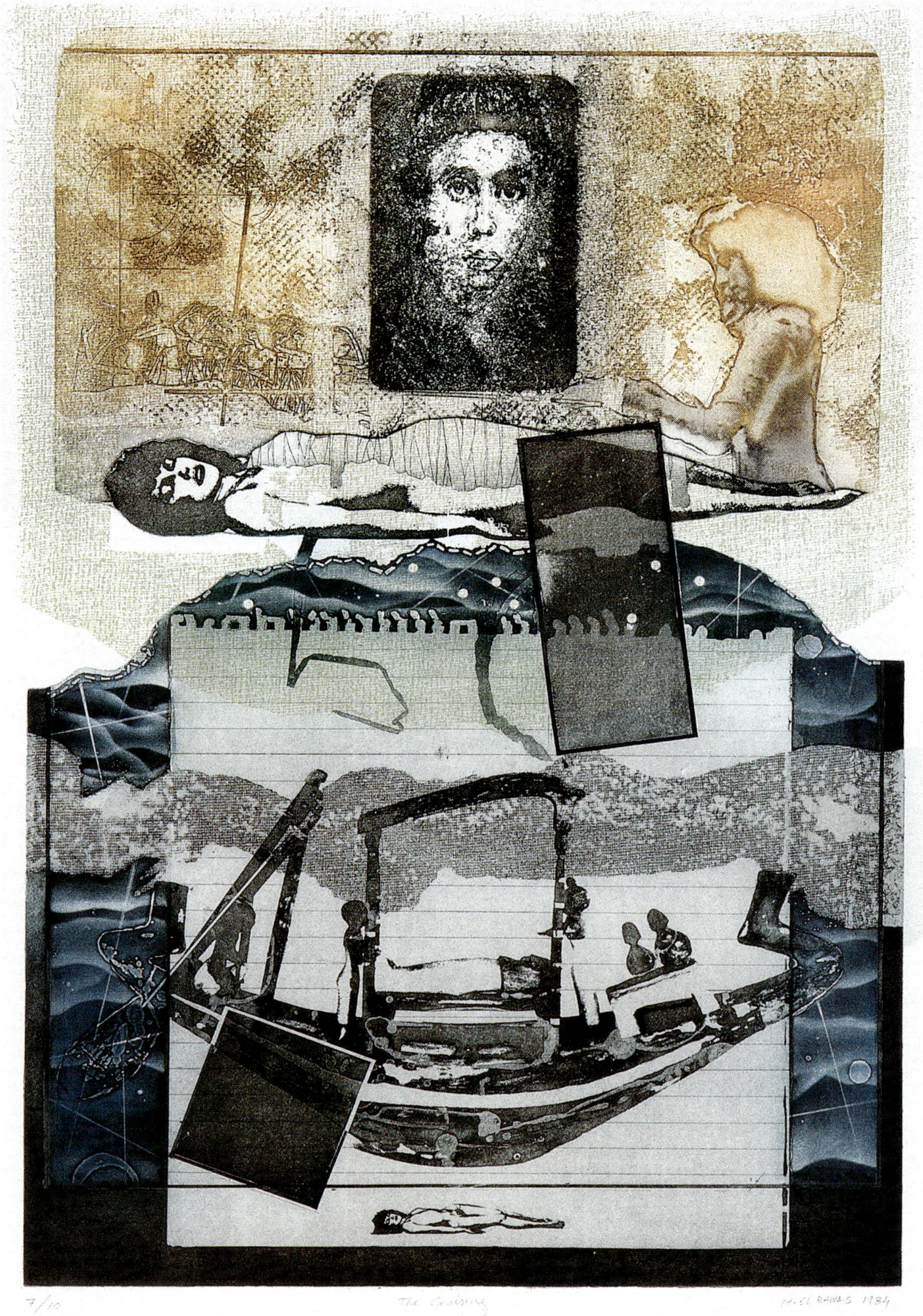
7/10
The Cruising
M. El Rawas 1984

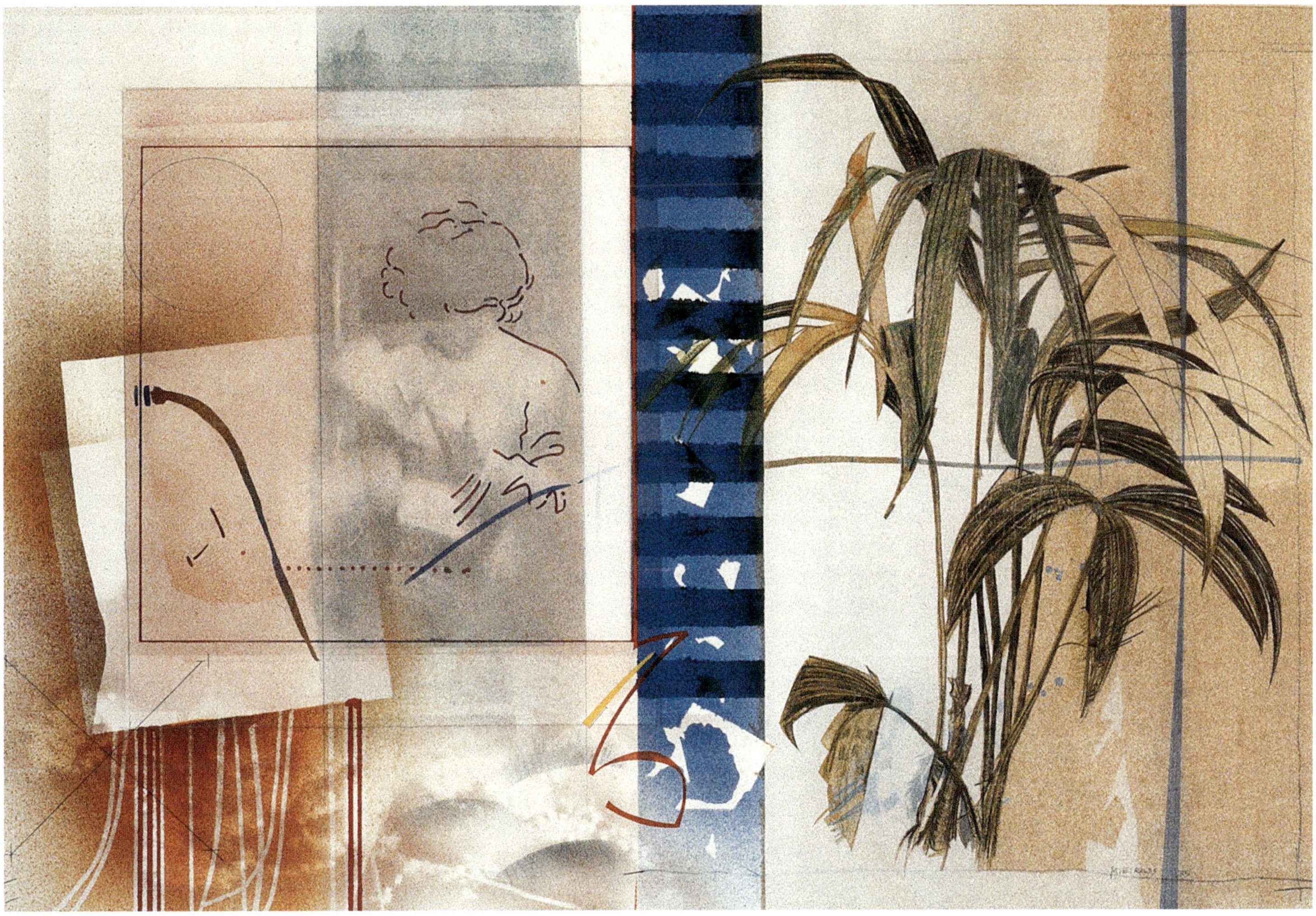

BLUE IN BETWEEN,1985
Mixed media and gum printing on paper
64 x 94 cm
Private collection

Opposite page
THE CRUISING, 1984
Etching and silkscreen
62 x 42.5 cm

Exhibited at:
– Eleventh International Independent Exhibition of Prints, Kanagawa, Japan, 1985
– Ninth British International Print Biennale, Bradford, 1986

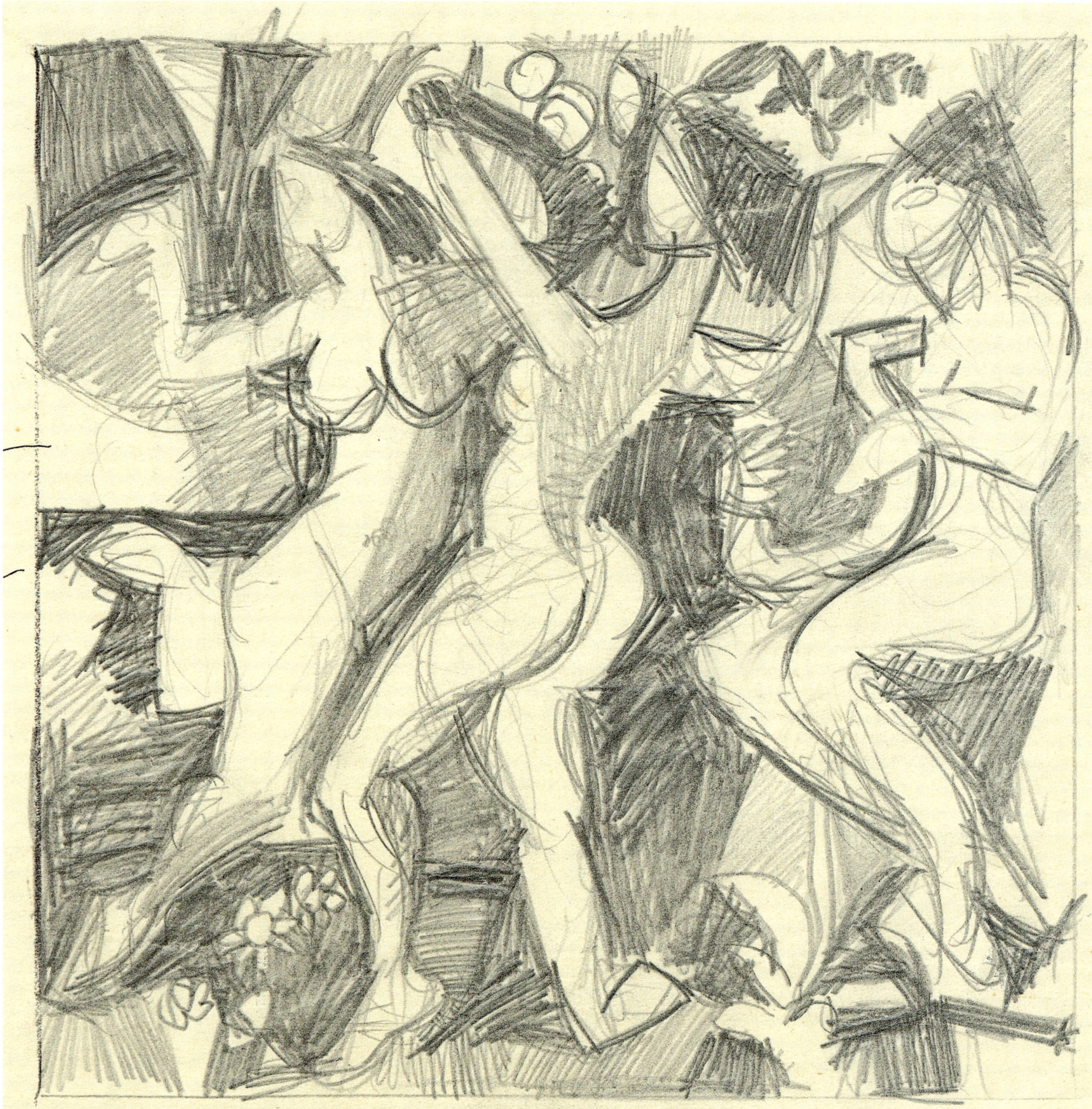

A COMPOSITION WITH THREE DANCING NUDES, 1971
Pencil on paper
23 x 23 cm
Artist's collection

The Lebanese University: The Institute of Fine Arts

On finishing high school, I enrolled at the Lebanese University to study English literature. After one year I decided to change majors and joined the Institute of Fine Arts in that University.

I do not think that any teacher at that Institute taught me much. This is not out of the ordinary, for it is a well-known fact in art schools all over the world that one does not necessarily learn from the teachers. What leads to developing one's own work is the surrounding atmosphere created by seeing other students' work, learning from their mistakes and then from one's own. But what bothered me most was the subjectivity of the tutorials: the teachers' comments and observations were made without convincing justifications. However, I did manage to learn something from a tip passed on by the artist Rashid Wehbi. We were drawing from a plaster cast of grapes. He showed me, on the margin of my paper, how to render the effect of a three-dimensional, oval-shaped grape by not extending the shading to the very edge, leaving a lighter area at the rim.

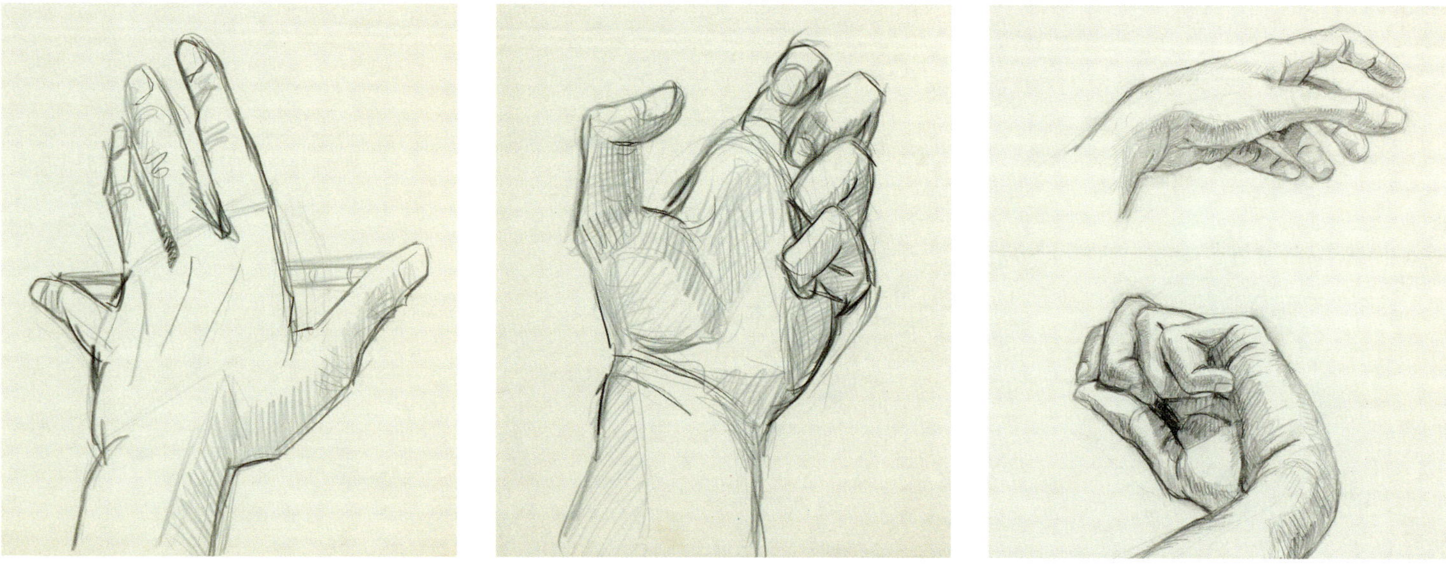

STUDIES OF HANDS, 1973
Charcoal on paper
30 x 26 cm
Artist's collection

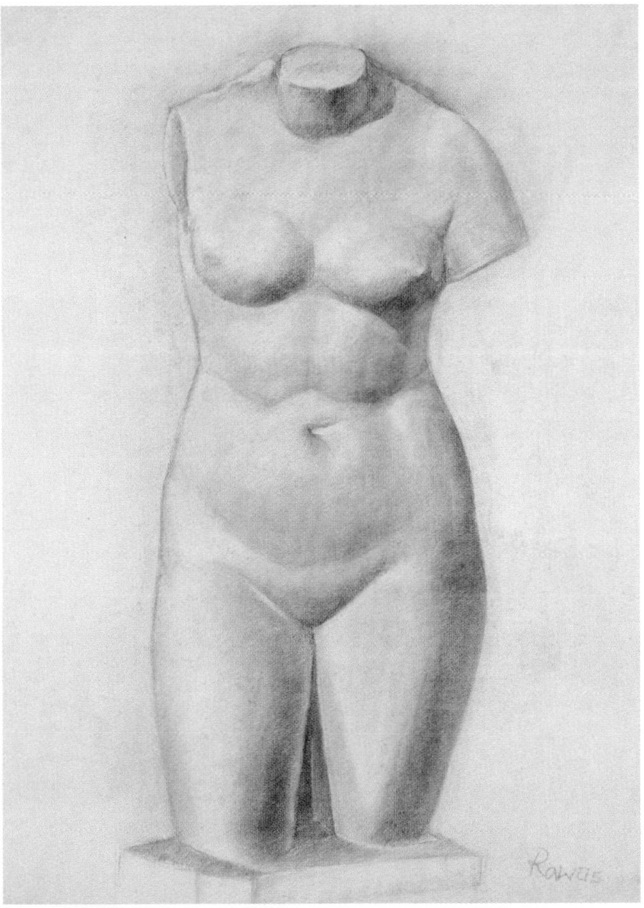

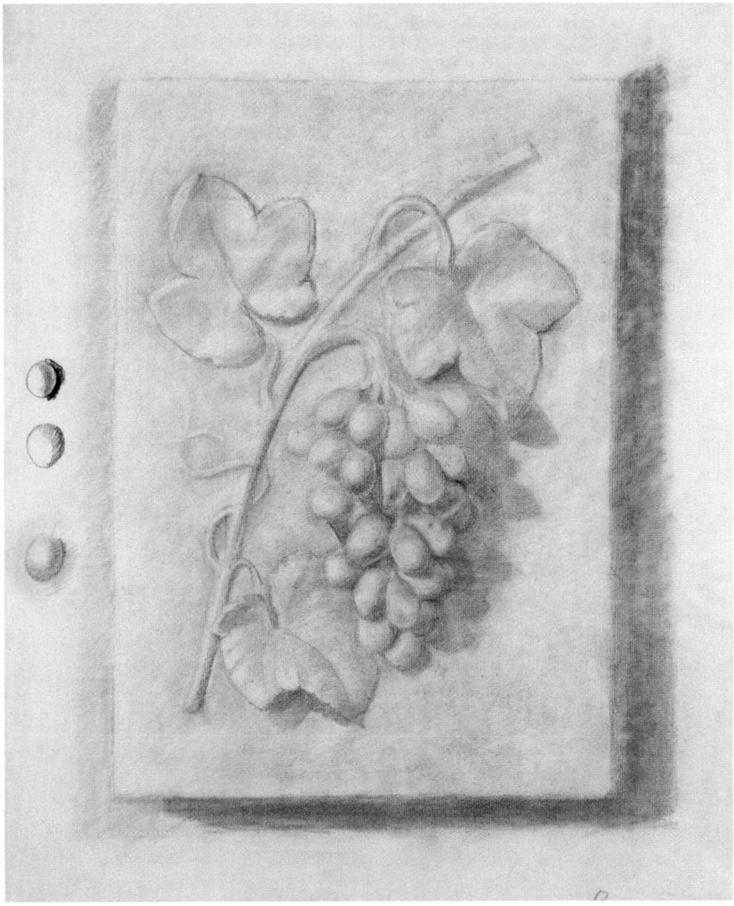

Top left
VENUS, 1971
Charcoal on paper
65 x 50 cm
Artist's collection

Top right
A STUDY FROM A PLASTER CAST, 1971
Charcoal on paper
65 x 50 cm
Artist's collection

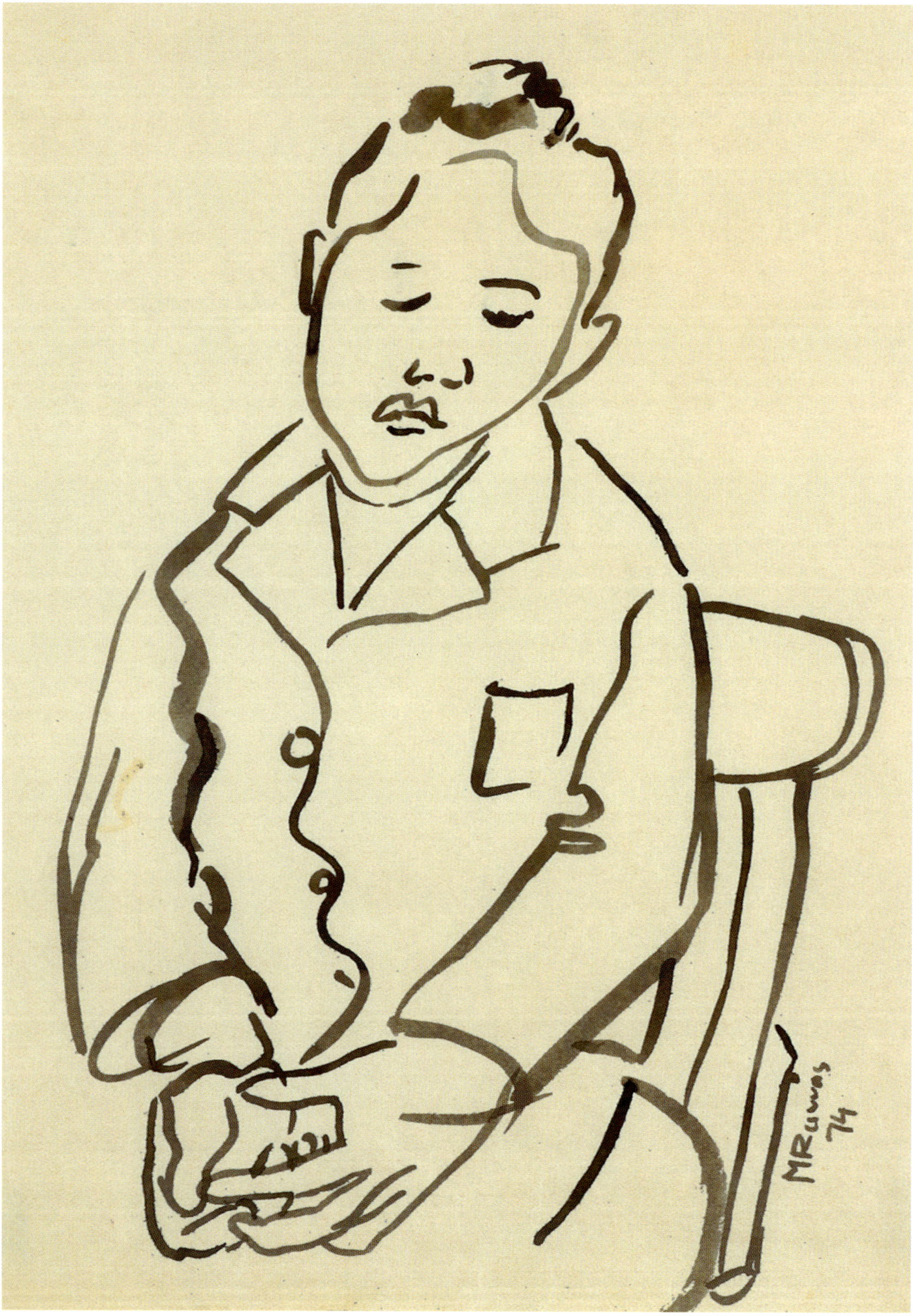

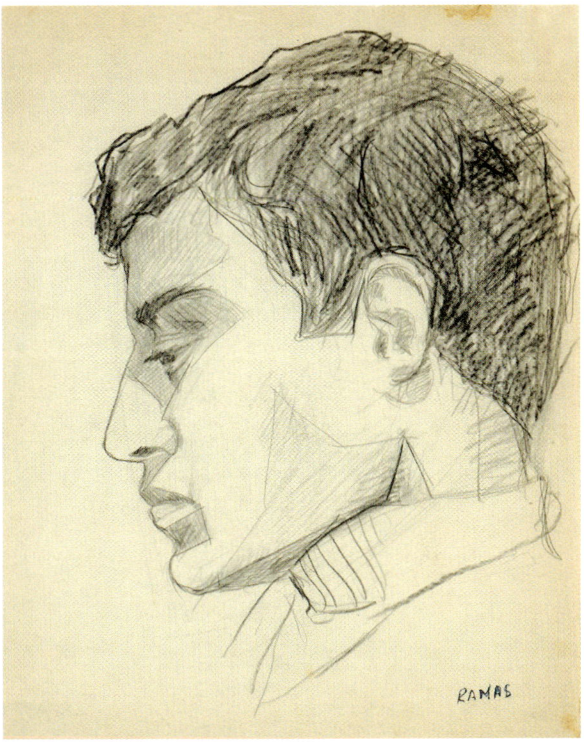

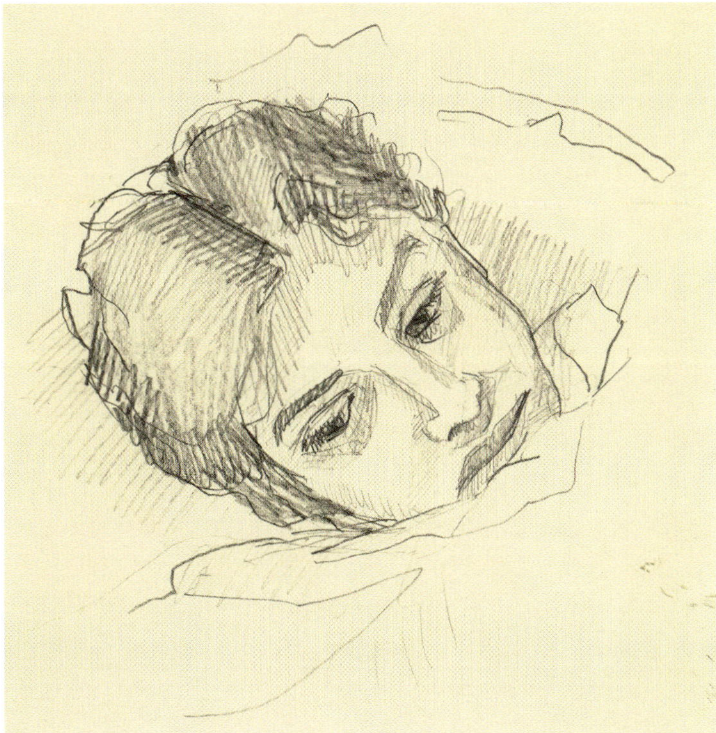

Top left
THE ARTIST'S BROTHER; ABED, 1972
Charcoal on paper
33 x 25 cm
Artist's collection

Top right
THE ARTIST'S BROTHER IN BED, 1970
Crayon on paper
25 x 28 cm
Artist's collection

Opposite page
THE ARTIST'S BROTHER; JAWHAR, 1974
Ink wash on paper
44 x 31 cm
Artist's collection

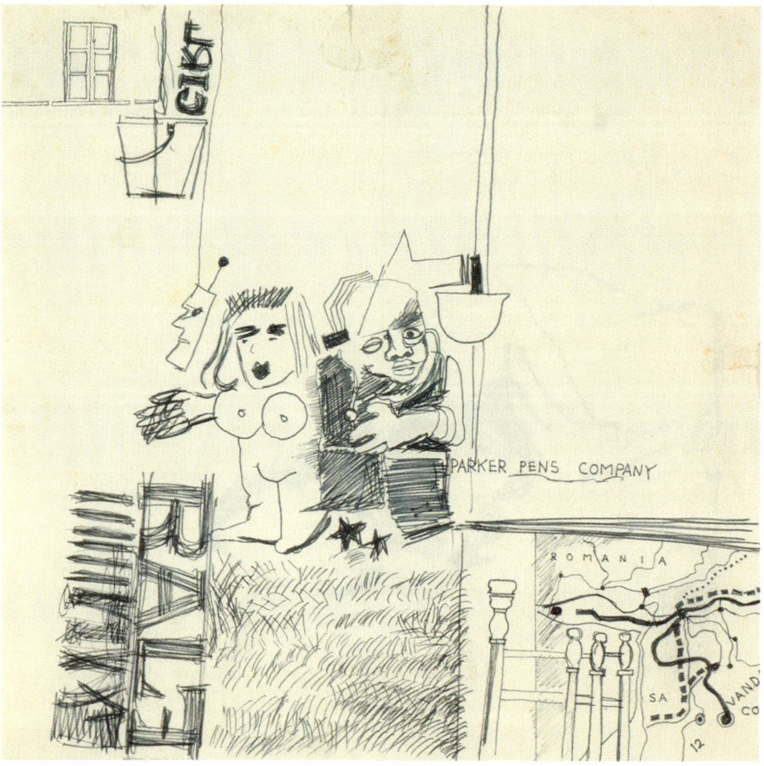

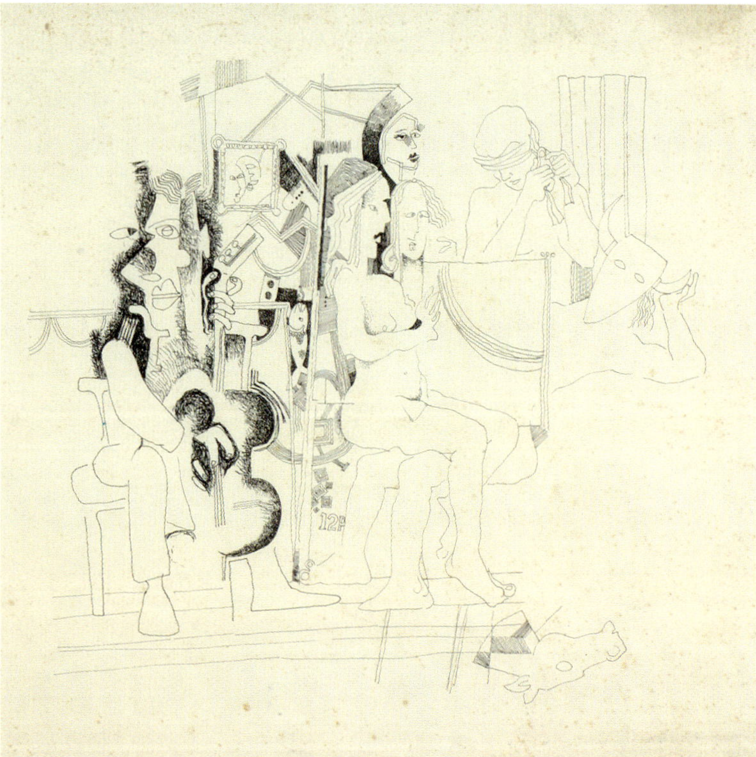

Top
A COUPLE IN A PARK, 1973
Felt pen on paper
30.5 x 30.5 cm
Artist's collection

Bottom
A SURREALISTIC COMPOSITION, 1974
China ink on paper
35 x 35 cm
Artist's collection

Opposite page
THE BOOK OF LIFE, 1973
Etching
32.5 x 24.5 cm

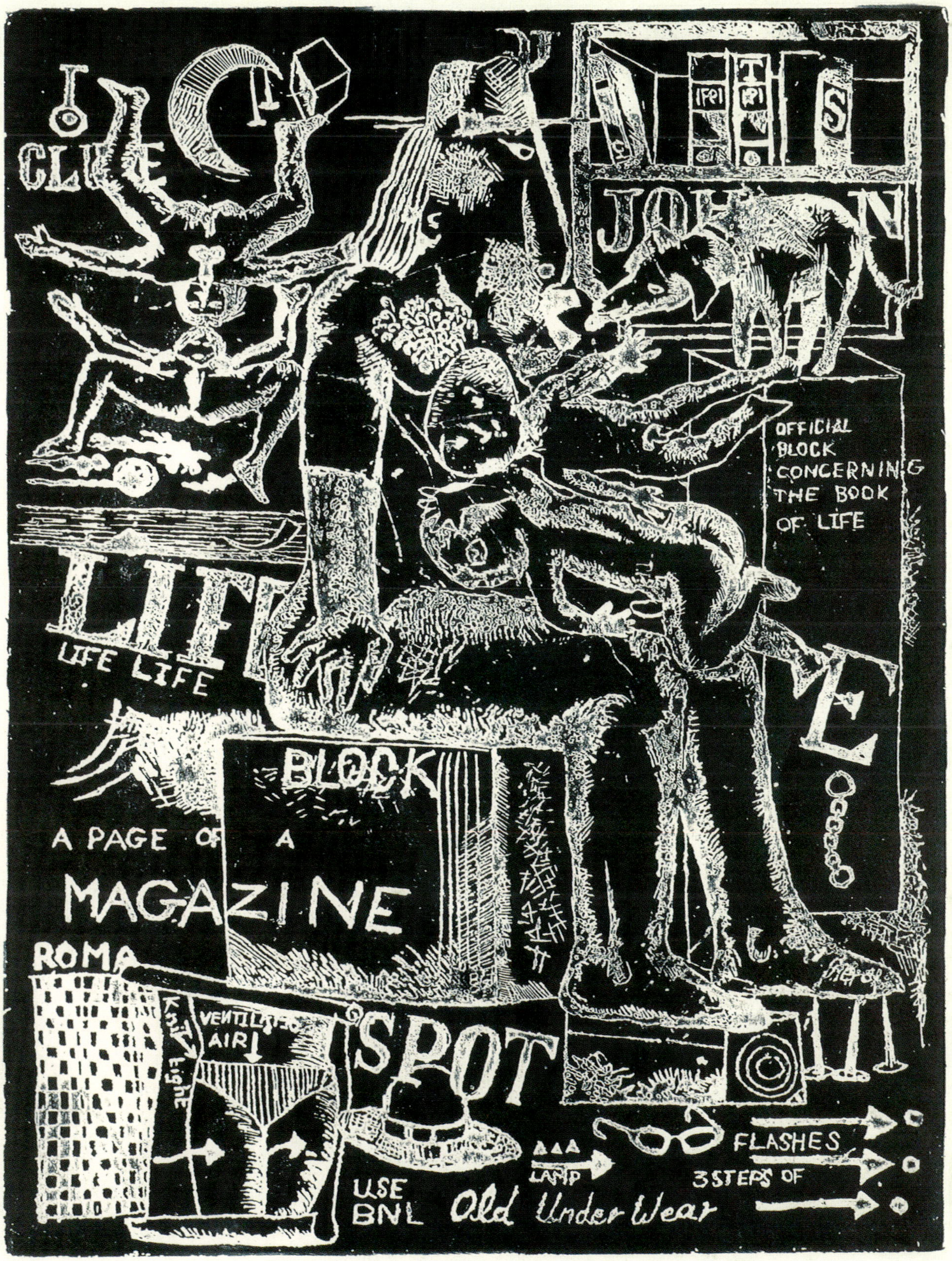

JOHN
OFFICIAL BLOCK CONCERNING THE BOOK OF LIFE
LIFE LIFE
BLOCK
A PAGE OF A
MAGAZINE
ROMA
VENTILATED AIR
SPOT
LAMP
FLASHES
3 STEPS OF
USE
BNL Old Under Wear

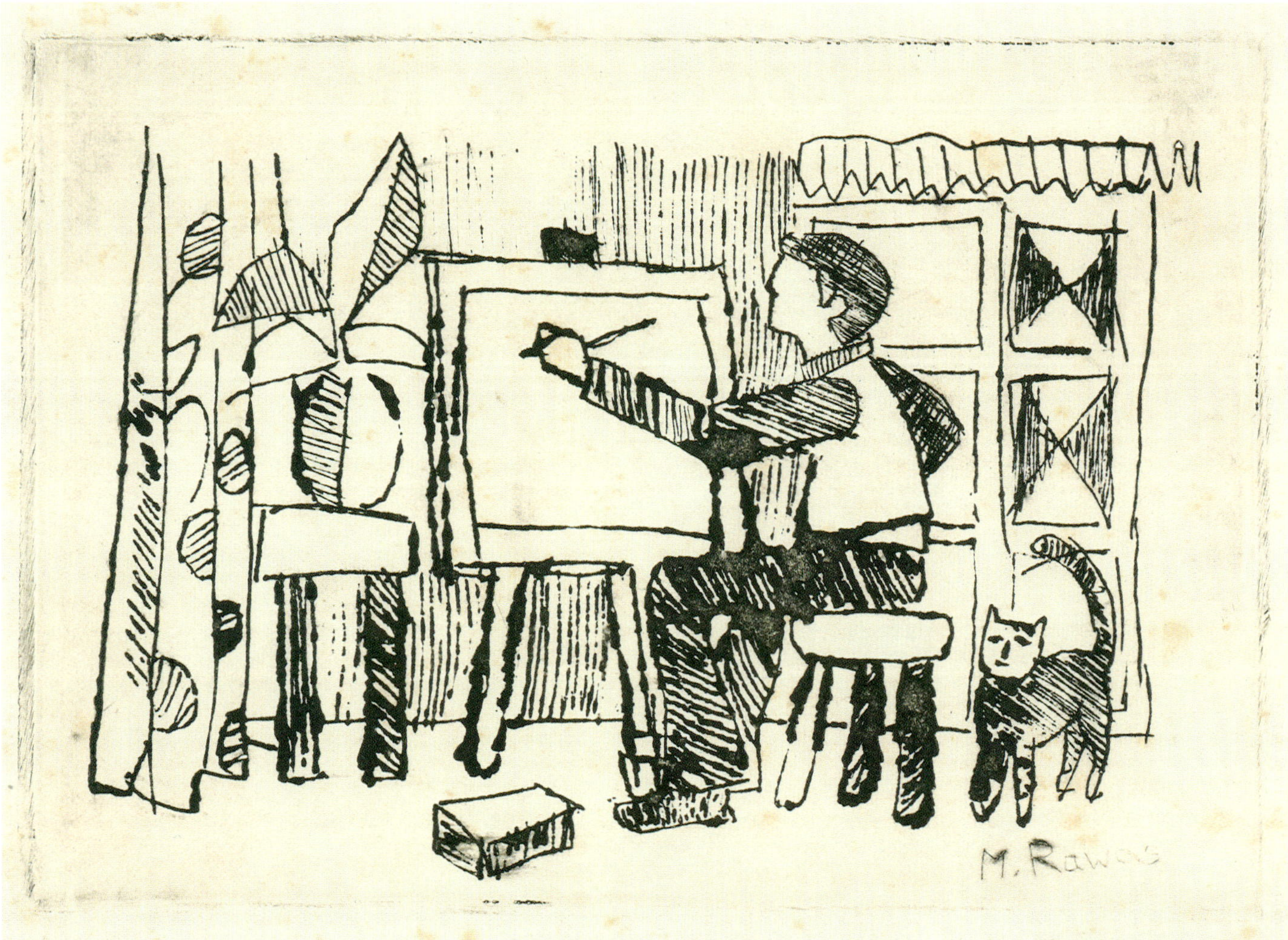

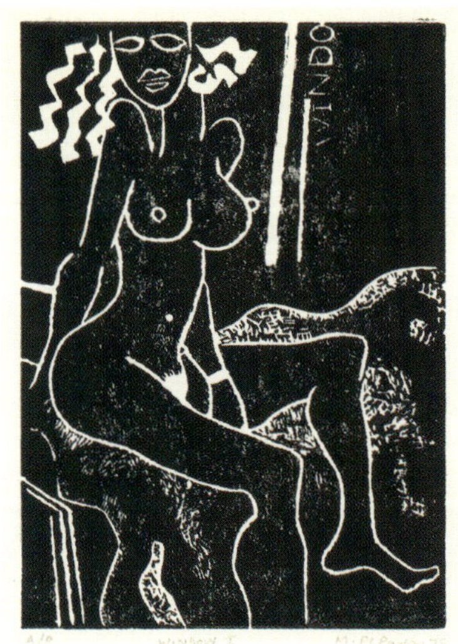

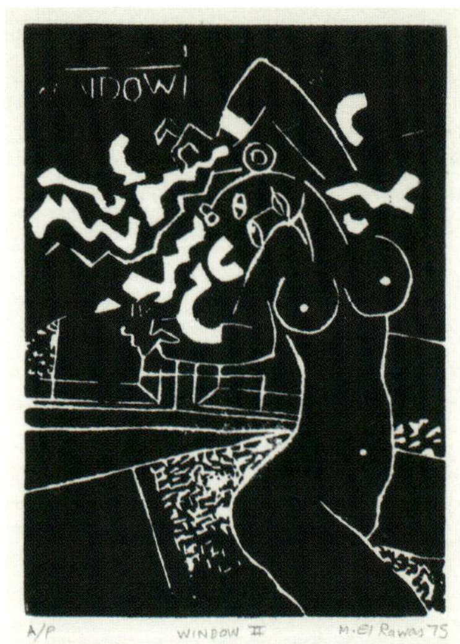

A FIGURE PAINTING WITH A CAT, 1972
Etching
11.5 x 16.5 cm

The first etching I did at Halim Jurdak's printmaking class at the Lebanese Universitry

Bottom left
WINDOW I, 1975
Linocut
18 x 12.5 cm

Bottom right
WINDOW II, 1975
Linocut
18 x 12.5 cm

Opposite page
POLOGNE, 1973
Etching
32 x 25 cm

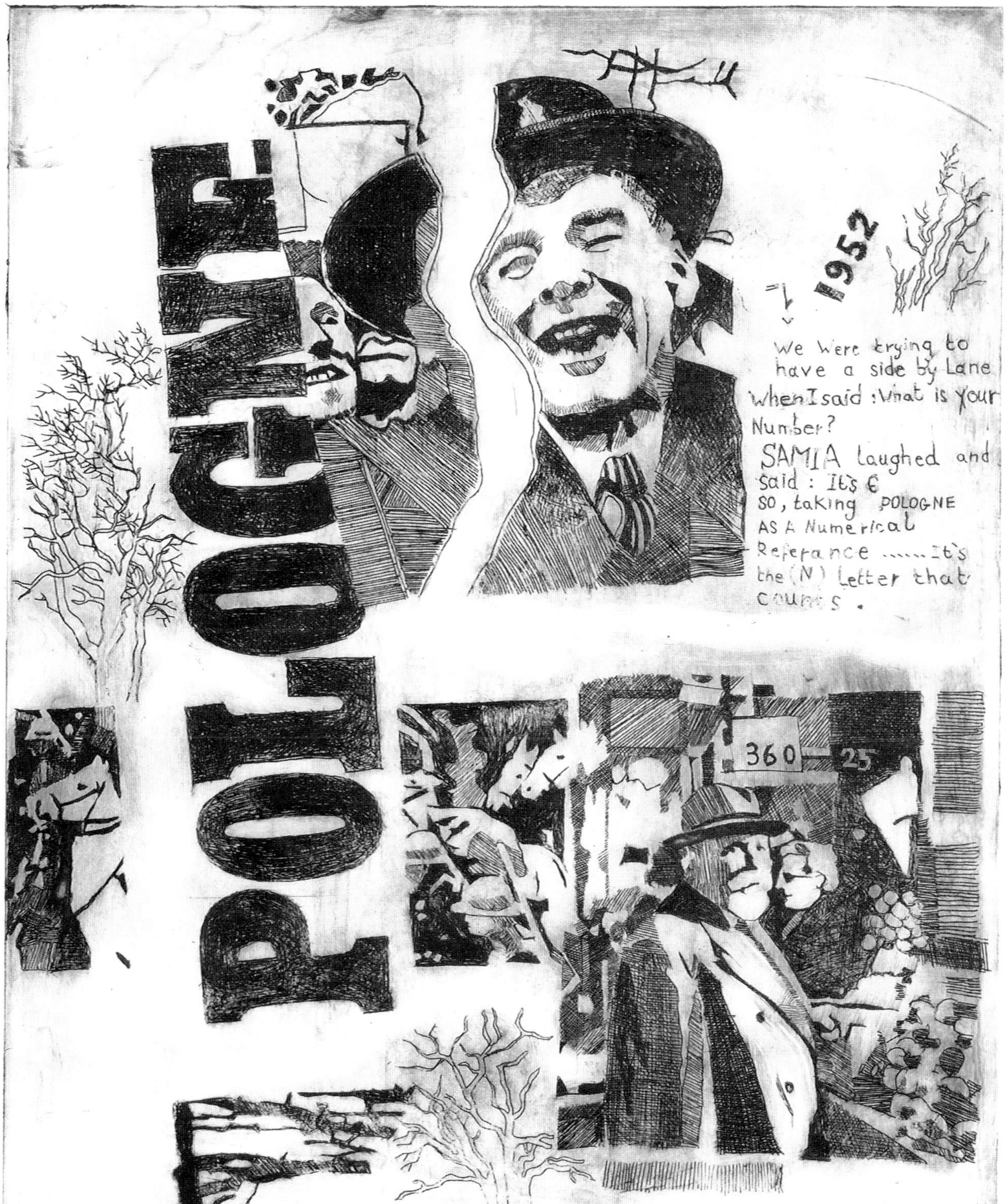
POLOGNE
1952
We were trying to
have a side by Lane
when I said : What is your
Number?
SAMIA laughed and
said : It's 6
so, taking POLOGNE
AS A Numerical
Referance ...... It's
the (N) Letter that
counts .
360
25

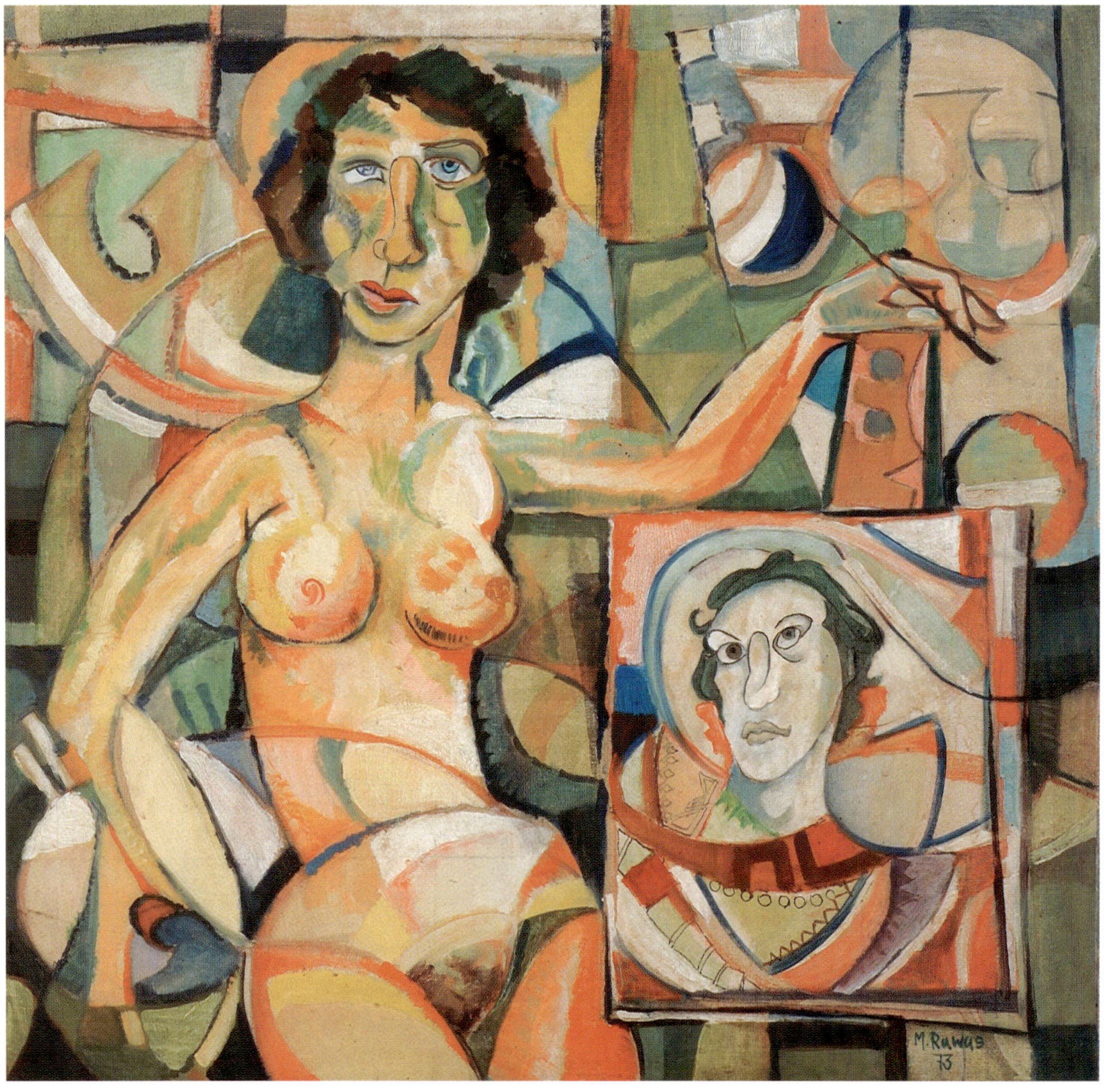

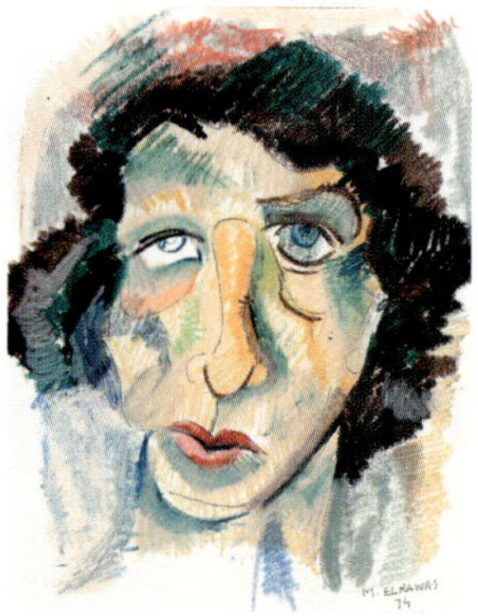

Top left
NUDE WITH SELF-PORTRAIT, 1973
Oil on canvas
72 x 72 cm
Collection Ms. M. Daou

Top right
PORTRAIT, 1973
Pastel and Ink on paper
30 x 20 cm
Artist's collection

Opposite page
RUE 26, 1974
Oil on canvas
69 x 57 cm
Collection Ms. M. Daou

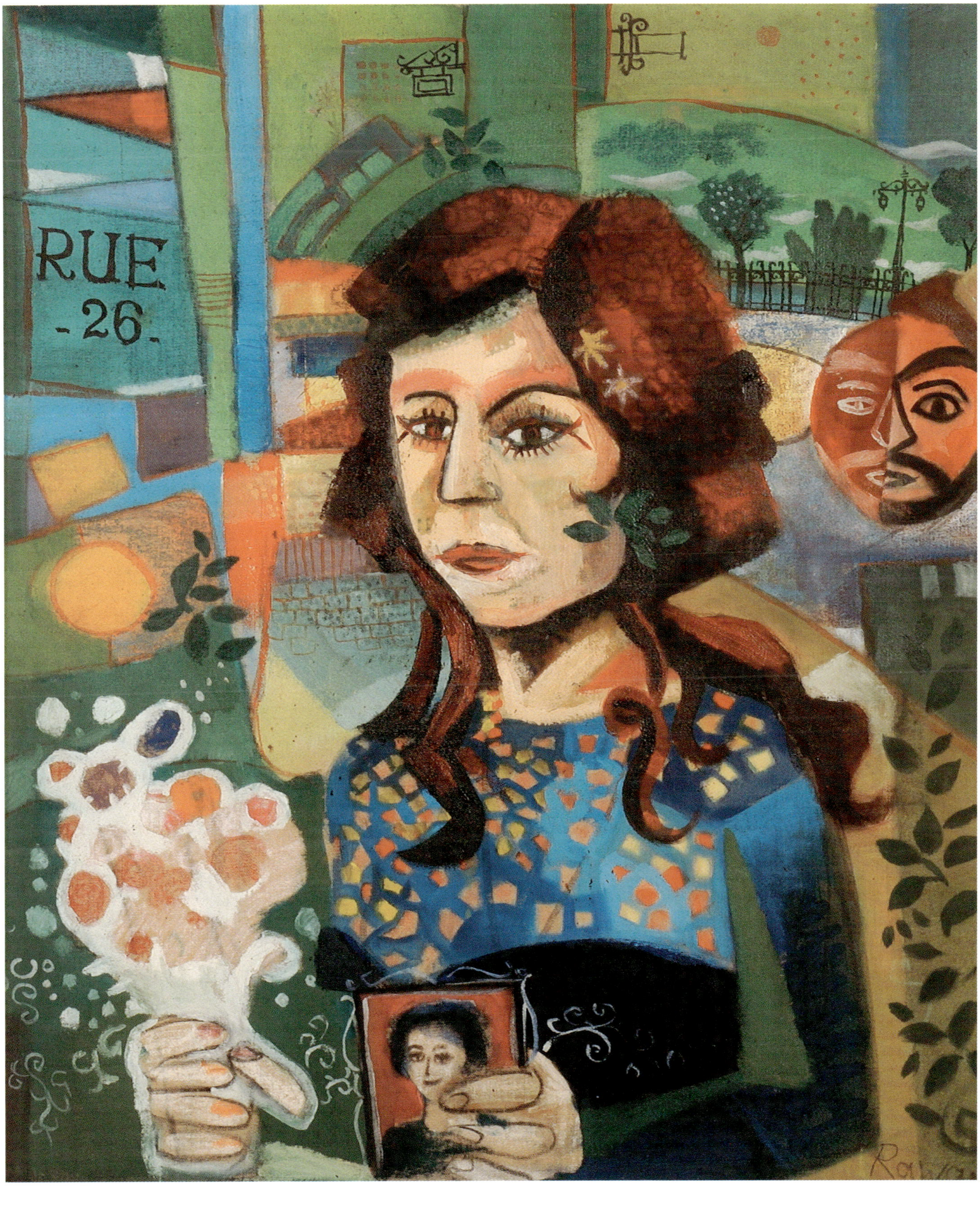
RUE
-26-

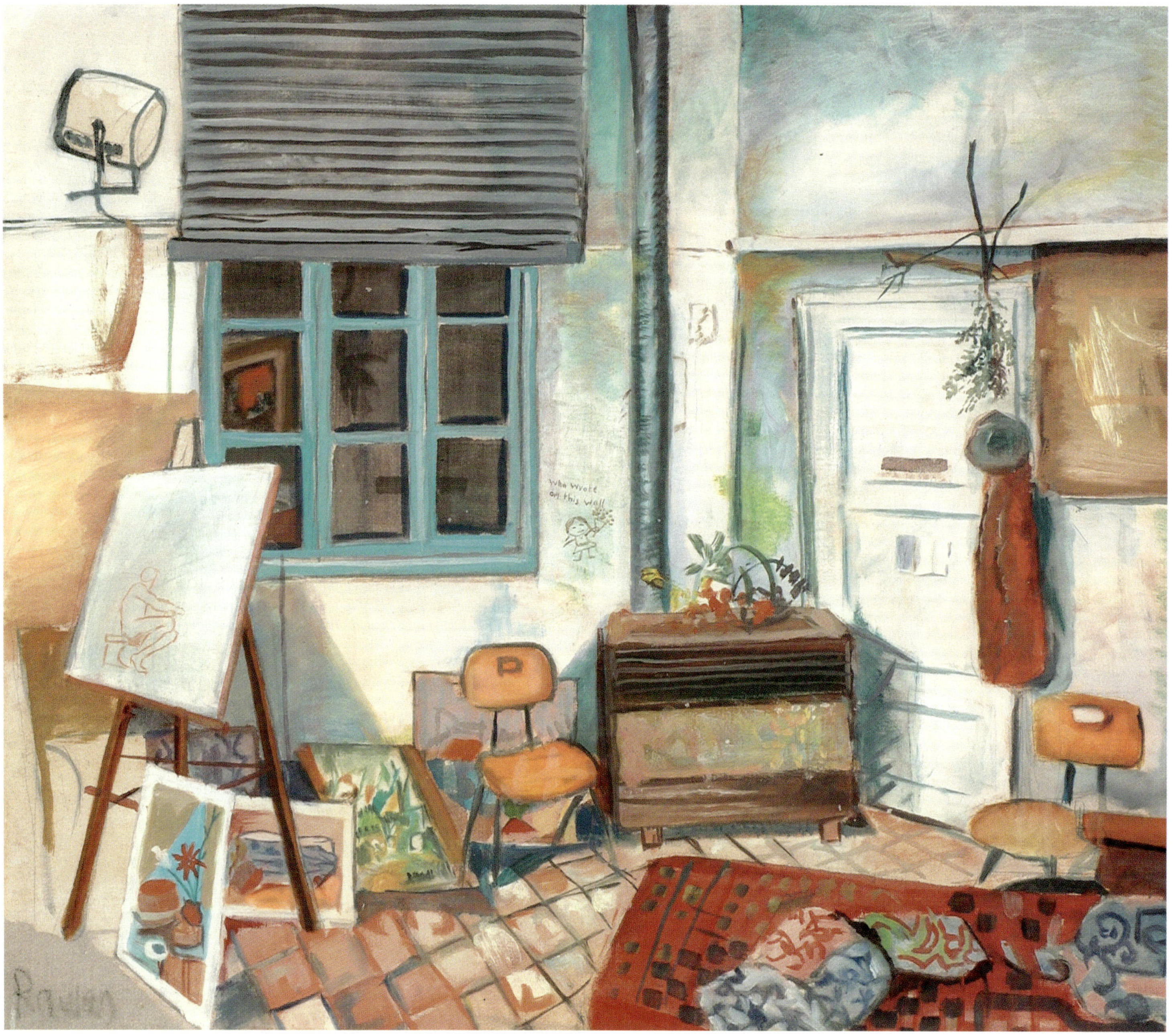

THE PAINTING STUDIO AT THE LEBANESE UNIVERSITY, 1974
Oil on canvas
65 x 75 cm
Artist's collection

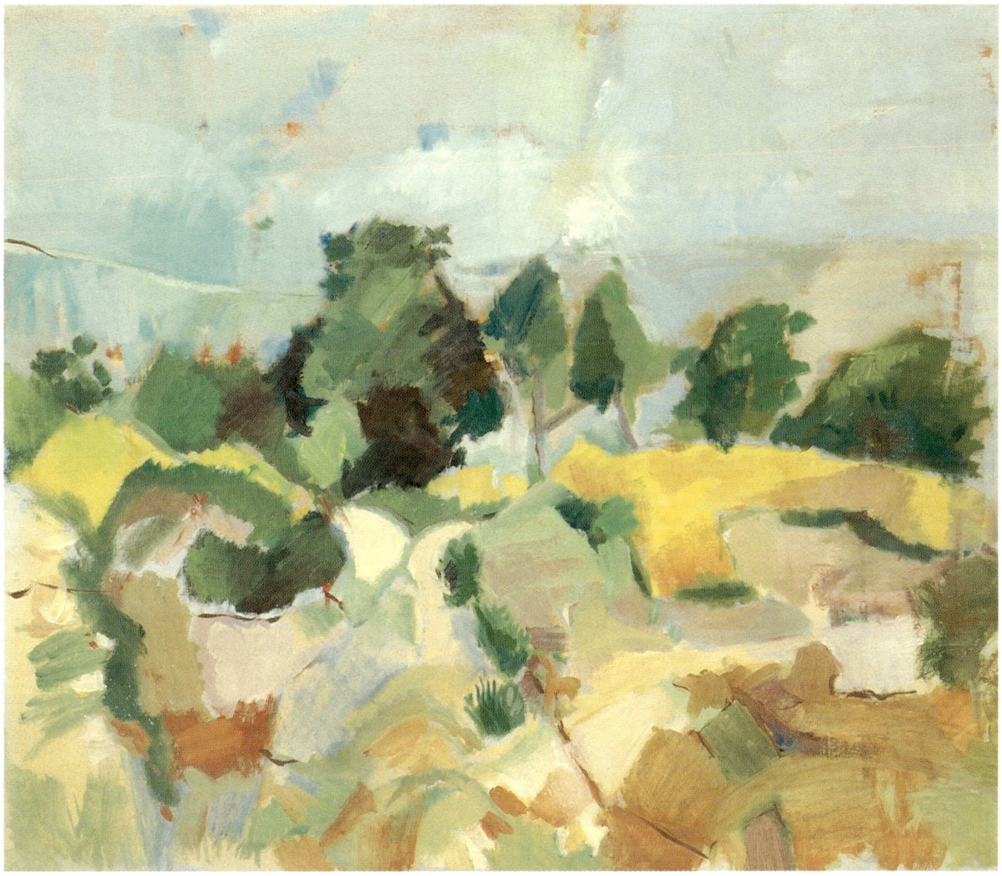

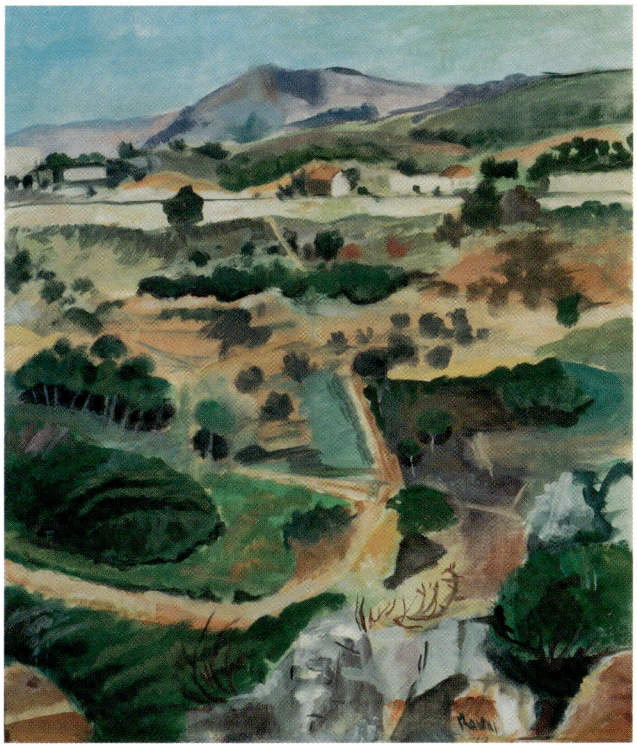

Top
A LANDSCAPE, 1974
Oil on canvas
65 x 75 cm
Artist's collection

Bottom
A LEBANESE MOUNTAINOUS LANDSCAPE, 1973
Oil on canvas
60 x 50 cm
Artist's collection

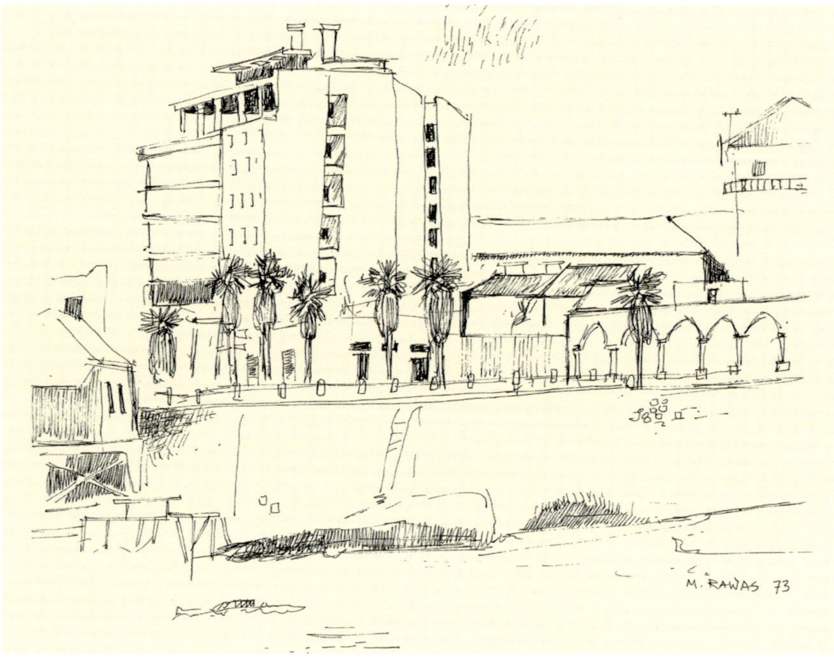

A SCENE FROM AIN AL-MRAISSEH
CORNICHE IN BEIRUT, 1973
China ink on paper
20 x 27 cm
Artist's collection

Opposite page
ABSTRACT COMPOSITION, 1975
Oil on canvas
80 x 80 cm
Collection Ms. M. Daou

In those days most of the professional and renowned local artists were teaching at the Lebanese University. Besides the late Rashid Wehbi and Rafic Charaf, we were taught by Aref Rayess, Jean Khalifé and Chafic Abboud (who, as a member of the École de Paris and residing in Paris, used to be a visiting professor). I particularly admired Abboud's work. Among the other artists who taught me were Amin al-Basha and Halim Jurdak, the latter introducing me to the very first notions of printmaking techniques, mainly etching. His course, however, was an elective one and the etching studio at the Lebanese University was poorly equipped: apart from a vintage etching press, the studio only had a small, household electric hotplate. This was somewhat compensated for by the studio's location in the vaulted basement of a beautiful nineteenth-century Ottoman building, originally a hospital but later used by the French as a courthouse until it became, in 1965, home to the Lebanese University's Institute of Fine Arts.

It was in Yvette Achckar's classes in particular that I encountered the notion of space and the dynamic movement of the visual components of a painting. I remember that, at the time, I was not fully capable of understanding the notion of pictorial expressive dynamics, so I used to take a shortcut, by

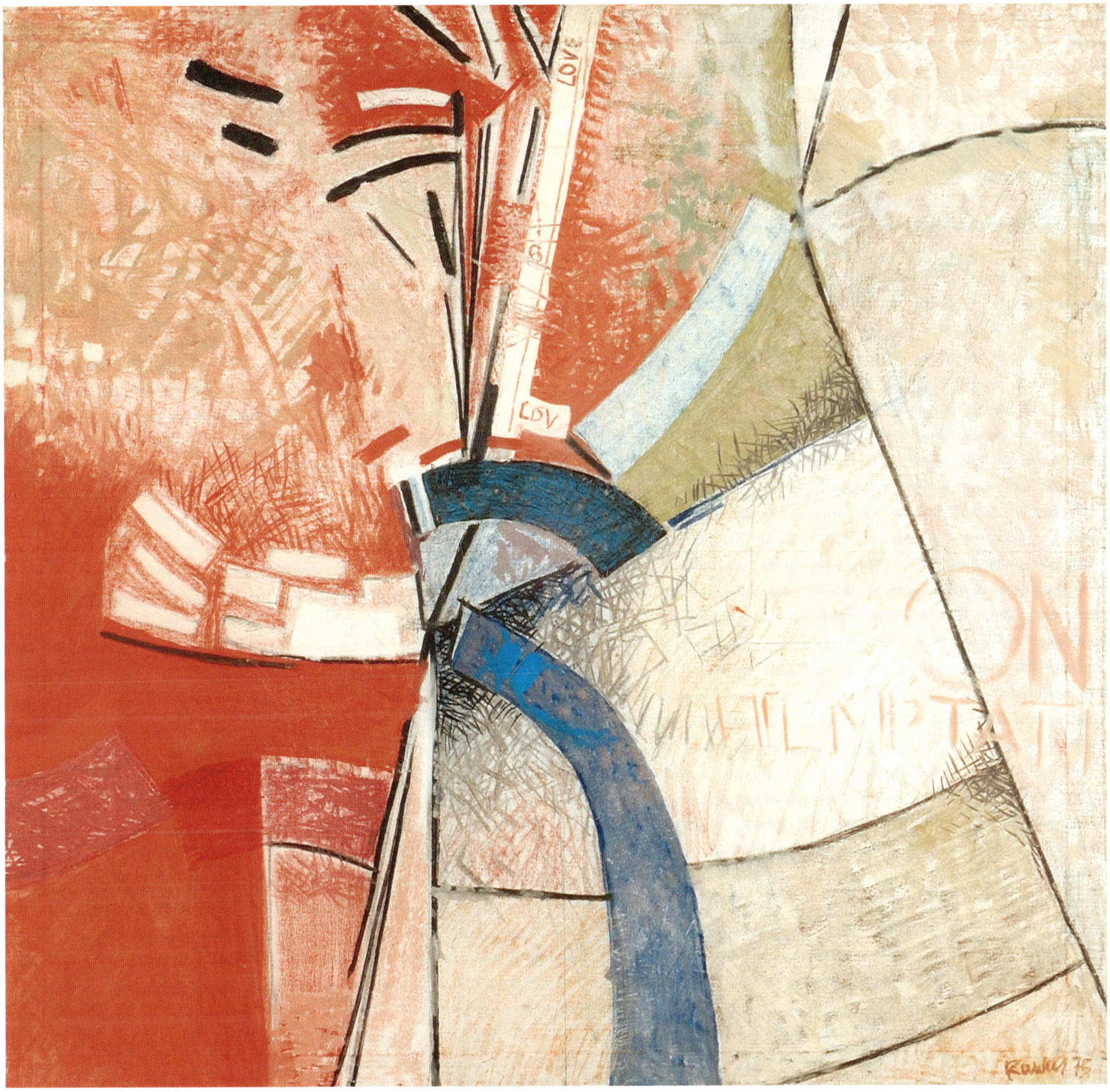
LOVE
LOV
ON

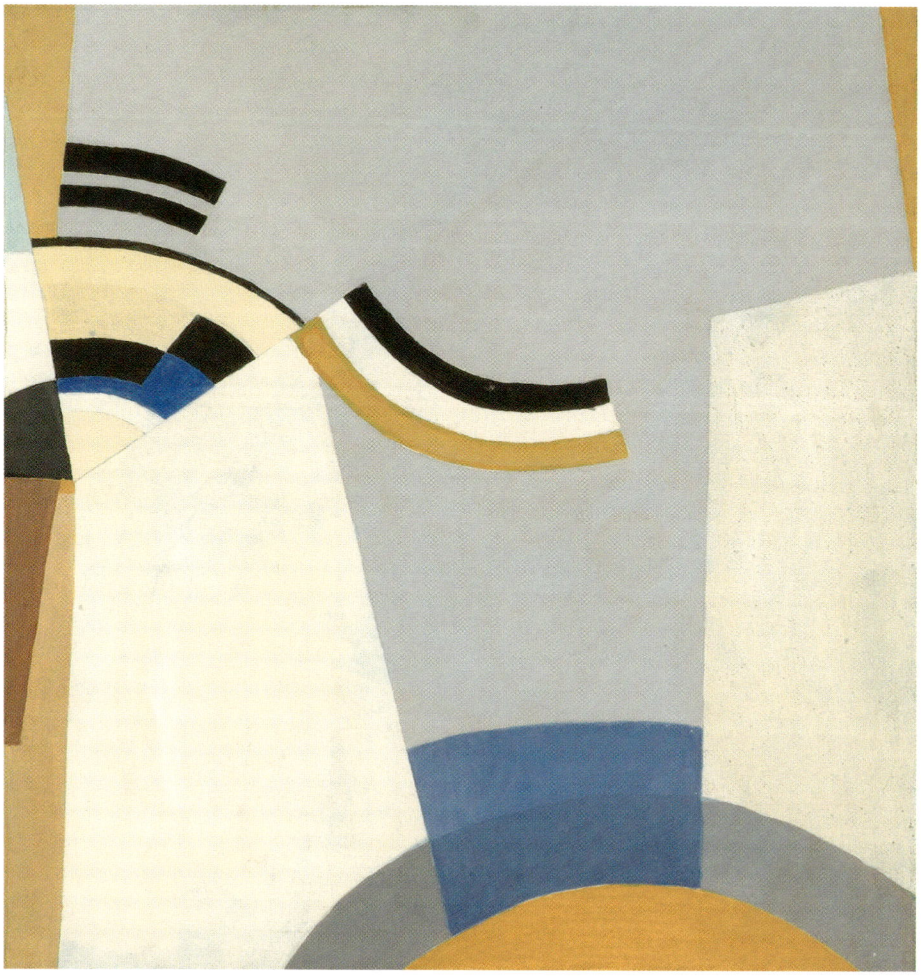

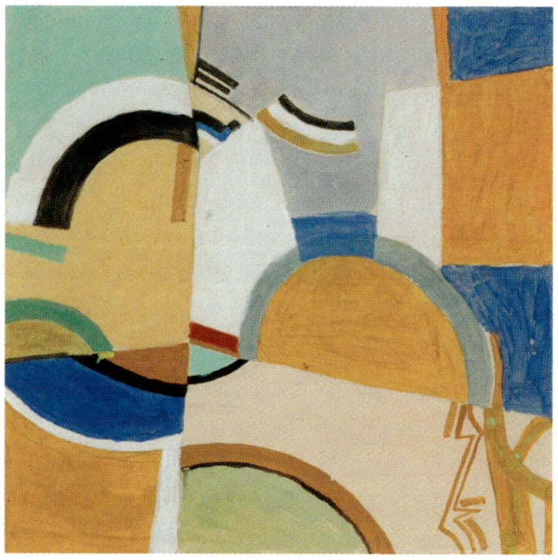

Top
THE FALLING BRIDGE, 1972
Oil on canvas
64 x 59 cm
Artist's collection

Bottom
STUDY FOR 'THE FALLING BRIDGE', 1972
Oil on paper
31.5 x 31.5 cm
Artist's collection

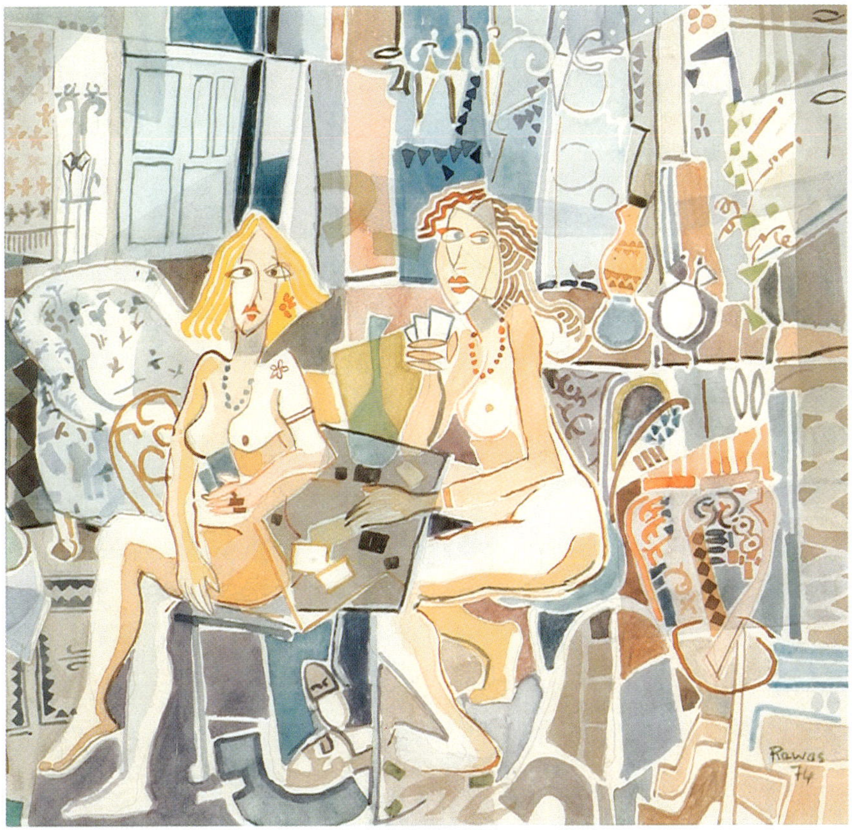

TWO NUDES PLAYING CARDS, 1974
Watercolor on paper
28.5 x 29 cm
Collection Ms. M. Daou

looking at one of her works in a catalogue and imitating it. Later – through my own outside readings – I came to understand fully the elements and principles of design and the rules of visual perception in the arts.

In general, the type of art I was doing at the Institute of Fine Arts was painting from still life and live models, and working on various landscape themes. On another level, I did watercolor paintings depicting simple themes of still life and interiors. These paintings were done in a decorative and oriental arabesque style. No matter how varied the stylistic manipulations I attempted, my work in general, remained limited to an exercise in observation. Although such exercises helped in developing and strengthening one's skills of visual and pictorial composition, they did not include much in the way of ideas or concepts.

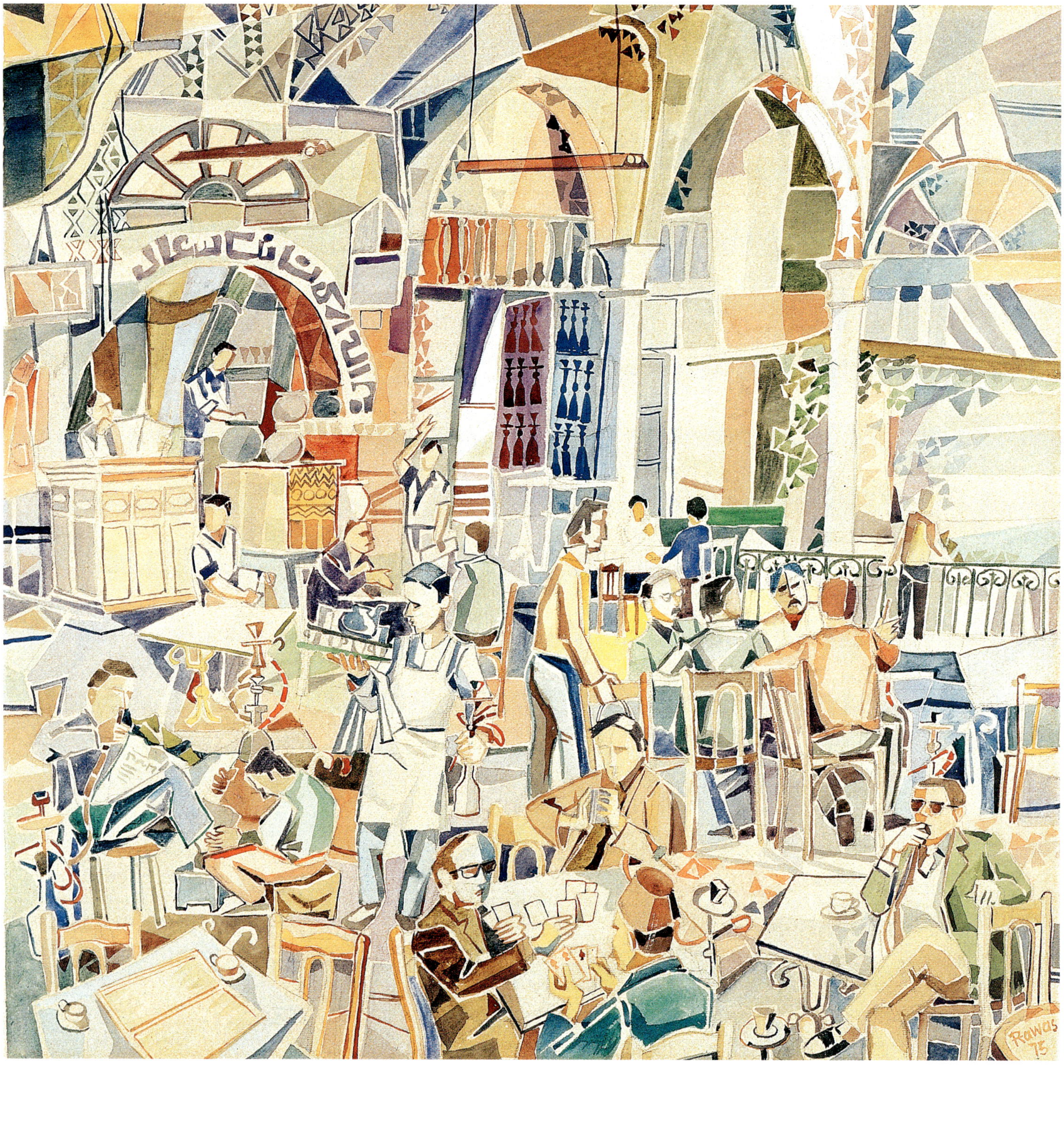
Rawas
75

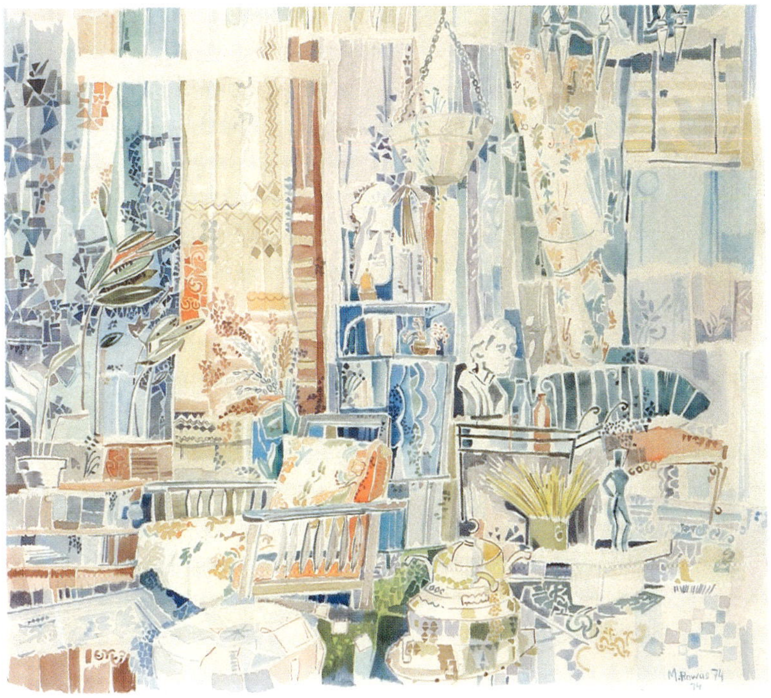

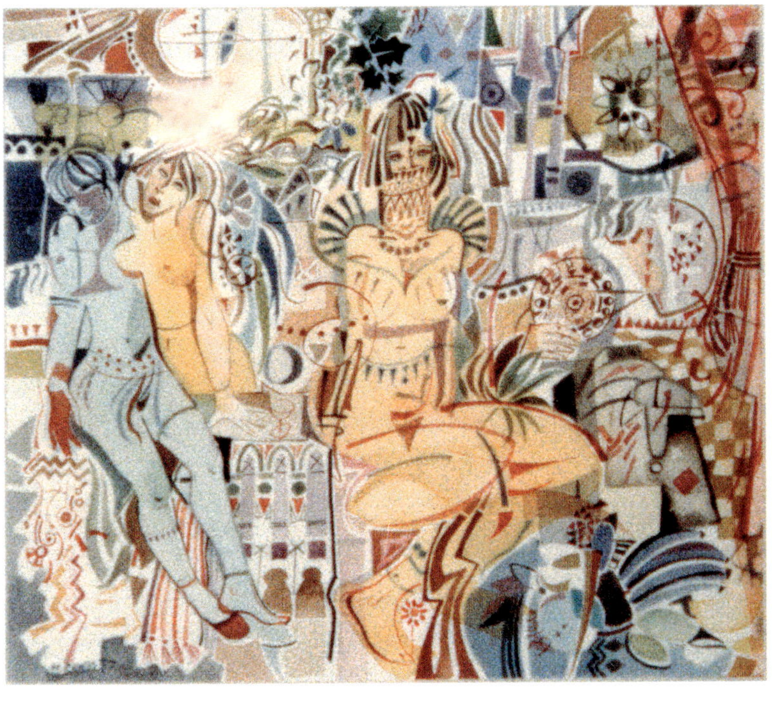

Top
AN INTERIOR, 1974
Watercolor on paper
43.5 x 47.5 cm
Collection Ms. M. Daou

Bottom
HAREM, 1977
Watercolor on paper
50 x 60 cm
Private collection

Opposite page
THE COFFEE HOUSE, 1975
Watercolor on paper
47 x 47 cm
Collection Mr. & Mrs. G. Mekdashi

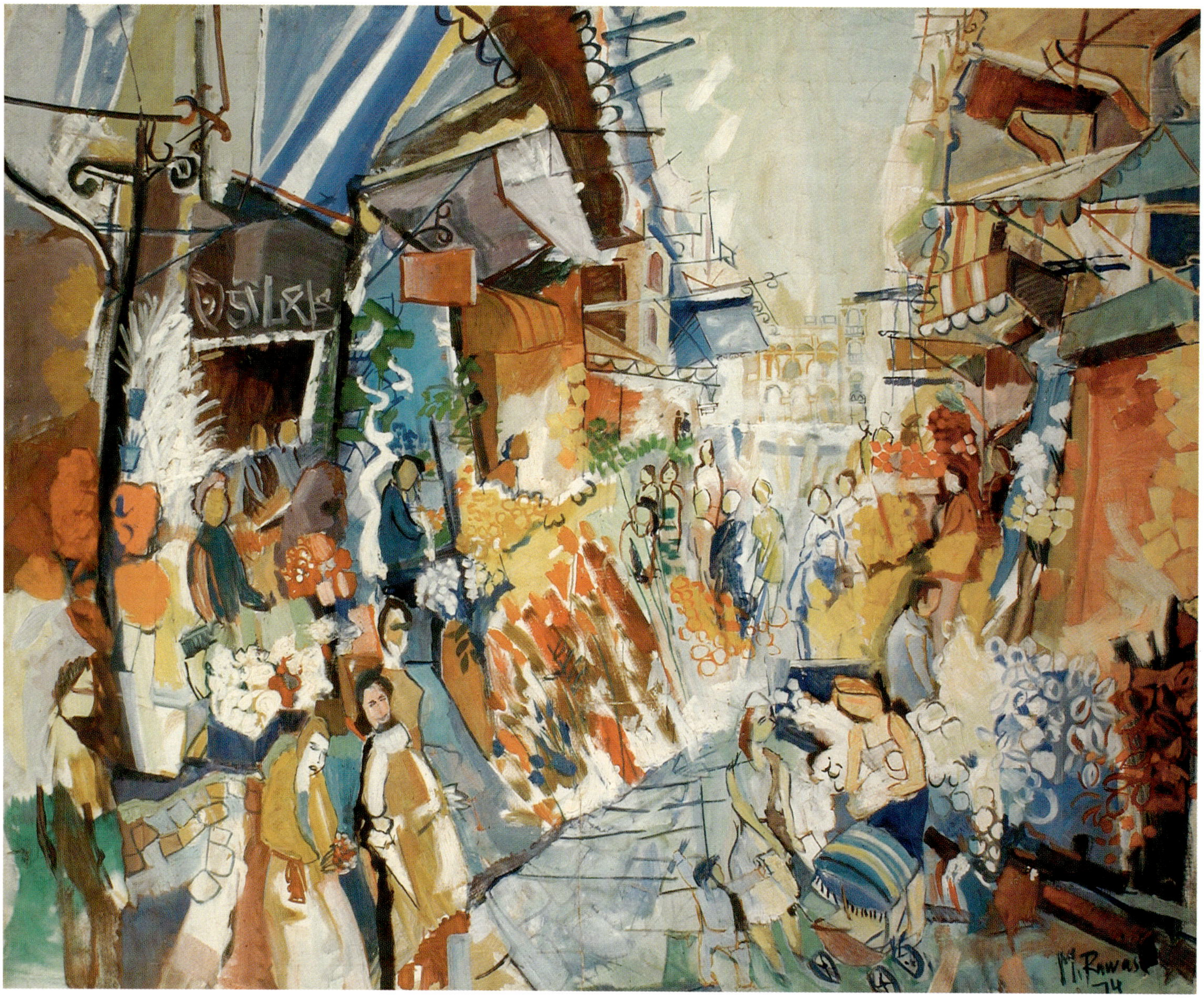

BEIRUT VEGETABLE MARKET, 1974
Oil on canvas
133 x 161 cm
Collection Ms. M. Daou

Opposite page
WHITE, 1975
Oil and pencil on paper mounted on plywood panel
120 x 86 cm
Artist's collection

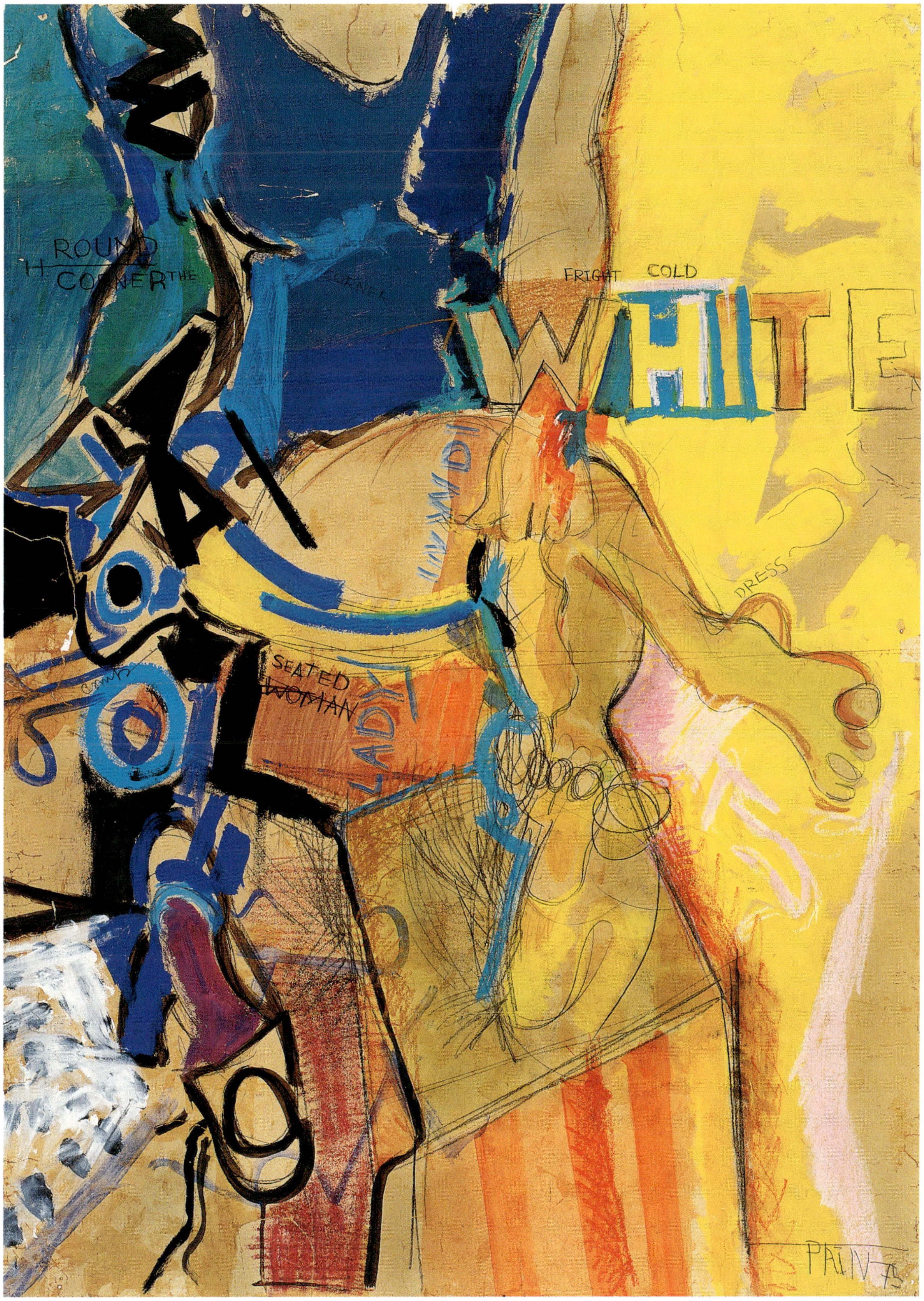
ROUND
CORNER THE
FRIGHT COLD
WHITE
DRESS
SEATED
WOMAN
LADY

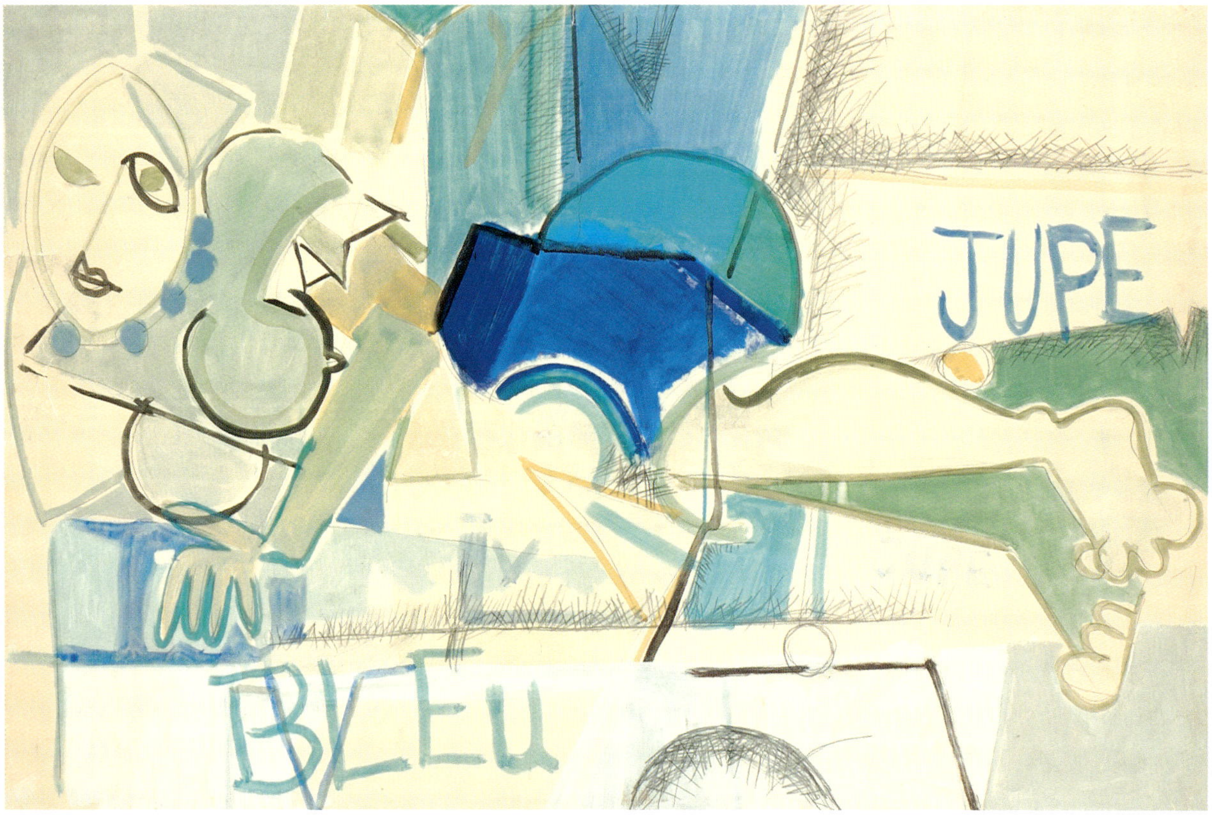
JUPE
BLEU

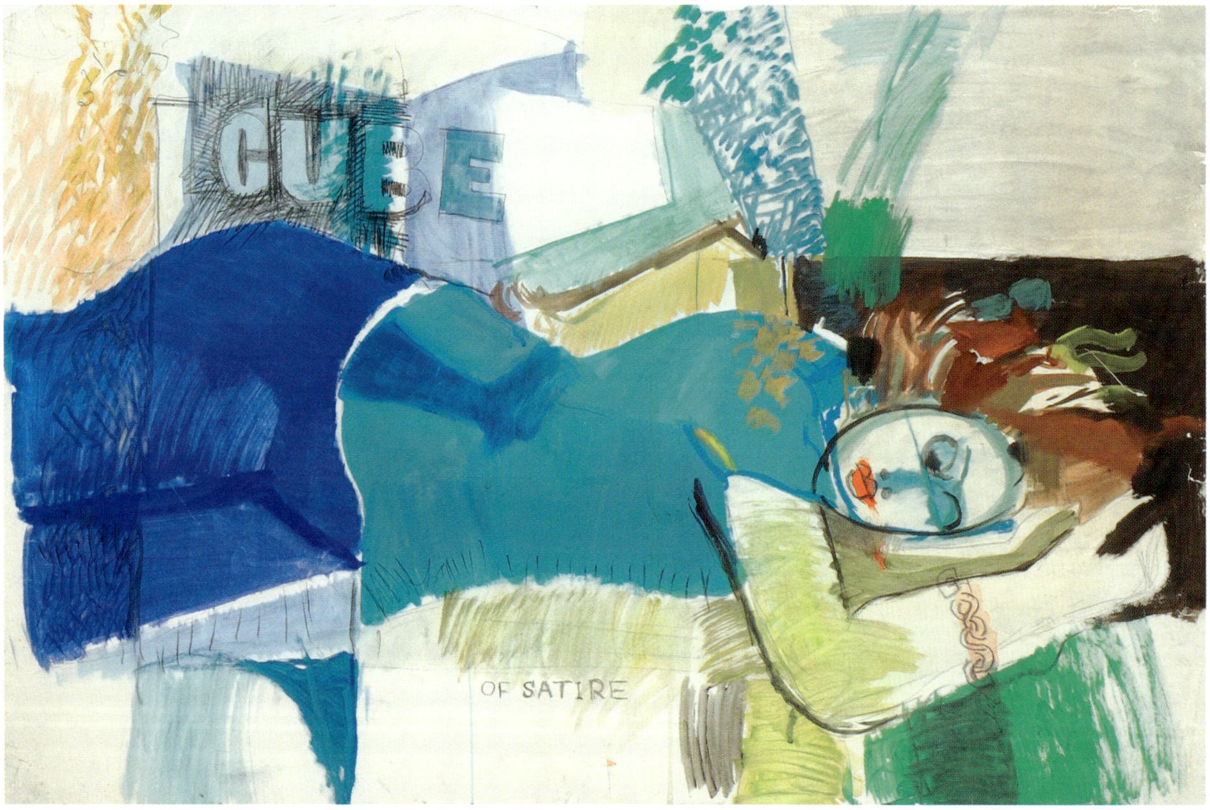
CUBE
OF SATIRE

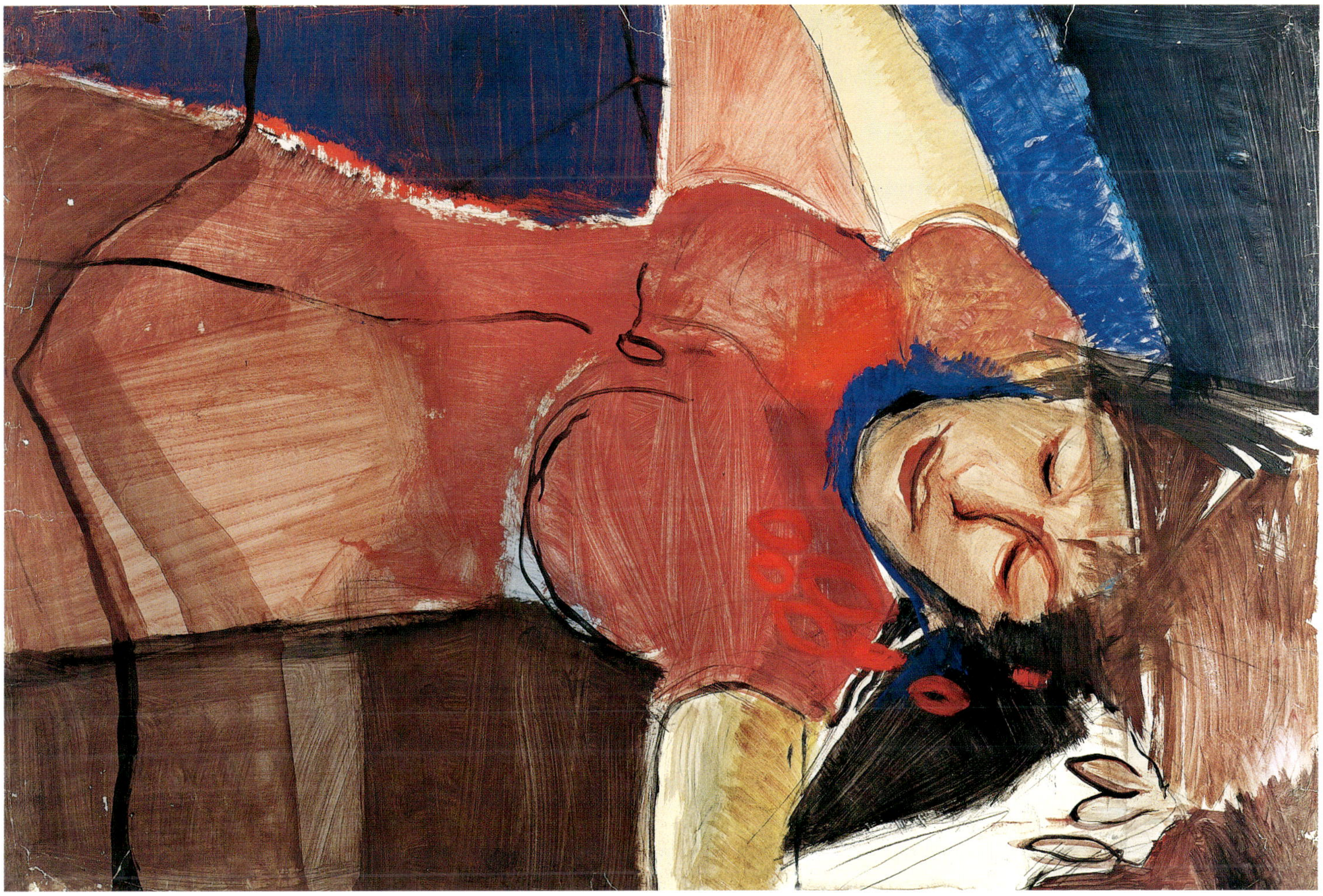

A LYING WOMAN IN RED, 1975
Oil and pencil on paper mounted on cardboard
68.5 x 100 cm
Artist's collection

Opposite page

Top
JUPE BLEUE, 1975
Oil and charcoal on paper mounted on cardboard
70 x 100 cm
Artist's collection

Bottom
CUBE, 1975
Oil and charcoal on paper mounted on cardboard
70 x 100 cm
Artist's collection

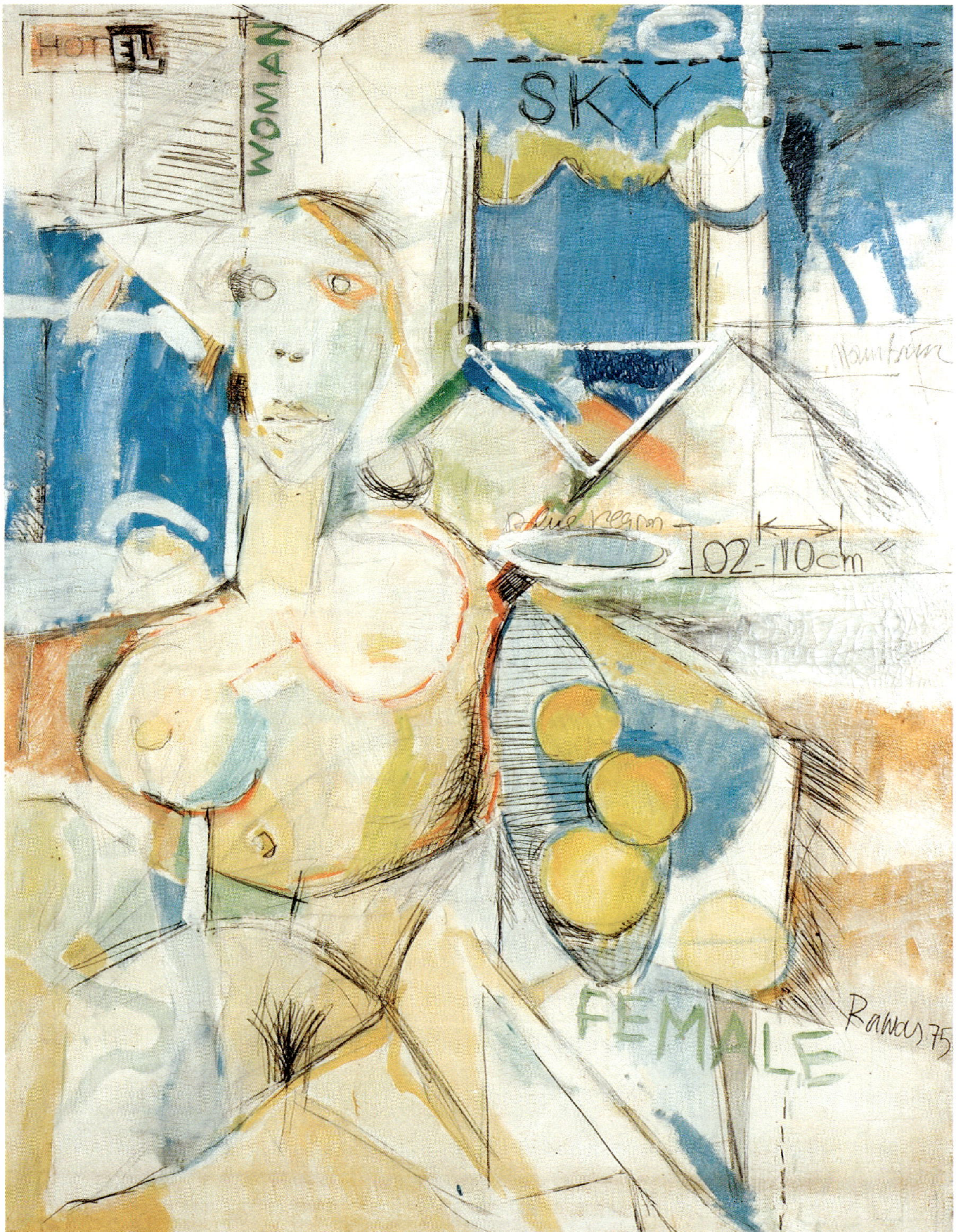
HOTEL
WOMAN
SKY
102-110cm
FEMALE

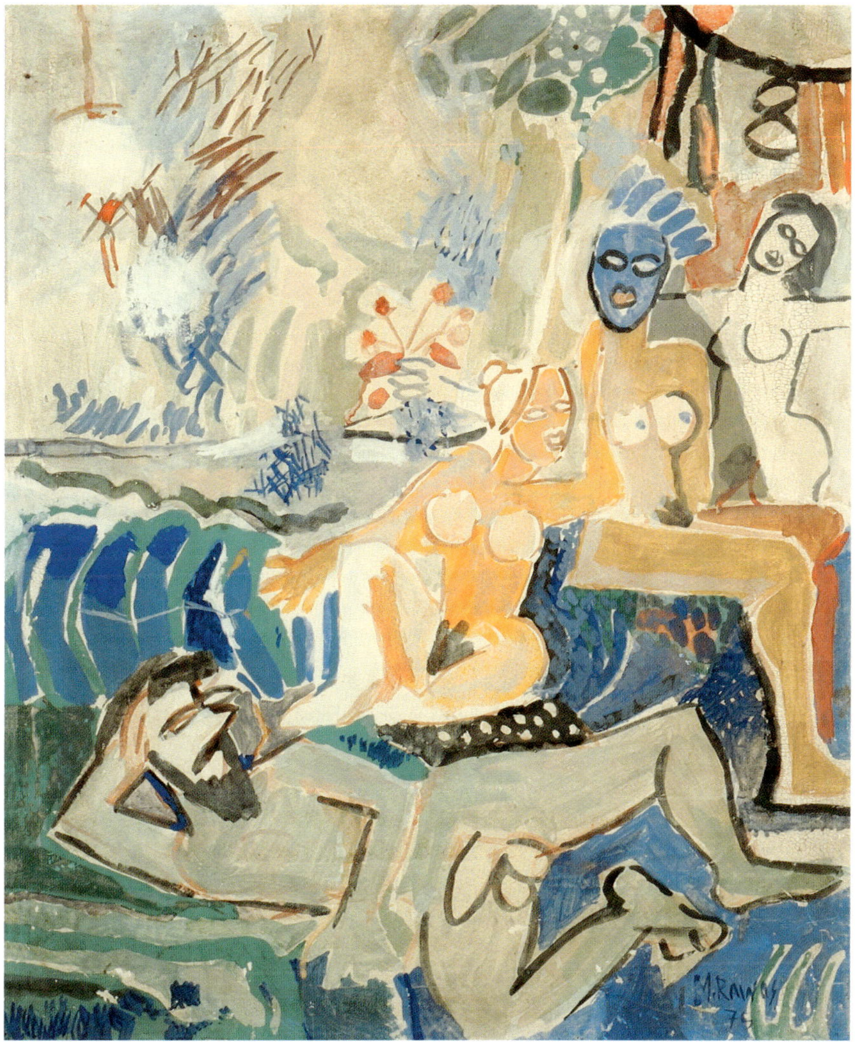

NUDE FIGURES IN NATURE, 1975
Oil on canvas
52 x 42 cm
Collection Ms. M. Daou

Opposite page
SKY, 1975
Oil and charcoal on canvas
100 x 74 cm
Collection Ms. M. Daou

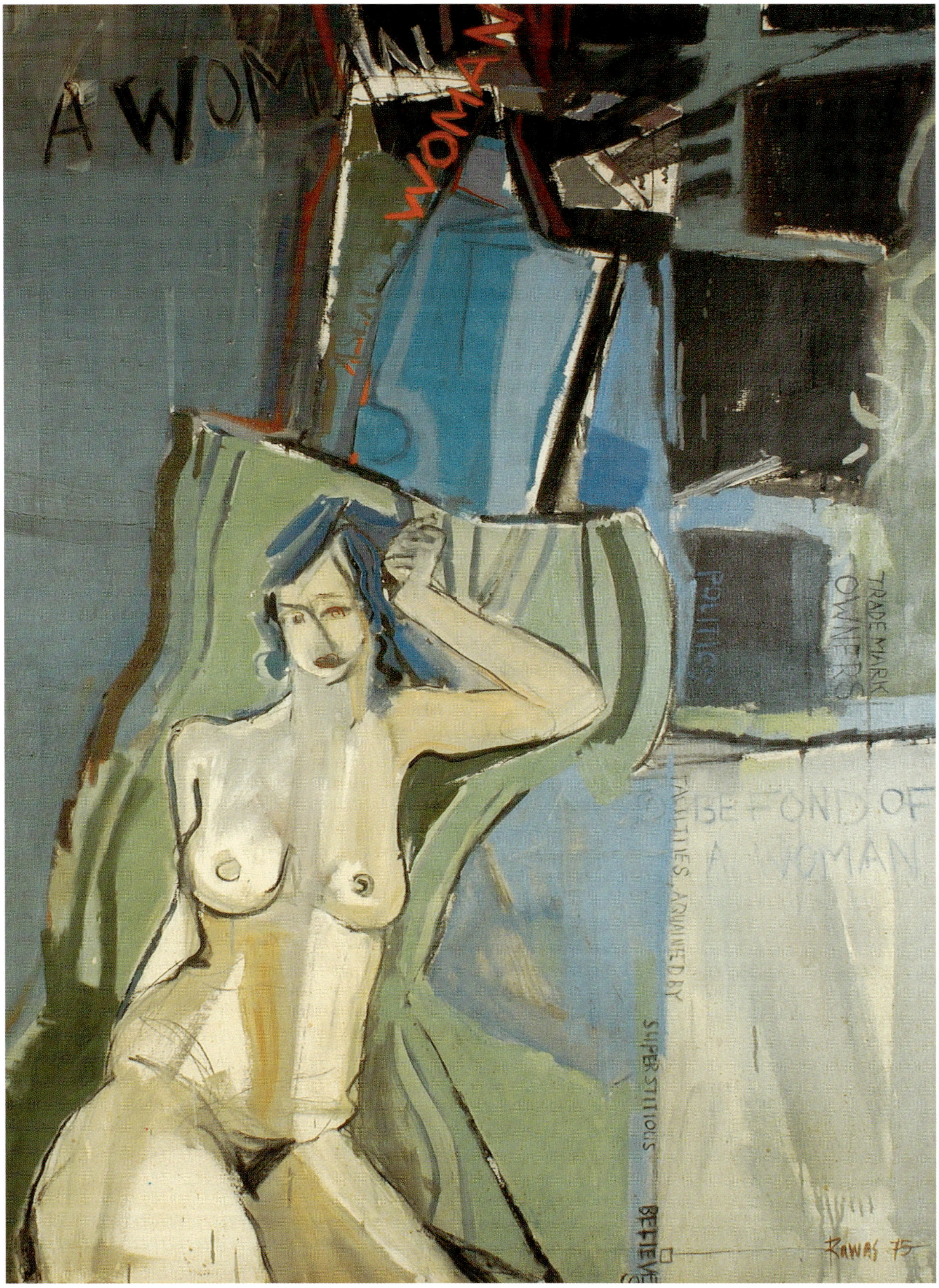
A WOM
TRADE MARK
OWNERS
POLITICS
TO BE FOND OF
A WOMAN
SUPERSTITIOUS
BELIEVE
Rawas 75

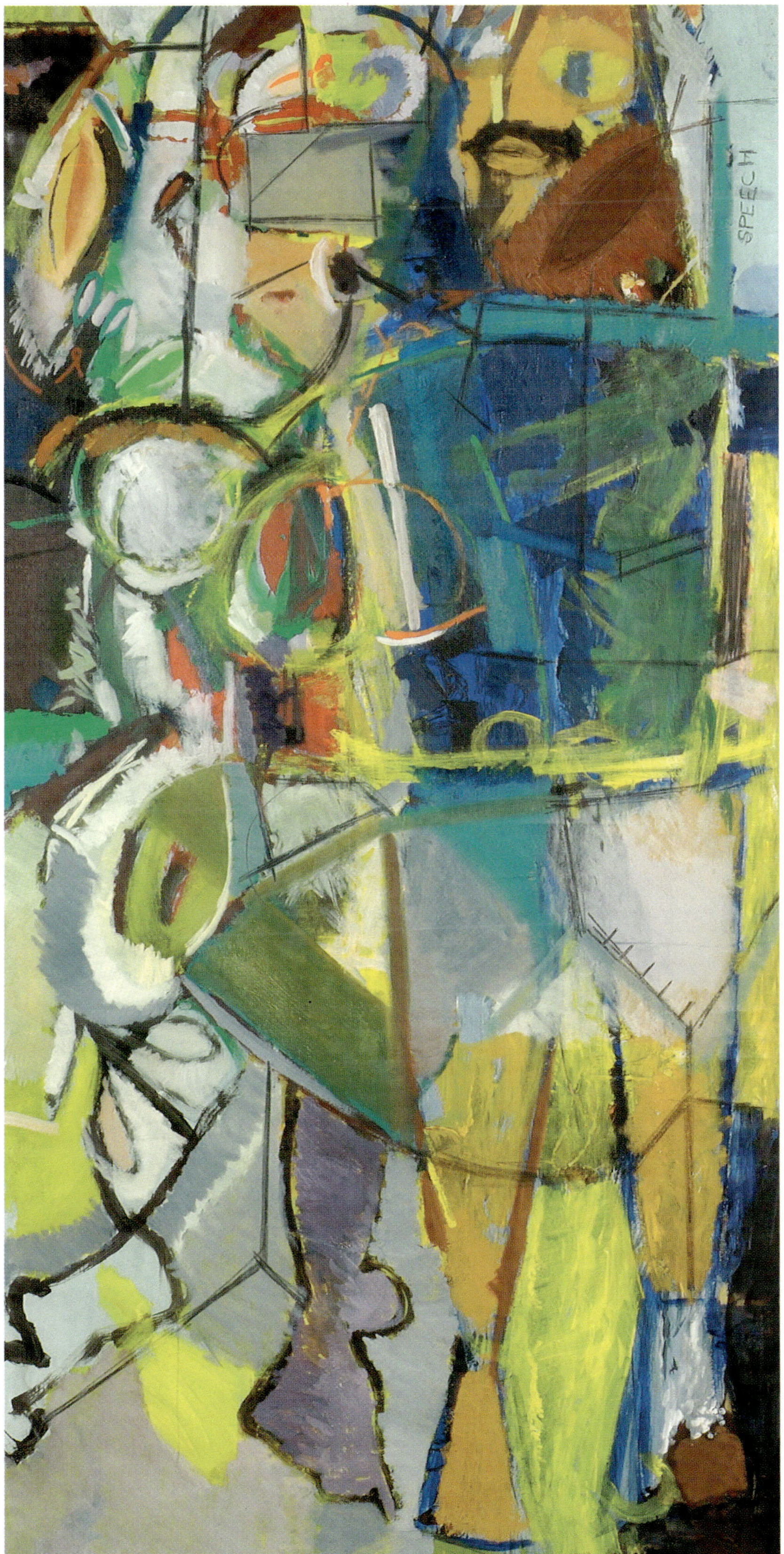

A COUPLE, OR HOMAGE TO ARSHILE GORKY, 1975
Oil and charcoal on canvas
148 x 70 cm
Artist's collection

Opposite page
WOMAN, 1975
Oil on canvas
128 x 91.5 cm
Collection Ms. M. Daou

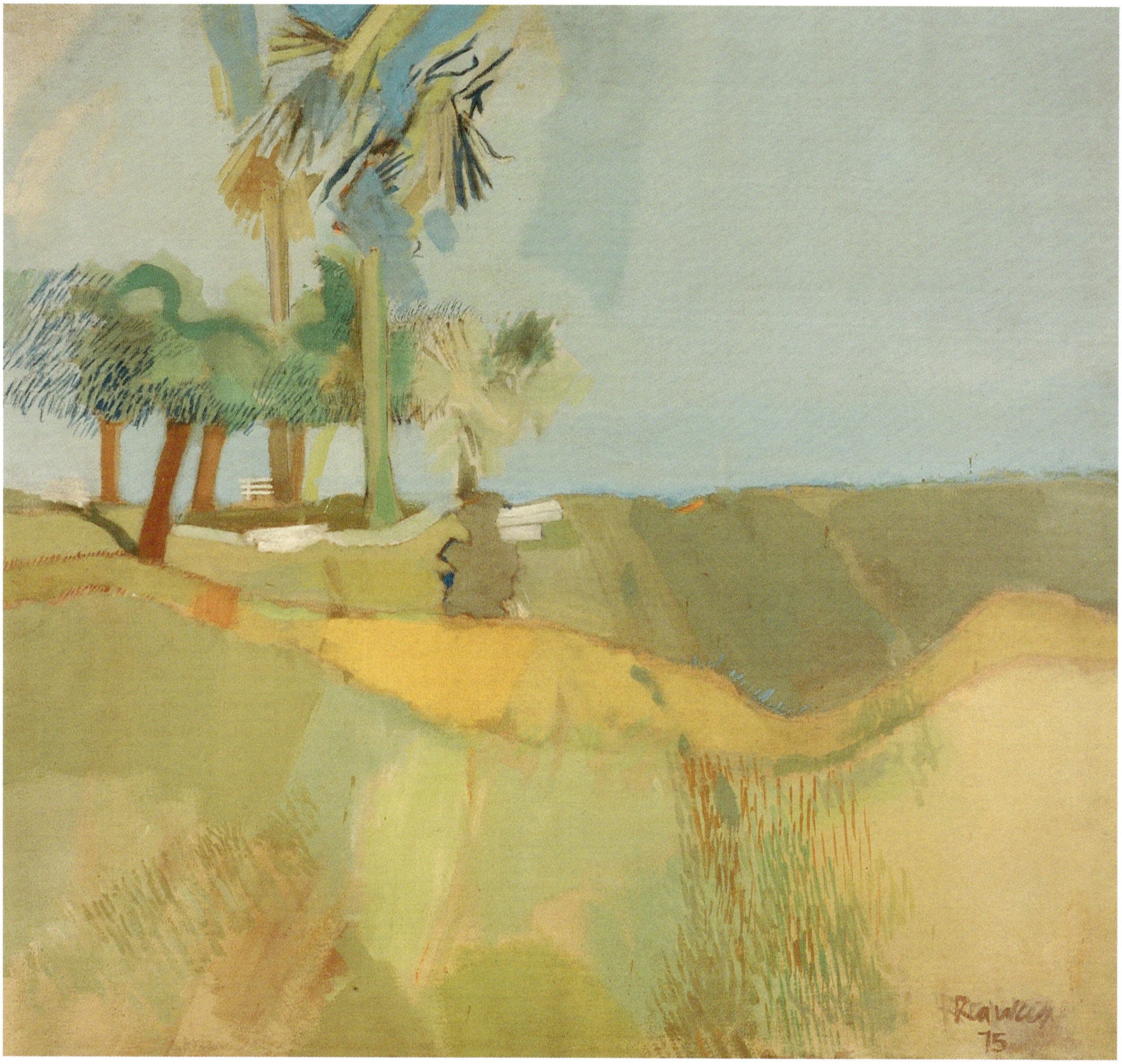

LANDSCAPE, 1975
Oil on canvas
68 x 73 cm
Collection Ms. M. Daou

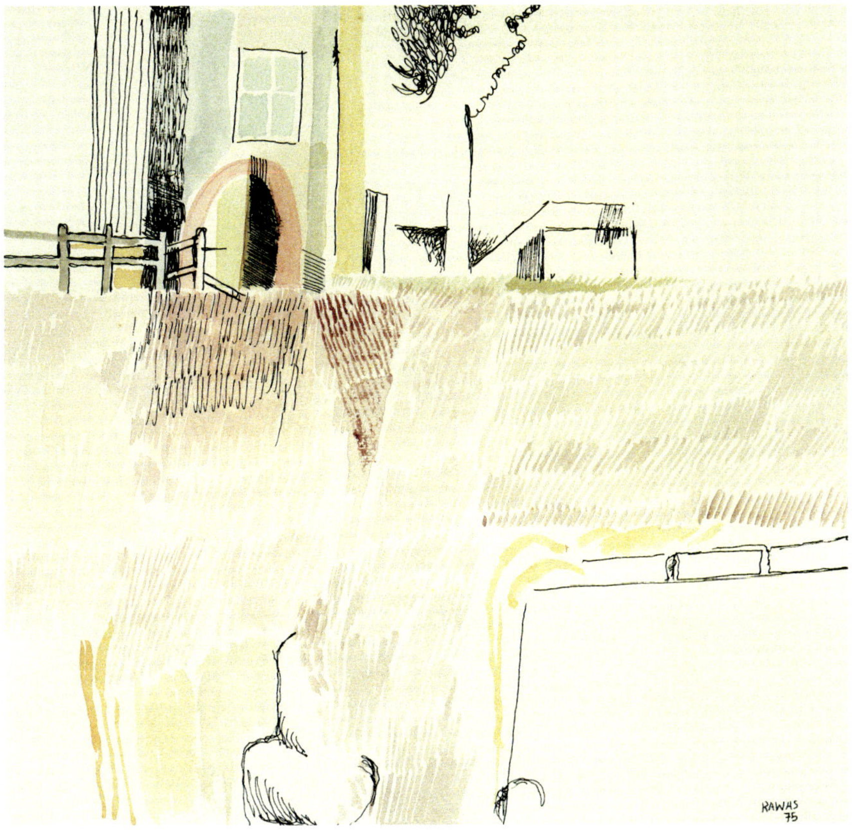

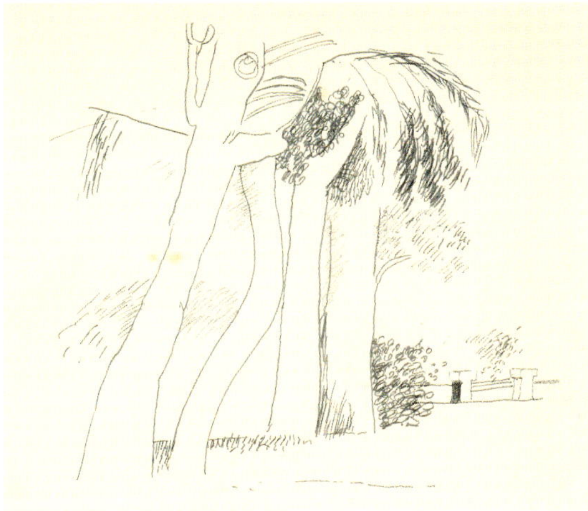

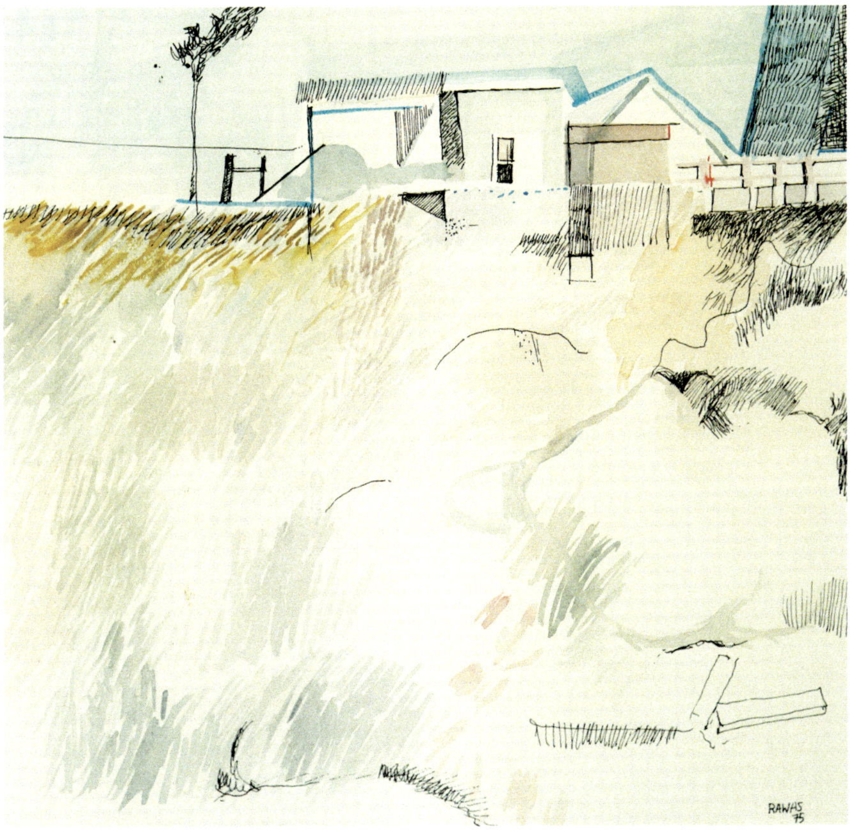

Top left
LANDSCAPE I, 1975
Watercolor and china ink on paper
20 x 20 cm
Collection Mr. & Mrs. R. Saidi

Top right
THE GARDEN AT THE LEBANESE UNIVERSITY III, 1974
Felt pen on paper
25 x 29 cm
Artist's collection

Bottom
LANDSCAPE II, 1975
Watercolor and china ink on paper
20 x 20 cm
Collection Mr. & Mrs. R. Saidi

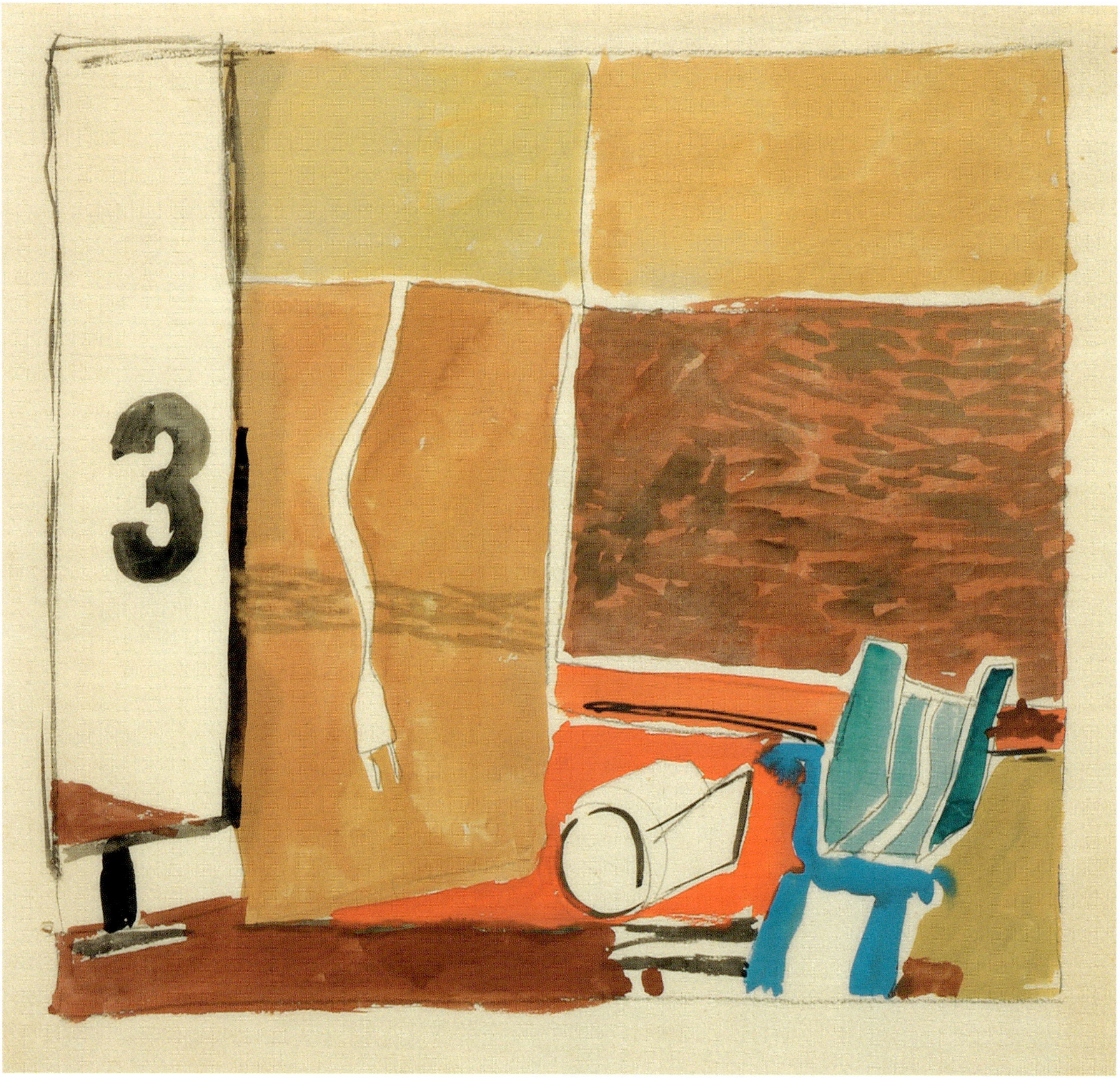

INTERIOR 3, 1974
Gouache and charcoal on paper
38 x 40 cm
Artist's collection

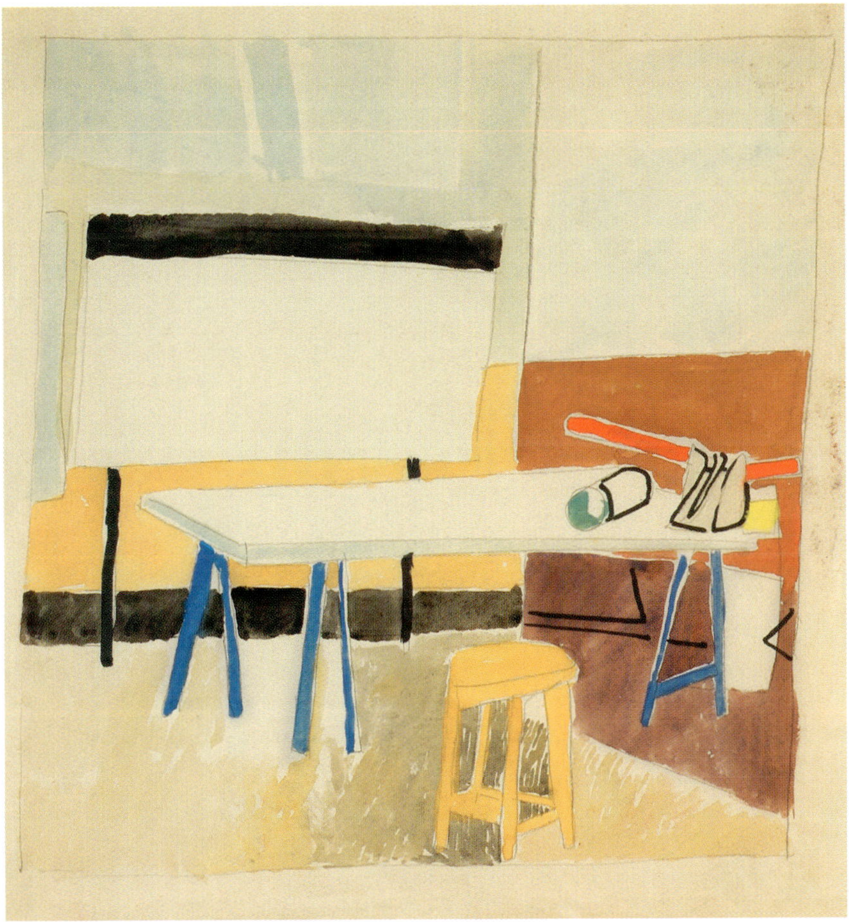

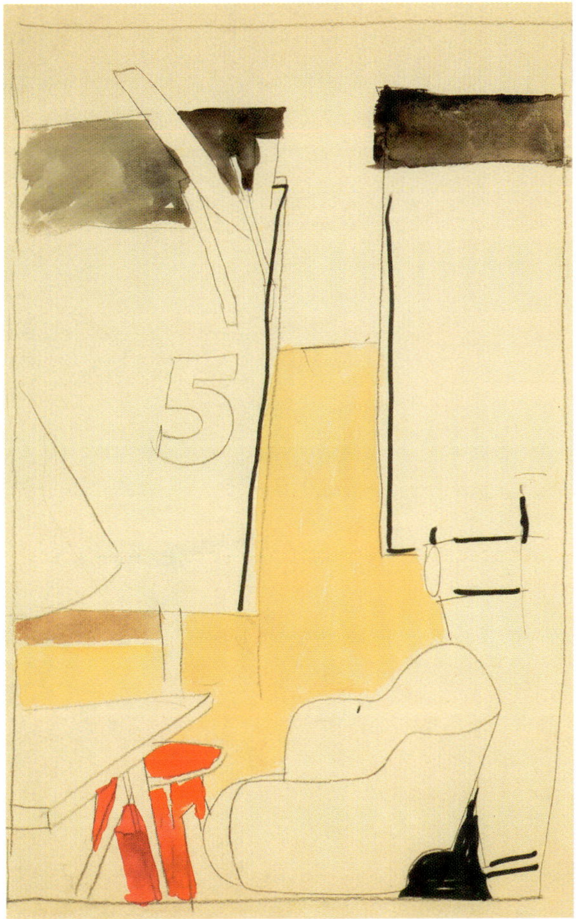

Top left
STUDIO INTERIOR, 1974
Gouache and charcoal on paper
42 x 38.5 cm
Artist's collection

Top right
INTERIOR 5, 1974
Gouache and charcoal on paper
44 x 30 cm
Artist's collection

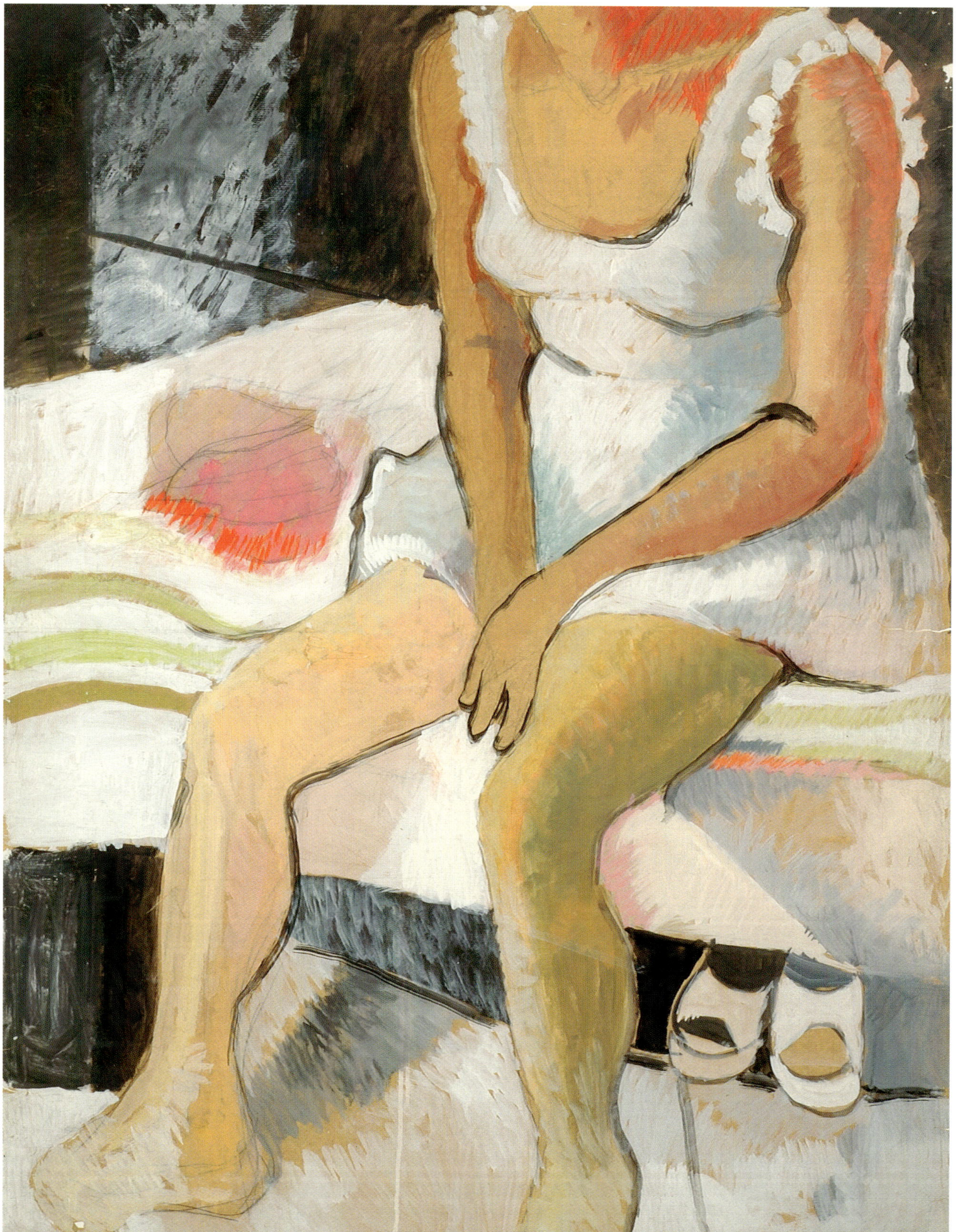

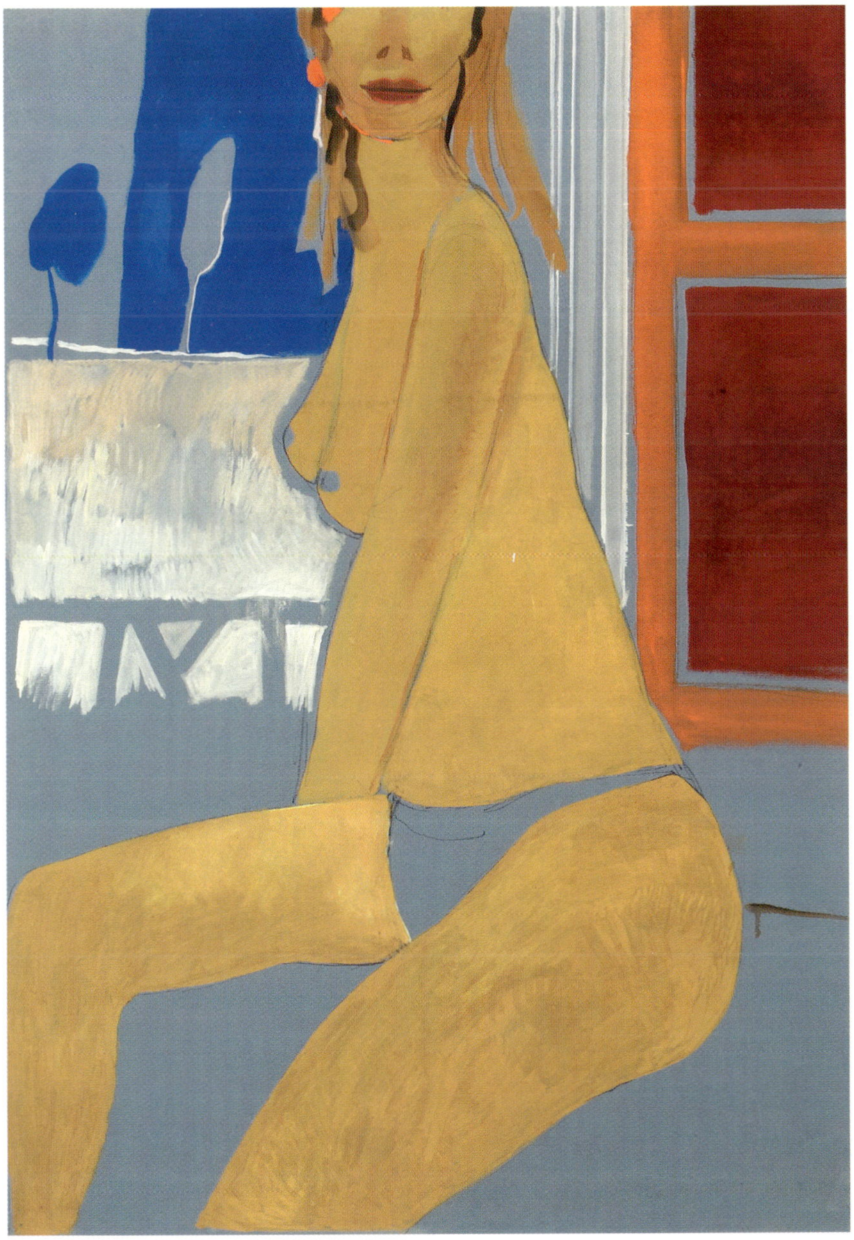

A NUDE BY A WINDOW, 1975
Oil and charcoal on colored cardboard
100 x 70 cm
Artist's collection

Opposite page
A SEATED WOMAN IN WHITE, 1975
Oil and crayon on paper mounted on cardboard
120 x 90 cm
Artist's collection

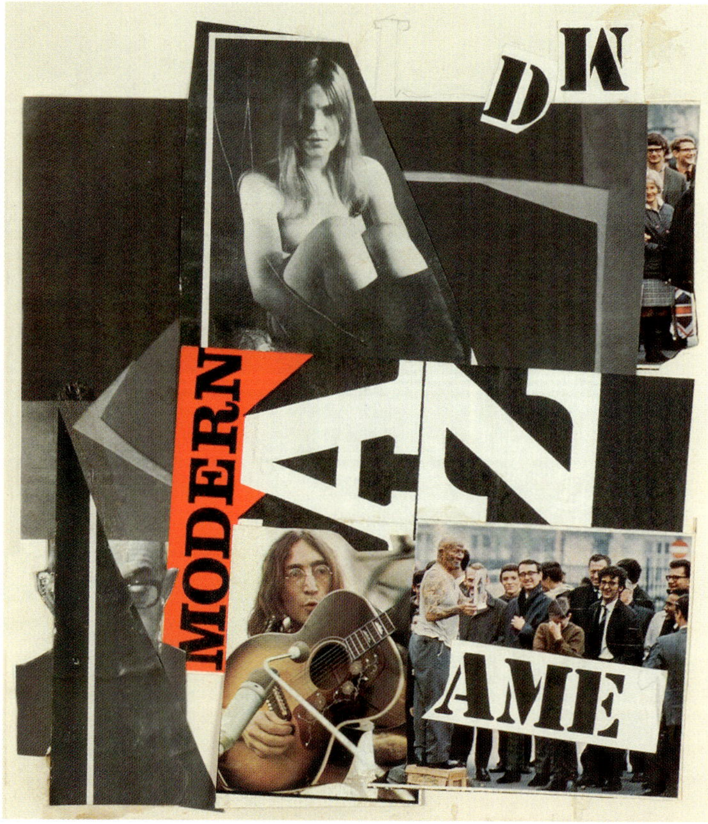

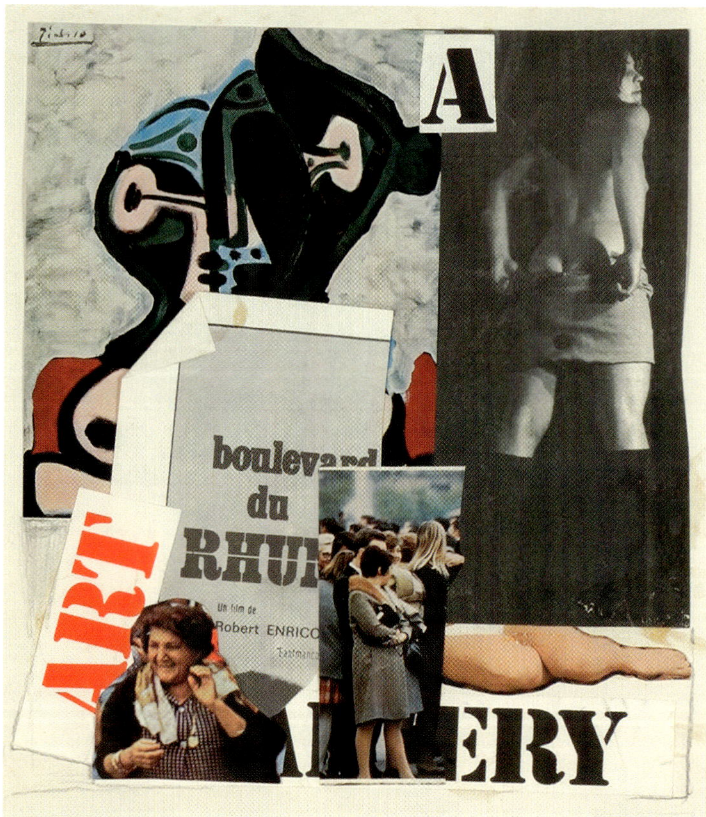

Top
MODERN AZ, 1975
Collage on paper
23 x 19 cm
Artist's collection

Bottom
ART, 1975
Collage on paper
18.5 x 16 cm
Artist's collection

New Directions

The need to push my work in a direction that would encompass intellectual content increased after coming across two books: *Art Without Boundaries: 1950–1970*, by Gerald Woods, Philip Thompson and John Williams (Thames and Hudson, London, 1972) and *Movements in Art Since 1945* by Edward Lucie-Smith (Thames and Hudson, London, 1984). These two books became my precious points of reference and my constant companions. I was always looking through them, intrigued by the versatile means of expression artists used, particularly photography. My earliest attempts to introduce photography into my work (in 1973, while still an art student) used collaged pictures from magazines.

My notion of the importance of the textural manipulation of the painted surface of the canvas was triggered and developed by my discussions with Michael Fani, whom I first met as a fellow student at the Institute of Fine Arts. He was well-read and more knowledgeable about art than any of us then, and although he dropped out of the Institute, he remained my friend. It was through discussions with Fani that I came to understand the meanings and theoretical justifications of modern art movements. I worked with him on preparing my final graduation paper on American Abstract Expressionism, a movement which greatly influenced me, particularly the work of Arshile Gorky. My final graduation project was inspired by one of this artist's paintings, *The Liver is the Cock's Comb* (1944).

Although ranging between Abstract Expressionism and Pop Art, Robert Rauschenberg's work fascinated me too, particularly his

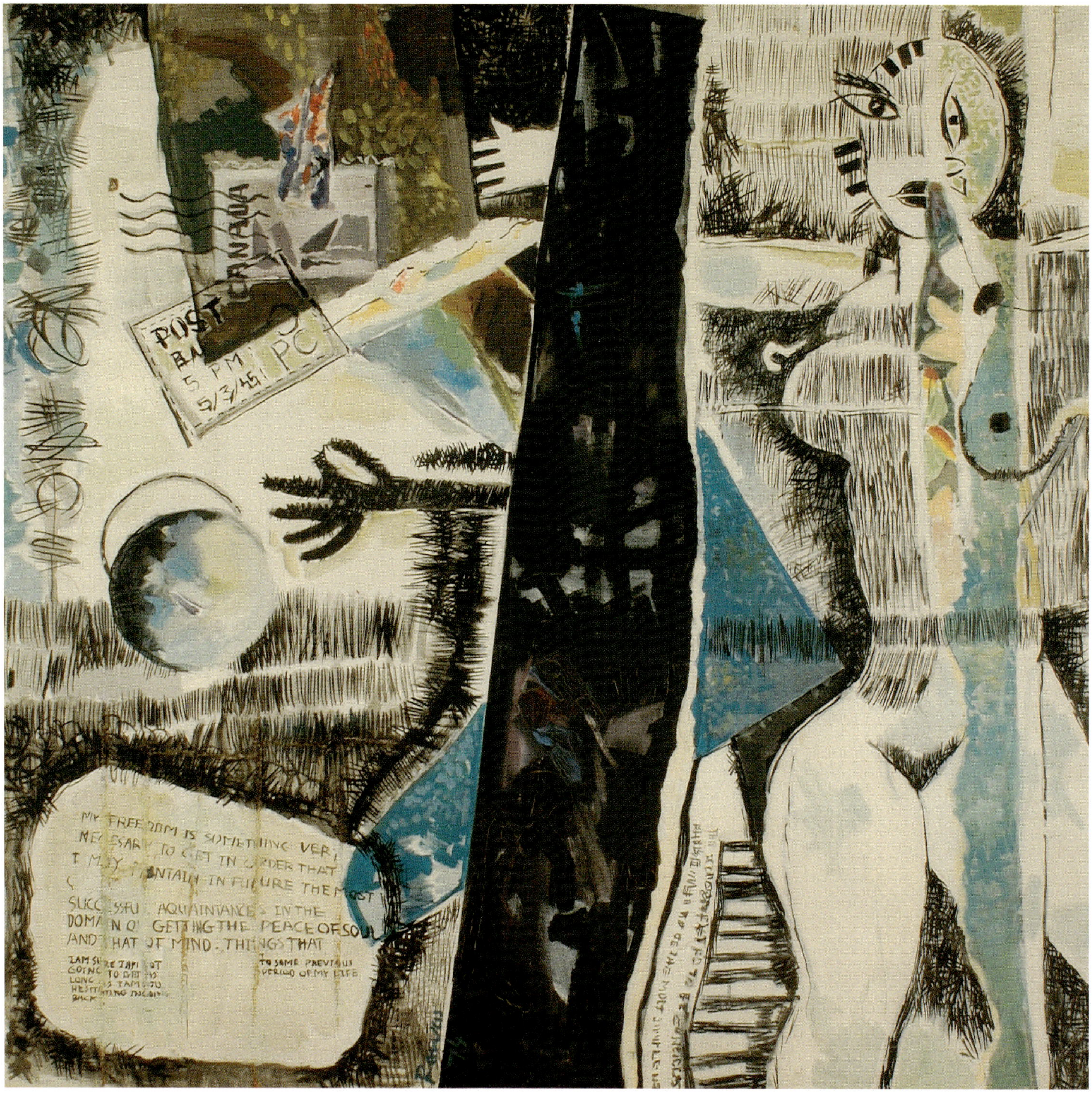

A POSTED LETTER, 1974
Oil on canvas
100 x 100 cm
Collection Ms. M. Daou

use of photographic images. I wanted to use photographs because of their quality of complete objectivity in terms of representing the real world. A photograph placed next to an image painted in a realistic style offered a variety of visual and conceptual sensibilities that attracted me – and still does. I began by using collaged photographs, and I consider that my personal style started taking shape during this period. I also started introducing written words and texts into my work, realizing the richness of using both means of communication: the visualized and the read.

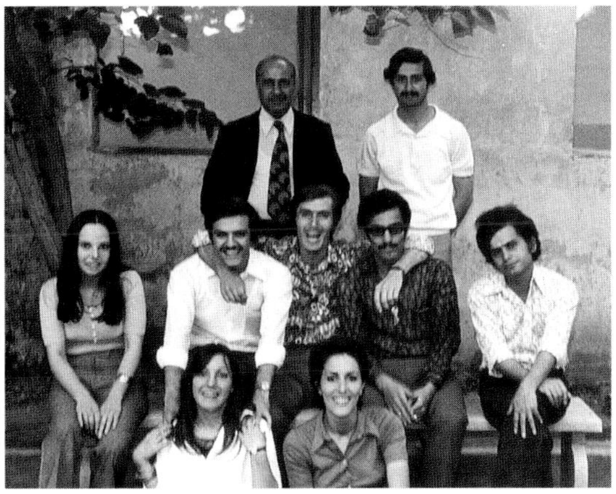

The artist with classmates at the Institute of Fine Arts, 1971
From L. to R. standing, Prof. Samih al-Attar, M. Hakim
Second row, A. Kabbani, M. Rawas, E. Isaak, O. Samra, I. Abou Ajram
Third Row, C. Buissière, L. Majdalani

At this time I was shifting between two main schools: Impressionism and Cubism. I did not like Surrealism as a style of painting, although I liked the way it gave full rein to the imagination. Later, I realized how much I enjoyed Salvador Dali's cinematographic work while at the same time disliking his paintings. I also hated the idea of my art merely stylizing what the eye sees. I felt an urgency to introduce thoughts and ideas through the visual. For me, a complete work of art needs to encompass both. However, the bulk of what I did at the Lebanese University represented the typical training of an art student: freely testing and experimenting, influenced by selected styles and schools. In retrospect, it appears to me to have been a crash course in painting covering the last century's art movements. It was like a four years' sieving process after which one ended up with what is left at the bottom of the sieve – a material amalgamated into a single body, forming the seeds of one's own artistic personality which later grow into a new, individual and personal style.

But one good thing about the Institute of Fine Arts at the Lebanese University is that we lived in an atmosphere of pure liberal thought. I do not know whether all the students shared my liberal thinking, but this was the way I felt. I was very happy there; the ambiance was a healthy one, I could paint freely, our life was leisurely and I was doing what I liked to do. We used to visit many exhibitions, since Beirut was full of art galleries such as Contact Art Gallery, Gallery One, Deco 27, Brigitte Shehade Centre d'Art, Alecco Saab Gallery, Galerie L'Amateur, Galerie Manoug, Galerie Le Point, Delta International Gallery and Galerie Contemporaine. In addition, the works of major contemporary sculptors and painters could be seen in the J. F. Kennedy Cultural Center, where I used to spend hours looking at art books. This center provided a

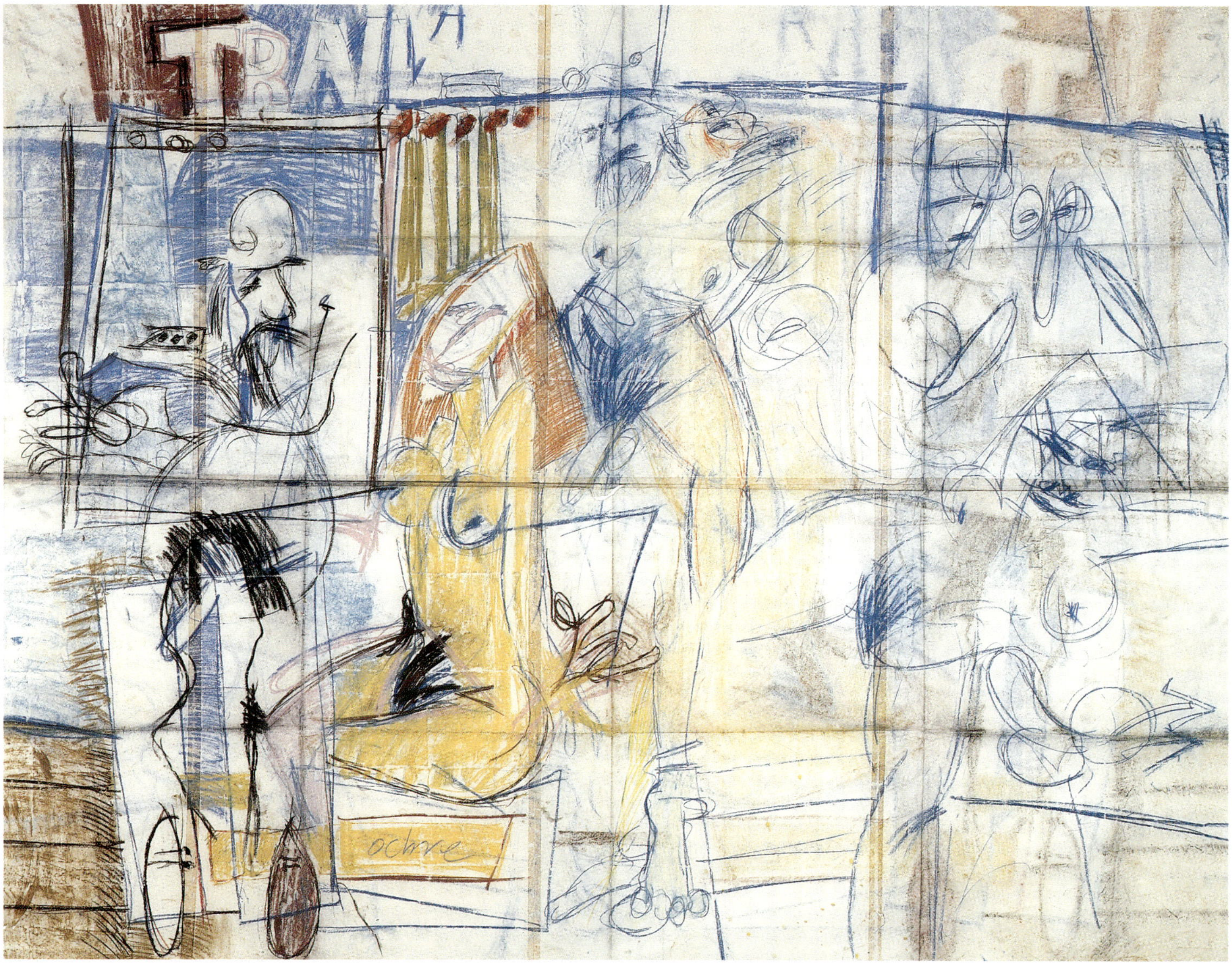

STUDY FOR 'TRAIN', 1975
Pastel on paper
200 x 250 cm
Artist's collection

wealth of exposure to the American international art scene. Among the most memorable exhibitions hosted by the center I particularly recall 'R. B. Kitaj's Graphics' and 'New American Sculpture' – an exhibition of work by 44 artists including Louise Nevelson, Robert Richards, Ernest Trova and Larry Rivers.

While studying, I earned money for art materials and the university's nominal tuition fees by working as a government employee, initially in the Ministry of Interior, from 8 AM to 2 PM daily. Fortunately, the main courses at the university ran in the afternoons so, after work, I would simply go and join my classes. The courses in 'human anatomy' and 'perspective drawing principles' were taught in French, as the tutors found it easier to give instruction in the language they had used during their own art training in France. For me this was very frustrating as I knew not a word of French, and had to take an intensive course in the language in order to benefit fully from the teaching.

I moved on to two other government departments – the prime minister's department and finally the Ministry of Finance – but my whole experience as an employee in that type of work was as a 'misfit'. I still have the letters of reprimand (for not showing up at work in many instances) from my boss at the Ministry of Finance in Saida (a city 40 kilometers south of Beirut), to which I was transferred in 1977, a few months before my final resignation.

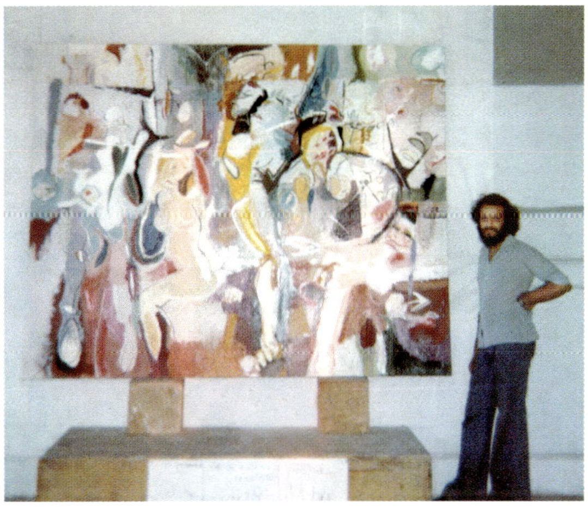

The artist next to 'TRAIN' (1975, oil on canvas) at the Lebanese University

This polaroid photograph is the only surviving evidence of the painting, which was destroyed during the war.

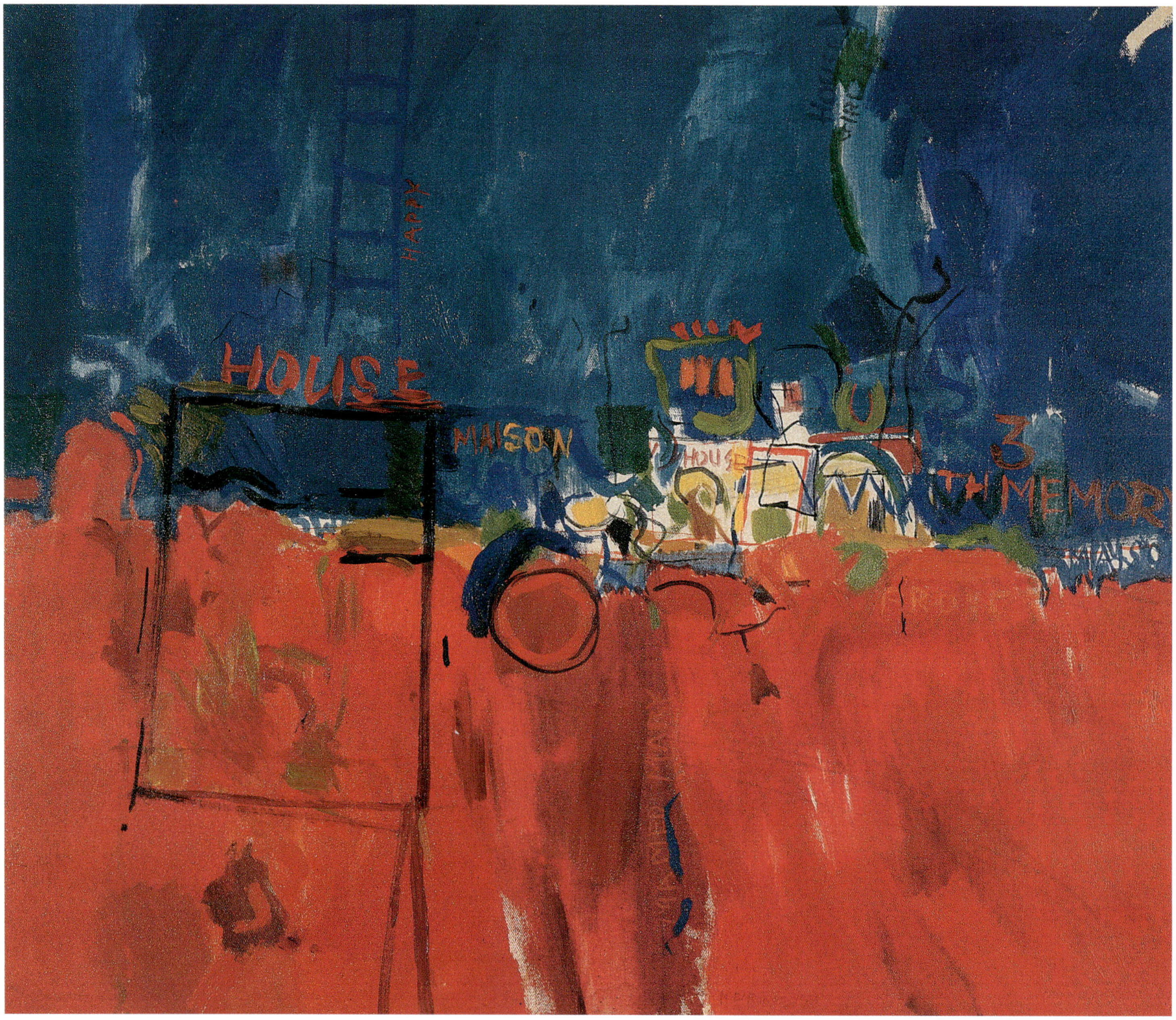

HOUSE, 1975
Oil on canvas
60 x 75 cm
Private collection

Trauma, Change ... and Crucial Developments

Neither at the Institute nor at home was the question of one's 'faith' ever raised, and it never occurred to me to ask about my fellow students' religion. I was never involved in politics, the more so because most of the political parties in Lebanon are affiliated with certain religious sects. If one's own thoughts are not sectarian, then one tends not to be aware of sectarianism in others. But the liberal, tolerant, 'normal' atmosphere in which I lived and believed was suddenly challenged by the Lebanese civil war.

The war in Lebanon broke out in April 1975 between armed Palestinians and the Lebanese Christian militia. It soon turned into a sectarian battle between Muslims and Christians, a situtation I could not tolerate. Could things turn upside down so suddenly? Had I been living a big lie? Or had I been so naive as to not realize the political struggle for power that was going on behind our apparently stable and liberal-minded society? I was deeply shocked to realize that things were not what I had imagined them to be, and I was left with a very bitter feeling that shook my belief in liberty, freedom and culture. Besides the physical threat of bombs and rockets, this traumatizing cultural shock caused me to stop painting for one and a half years. The last painting I did before stopping was *House* (1975), which I painted while confined to our home, using the only paints that were available to me there. It was a spontaneous and nervous application of mainly blue and red. All the paintings that I had left at the Institute were destroyed by the war.

Because staying in Beirut became dangerous, my parents decided to flee to Damascus, where I stayed until 1976. I found a job

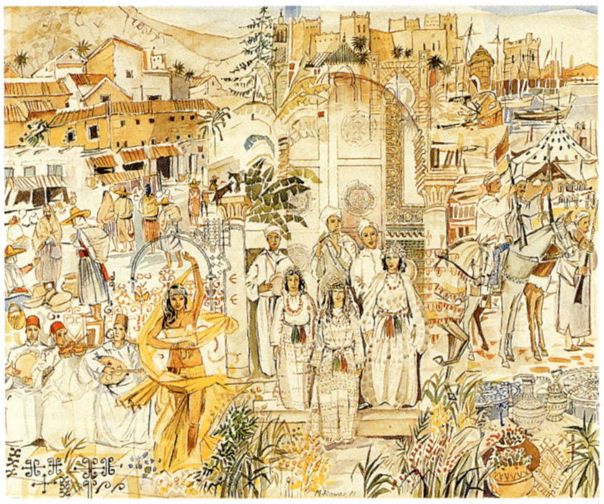

MOROCCAN SCENE, 1979
Watercolor on paper
47 x 56.5 cm
Collection Dr. & Mrs. A. Diab

Opposite page
LIBERTY, 1977
Gouache, pencil and china ink on paper
62 x 47 cm
Artist's collection

at the Syrian television station designing the sets for children's programs. It was a job I performed with no great enthusiasm. (I never had the chance to do serious work for the theater. During one summer in Lebanon I had done a couple of stage sets for some minor plays performed in the mountain villages, but that was all.) While in Damascus I read the works of Albert Camus, and I remember the tremendous contrast between the time I was spending with his challenging existential questions and my job at the TV station painting trees, fences, fountains and sheep for children's plays of the most naive kind. But the job was necessary at the time: I needed to make some money.

After three months I left for Morocco. A classmate of mine and fellow artist, Maroun Hakim, had been teaching art there in the École Normale in Rabat and wanted to return to Lebanon, so he phoned me asking if I could replace him. I could hardly believe my ears! I was overjoyed, left Damascus within a few days, and spent the following two years in Rabat.

In Morocco I led a peaceful and free life which contrasted with both dangerous, war-torn Lebanon and the limited – and limiting – Damascus. In Morocco I felt relaxed, and I could finally unwind. The people are easy-going, tolerant and straightforward, without a sense of the complex social stratifications that we have in Lebanon. I made many acquaintances during this time, although the only one with whom I remained in contact was the Moroccan artist Fouad Bellamine.

My stay in Morocco was wonderful – mainly because it gave me the chance to go back to painting. Suddenly I felt the peace of not being close to the Lebanese war, of not having my day-to-day life directly affected by it. So, three months after my arrival there, I started painting again. I always believed that the agonies, disasters, problems and harshness an artist might endure are elements that enrich his or her art; but, at the same time, I cannot work under stressful conditions. I had to let some time elapse before I could work again. I could not just spontaneously start to paint while in a state of trauma and general emotional turmoil. I needed time to think clearly about the visual and conceptual statements I wanted to make.

Some of the paintings I produced in Morocco were like the arabesque, decorative watercolor work I used to do in Lebanon. I painted one or two pictures depicting traditional Moroccan weddings

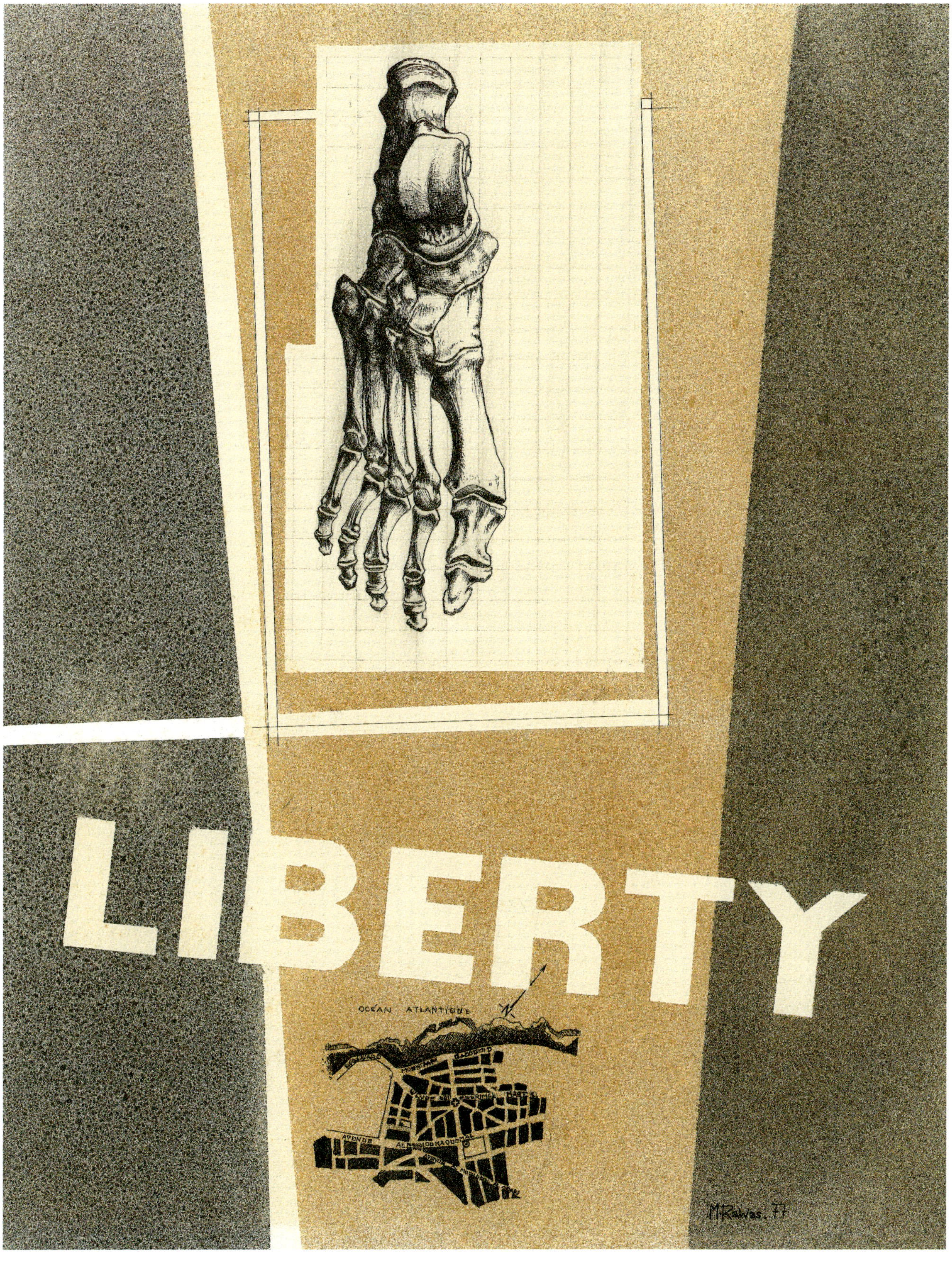
LIBERTY
OCEAN ATLANTIQUE
M.Rawas. 77

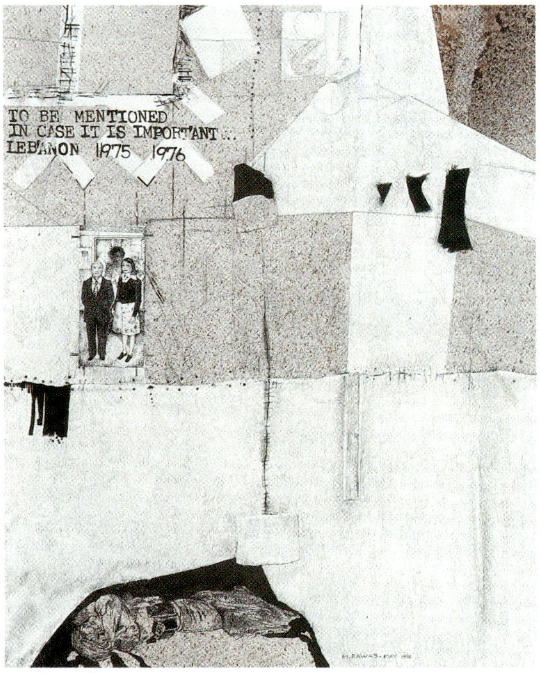

TO BE MENTIONED IN CASE IT IS IMPORTANT, 1976
Gouache and ink on paper
70 x 50 cm
Artist's collection

Opposite page
MATRIMONY AND MATERNITY, 1978
Gouache and ink on paper
61 x 47 cm
Collection Mr. & Mrs. T. Tohmé

I had been invited to, but then I moved to more serious work. All the paintings of still life that I had done in Lebanon, and now in Morocco, were sold quickly because people liked them: they are pretty to look at, and appreciating them does not demand a lot of effort. The public enjoyed them as a reminder of our oriental heritage. However, I was not fully satisfied by my paintings that were merely nice visual statements. I thought that being an artist was not simply to render cleverly what your eyes see, even if stylized. I did not want a split between my art and my life; I wanted to preserve my integrity as a human being. I began to see that there were two ways of involving thought in a work of art: either by creating a new and innovative pictorial solution to the problem of representing reality as Matisse, Picasso and others had done, or by adapting the medium of art to the expression of ideas, directly or indirectly, as in the majority of modern conceptual art movements.

Once I started painting seriously again in Morocco, I wanted my work to involve 'concepts', to express my ideas – which had been the case before, when I did *A Posted Letter* (1974) (page 60), *Pologne* (1973) (page 33) and *The Book of Life* (1973) (page 31), to name a few. Thus the themes of my paintings became related to the events in Lebanon and their consequences for me. To break down the realistic pictorial space, and to negate and avoid the physically realistic arrangement of things as I saw them was, for me, the first necessary change. My images no longer obeyed the rules of visual perspective. The various elements of the painting were no longer arranged according to the conventions of 'realistic' painting. I did not want the eye alone, but analytical and synthetic thought as well, to be involved in the appreciation and reading of my work of art.

I increasingly used in my paintings at that time words and text as both communicative and compositional elements of expression. The technique I used for applying the letters was to stamp them onto the surface of the picture. Words have a different flavor of expression, a different discipline of communication, and they helped a lot in constituting the full idea I wanted to express. I was and still am fascinated by the two levels of expression, the written and the pictorial – not forgetting that you cannot isolate the pictorial aspect from the written word, for the word is presented in a specific typeface, size or color, so you are once again viewing it as a pictorial element. A visual compositional need would make me choose a certain size or color for the letters. The words have a double role: first, they are read for their

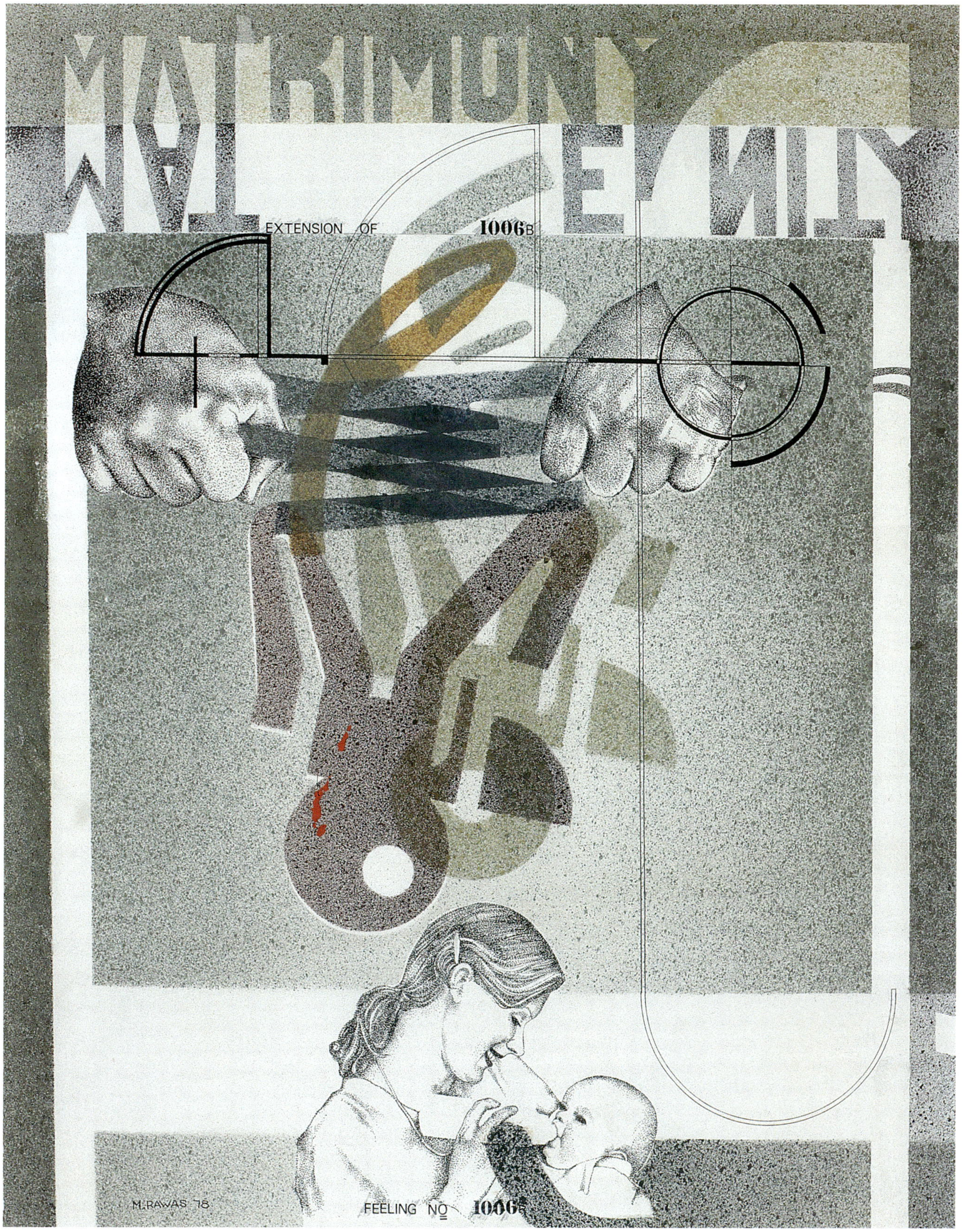
EXTENSION OF 1006B
M.RAWAS 78
FEELING NO 1006

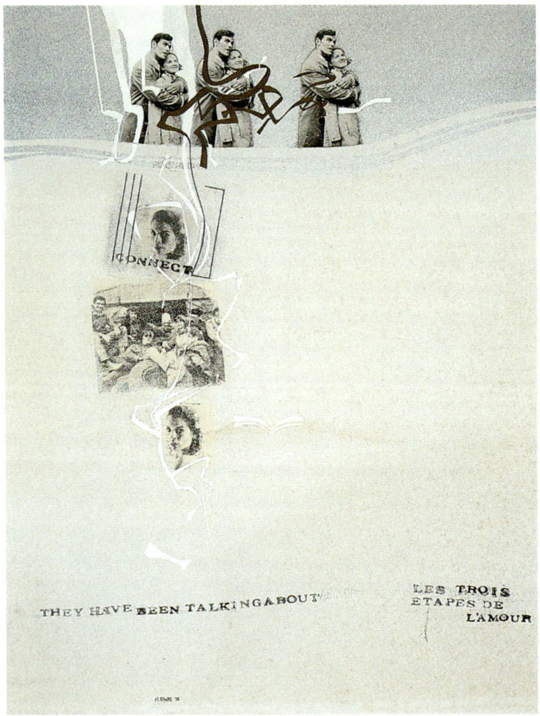

LES TROIS ÉTAPES DE L'AMOUR, 1978
Gouache, transfer and collage on paper
63 x 47 cm
Artist's collection

Opposite page
THE REAL CAUSE TO RUN, 1978
Gouache and collage on paper
63 x 48 cm
Artist's collection

semantic content, their 'meaning', but they are also part of the pictorial, visual composition. My paintings from this time might be described as rather dry, cold, cerebral statements.

A reduction in color is also noticeable during this period. My work started looking very subdued, using grays and desaturated colors. Perhaps I had become more conservative in my approach, subtler in my statement. It might also have been that I wanted to use images that were less distracting – less busily colorful – in order to allow the mind to operate. Then, too, I might have been affected by the Moroccan artist Fouad Bellamine's abstract minimalist paintings. When I compare *House* (1975) (page 64) to *Liberty* (1977) (page 67), two successive paintings with two years between them (during which I did not paint), I am astonished by the considerable shift in style and content that took place.

Another important change was my ever-growing interest in photographic images. An image taken by the camera retains the objective reality of the thing that is photographed, and such images became increasingly present and significant in my painting. By photos I do not mean 'artistic' photographs. I do not normally use them in my work, because they are complete works of art in their own right. What I use are the most ordinary and casual photographs, because they can lend themselves to borrowing, adding to and working on.

I had already been greatly affected by works of art that integrated photographs, such as those by Robert Rauschenberg, Peter Blake, Andy Warhol and others. However, I also felt the need to grasp reality with the least possible personal interference. Some of the works I produced while living in Morocco (those of 1976 and 1977), besides including photos, introduced another innovation: I refrained from applying the paint by brush. Using a brush necessarily expresses the painterly sensibility of the artist's 'hand marks'. Instead I used a method of spraying paint onto the surface with a primitive type of airbrush. By doing this I was eradicating the artist's personal signature and all rhetorical or gestural practices. The lines, too, were not drawn with a medium that could communicate 'feelings': I used a technical drawing pen which would give the same thickness all the way through and produce a line with a consistent, homogeneous quality. And my painting now contained shapes that were more geometric than organic.

Although the topics I dealt with at that time were mainly linked to the events in Lebanon, they also included commentaries on human

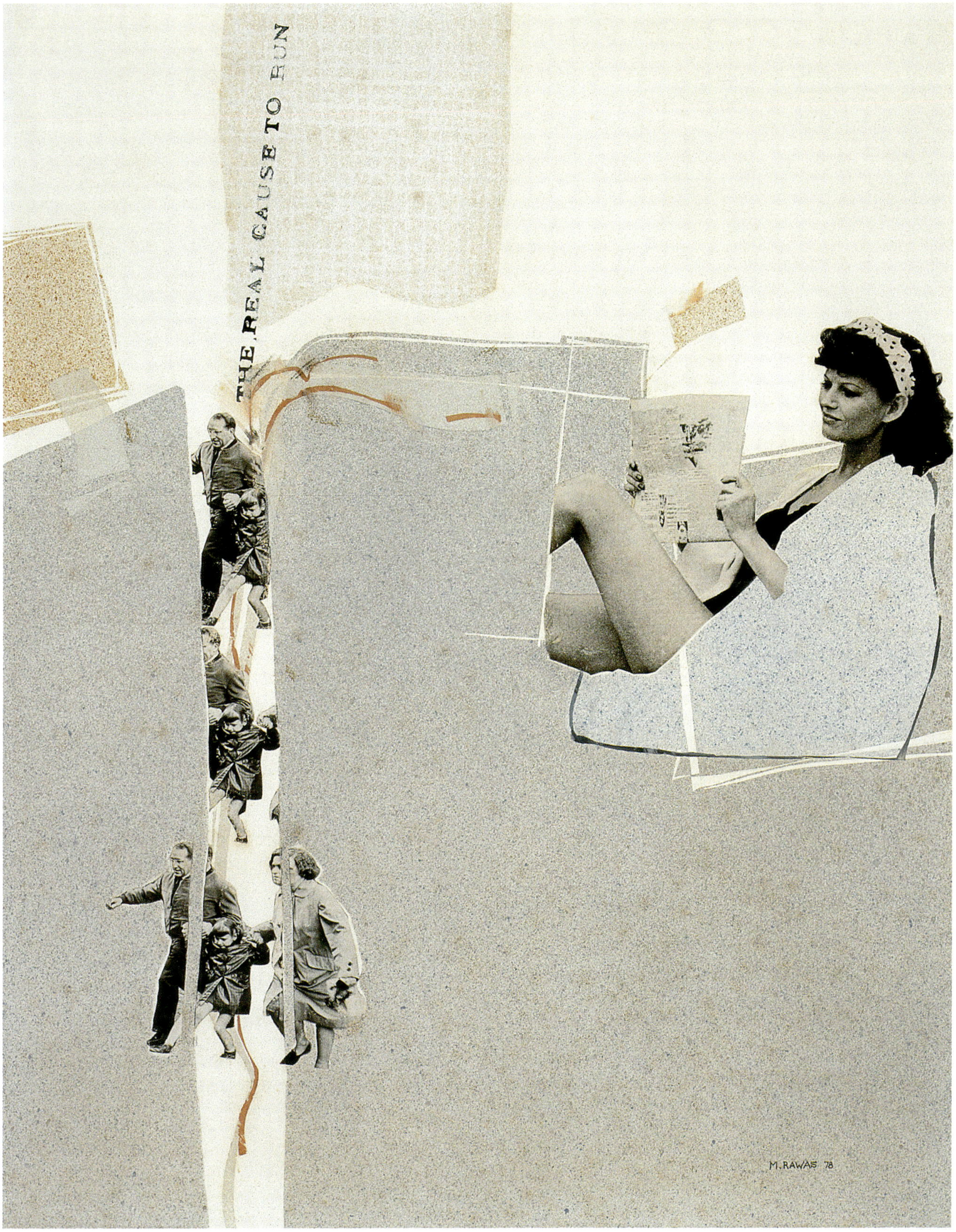
THE REAL CAUSE TO RUN
M.RAWAS 78

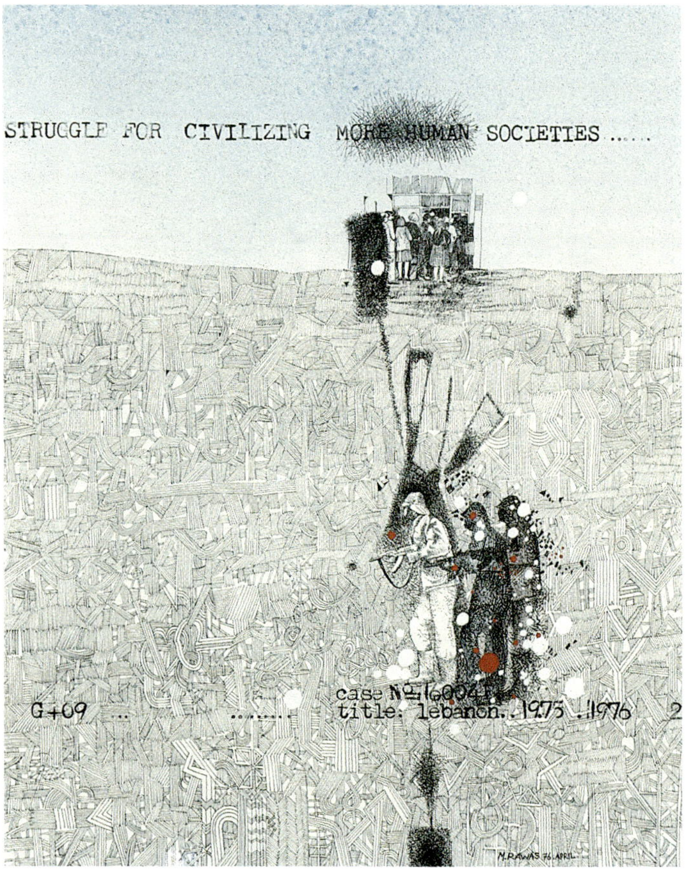

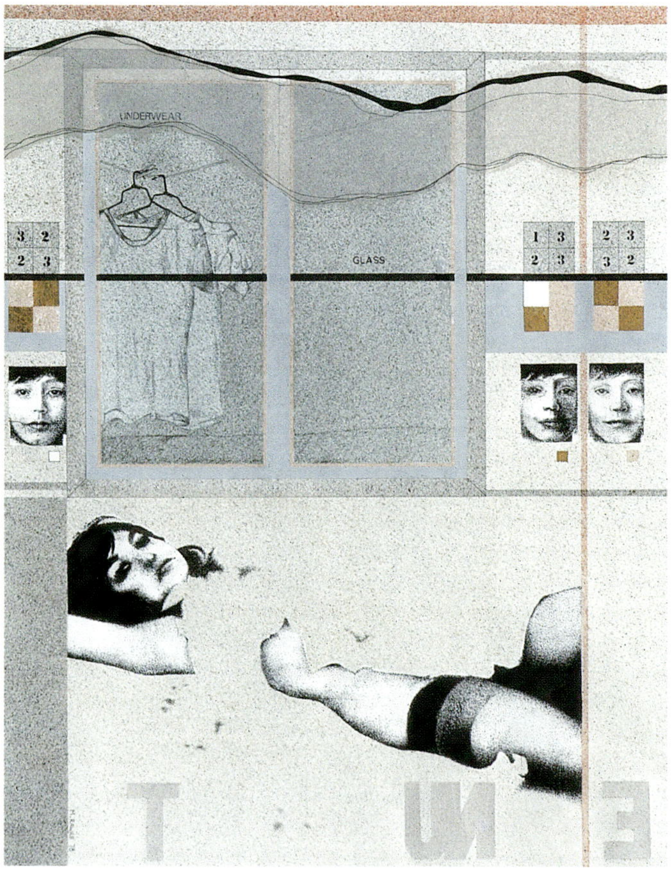

Top left
STRUGGLE FOR CIVILIZING MORE HUMAN SOCIETIES, 1976
Gouache and china ink on paper
70 x 50 cm
Artist's collection

Top right
TUNE, 1978
Gouache and china ink on paper
70 x 50 cm
Artist's collection

behavior and reactions. But this emotional and conceptual content was expressed in a subtle, indirect manner, often charged with sarcasm and cynicism. I recall that when I painted *Liberty* (1977) it was less a celebration of my return to freedom of expression and movement (represented by the skeletal foot) as a result of being out of the war zone than a cynical commentary on my situation. Soon after settling in a small apartment in Le Quartier Océan in Rabat, I started my teaching job at the École Normale des Institutrices, situated within walking distance of my flat, and found myself confined by a new regime – that of regular routine and a strict work schedule, including the repetitive walking to and fro between the school and the flat at exactly the same time six days a week! A map of the region appears at the bottom part of *Liberty*, the location of both ends of that daily, obligatory trip marked on it.

Struggle for Civilizing More Human Societies (1976) refers to an incident from the time when I was still in Beirut. The work features an image of a group of people in the top part of the painting queuing in

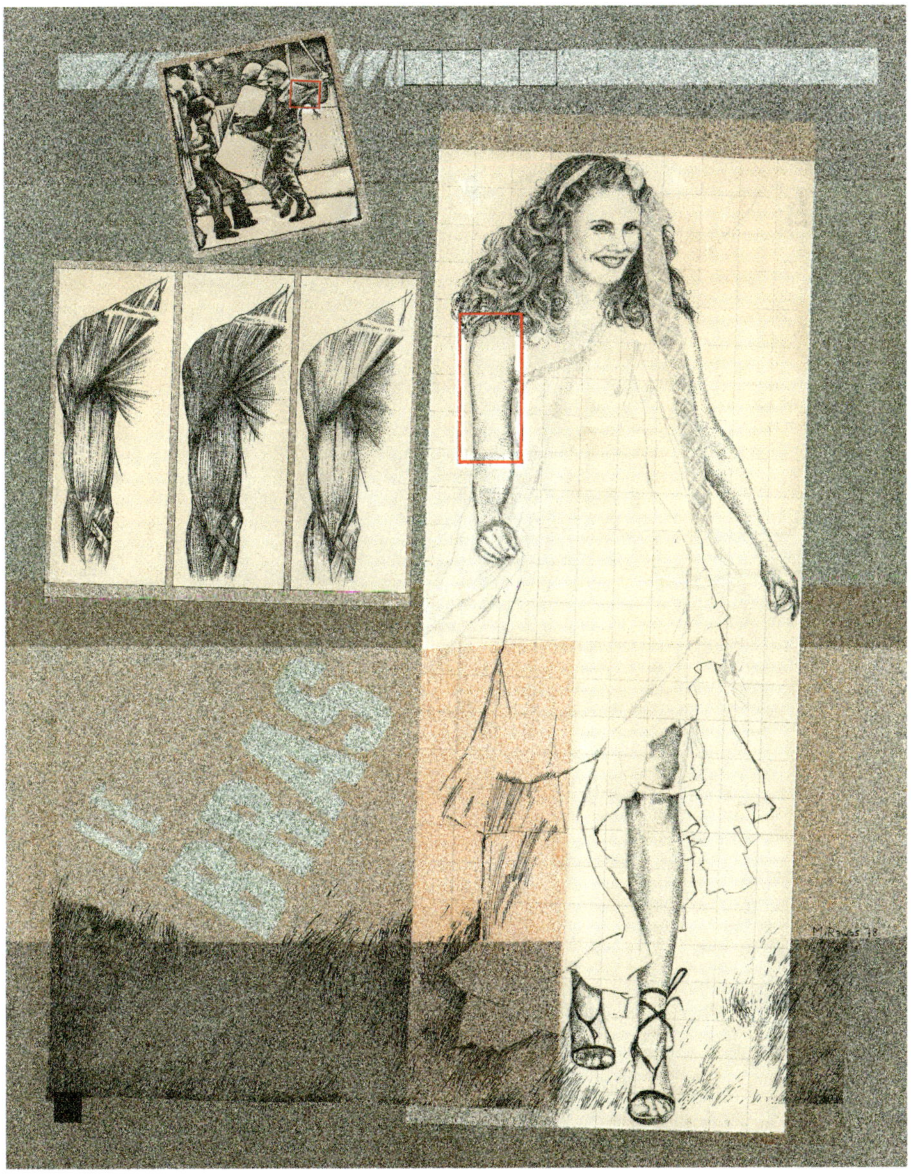

LE BRAS, 1978
Gouache, pencil and china ink on paper
62 x 47.5 cm
Artist's collection

front of a bakery for their 'daily bread' when a mortar bomb fell, killing most of them, including a fellow painter and friend, Ibrahim Marzouk. Such atrocities were justified by Lebanese warlords and leaders of the various fighting factions as an inescapable price for a free, prosperous and civilized future. It seems to me a warping of human nature to try to impose one's own beliefs on others, especially in such a violent way.

In another painting from this period, *Le Bras* (1978), I was simply commenting on the intriguing subject of the relative functions of the human arm. The painting shows a beautiful model displaying a dress by Yves Saint-Laurent (a 1978 design), and a picture of an Italian

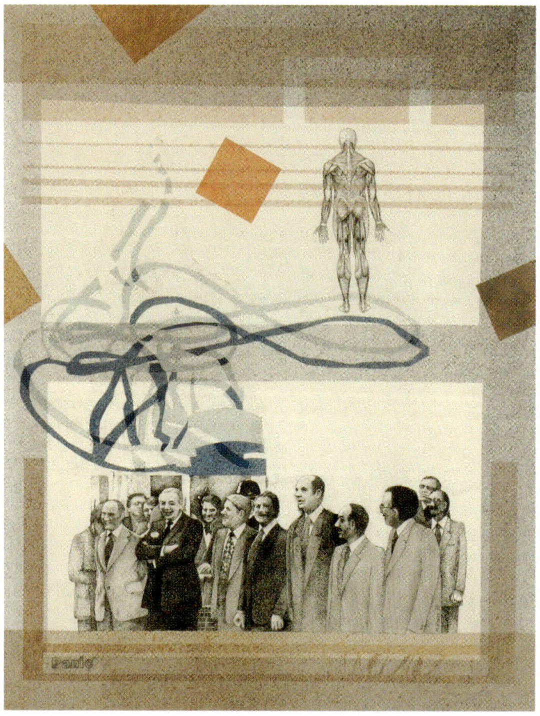

PANIC, 1978
Gouache and china ink on paper
63 x 48
Artist's collection

Opposite page
NEGATIVE, 1978
Gouache and transfer on paper
62 x 48 cm
Artist's collection

anti-riot policeman holding a truncheon during a demonstration in Italy in the same year (I do not remember the specific details of the event). The arm of the model, as well as that of the policeman, is marked with a red rectangle, while a drawing of the anatomy of the human arm, repeated three times, hints at the idea that with the skin removed, both arms display the same structure. It is interesting how the same device ('*le bras*' – the arm) can appear so radically different – when in brutal action, and when at rest.

I believe that a major part of the process of making art lies in the way the artist applies paint or other elements during the process of creating a work. It is not so much *what* you paint as *how* you paint it. In an important sense, the technique becomes part of the content, the meaning. An example would be the particular use I make of photography. If I were to use an actual photograph and attach it to the surface or support I was painting on, I would be aware of the visible photograph's edges. Do I need this edge, or is it forced upon me because I have attached the photo? The need for meticulous attention to the texture of the painterly surface made me worry about the 'imposed' physical presence of a picture collaged onto the canvas. My solution to this was to try to imitate the photographic image by redrawing it in terms of dots, using a fine technical drawing pen and achieving, through the dotting process, what looked like a screen-printed photo from a magazine. Of course it did not look exactly like a photo, but at least this technique created a semi-mechanical appearance with some resemblance to the mechanical look of the printed photograph.

I also used the transfer technique of simply rubbing a printed photographic image onto my art paper, using an ink solvent. I discovered this technique by accident in Morocco when I came across a street vendor in the Rabat *souk*. He was selling what he claimed to be a 'magic' product, and performed his 'magic' by transferring printed pictures from a magazine to a blank sheet of paper. Fascinated and intrigued, I bought all the little bottles of his 'magical' product, only to discover, when I got home, that it was nothing but paint thinner.

Inserting the photographic image using the transfer technique took only a few minutes, as opposed to the hours I had spent copying it with a fine technical drawing pen. Stupidly enough, this made me feel guilty since, for me, a work of art had to be time-consuming. After

TIVE 1
NEGATIVE 2
M. RAWAS 78

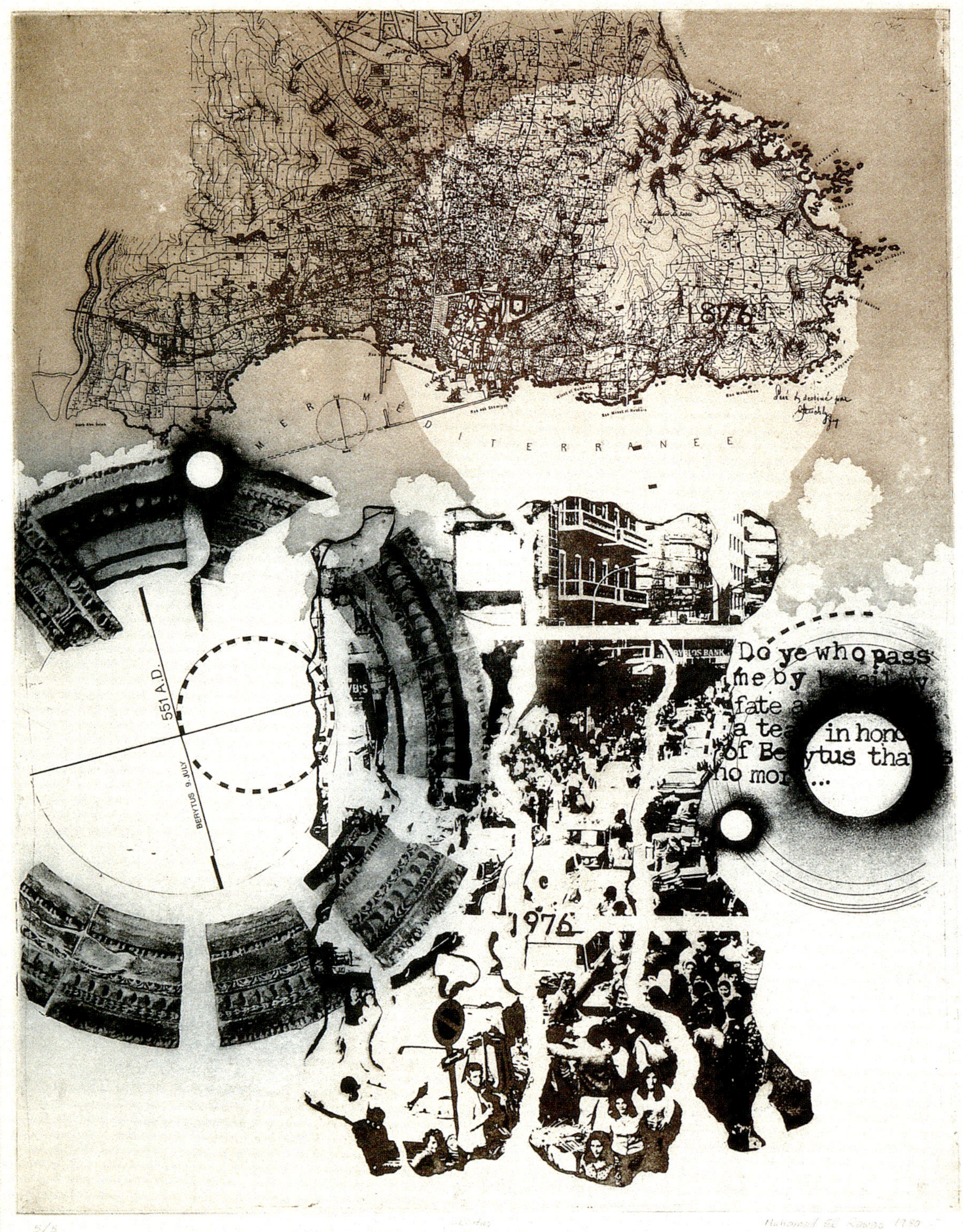

BERYTUS, 1980
Etching
68 x 53 cm

Exhibited at the Third World Biennale of Graphic Art, London, 1980 (Honourable Mention).

London

The work I did in Morocco became my admission portfolio to the Master's program at the Slade School of Fine Art, University College, London.

I had obtained a scholarship from the Lebanese University to study abroad and applied to the Slade for a Master's degree in printmaking. In 1981 I went to London, a city I had visited once before, during a study tour in 1974, and which I remembered having liked a lot – more than Paris (which was included in that same trip). When I arrived in London, I stayed first with a close friend and then moved to a one-room flat near Victoria Station.

At the Slade I was introduced to the elaborate techniques of printmaking that included etching on metal plates, stone and plate lithographic printing and silkscreen printing. I was overwhelmed by all the facilities and workshops that were at the disposal of the students, and would spend eight to ten hours a day in the workshop, working and learning a lot, because I felt this to be a rare period in my life which offered me so many opportunities for extending my knowledge.

Yet I remember that the first couple of months there were problematic, mainly because I experienced an 'artist's block'. It was difficult for me to cope with these new techniques and to adopt them as a means of personal artistic expression, for there is a great difference between the method of planning and designing a painting and that of a fine art print. On the other hand, printmaking opened up vast

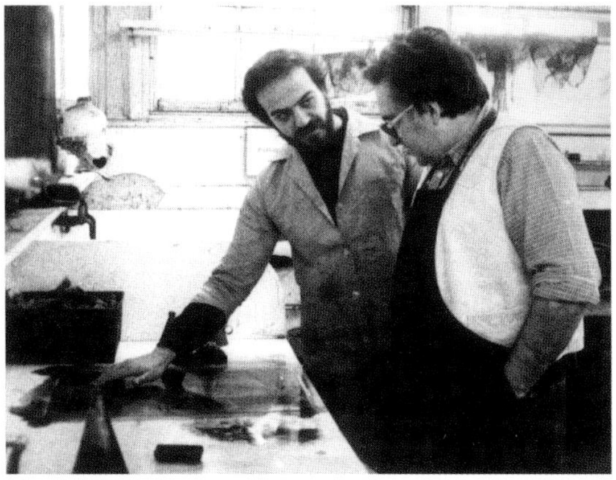

The artist with Bartolomeo Dos Santos in the Slade Printmaking Department, London 1981

horizons and enabled me to use the photographic image in ways I had not experienced before. My tutor, Bartolomeo Dos Santos, was the head of the printmaking department, and he helped me overcome my block and start working meaningfully again. I am greatly indebted to him in another way, too: as he produced his own work in the school workshop, I was able to observe and learn directly from him. Dos Santos used photographs extensively in his etchings, and my vision – in terms of work – was similar to his. Stanley Jones and Peter Daglish taught me lithography and David Leveritt, silkscreen. And I particularly remember Julia Farrer and Paul Coldwell, who were a source of great assistance and guidance in the etching and lithography workshops.

In England I was also exposed to the actual masterpieces of Western art in museums and art galleries. One learns a lot from being directly exposed to works of art: one can observe the texture and have immediate access to the surface of the painting, something one cannot gain from looking at the printed reproduction in a book. Such reproductions can only be a faint reflection of what a painting is in reality. For, once again, what is very important in visual art is to see how the paint is treated on the surface, how it is applied with different brushes and tools to yield a variety of textures. One does not react to a spontaneous, rather aggressive and free brush-stroke application as one would react to the same color, the same value and saturation of the paint, when applied by carefully covering the surface with a slow movement of the hand, or when the paint is sprayed onto the surface. It is these variations of painterly qualities that are capable of transmitting different messages and feelings, and of eliciting different reactions from the viewer. This also applies, of course, to the various printmaking practices and production choices when making a fine art print in any of the texturally varied disciplines of block printing, etching, lithography or silkscreen. Each technique has its own significant sensibilities with regard to texture, and in most cases I combined more than one printing technique in the making of a single print – as in *The Dream of Wartime* (1980), *The Conversation* (1980) and *The Play* (1981).

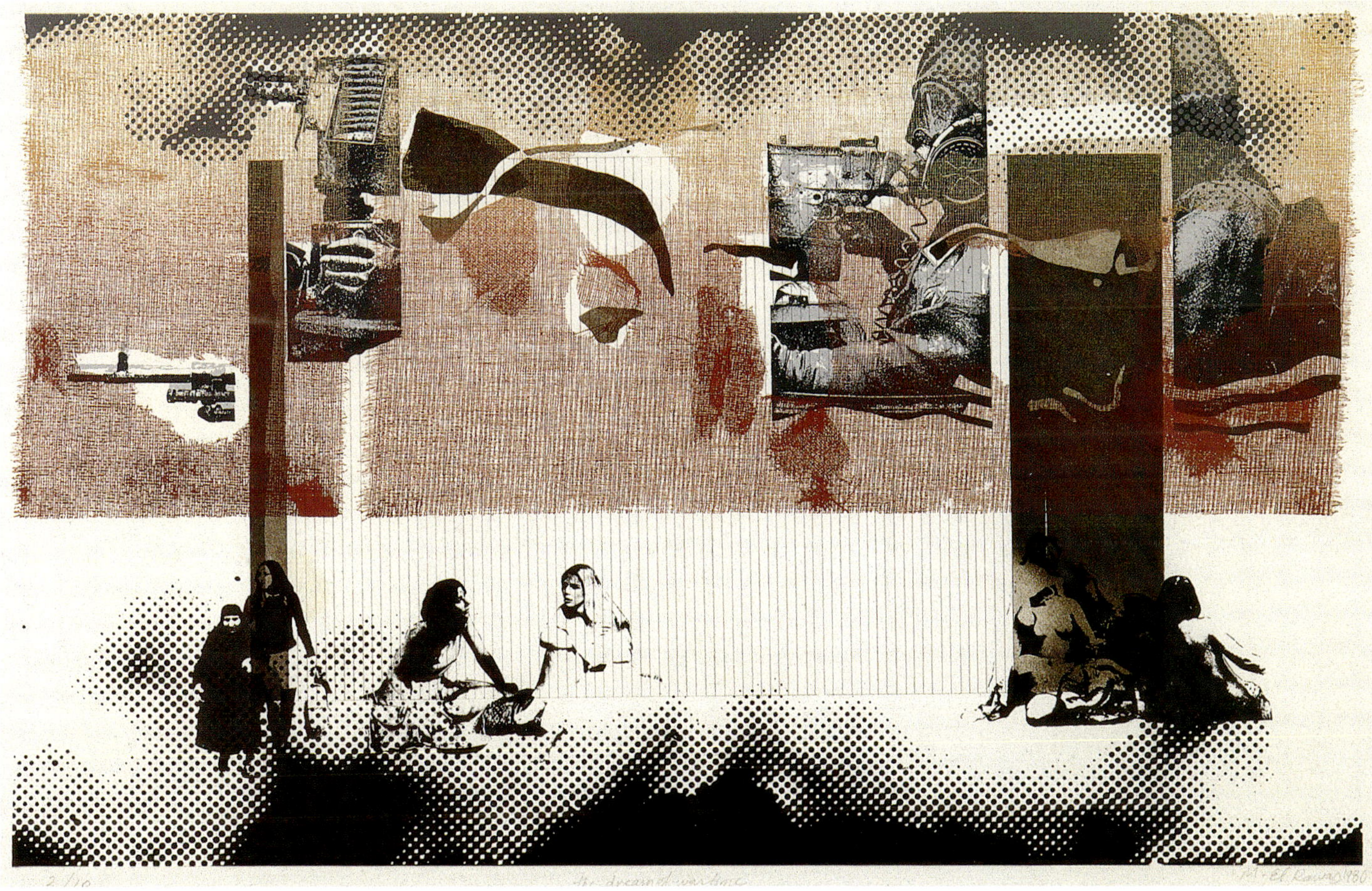

THE DREAM OF WARTIME, 1980
Silkscreen and etching
47.5 x 72 cm

Exhibited at the Eleventh International Independent Exhibition of Prints in Kanagawa, Japan, 1985

During my time at the Slade, the themes I tackled in my work were related to the ongoing war in Lebanon, the atmosphere of uncertainty it created and the absurdity of it all. This choice was not triggered by any direct involvement or affiliations on my part as much as by the simple fact that the war was something I had experienced: I was familiar enough with it to be able to reflect upon it in my work.

I can honestly say that I did not feel homesick during my stay in England. I had no heightened sense of 'belonging to a tribe' in the way that many people seem to when they leave their country to live elsewhere. For me, such 'tribal' feelings are another facet of those national or communal affiliations which are alien to me.

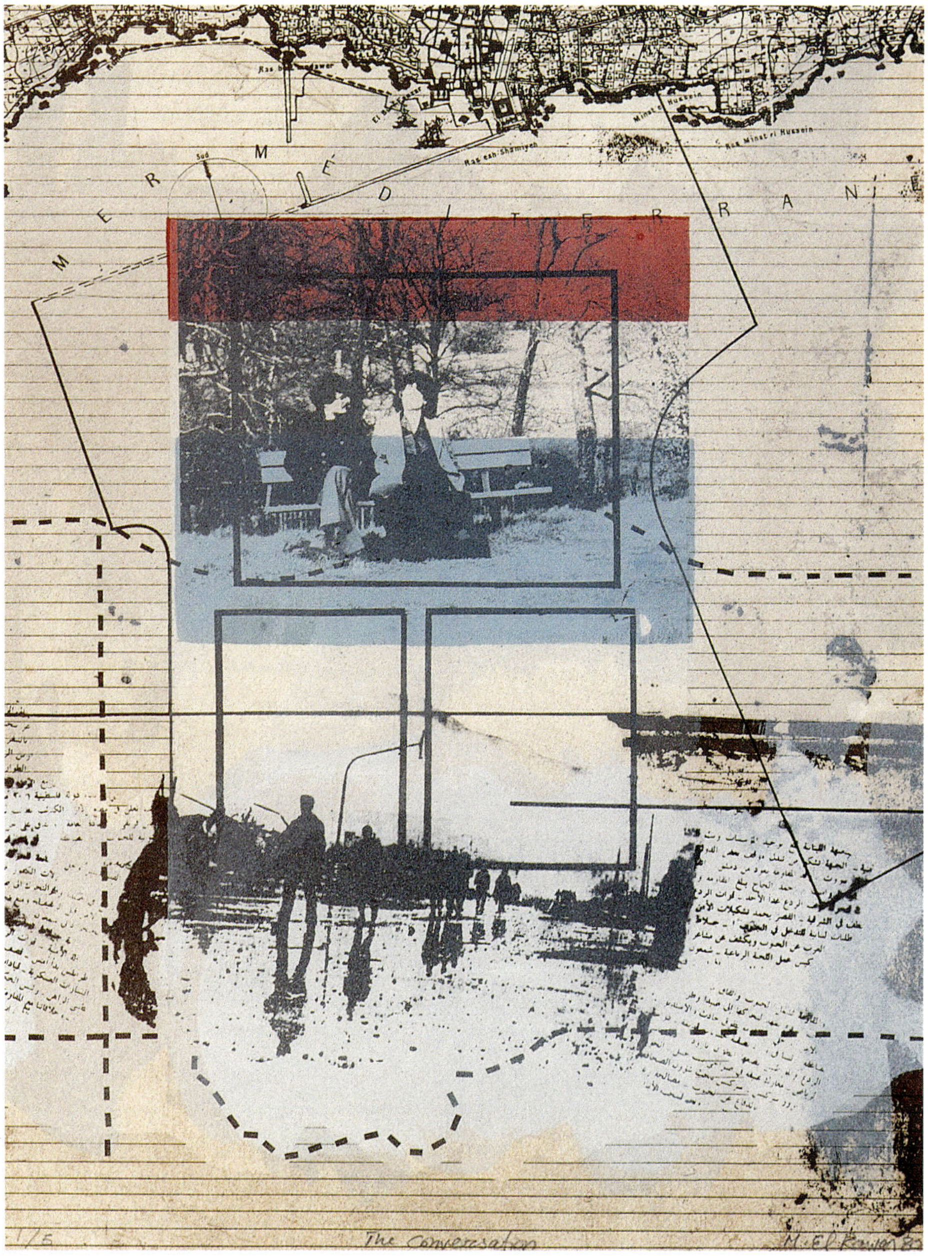

THE CONVERSATION, 1980
Etching and lithography
37.5 x 28 cm

Opposite page
THE PLAY, 1981
Etching and silkscreen
59.5 x 44.5 cm
Collection Centre d'Art Vivant de la ville de Tunis, Tunisia

Exhibited at:
– Sixth Norwegian International Print Biennale, Fredrikstad, 1982
– Sursock Museum Salon d'Automne, Beirut, 1982
– First Contemporary Arab Art Exhibition, Centre d'Art Vivant de la ville de Tunis, Tunisia, 1984 (Third Prize)

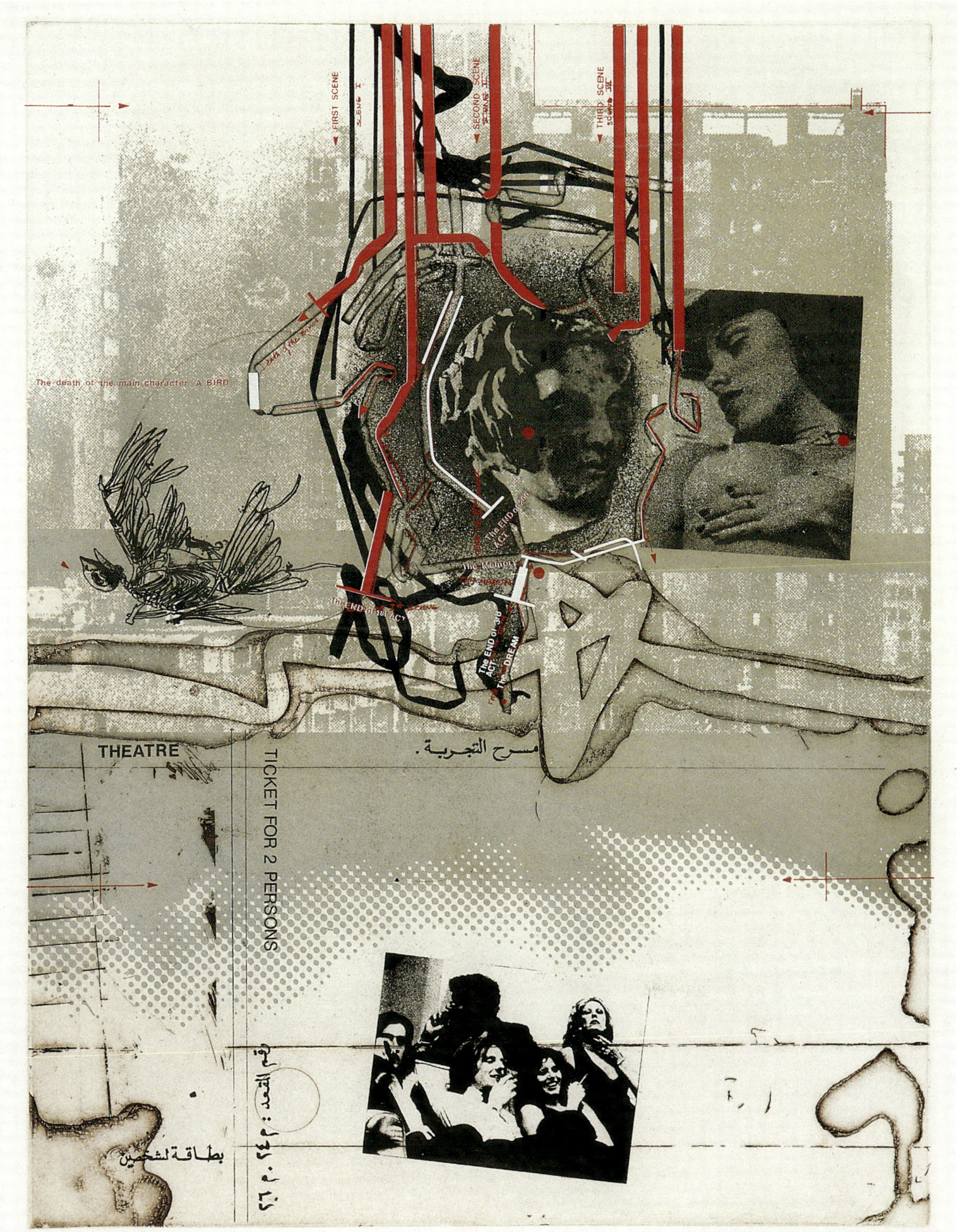
FIRST SCENE
SECOND SCENE
THIRD SCENE
The death of the main character: A BIRD
THEATRE
TICKET FOR 2 PERSONS
مسرح التجربة .
بطاقة لشخصين
2/4
THE PLAY
M. EL RAWAS 1981

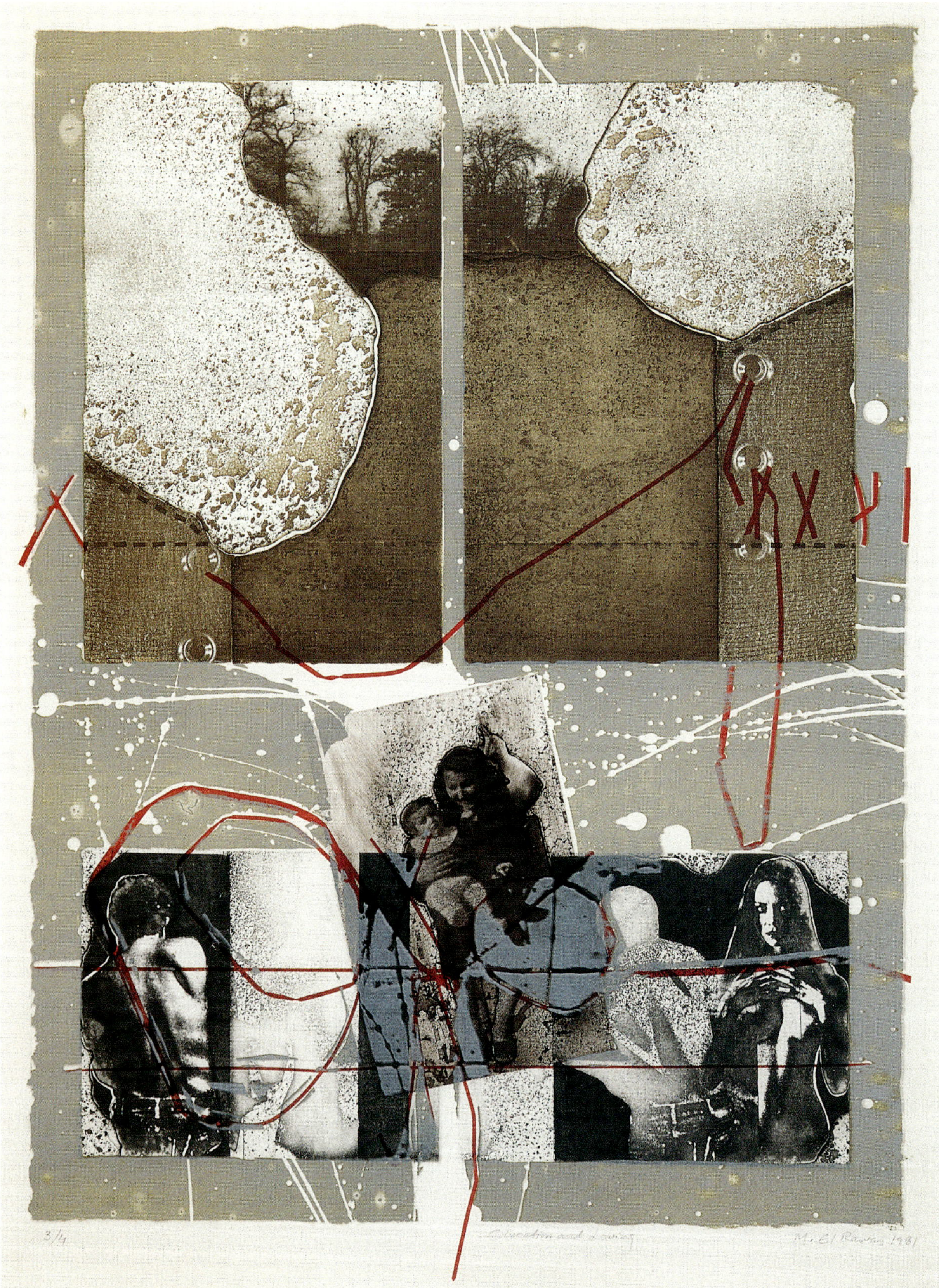
3/4
M. El Rawas 1981

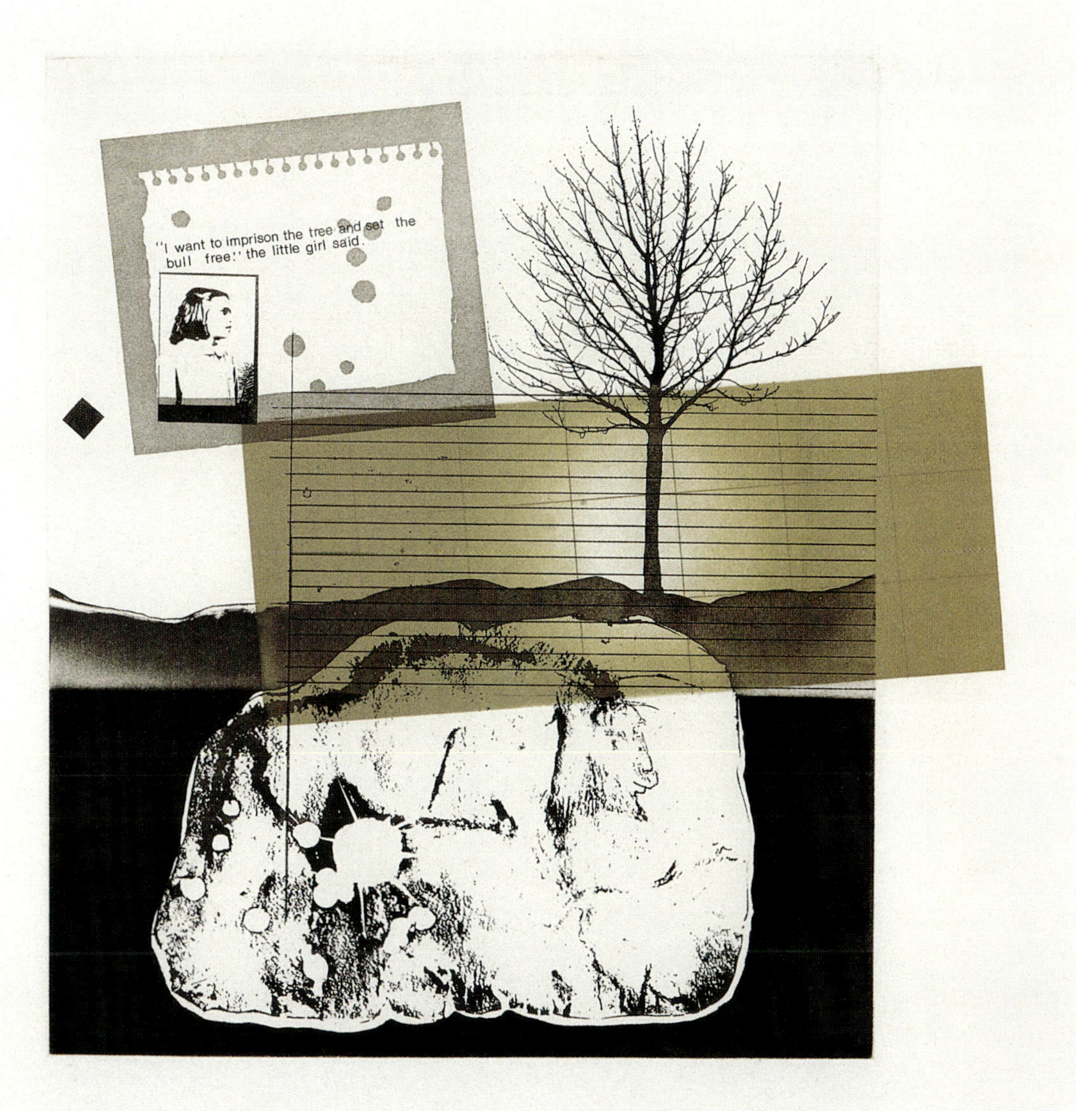

THE LITTLE GIRL'S WISH, 1981
Etching
31 x 29.5 cm

Opposite page
EDUCATION AND LOVING, 1981
Etching and lithography
61 x 43 cm

The question 'Where do you come from?' is, for me, no more significant than any other item of knowledge about a person. My interest in this idea of foregrounding or valuing certain pieces of knowledge and disregarding others – whether concerning a person, a situation, or a history – is reflected in *Relatively Unknown* (1981). The context of this work was a difference I noted between the reporting in two daily newspapers on 14 April 1981: both the English *New Standard* (now the *Evening Standard*) and the Lebanese *al-Nahar* were papers that covered what was supposed to be worth knowing about. Both reported the riots then taking place in Brixton, South London, but only *al-Nahar* covered news from the Lebanese civil war. This made me think about how we decide which issues are worth knowing about and which are not, and about who makes these decisions, in the personal as well as the national and international spheres. *Relatively Unknown* was intended as a commentary on this idea and included completed questionnaires that I had distributed to a number of people. (These questionnaires did not deal directly with the issue of what is reported and what is not: it was a more subtle assessment of what kind of information the majority of people 'took in' when reading newspapers.)

Something that influenced me strongly during my time in England was the people's mentality and their way of life. My experience there increased my inbuilt preference for discipline and order, and I found myself very much in tune with the manners and conduct that characterized British society as I experienced it at the time. I was tempted to stay there but, under the terms of my scholarship, I was obliged to return to teach at the Lebanese University.

Opposite page
RELATIVELY UNKNOWN, 1981
Silkscreen
81 x 58 cm

Exhibited at:
- Contemporary Arab Graphics, Graffiti Gallery, London, 1982
- Fourth World Print Council, fourth exhibition, San Francisco Museum of Modern Art, 1983.
- First Contemporary Arab Art Exhibition, Centre d'Art Vivant de la ville de Tunis, Tunisia, 1984, (Third Prize)
- Arab Art Exhibition, Tunis, Tunisia, 1984
- "Lebanon – The Artist's View: 200 Years of Lebanese Painting", Concourse Gallery, Barbican Center, London, 1989
- "Liban – Le regard des peintres: 200 ans de peinture libanaise", Institut du Monde Arabe, Paris, 1990

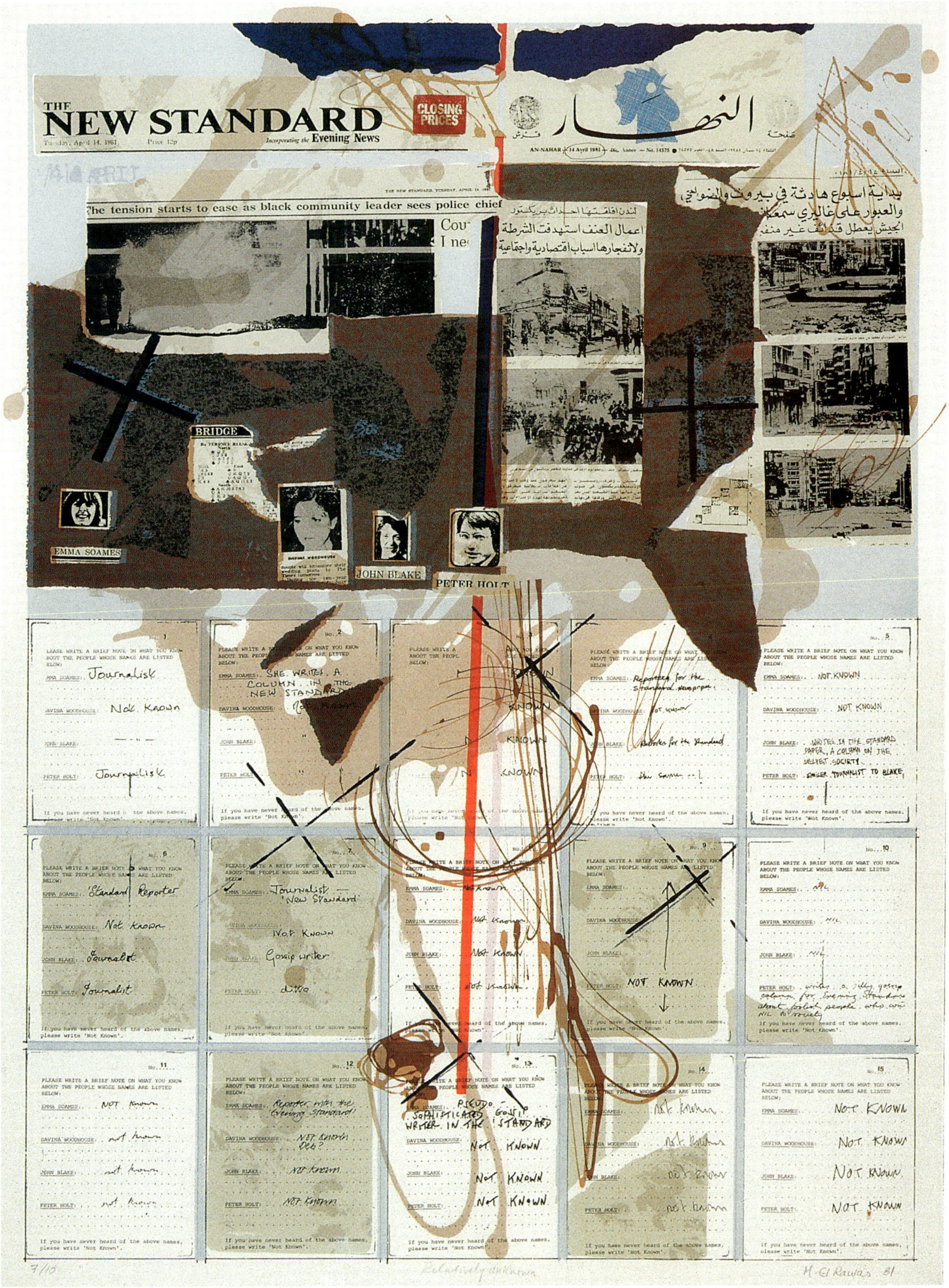
THE NEW STANDARD
CLOSING PRICES
Incorporating the Evening News
The tension starts to ease as black community leader sees police chief
النهار
BRIDGE
EMMA SOAMES
JOHN BLAKE
PETER HOLT

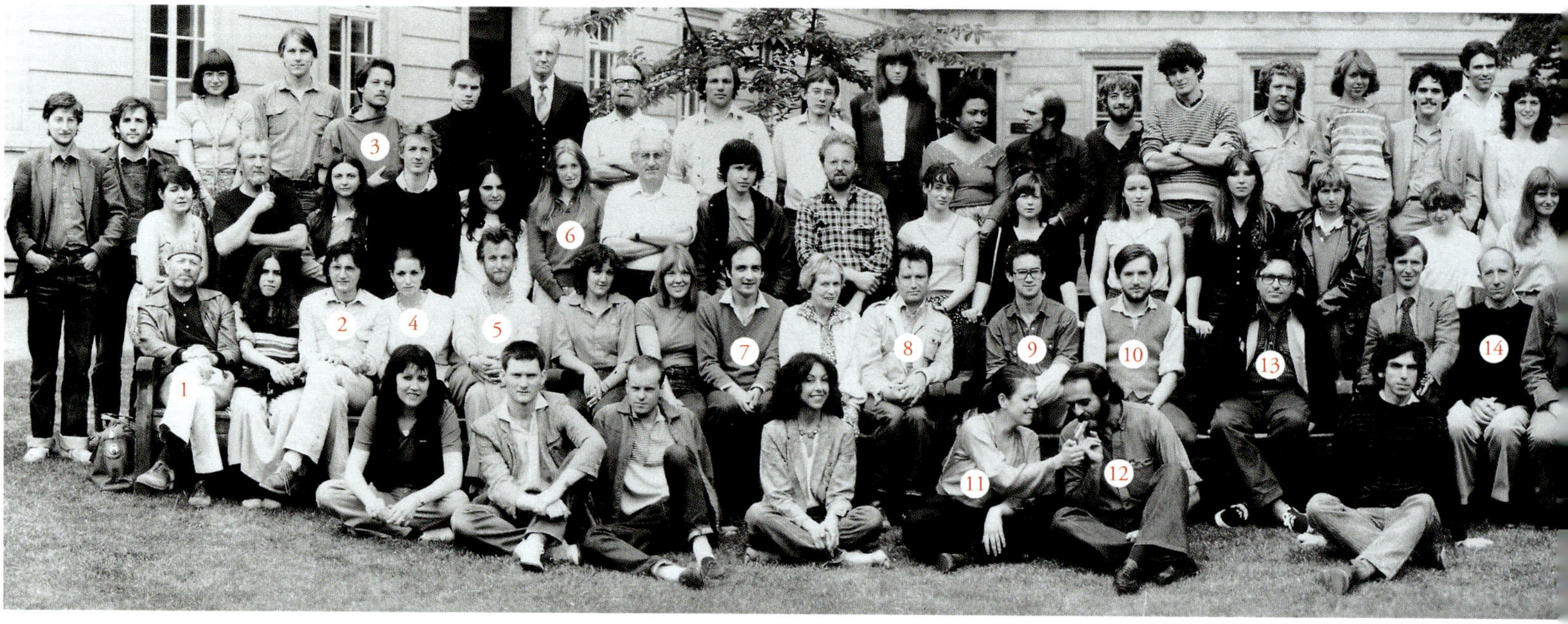

UNIVERSITY COLLEGE LONDON, SLADE SCHOOL, JUNE 1980. *Some of the faculty and students of the Printmaking Department:*
1. Peter Daglish, Lithography tutor 2. David Ferry 3. David Atherton 4. Arabella Jones 5. Paul Coldwell, Lithography instructor 6. Frances Edmonds 7. José Froufe 8. David Leverett, Silkscreen tutor 9. Andrew Folan 10. Christopher Lane 11. Julia Farrer, Etching instructor 12. Mohammad Rawas 13. Bartolomeo Dos Santos, Head of the Printmaking Department 14. Patrick George, Slade tutor 15. Sir Laurence Gowing, Dean of the Slade School 16. Bhajan Hunjan 17. Susie Johns 18. Sharon Firth Aivaliotis 19. Jeff Garrington, Silkscreen instructor

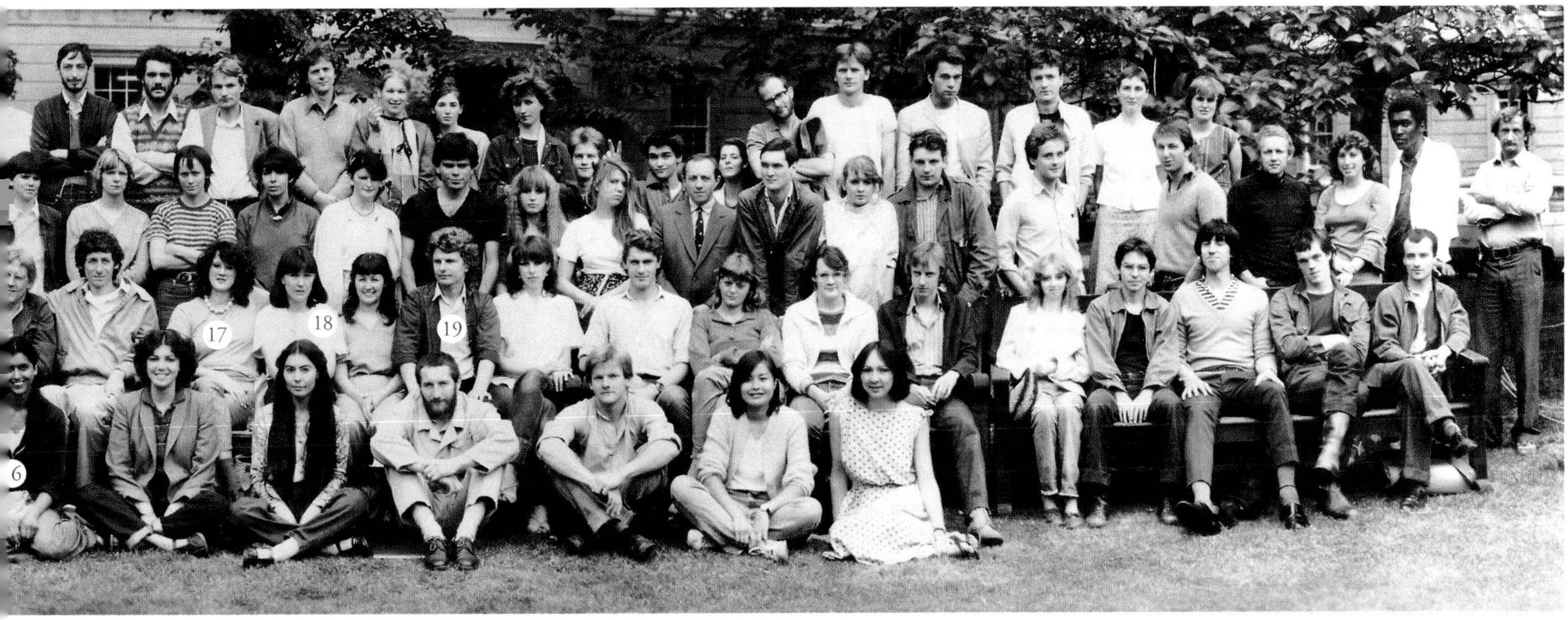
17
18
19
6

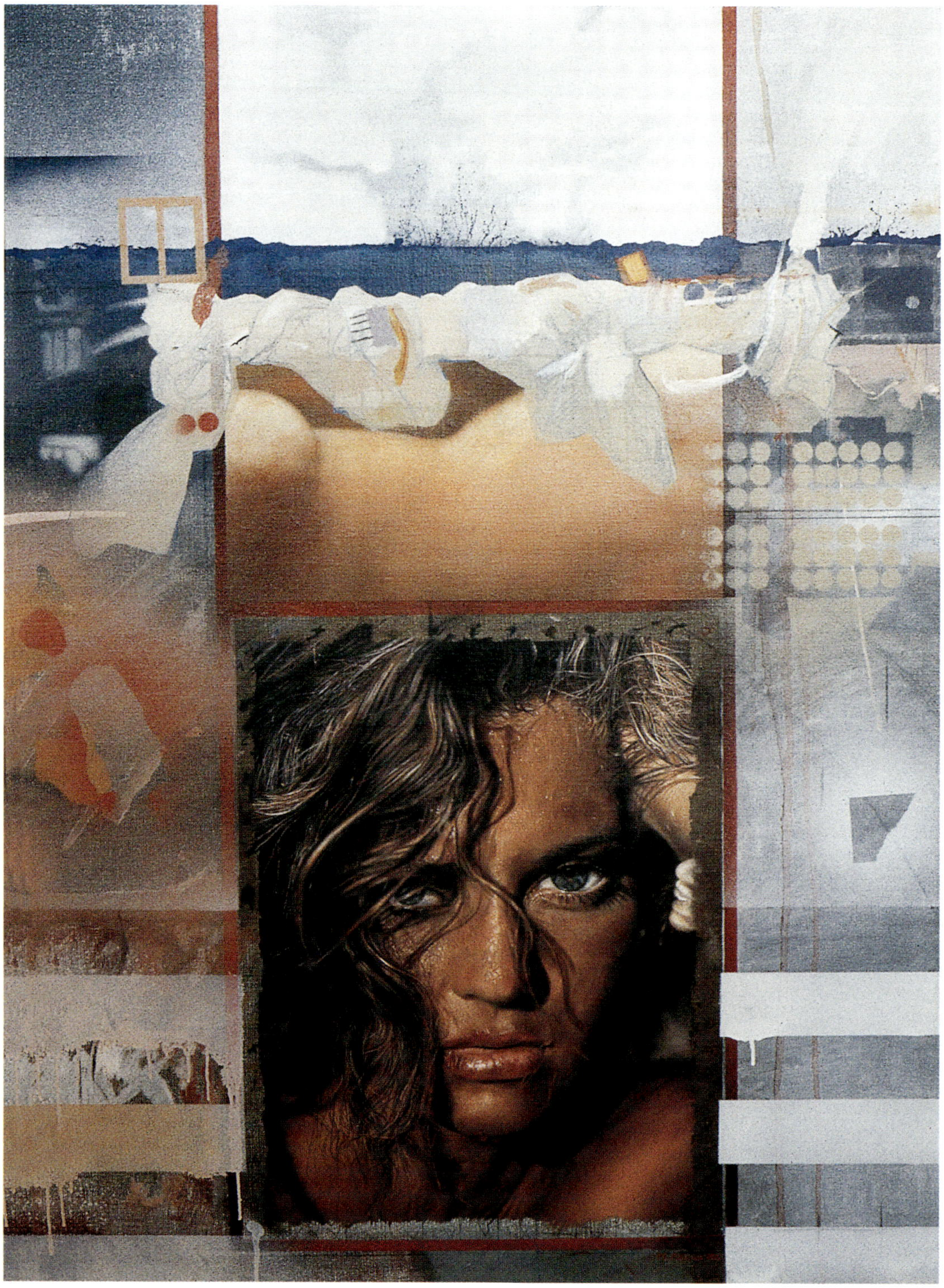

HER NEAR PAST, 1982
Oil on canvas
100 x 72 cm
Collection Mr. & Mrs. S. Chatila

Exhibited at the Sursock Museum Salon d'Automne, Beirut, 1982

Return to Beirut

On my return to Beirut in autumn 1981, I was unable to continue the work I had been doing in England: there was no chance of doing any lithography or silkscreen work due to the absence of any such workshops in Lebanon, and whatever was available for etching was at an extremely primitive level. I had to go back to painting.

My continuing obsession with the photographic image led me to attempt a new approach: the photorealism style of painting. This is when I produced *Her Near Past* (1982), my first work in photorealism. It was a new development in my career. However, it differed from the methods and approaches of the conventional photorealistic style of painting. I placed the painted photorealistic image adjacent to the other elements of the painting, which were given a more abstract treatment. This combination was a new experiment that enriched the vocabulary of my artistic experience. I still often use this style in my work. It is a time-consuming process but unique in its expressive qualities.

My first fine art print after returning to Lebanon was *A Childhood Moment* (1981), which used etching and 'gum printing' – a fascinating technique I had learned at the Slade. It involves coating the paper with a light-sensitive emulsion, mixed with watercolor paint. When this coating is dry, a photographic negative is placed on top and exposed to a source of ultra-violet (UV) light. In London I had used a professional 'light box': in Beirut, this was replaced by direct sunlight on the balcony.

When I started teaching at the Lebanese University I developed an etching studio and started producing my work there.

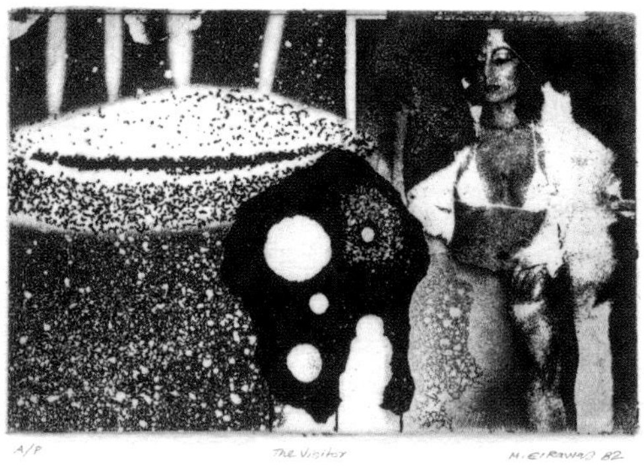

THE VISITOR, 1982
Etching
5 x 7 cm

Opposite page
A CHILDHOOD MOMENT, 1981
Etching and gum printing
52 x 41 cm

In 1990 I was asked by the American University of Beirut to establish an etching and engraving studio as well as a silkscreen studio in the Department of Architecture and Design. It seemed that practicing lithography, however, was going to be difficult once I was back in Beirut.

But then I met Rami al-Khal, the owner of a commercial printing press, who became a close friend. He was excited by my work and willing to put at my disposal a single-color 'Pearl' offset press on which I was able to produce my lithographic prints. The first one I produced on this press was *The Gentle Touch* (1986), which combined lithographic work with etching.

Producing lithographic fine art prints on a commercial press is generally neither practical nor feasible for the artist, and even less so for the owner of the printing firm. The specific printing practices required by fine art lithography, the detailed color testing and the frequency of plate-replacement – along with the 'limited edition' approach restricting the number of prints produced – lies beyond the pricing schedules and printing practices of ordinary commercial color-printing jobs which use four-color separation (CMYK) for print-runs of thousands. Conquering such difficulties demanded the printer's 'will' and an enthusiasm for art – qualities I was lucky enough to find in Rami al-Khal and later in Ali Chawraba, at whose press I produced lithographic prints from 1996 onwards. Dealing with the technical operators of the commercial presses proved interesting: they were both uneasy and fascinated at being able to break the rules they usually followed for producing spotless commercial work. My own approach was not that strict when it came to accidental spots of ink: mistakes of this kind were often welcomed by me as they registered part of the process by which the total work of art came into being. And the number of colors I used in my prints – often more than 50 – was another practice unfamiliar to the press operators.

Ever since I returned to Lebanon, teaching art has been my second profession. What gives me pleasure in teaching is that I am not only passing on technical expertise, but also my own personal experience – the result of my own discoveries. This is something I did not get from my teachers at the Lebanese University. And I feel tremendously rewarded when any student of mine excels in his or her chosen field.

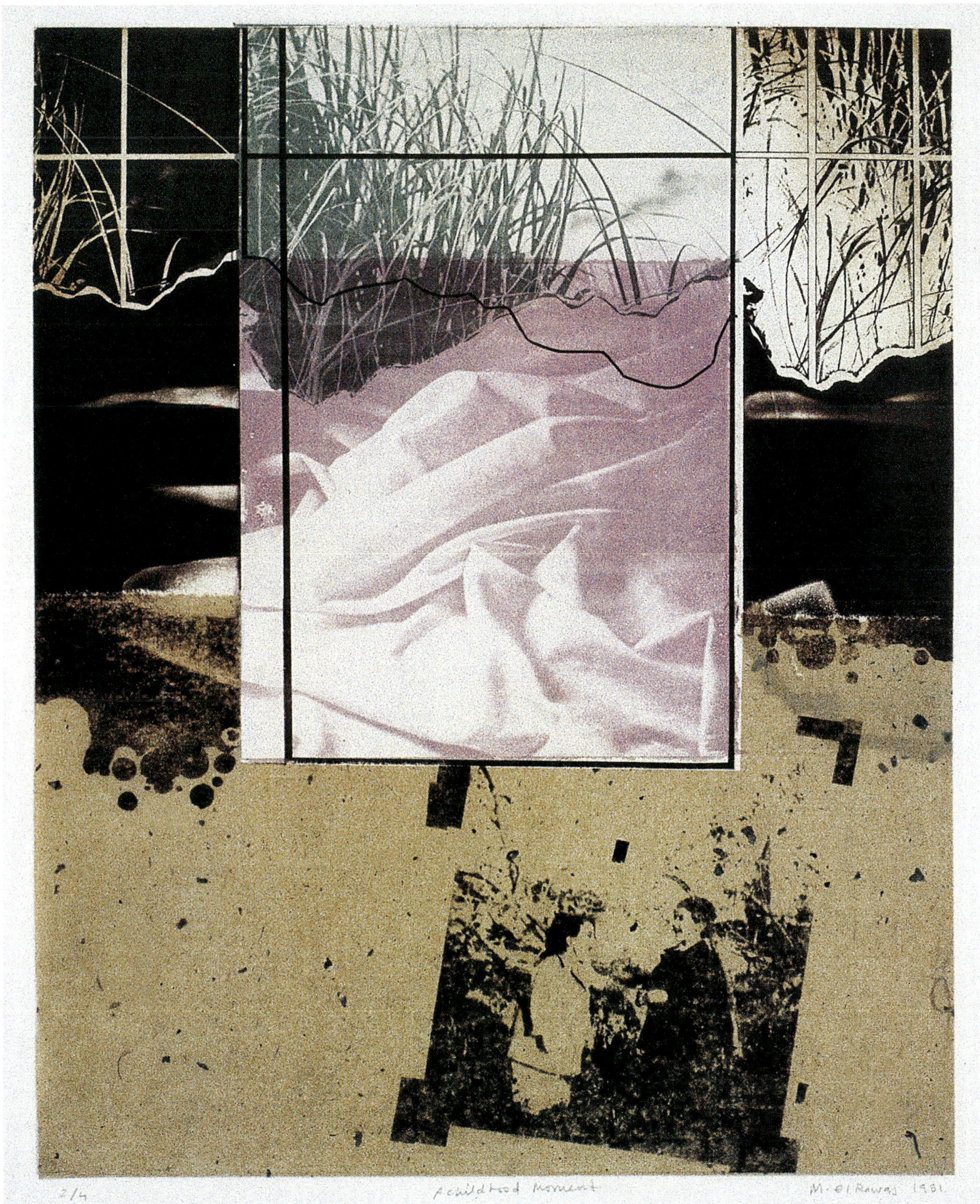
2/4
A childhood moment
M. el Rawas 1981

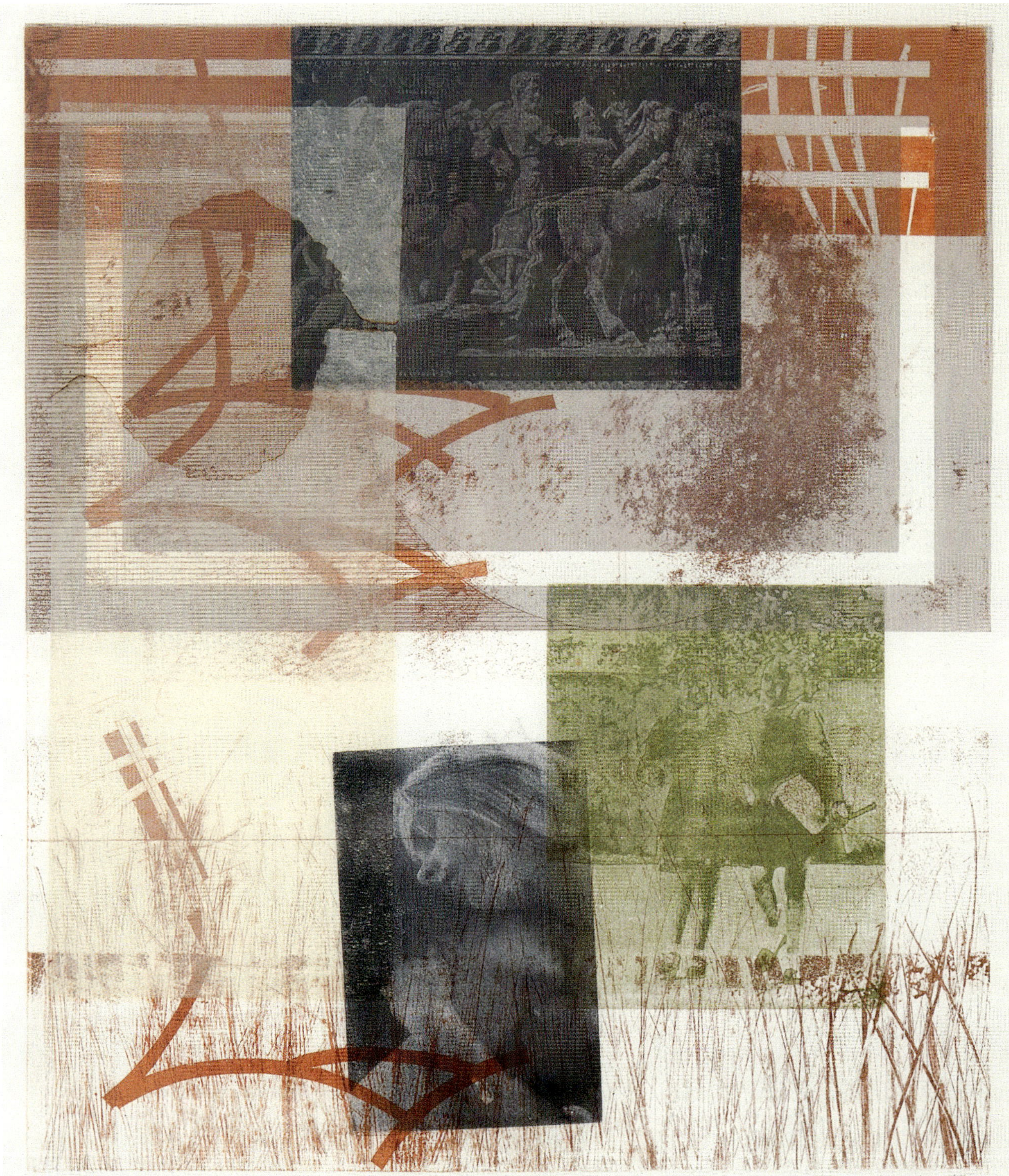
4/5
Images
M El RAWAS 1983

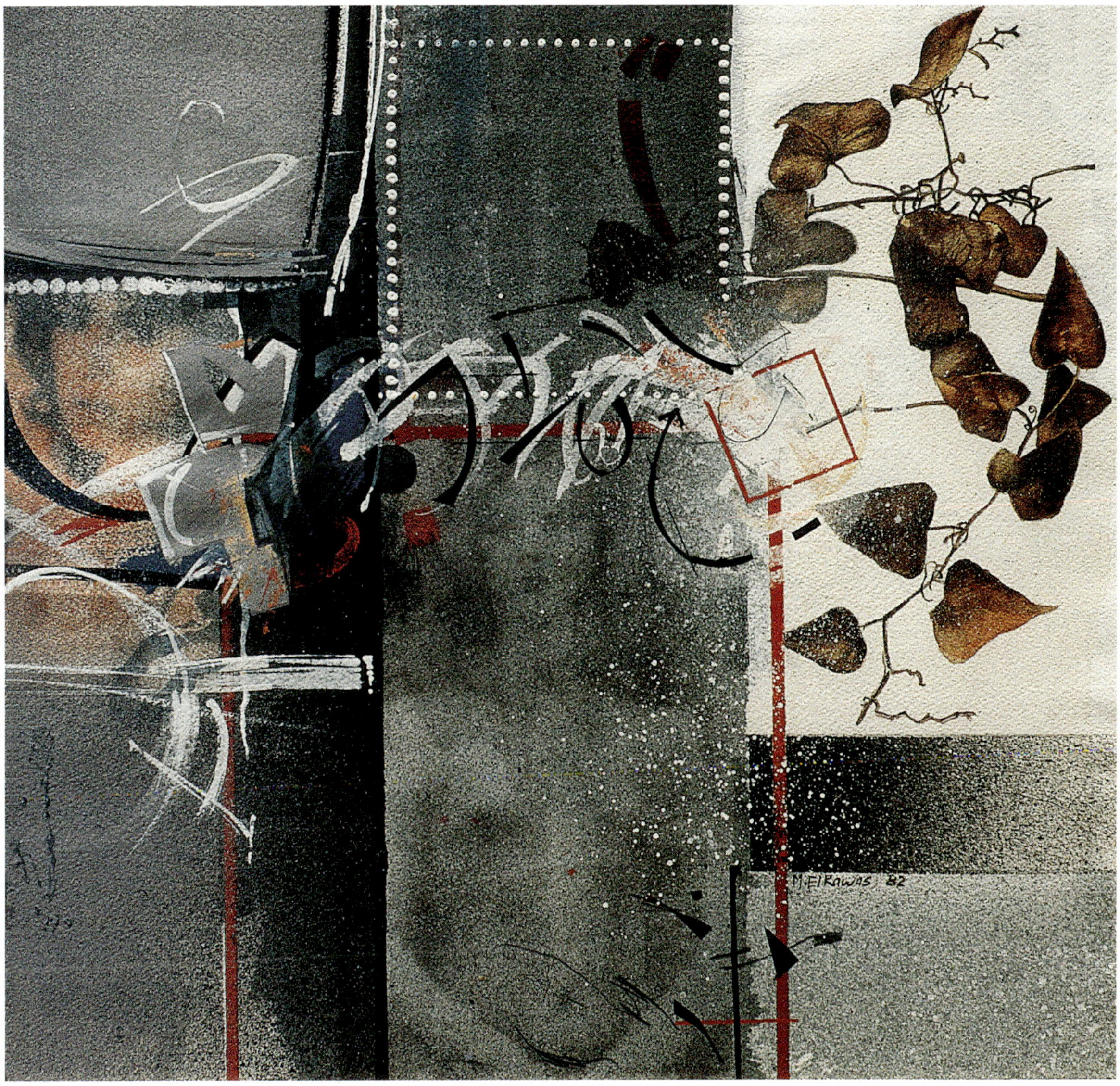

JEALOUSY, 1982
Transfer and mixed media on paper
31.5 x 32 cm
Collection Ms. V. Mokbel

Opposite page
IMAGES, 1983
Etching and collage
50 x 41 cm

Exhibited at the Second Cabo Frio International Print Biennale, Brazil, 1985 (Honorary Award)

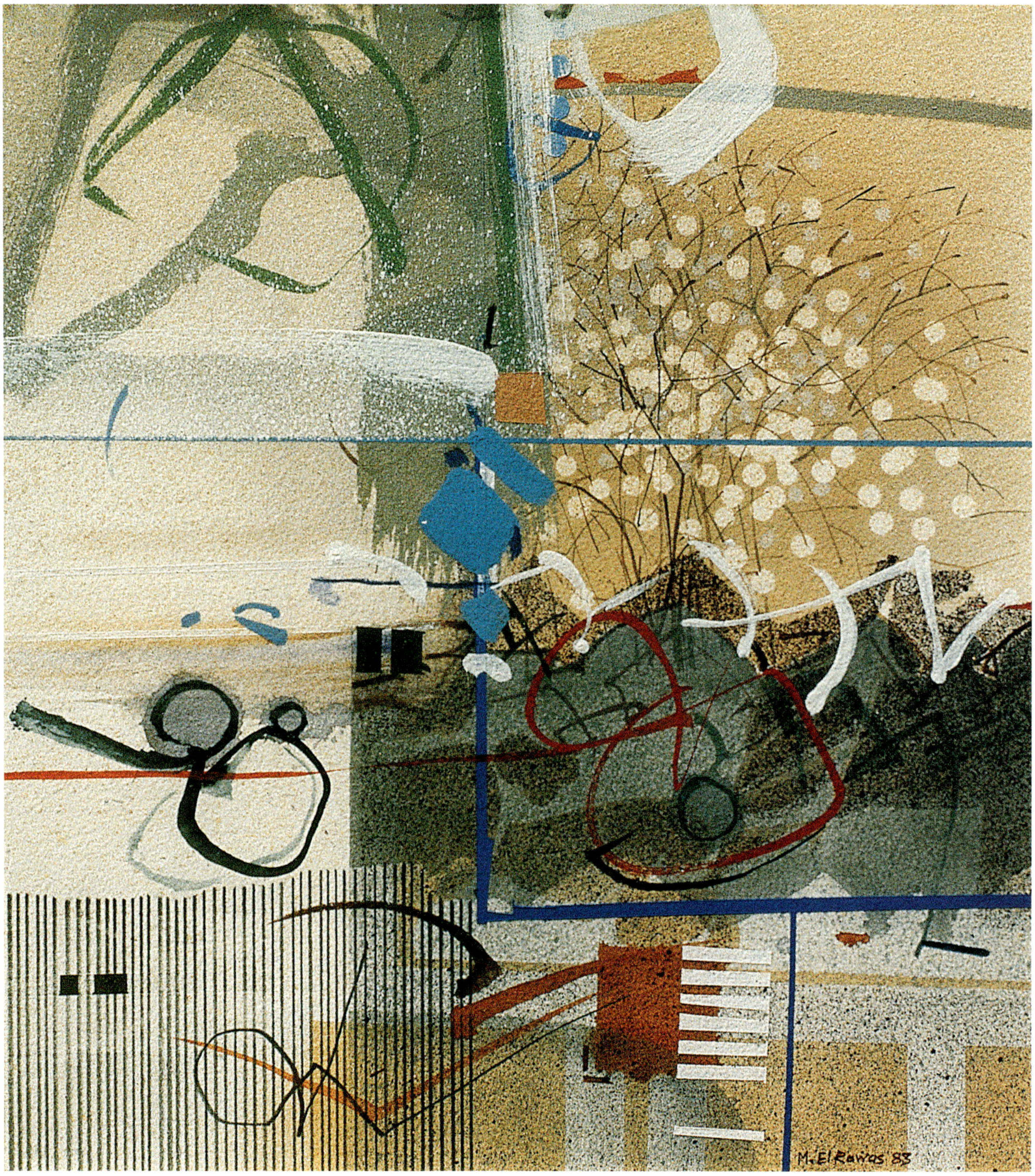

ALTERED PHASES, 1983
Mixed media on paper
24.5 x 21.5 cm
Collection Mr. & Mrs. A. Gaspard

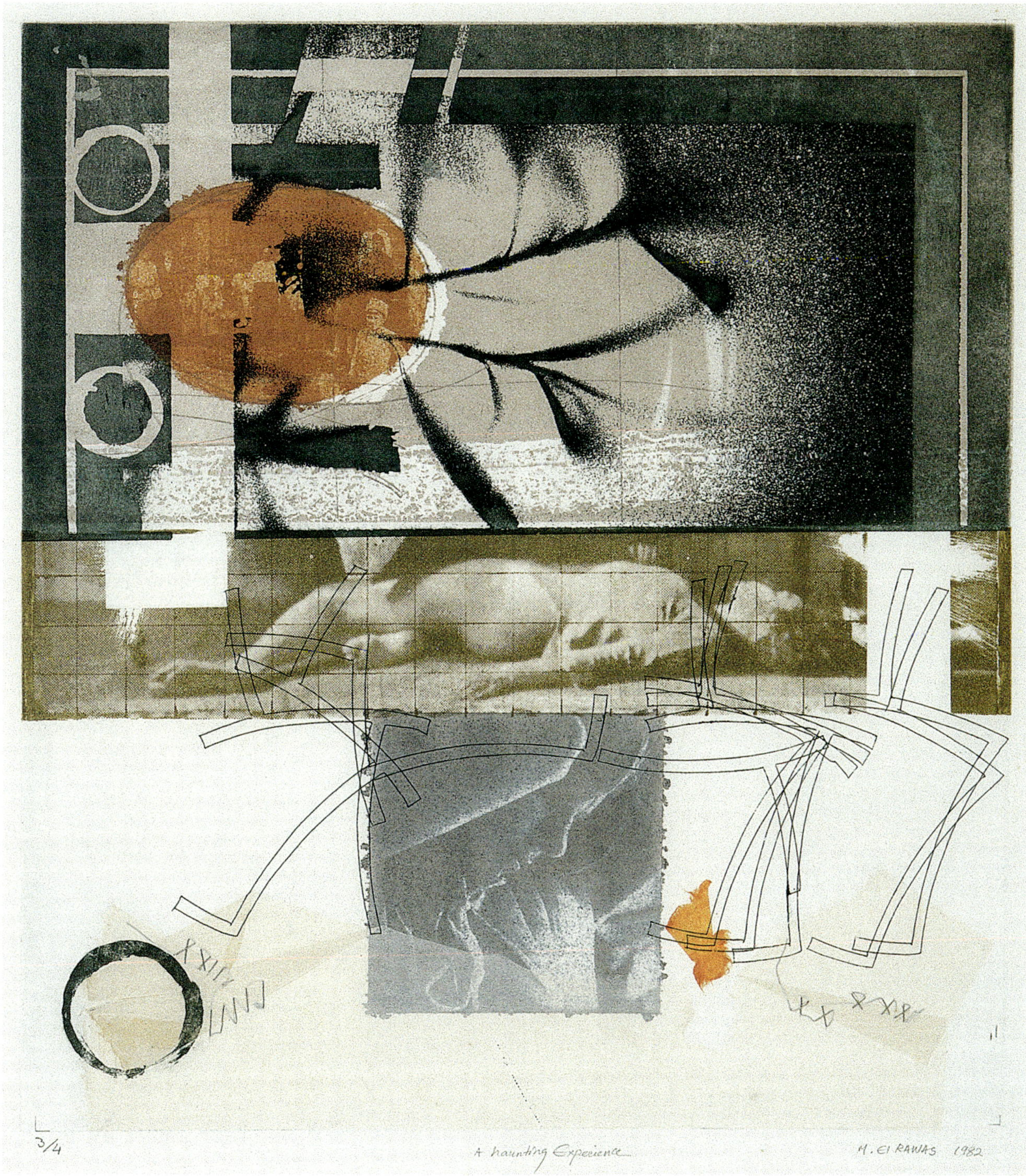

A HAUNTING EXPERIENCE, 1982
Etching and gum printing
45 x 41 cm

Exhibited at the Second Cabo Frio International Print Biennale, Brazil, 1985 (Honorary Award)

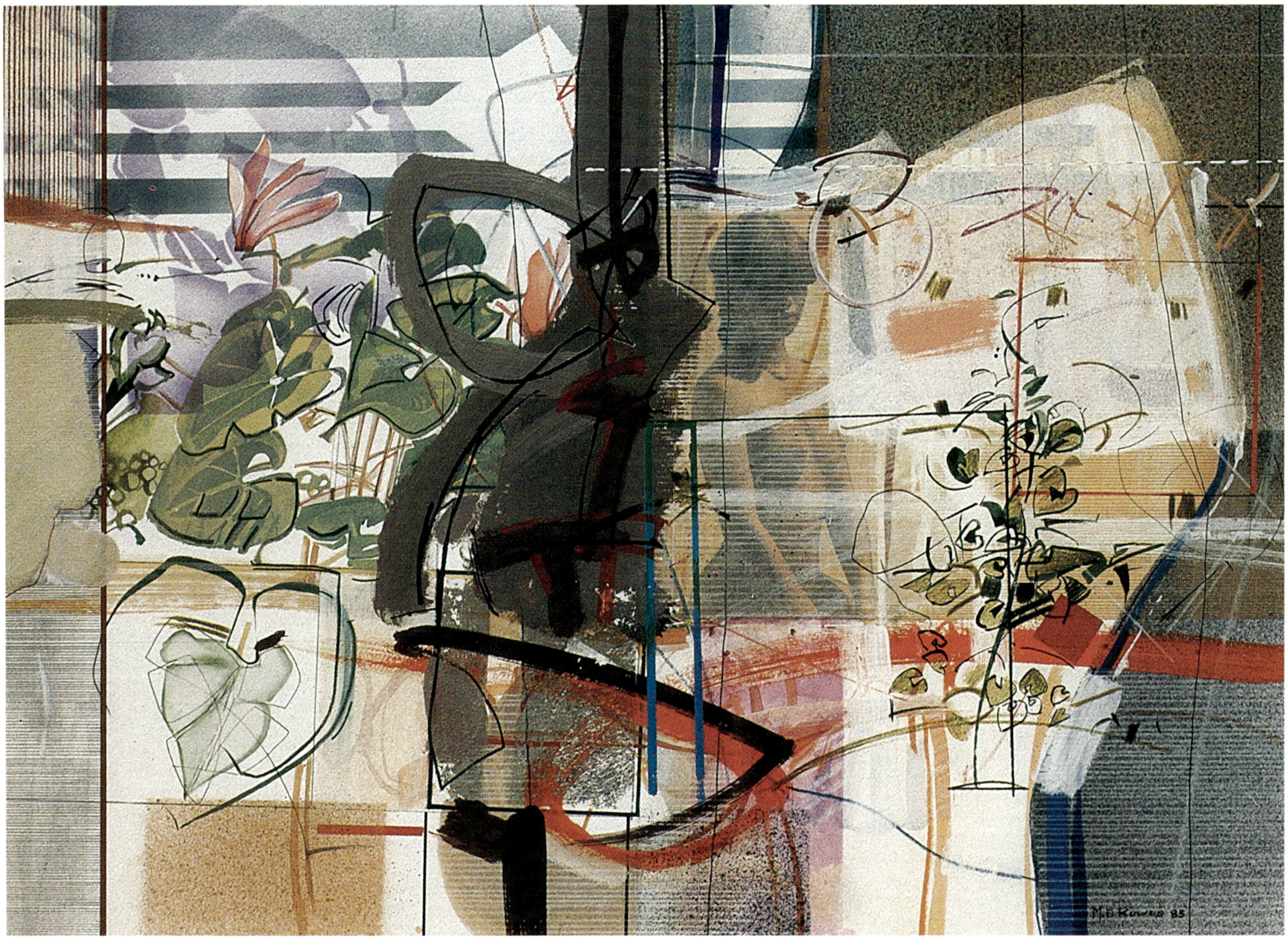

AWAKENING, 1983
Mixed media and transfer on paper
47 x 64 cm
Collection Mrs. A. Boulad

Opposite page
FRIENDS, 1983
Mixed media and transfer on paper
78 x 63 cm
Collection Mr. & Mrs. S. Chatila

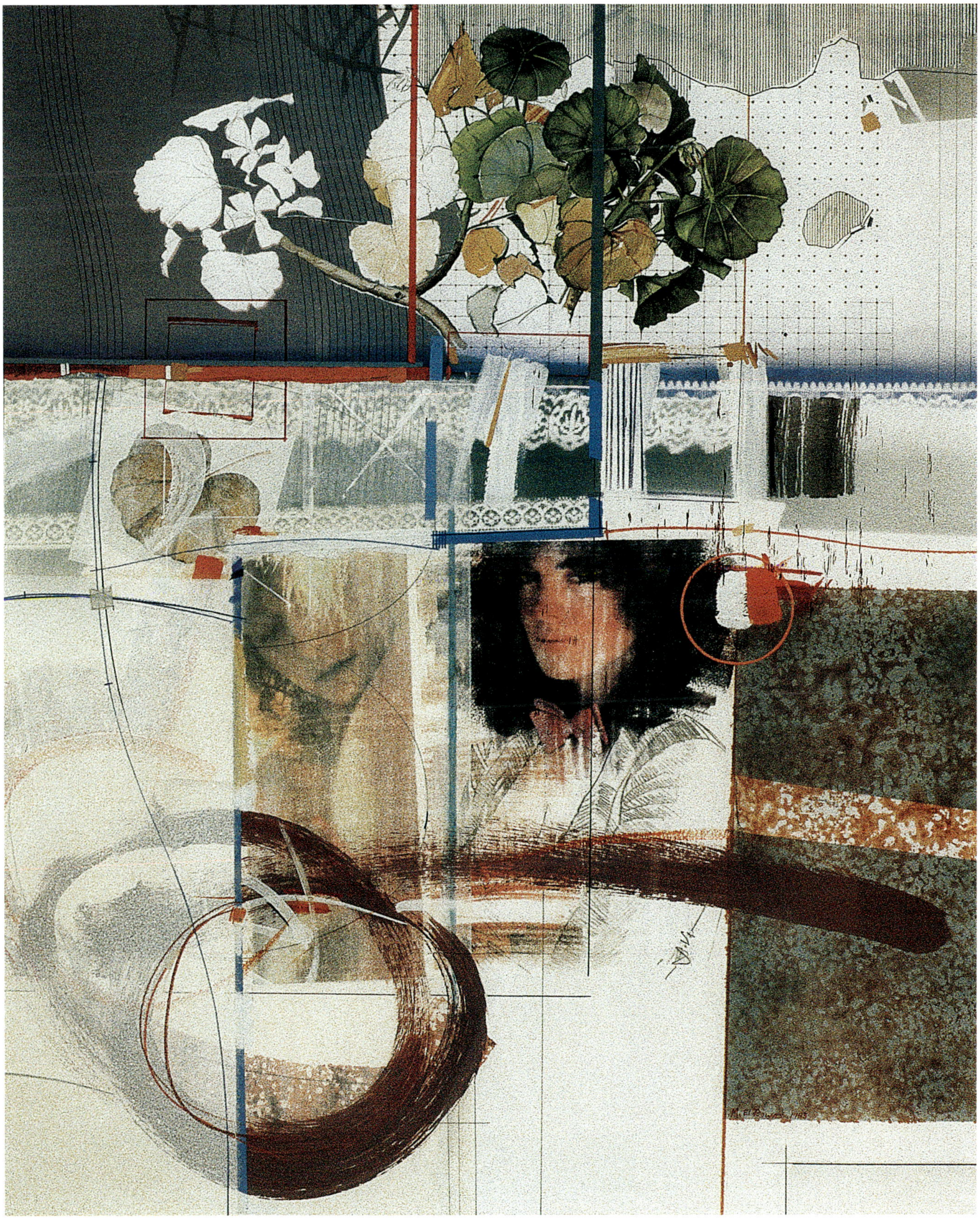

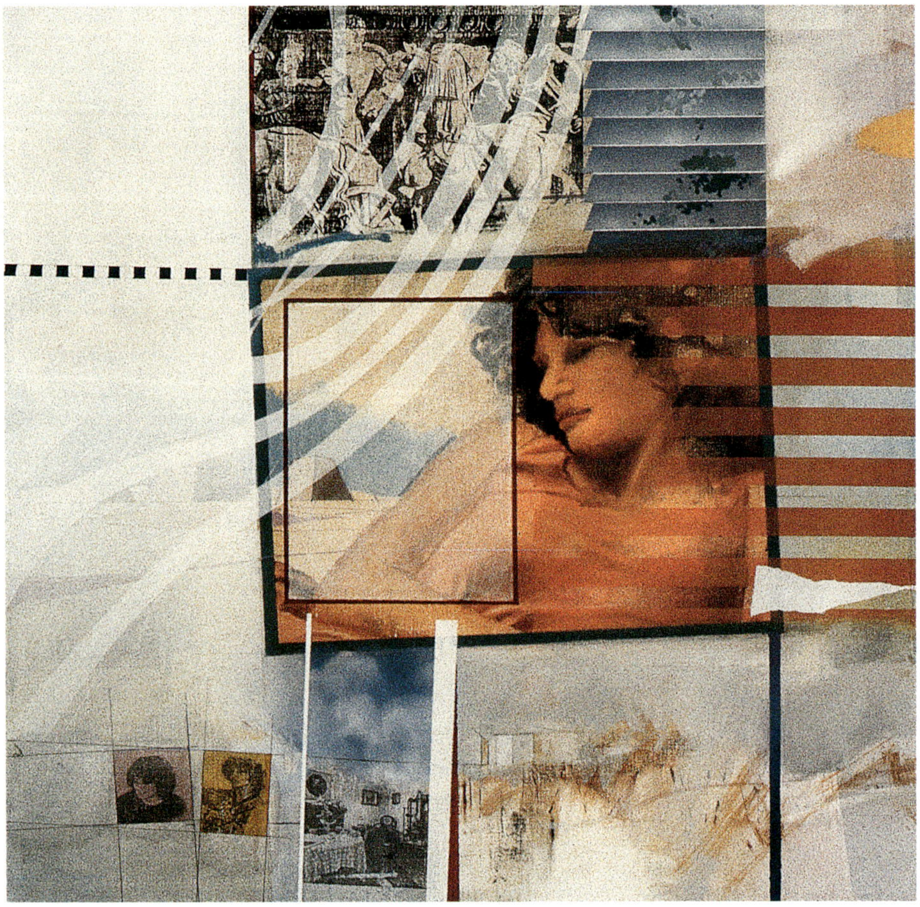

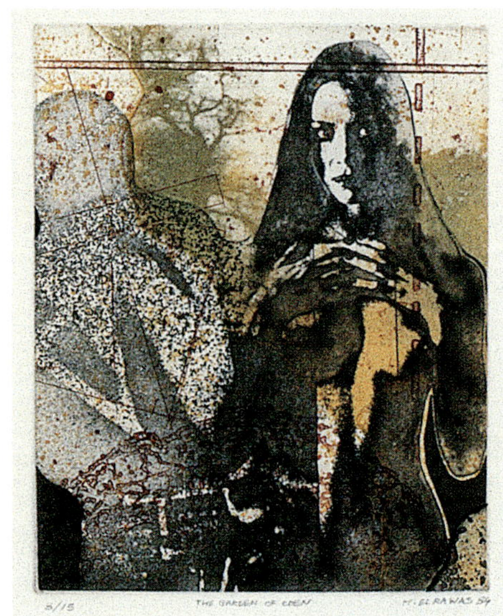

Top left
SALWA, 1984
Oil and transfer on canvas
79 x 79 cm
Collection Mr. & Mrs. A. Gaspard

Top right
THE GARDEN OF EDEN, 1984
Etching
14.5 x 12 cm

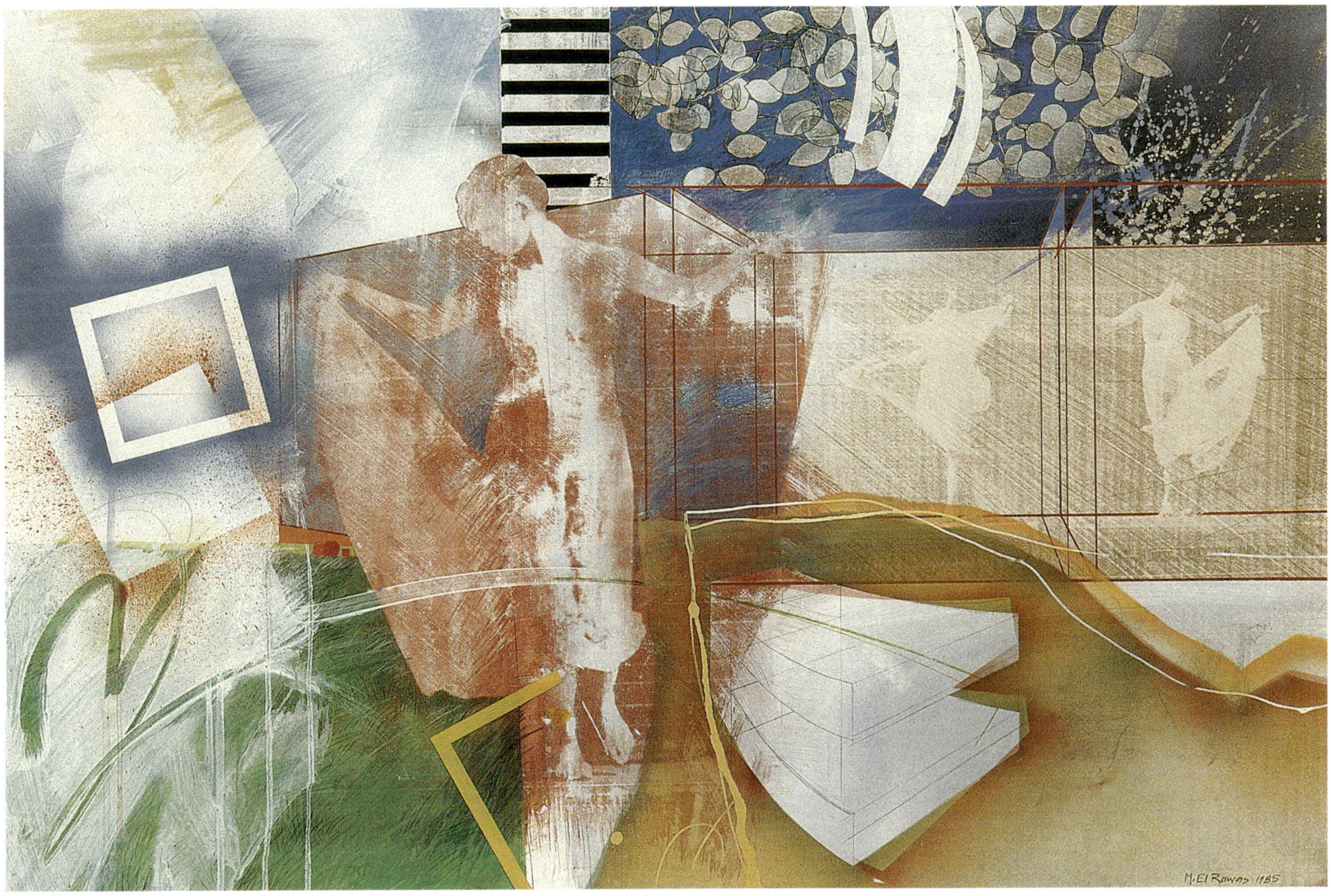

THE PLATFORM, 1985
Gum printing and mixed media on paper
65 x 94 cm
Private collection

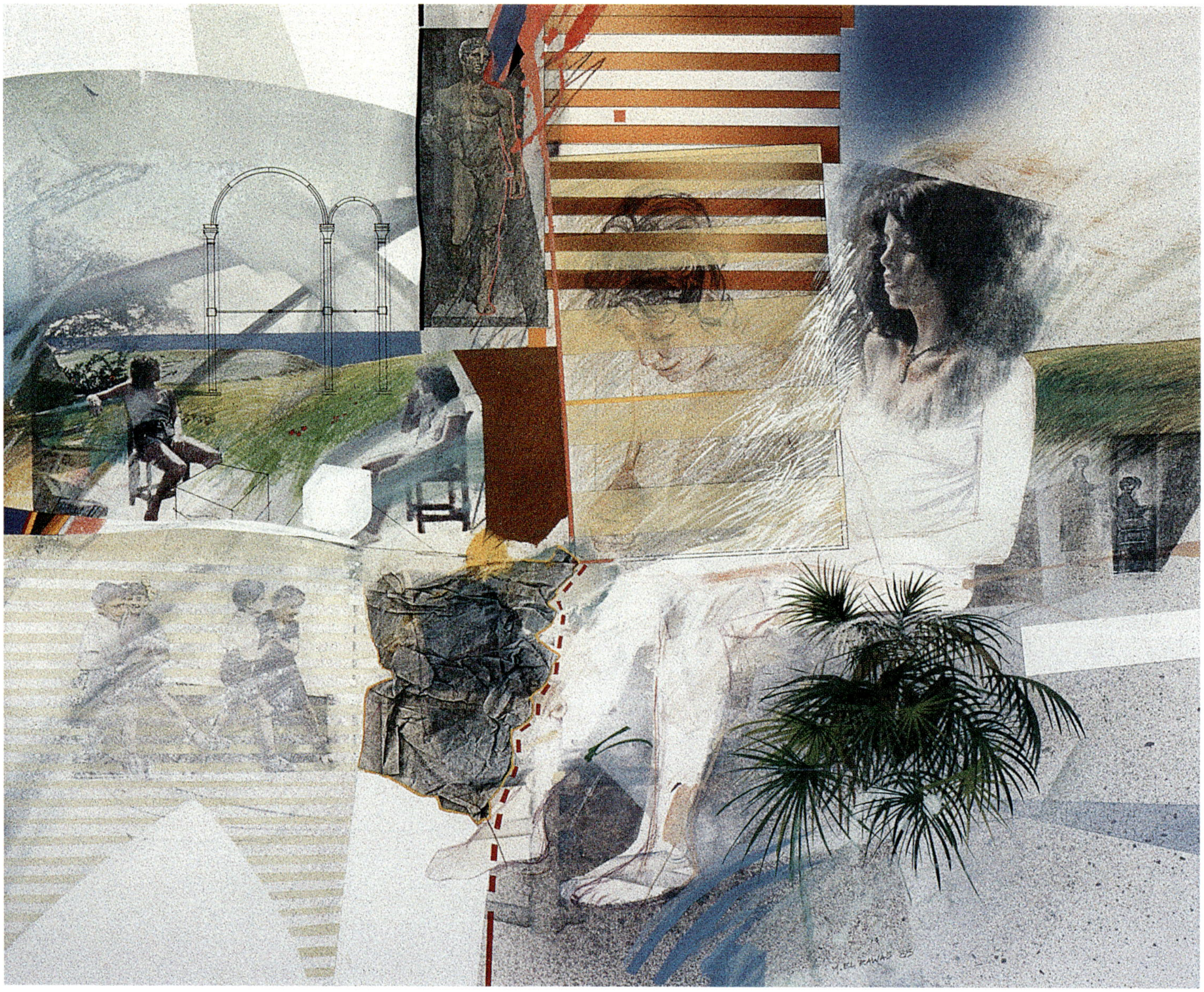

REMINISCENCE, 1985
Mixed media and transfer on paper
55 x 66 cm
Collection Mr. & Mrs. M. Atwi

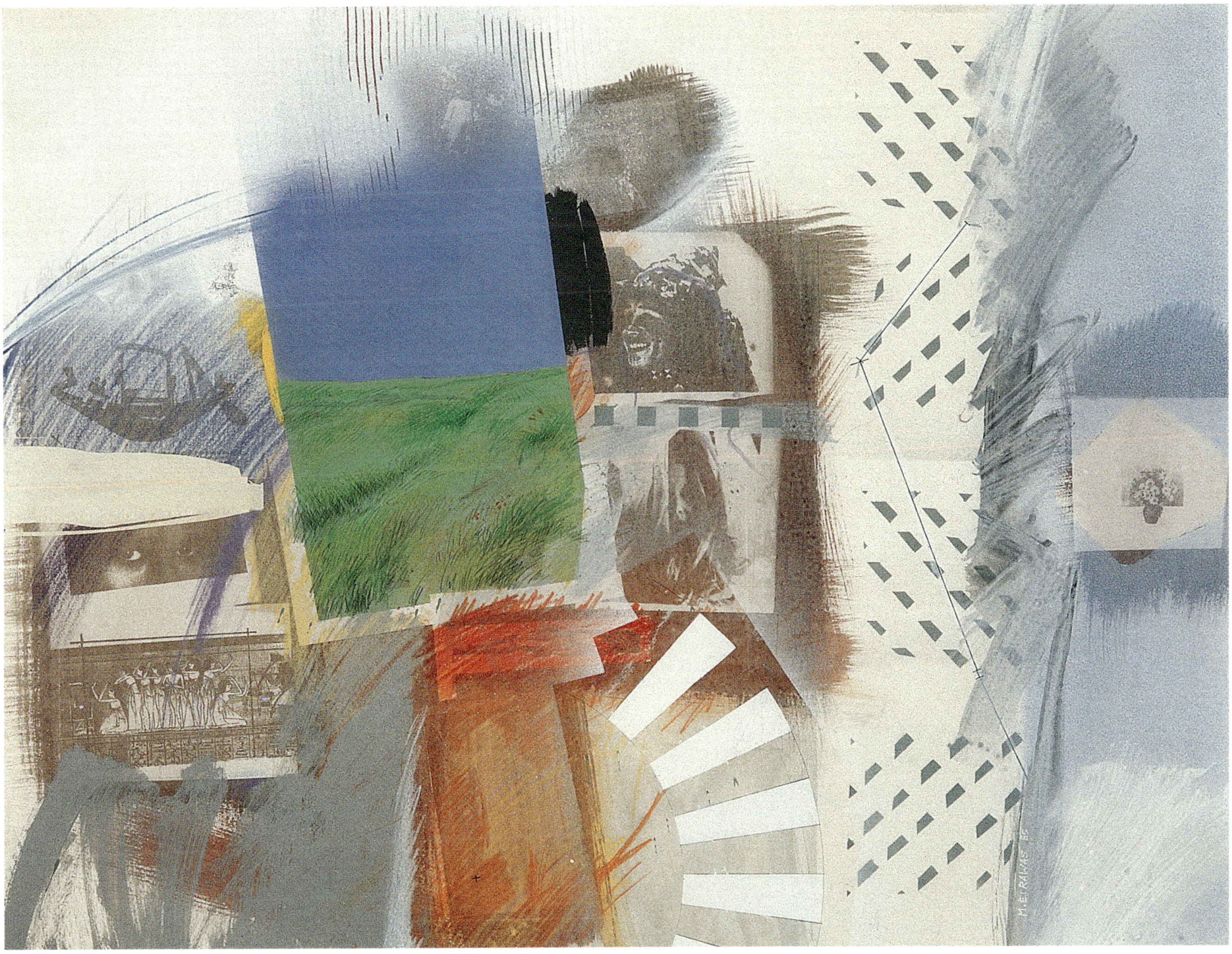

MEMORIES, 1985
Mixed media and gum printing on paper
49 x 63.5 cm
Collection Ms. F. Oueida

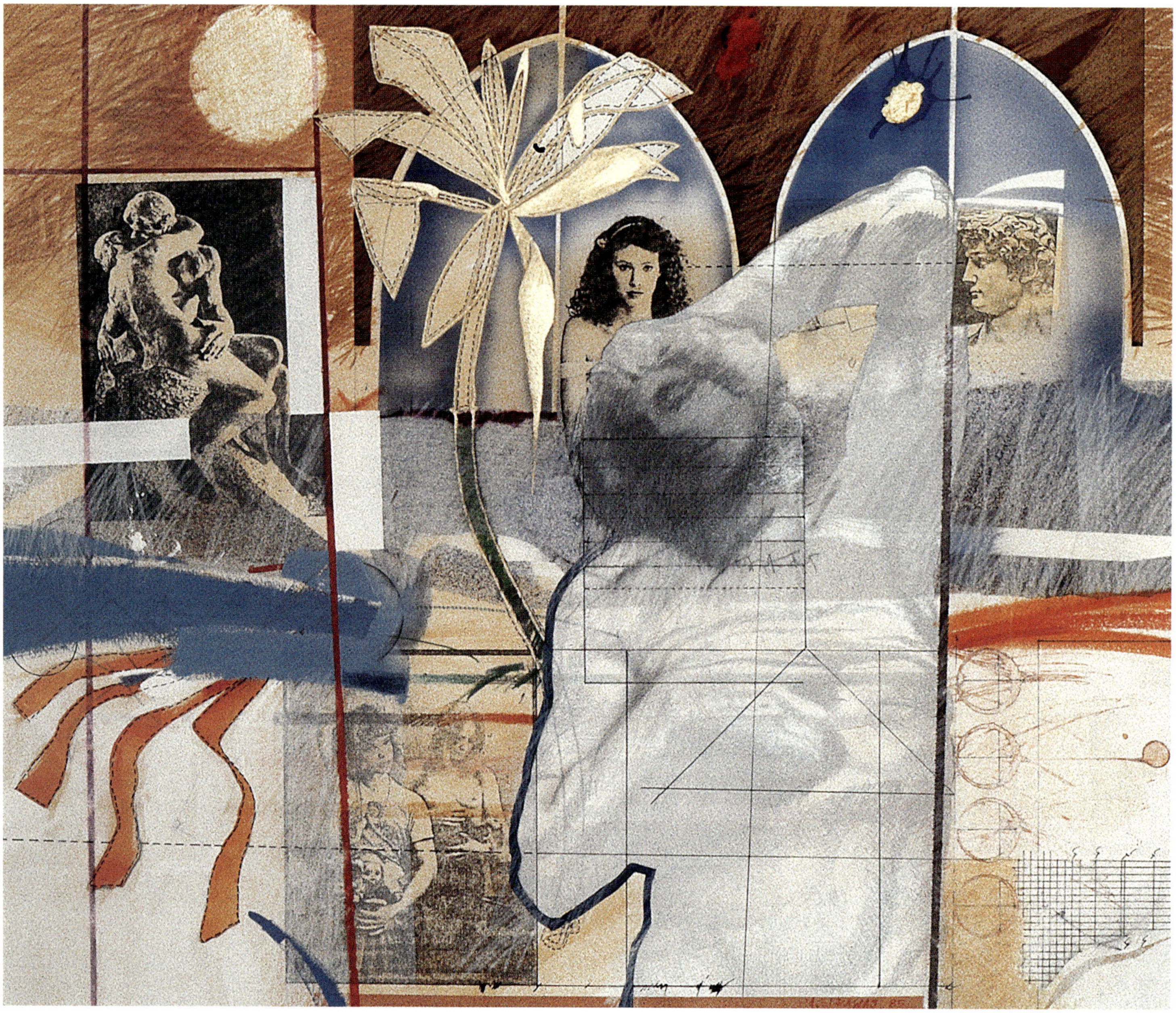

ADOLESCENCE, 1985
Mixed media and transfer on paper
44.5 x 52 cm
Collection Mr. & Mrs. O. Makki

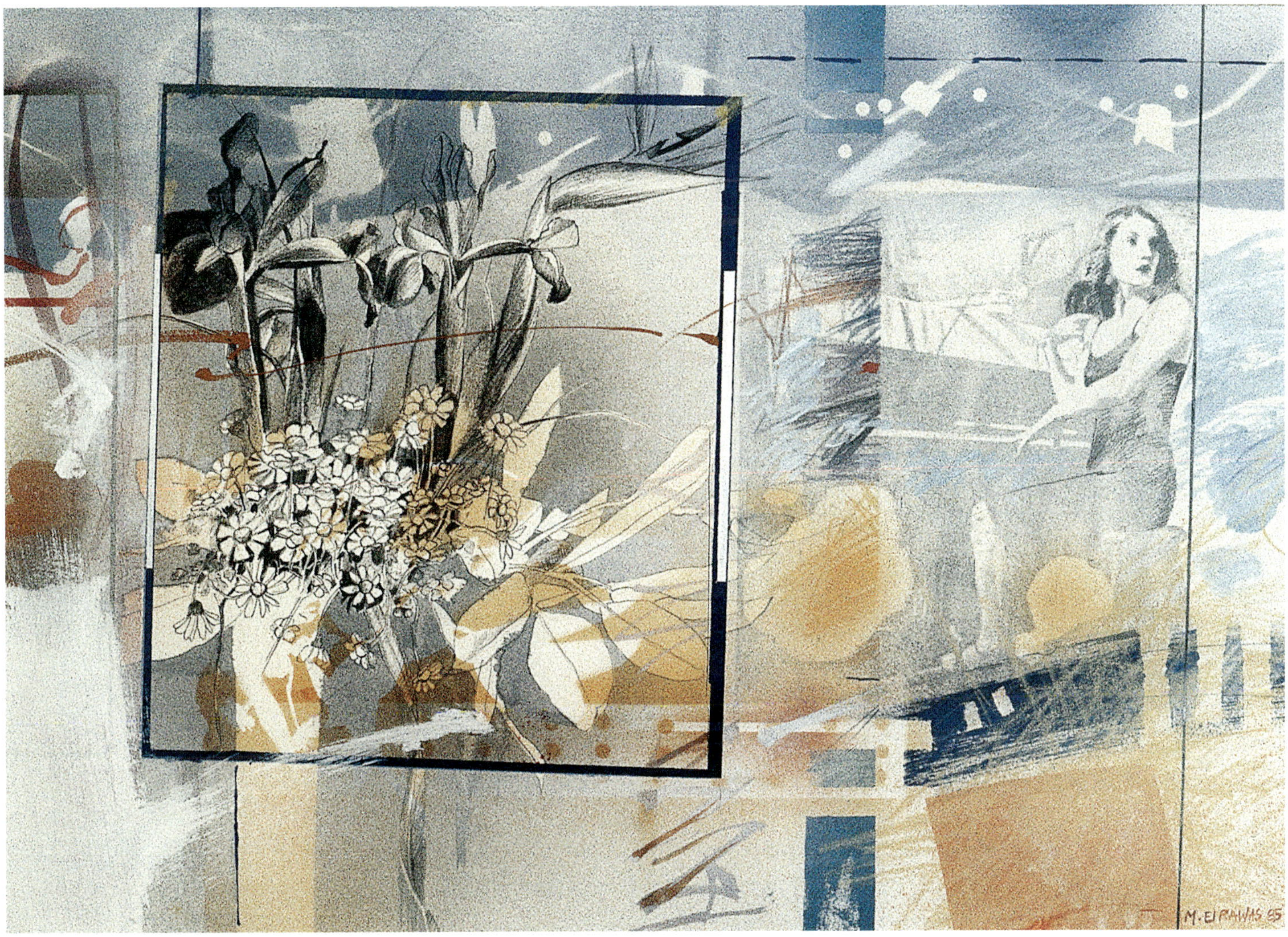

THE PIANO PLAYER, 1985
Mixed media and transfer on paper
32.5 x 44.5 cm
Collection Mr. M. Mekdashi

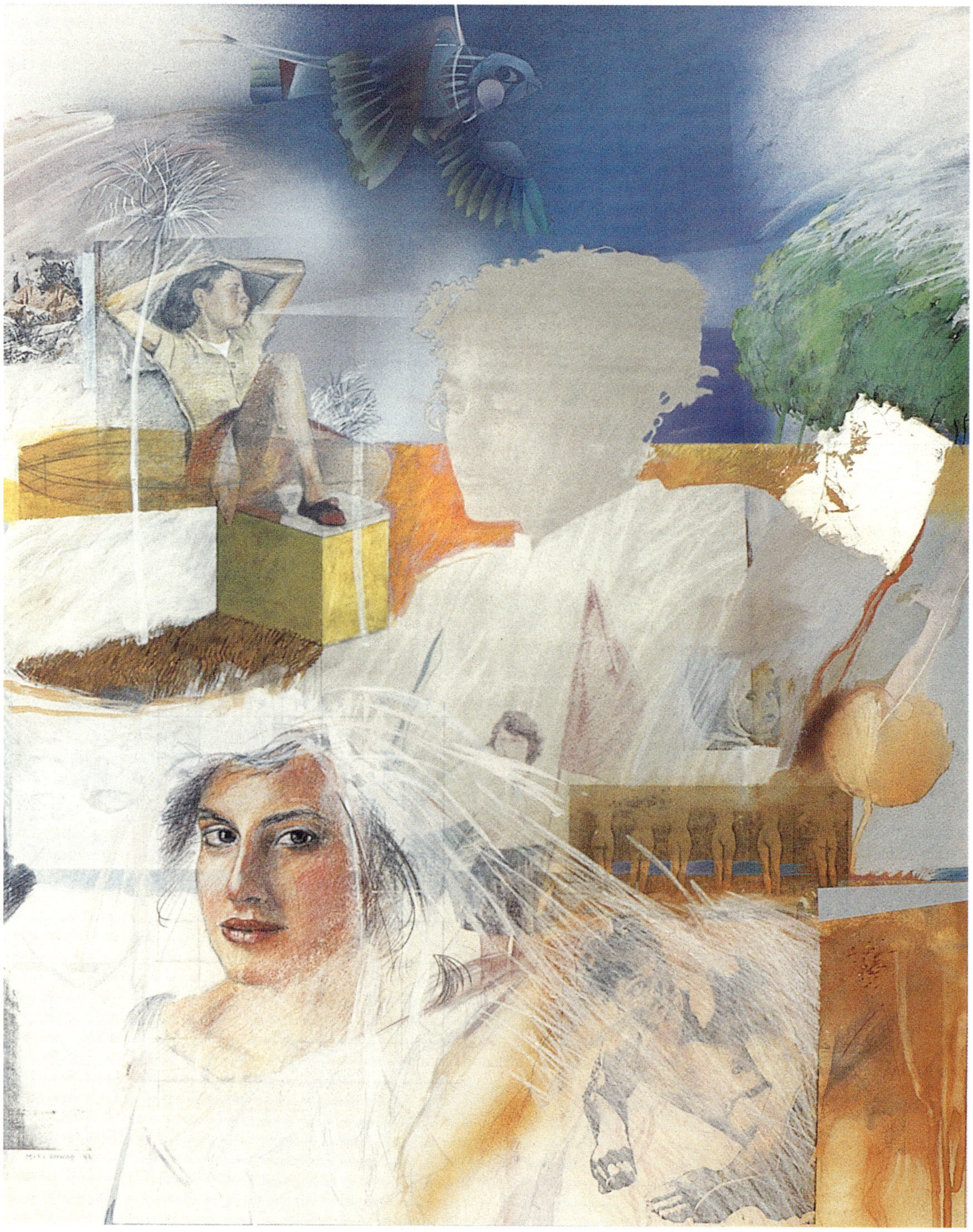

BRIDE AND TEMPEST, 1986
Mixed media and transfer on paper
68.5 x 53.5 cm
Collection Mr. & Mrs. R. Saidi

Exhibited at:
– Sursock Museum Salon d'Automne, Beirut, 1986
– "Lebanon – The Artist's View: 200 Years of Lebanese Painting", Concourse Gallery, Barbican Center, London, 1989
– "Liban – Le regard des peintres: 200 ans de peinture libanaise", Institut du Monde Arabe, Paris, 1990

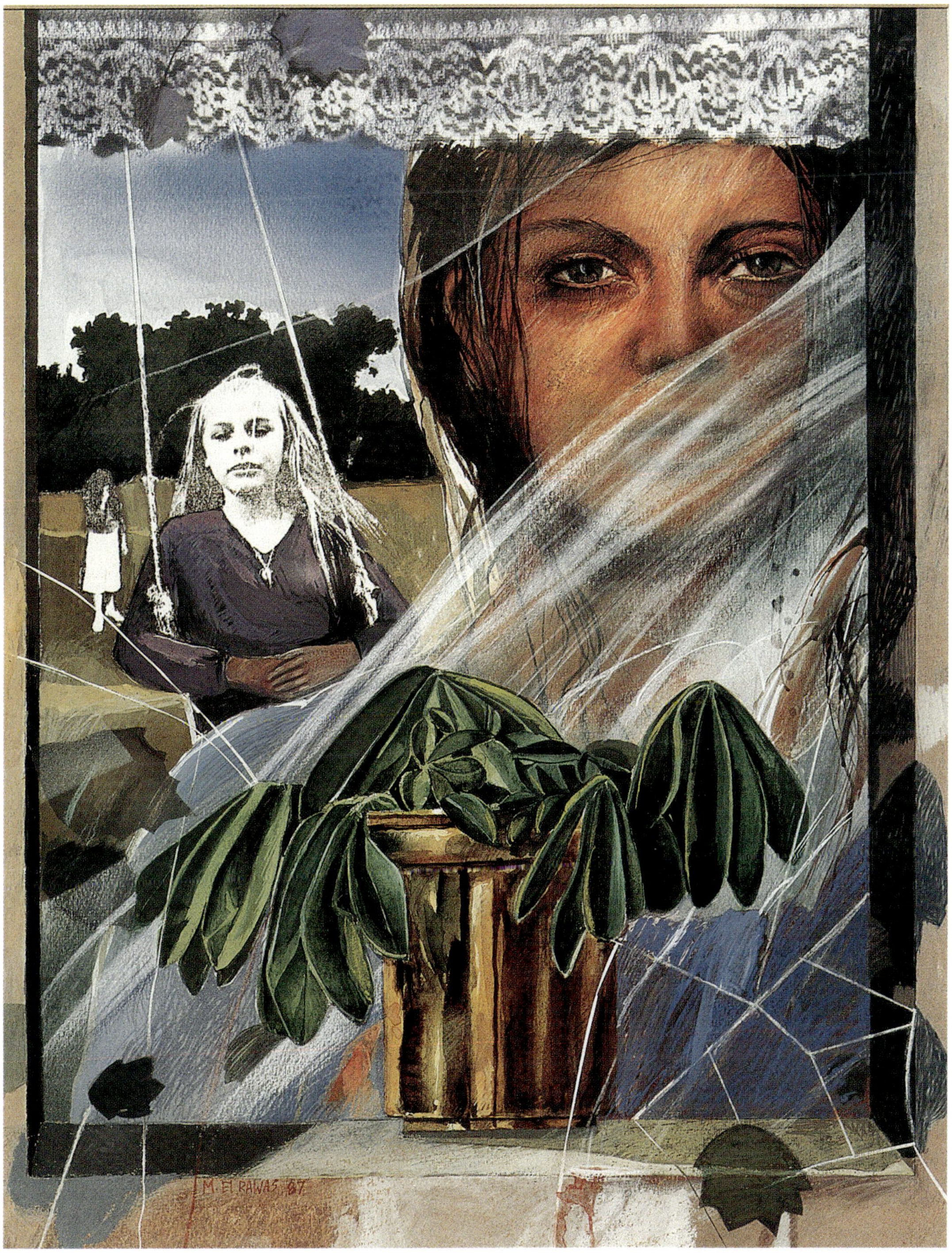

THE SWING, 1987
Mixed media and transfer on paper
45 x 30 cm
Collection Sursock Museum, Beirut

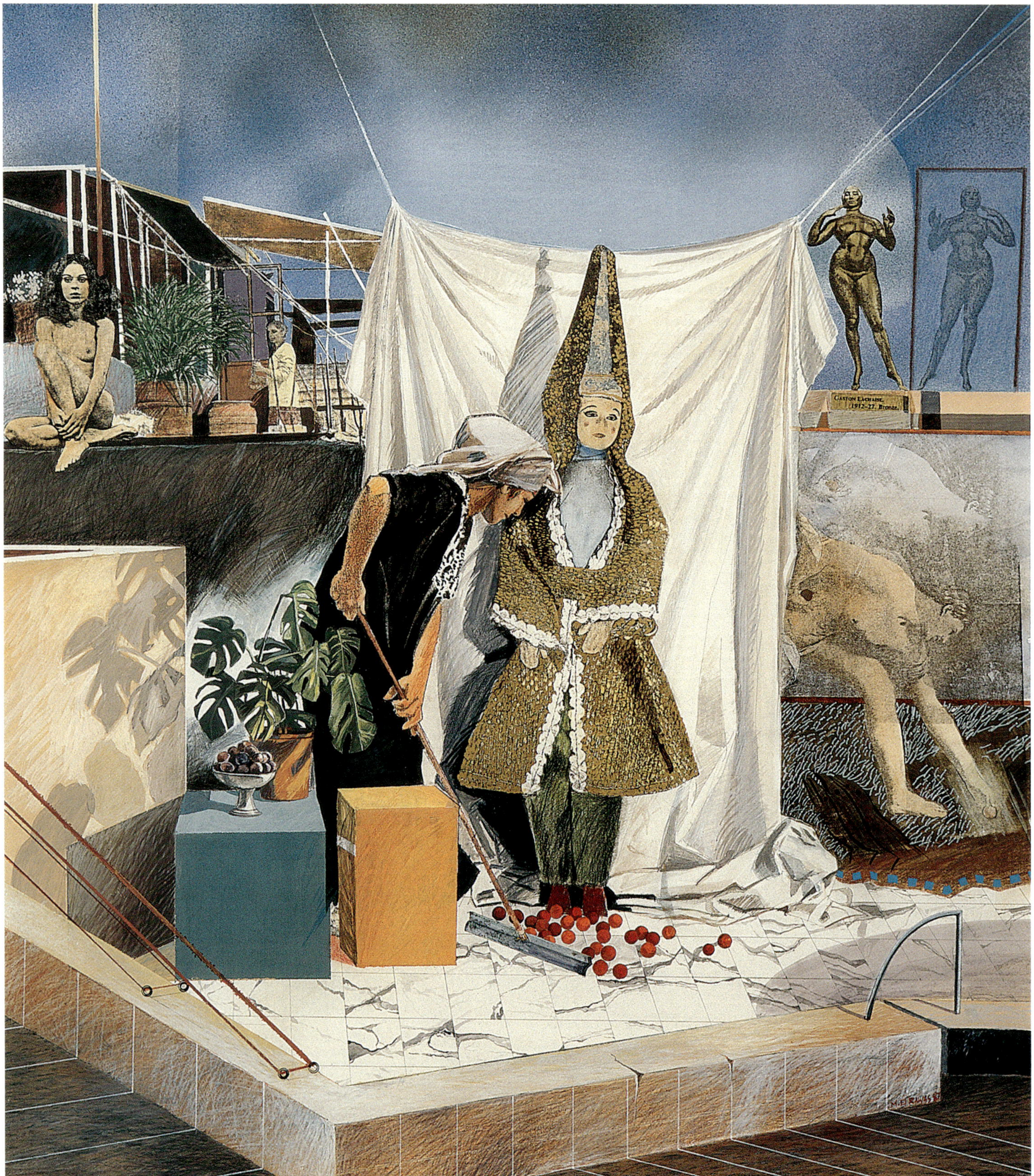

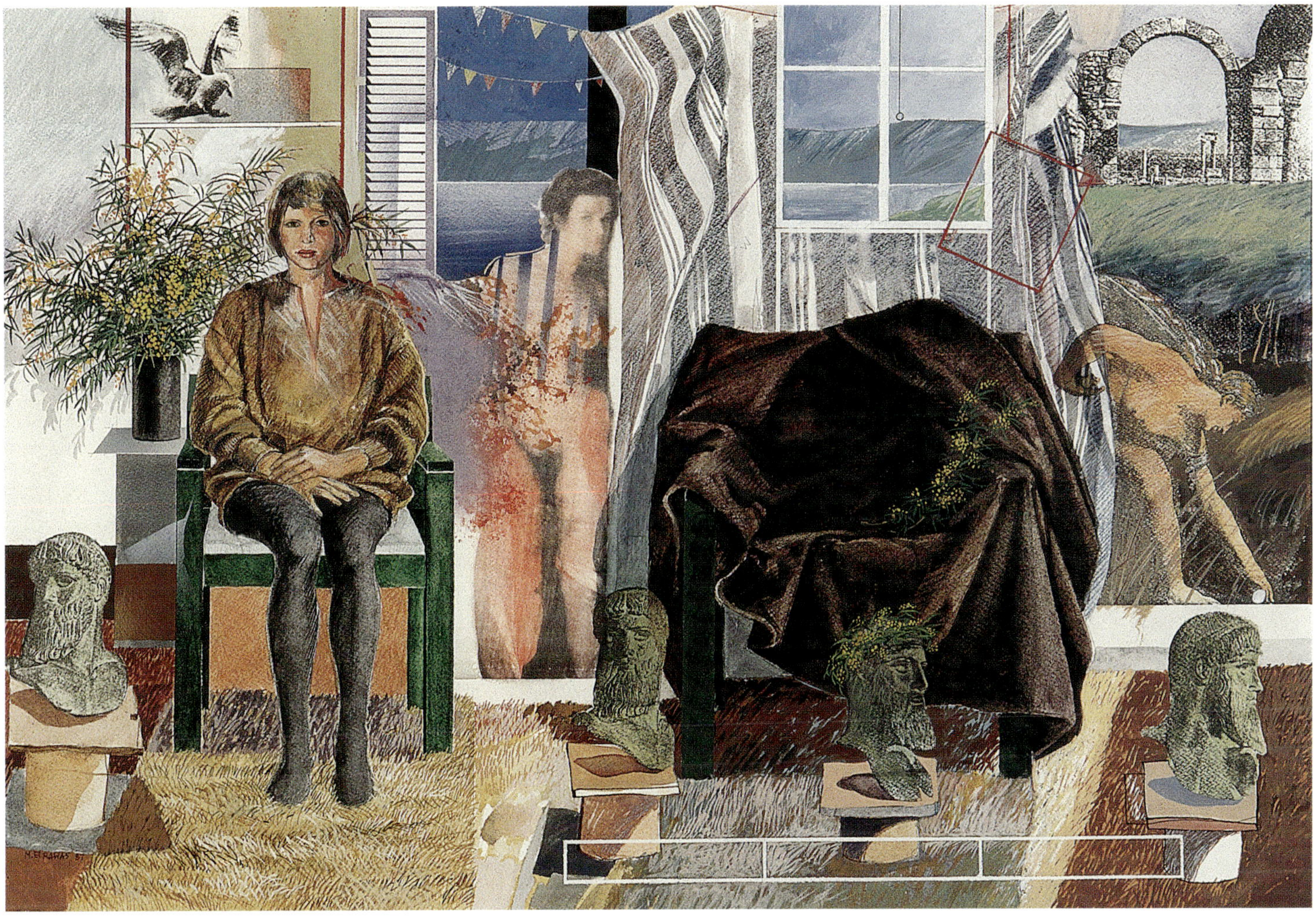

THE STILL AGE OF MIMOSA, 1987
Mixed media and transfer on paper
47 x 68 cm
Private Collection

Opposite page
LE QUARTIER, 1987
Mixed media and transfer on paper
64 x 55 cm
Private Collection

Exhibited at the Sursock Museum Salon d'Automne, Beirut, 1987

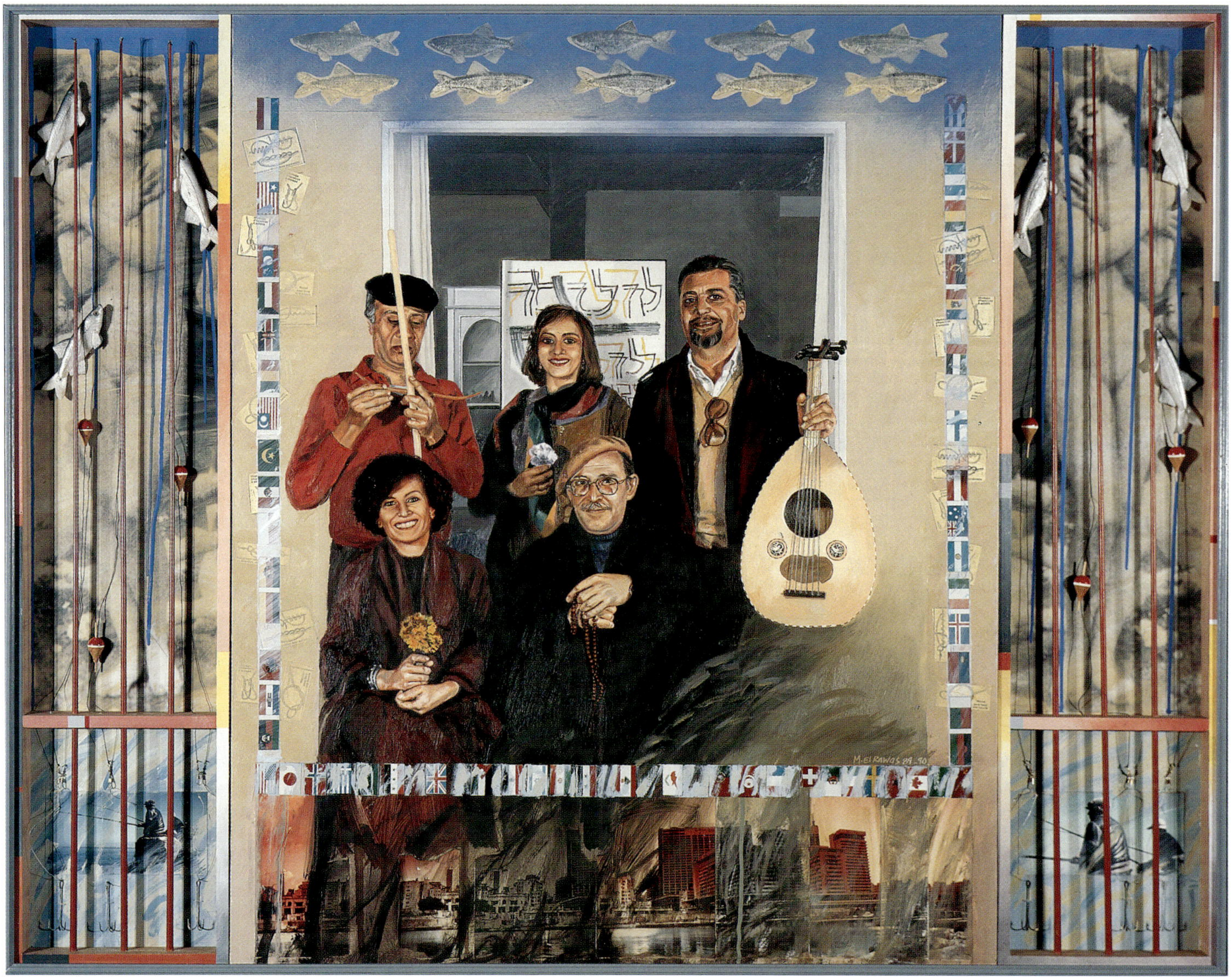

THE CONFERENCE OF THE FISH, 1989-1990
Oil, mixed media and assemblage on canvas and wooden panel
114 x 140 x 4 cm
Artist's collection

Exhibited at:
– Sursock Museum Salon d'Automne, Beirut, 1991–1992
– 93e Salon de la Société Internationale des Beaux-Arts (SIBA) Paris 2000

The Question of 'Identity'

Living and practicing my art in Lebanon, the question arises of how much I feel Lebanese or Arab. The answer is that I do not feel I belong to a certain nationality, and hate to be labeled by it. I believe nationalism to be an artificial construction, therefore I do not consider myself related to a specific nation or nationality. I do not feel I belong to any category. I care for individuals, no matter what their race, nationality or religion. I have never had any political interests, affiliation or tendency. I do not read the papers and usually rely on the BBC World Service for information on global events: following the local news is often a waste of time. True, I am aware of all the serious social problems in my country and feel that something should be done about them, but not by me: I have other aims in life. Thus I never felt the urge to become directly involved in any form of public service. But, ironically, many of my paintings reflect political issues in the broad sense of the word. Although the injustice in the world affects me deeply, I consider different individuals to have different tasks in different fields, and if individuals accomplish their tasks well, this will be an indirect improvement of the whole. If I am focusing on my art and doing it well, without jeopardizing my principles and standards, I am, in a way, serving society. I feel angry at all the injustice, misery and aggression, but I do not let it deflect me from my task, which is to do what I am doing to the best of my ability.

Naturally my art, in a way, reflects my attitude towards nationalism and belonging. What matters to me is the quality of

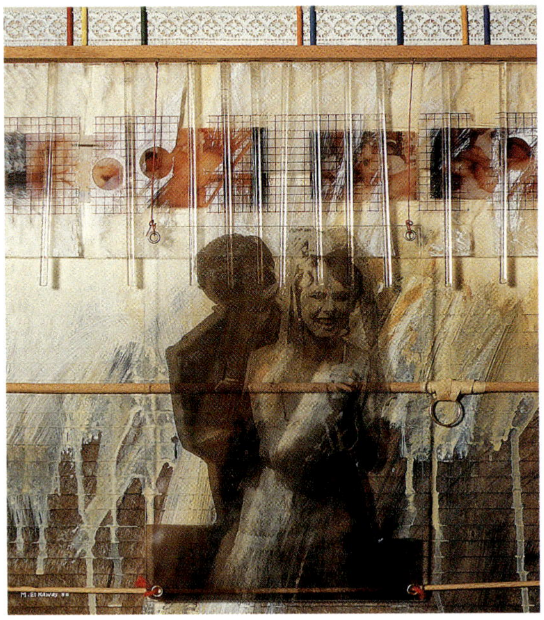

THE WEDDING AND ALL THAT JAZZ, 1988
Mixed media and assemblage on cardboard
48 x 41 x 4 cm
Private collection

Exhibited at the Sursock Museum Salon d'Automne, Beirut, 1988–1989

Opposite page
MAY GOD PRESERVE MY DAUGHTER, 1988
Mixed media and transfer on paper
95.5 x 65 cm
Private Collection

art, not whether it communicates a specific identity – although I strongly believe we do not have the choice as to whether or not our work manifests our identity. You are what you are. Whether I want it or not, my work will be deeply stamped by my culture, childhood, affinities and beliefs.

Displaying an Arab identity has, of course, been an issue on the Arab cultural scene. It has been implied that, if we did not make that identity obvious in our work, we would not be considered 'authentic' artists and our work would not be acknowledged by the international cultural authorities as being of any value. Some Arab artists fell victim to this brainwashing. In order to prove their oriental identity they forced into their paintings obvious symbols of our heritage, such as Arabic calligraphy or Eastern icons. This same tendency was seen in key Arab architects who, in the fifties, were educated in Europe (in England in particular). They reacted against Western teachings – by then, the Bauhaus international style – by incorporating oriental architectural patterns and icons into their designs. In most cases the outcome looked – in my opinion – pretentious and out of context.

I think that if proving your identity is what worries you when painting, you will no longer be producing true art. The most important thing in artistic creation is freedom of expression, and this freedom will naturally encompass your roots. I see no problem if an artist feels that his or her work should comprise icons or other symbols from our traditional culture, as long as this feeling is genuine. What bothers me is the element of 'unauthenticity'.

With regard to my paintings, I cannot really know how far they reflect my identity, whether consciously or unconsciously. In this connection a particular incident comes to mind. When asked by the director of the Kufa Gallery to exhibit in London (in 1990), a misunderstanding arose with the gallery's owner. He had not previously seen my work (unlike the director who had issued the invitation), so when I started unpacking my paintings he informed me that his gallery's aim was to promote Arabic art, not what I was unpacking which, he said, could have been painted by a Western artist. His comment took me by surprise, for I had never imagined that art was to be judged by criteria of

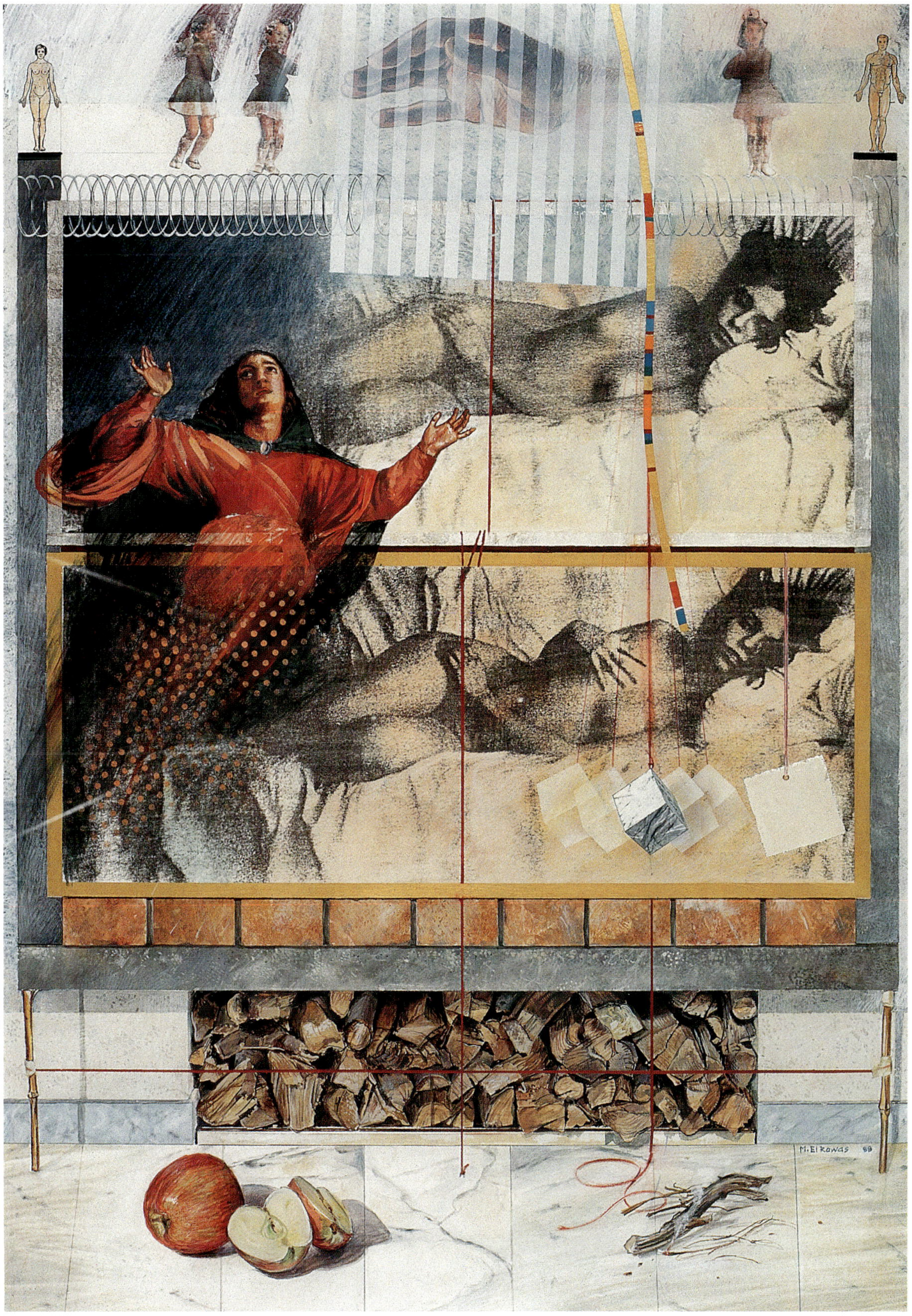
M. El Rowas 89

this kind. Before my show could go ahead, I had to explain that, when I paint, I do so honestly and freely, without ever thinking of my identity or whether my painting is going to look like Arab art or like anything else. But being Lebanese and having lived in Lebanon all my life, I considered myself to be an honest, possible reflection of certain cultural values and sensibilities that belong to that region, and that these were bound to be reflected in my paintings.

In trying to analyze in detail the various elements of my paintings, I cannot help wondering how credible and valid my reflections can be since I might be wrongly projecting onto my works certain explanations that were not intended at the time. Nevertheless, I offer the following tentative comments on my work in general.

My pictorial compositions involve a great many frames and windows, which I think could be the result of accumulated visual memories, having always lived in flats in the city and hardly ever in the country, and thus being familiar with the outside world mainly through a square or rectangle – the window frame. This, of course, is true for many people these days: living in the confined spaces of flats and apartment blocks, our perception of the world so often comes to us (though we are scarcely aware of it) through square and rectangular frames – the windows of our living spaces. My work always features horizons, too, which could be a sign of my longing for open spaces. And there are many historical and architectural elements and ruins in my paintings, representing different historical eras and civilizations – the result of my belief in the continuity of man's experience and in the non-existence of barriers between civilizations. This links with the point I made earlier about 'identity': if I am trying to express or illustrate any type of identity in my art, it is rather *non-identity*, or what may, perhaps, more accurately be called the identity of the borderland, of those marginal areas or frontiers where cultures blend or overlap. And in every one of my paintings there is a hybrid mixture of different cultural references. I do this intentionally because I like what this amalgam – this 'hybridity' – represents. I do not and cannot believe in a pure race or culture.

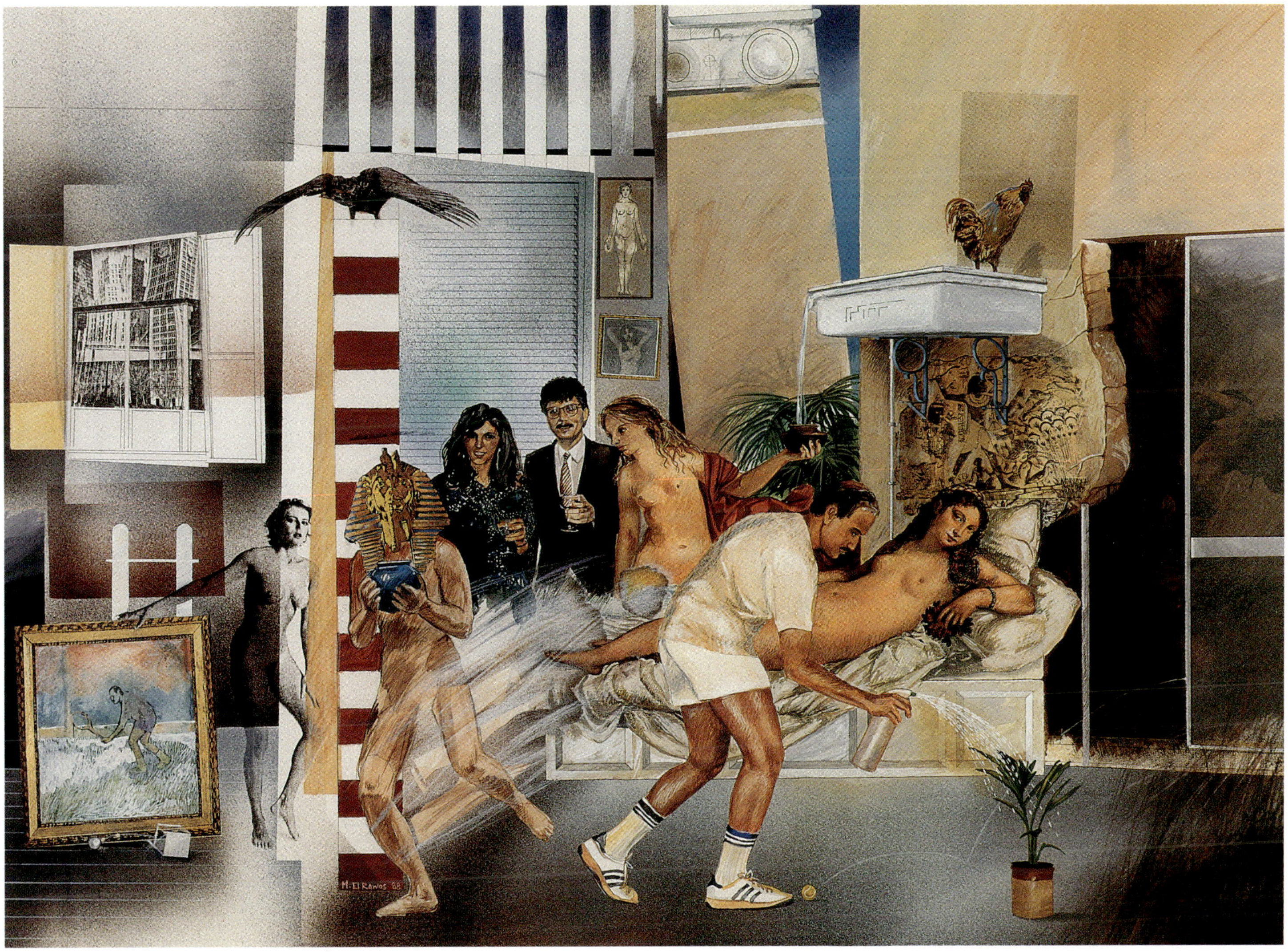

WATER OF LOVE, 1988
Mixed media and transfer on paper
65 x 88 cm
Collection Mr. & Mrs. H. Saghieh

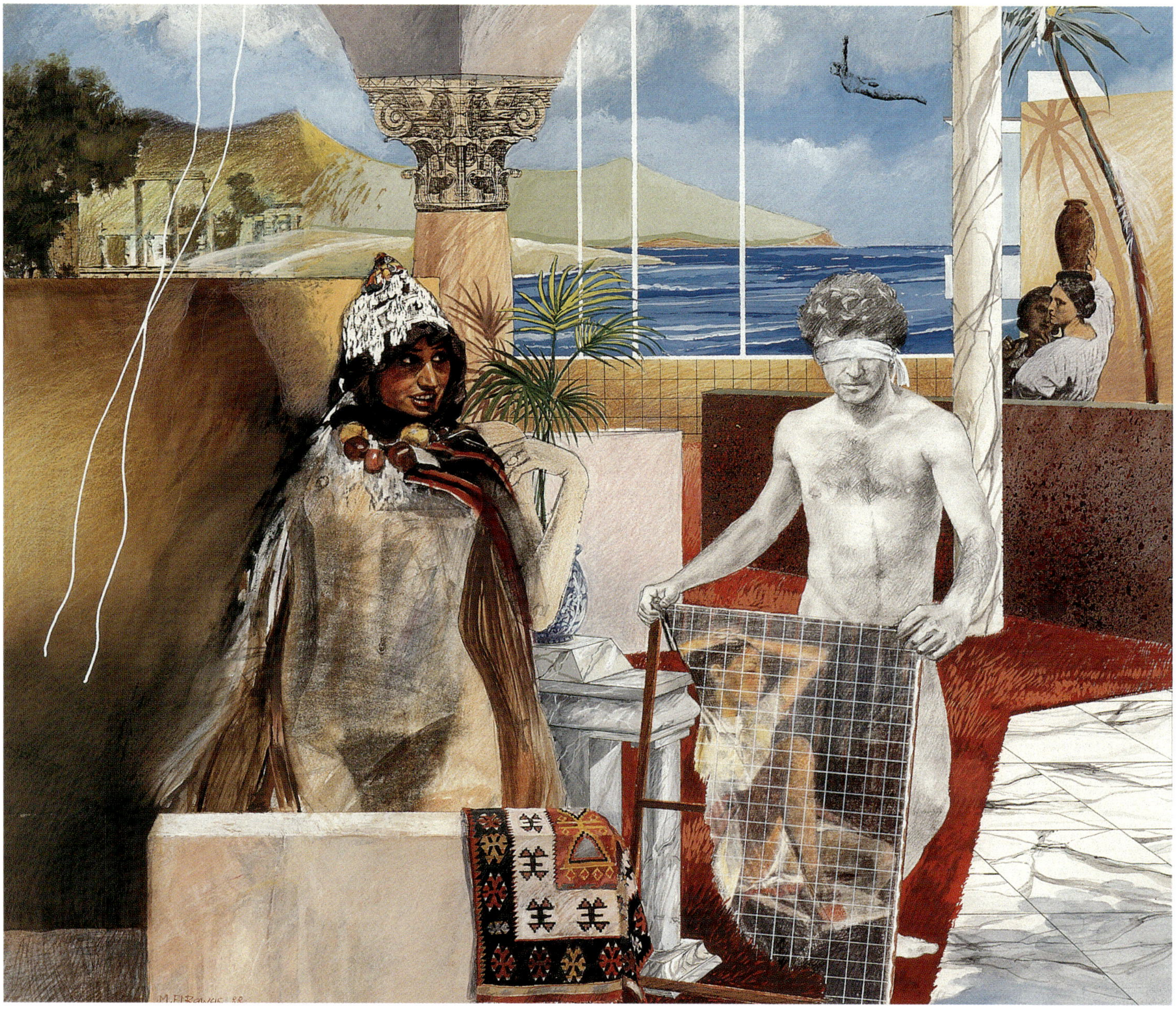

THE WHISPERER, 1988
Mixed media and transfer on paper mounted on masonite panel
54.5 x 64 cm
Private collection

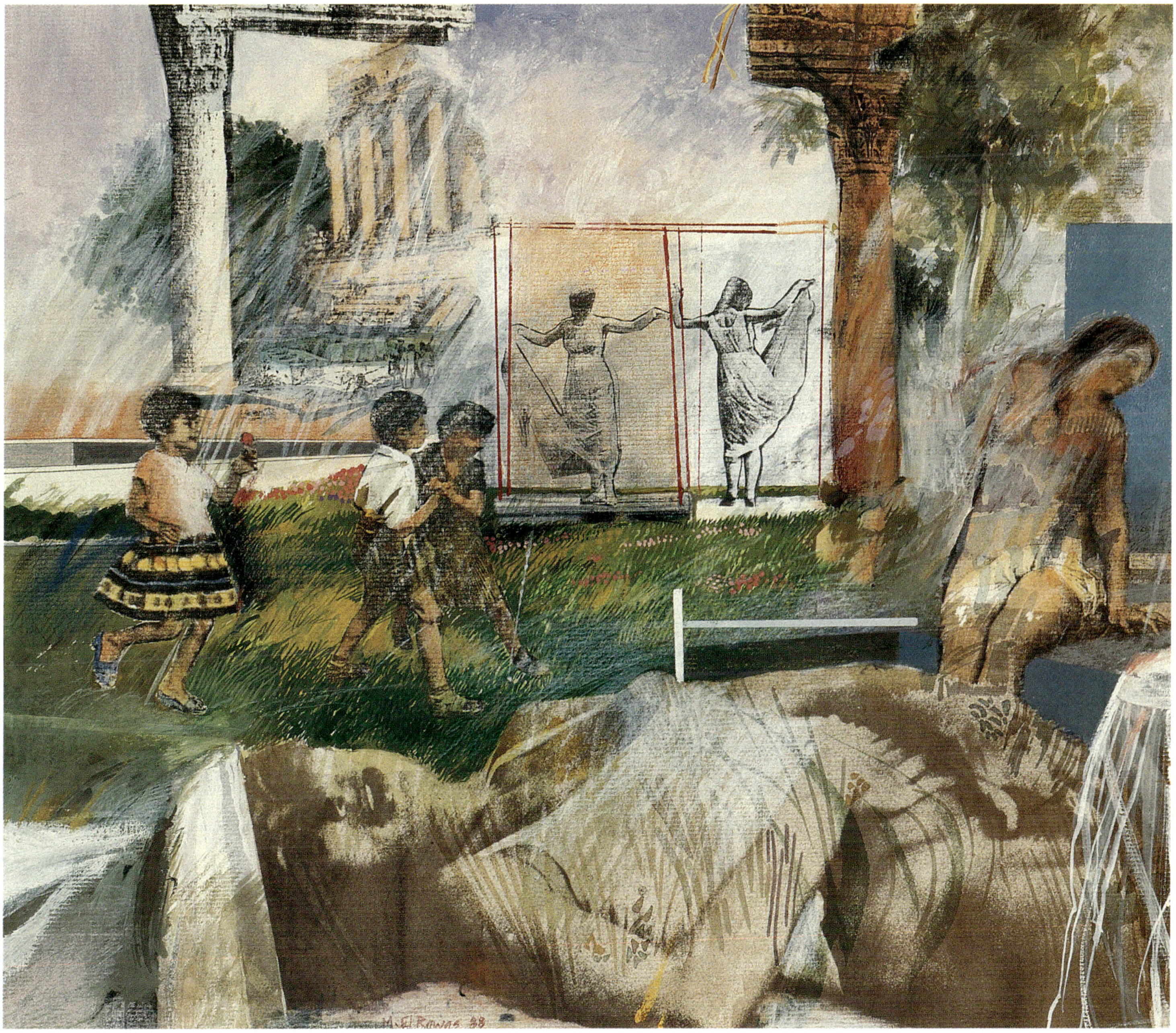

LE JARDIN, 1988
Mixed media, gum printing and transfer on paper
34 x 38 cm
Private collection

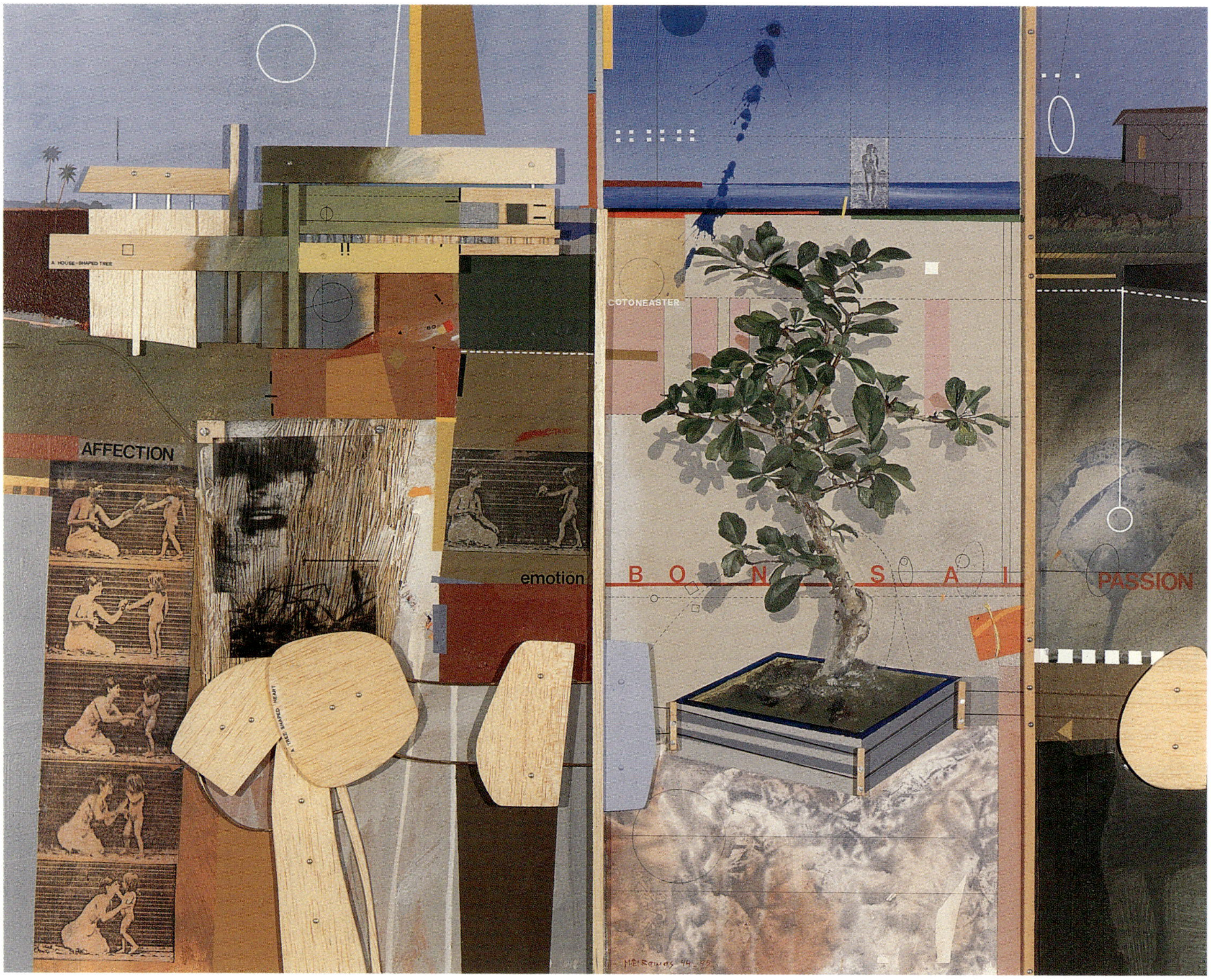

BONSAI PASSION, 1994
Mixed media and assemblage on cardboard
59.5 x 73.5 x 2 cm
Collection Mr. & Mrs. J. Mansour

Opposite page
WHY AN APPLE NOT A PEARL, 1989
Mixed media and assemblage on cardboard
78 x 63 x 4 cm
Collection Ms. R. Shhayel

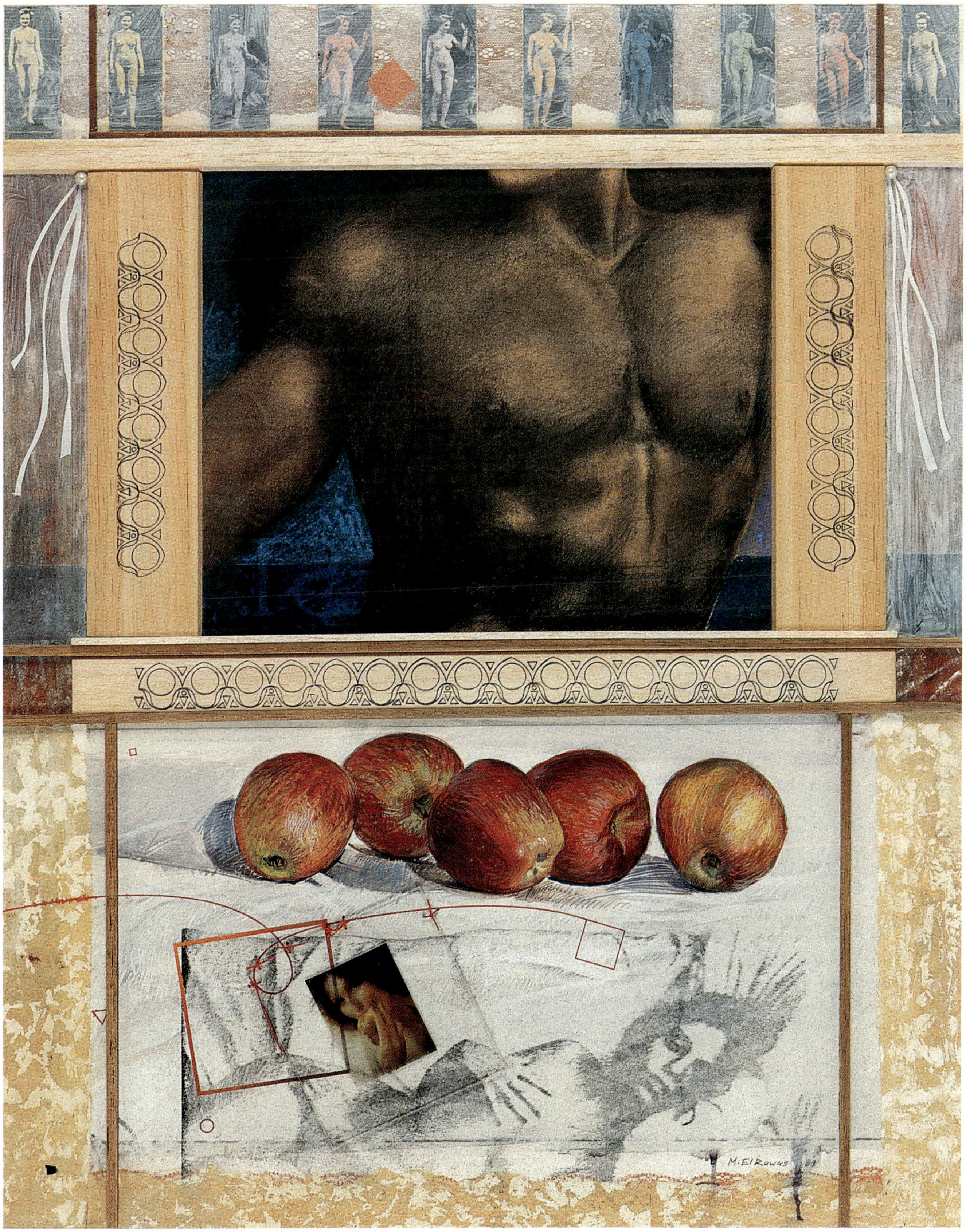
M. El Rawas 89

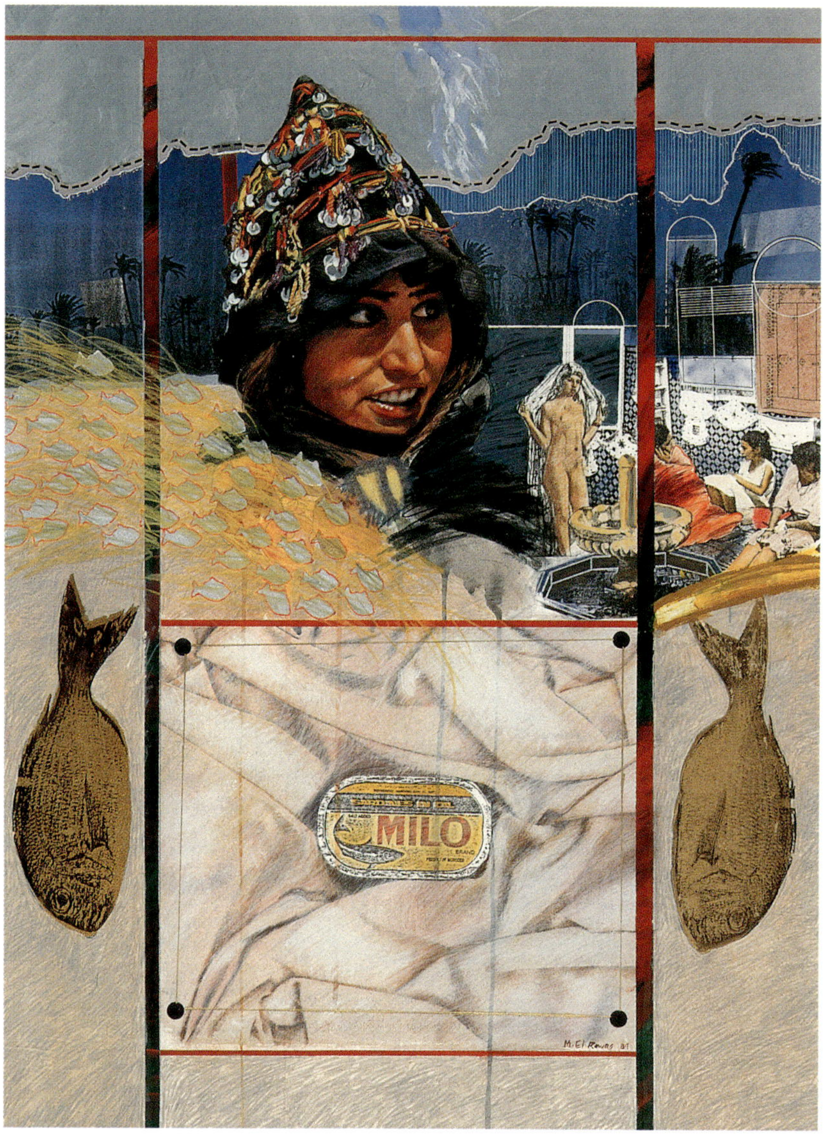

MOROCCAN FISHES, 1989
Mixed media and transfer on paper
67 x 48.5 cm
Private collection

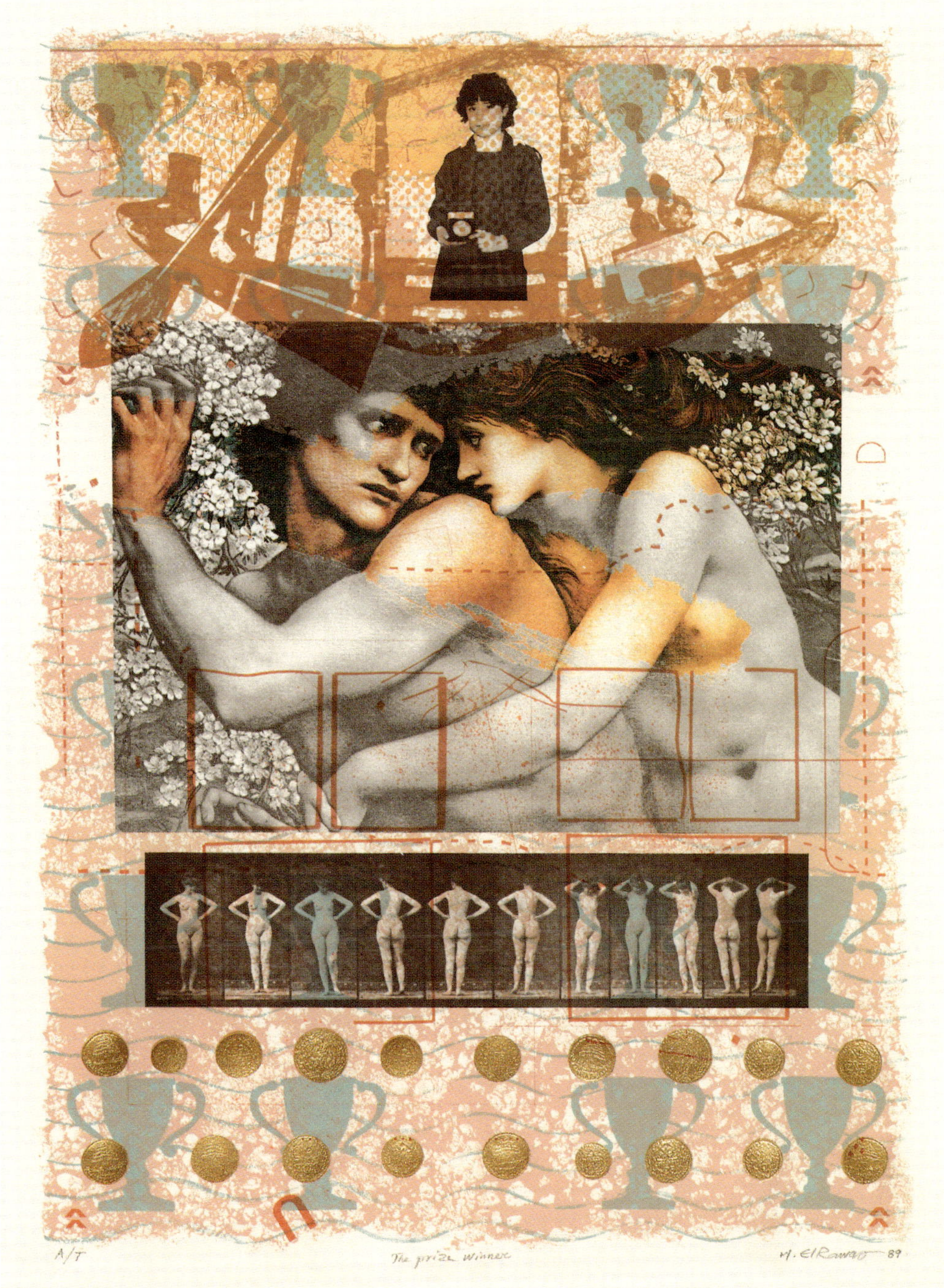

THE PRIZE WINNER, 1989
Lithography
60.5 x 43 cm

Exhibited at the Norwegian International Print Biennale 1989 (Honorable Mention)

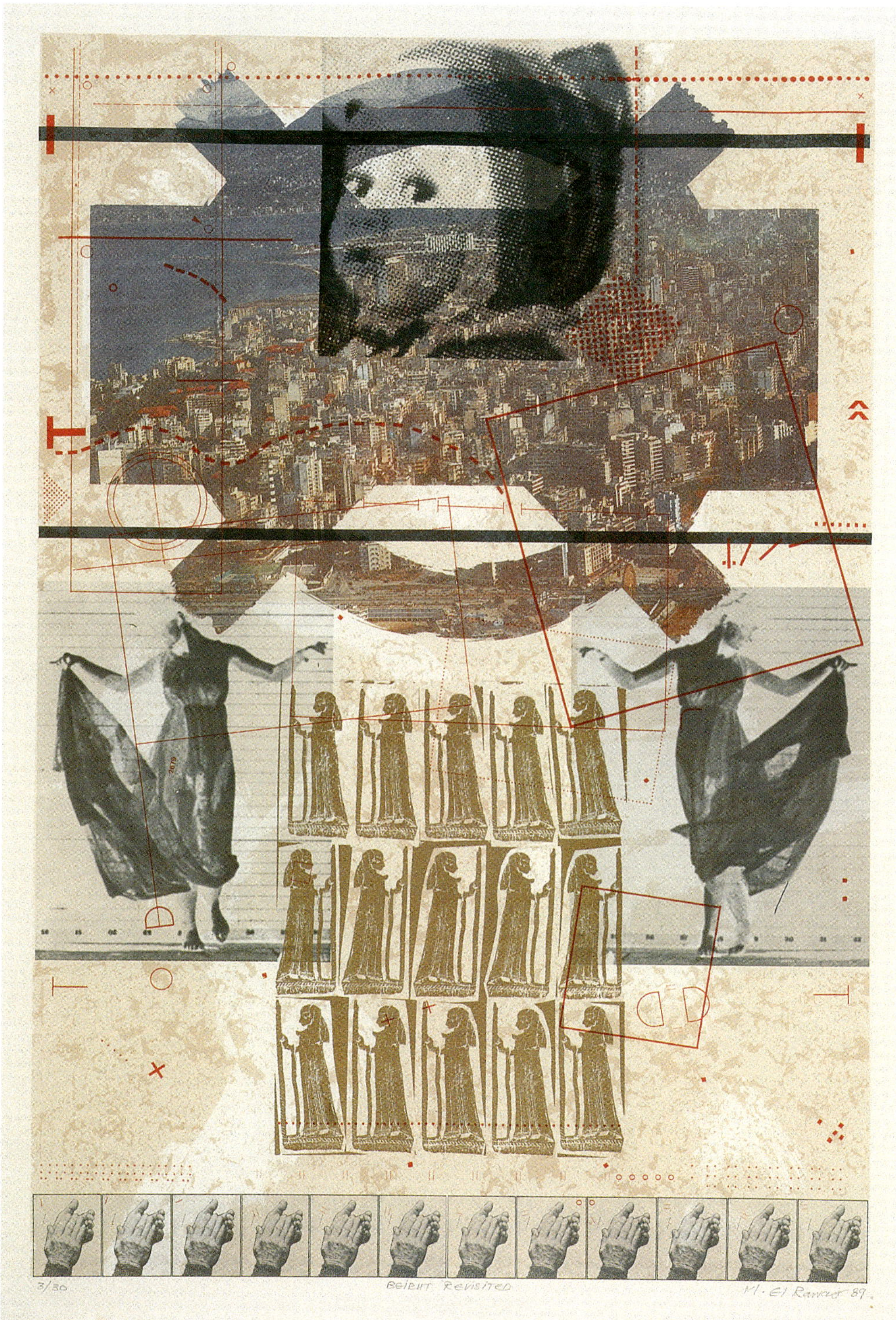

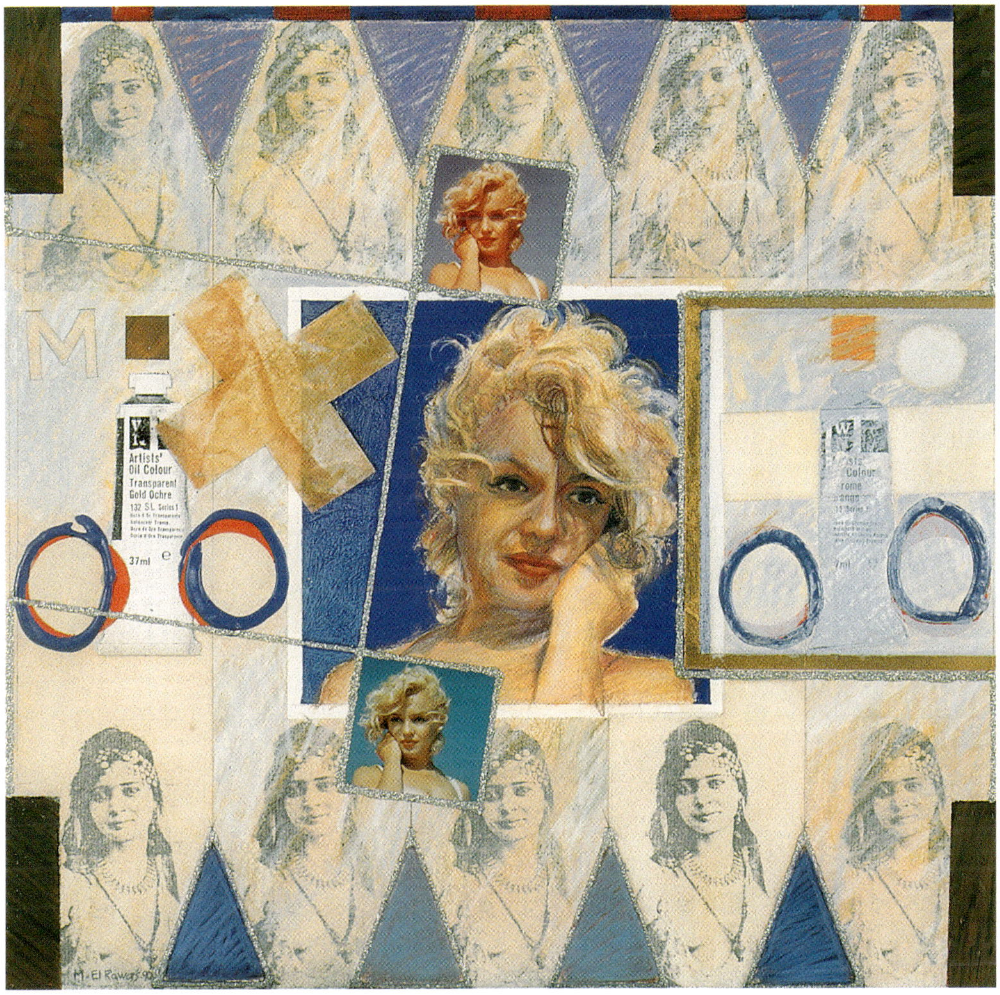

WITH PLEASURE, 1990
Mixed media and assemblage on cardboard
37 x 37 x 1 cm
Private collection

Opposite page
BEIRUT REVISITED, 1989
Lithography
62.5 x 41.5 cm

Exhibited at the Norwegian International Print Biennale 1989 (Honorable Mention)

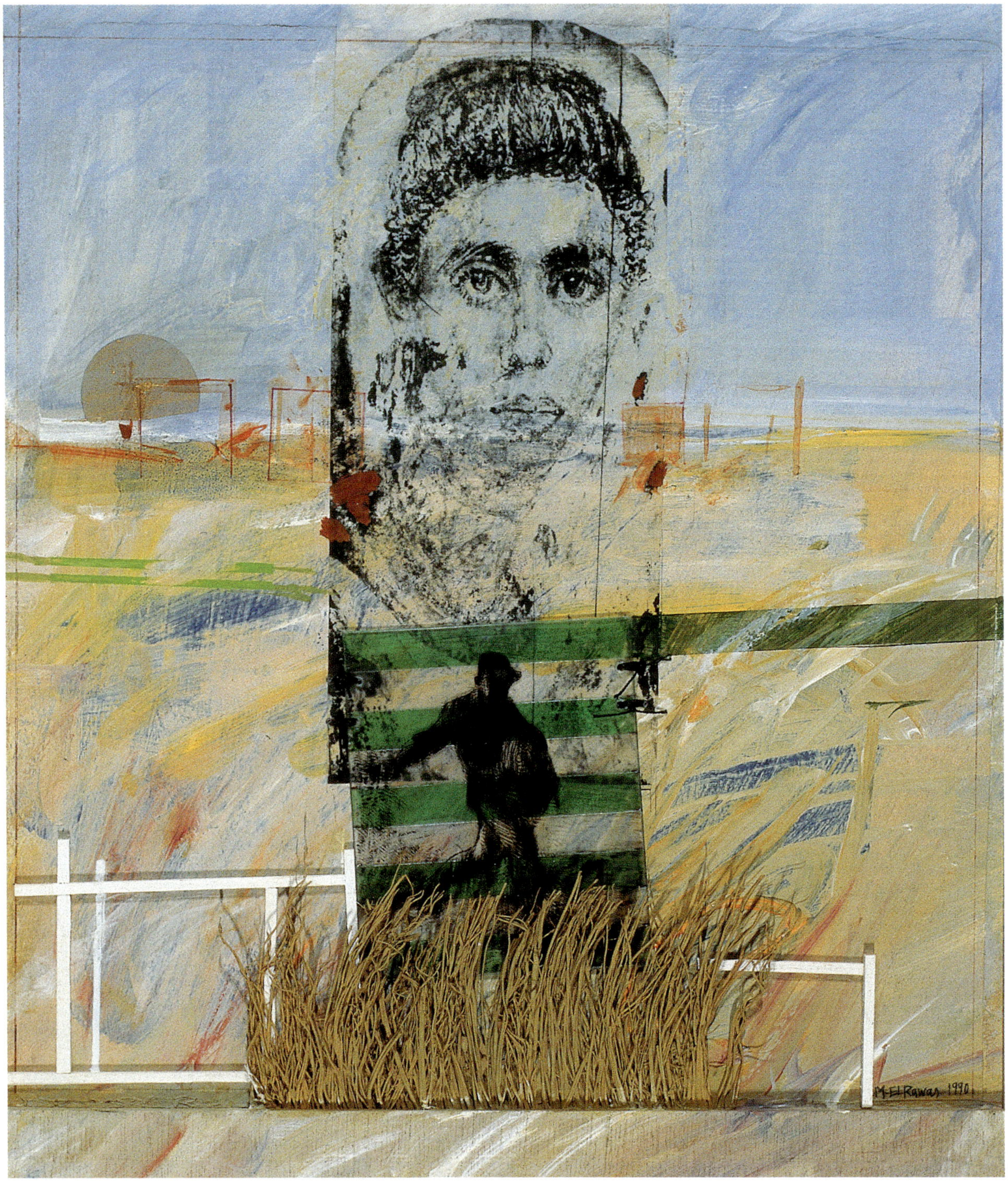

THE SOWER, 1990
Mixed media and assemblage on cardboard
30 x 25 x 1 cm
Collection Mr. & Mrs. M. Assi

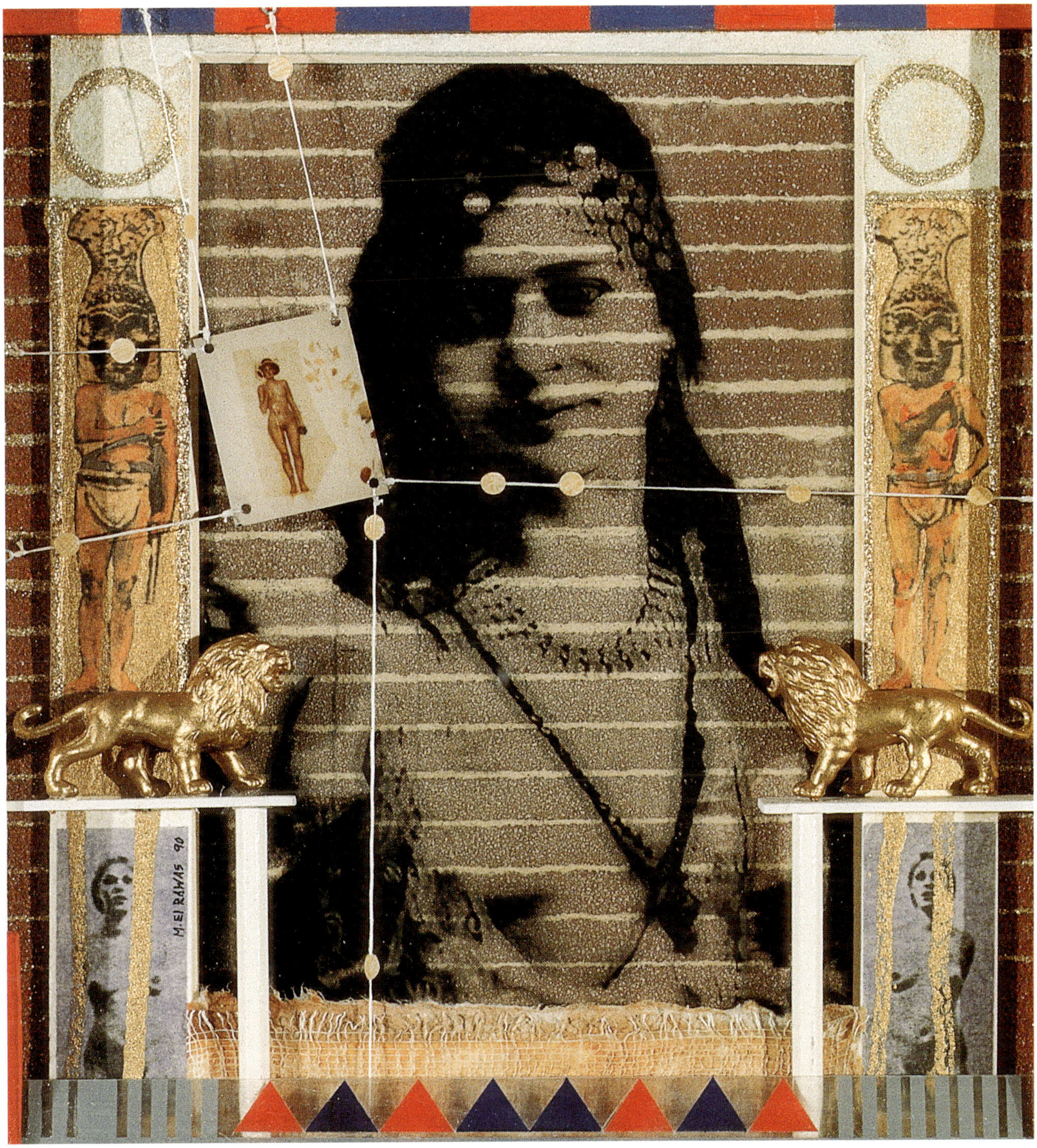

PRINCESS, 1990
Mixed media and assemblage on cardboard
32.5 x 30 x 4 cm
Collection Mr. & Mrs. D. Azzawi

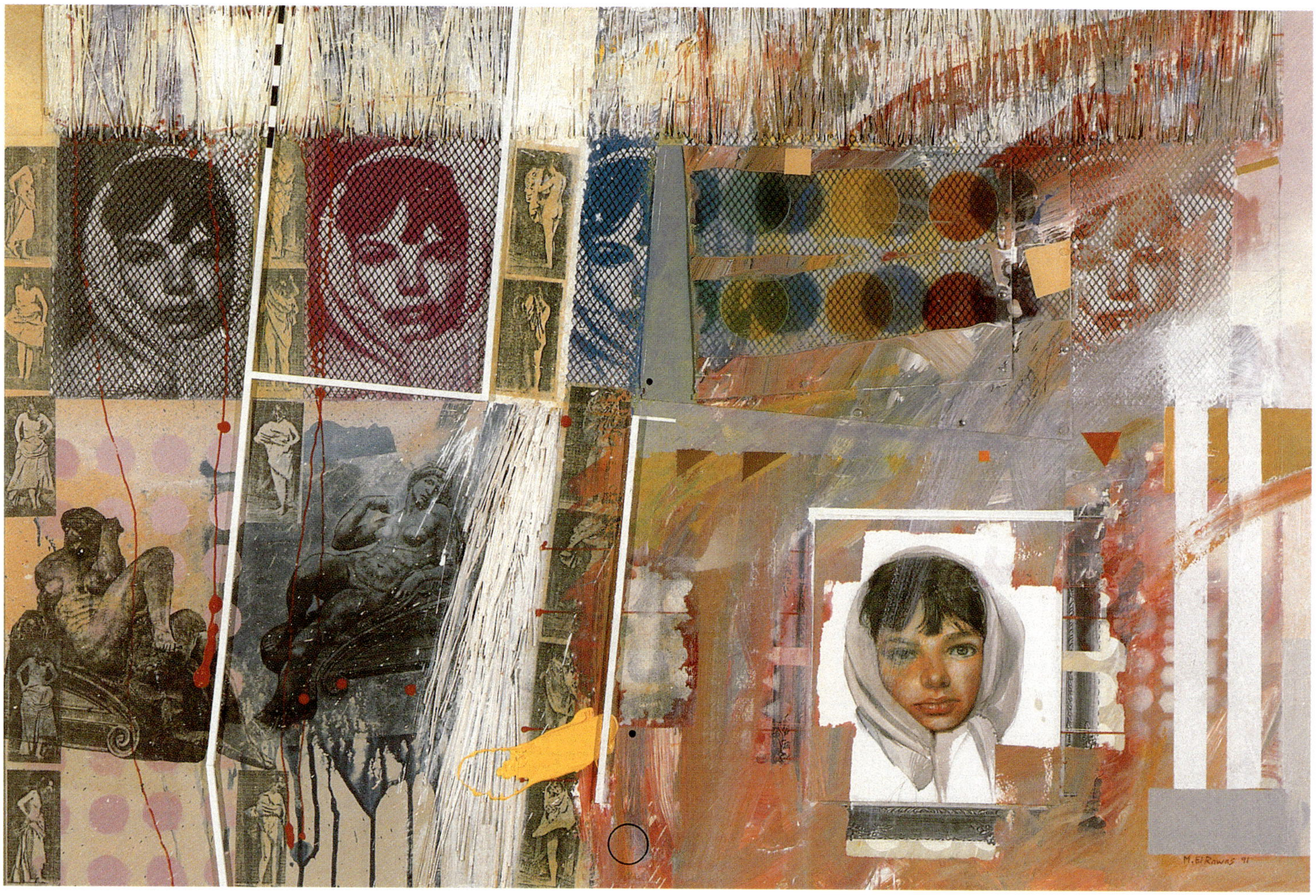

A COLORFUL SOCIAL ISSUE, 1991
Mixed media and assemblage on cardboard
67 x 96 x 2 cm
Private collection

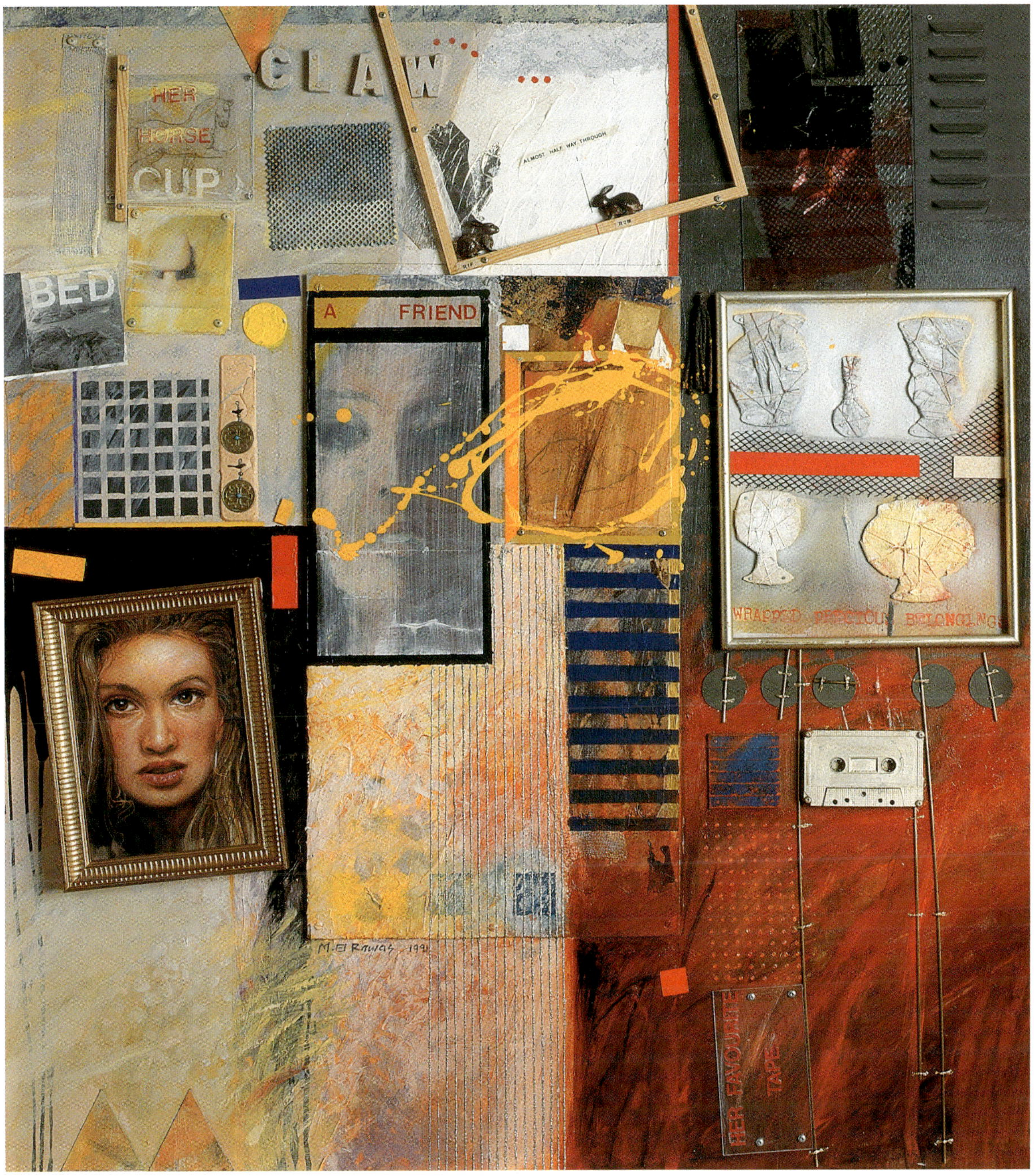

PERSONAL EFFECTS, 1991
Mixed media and assemblage on cardboard
100 x 87 x 2.5 cm
Private collection

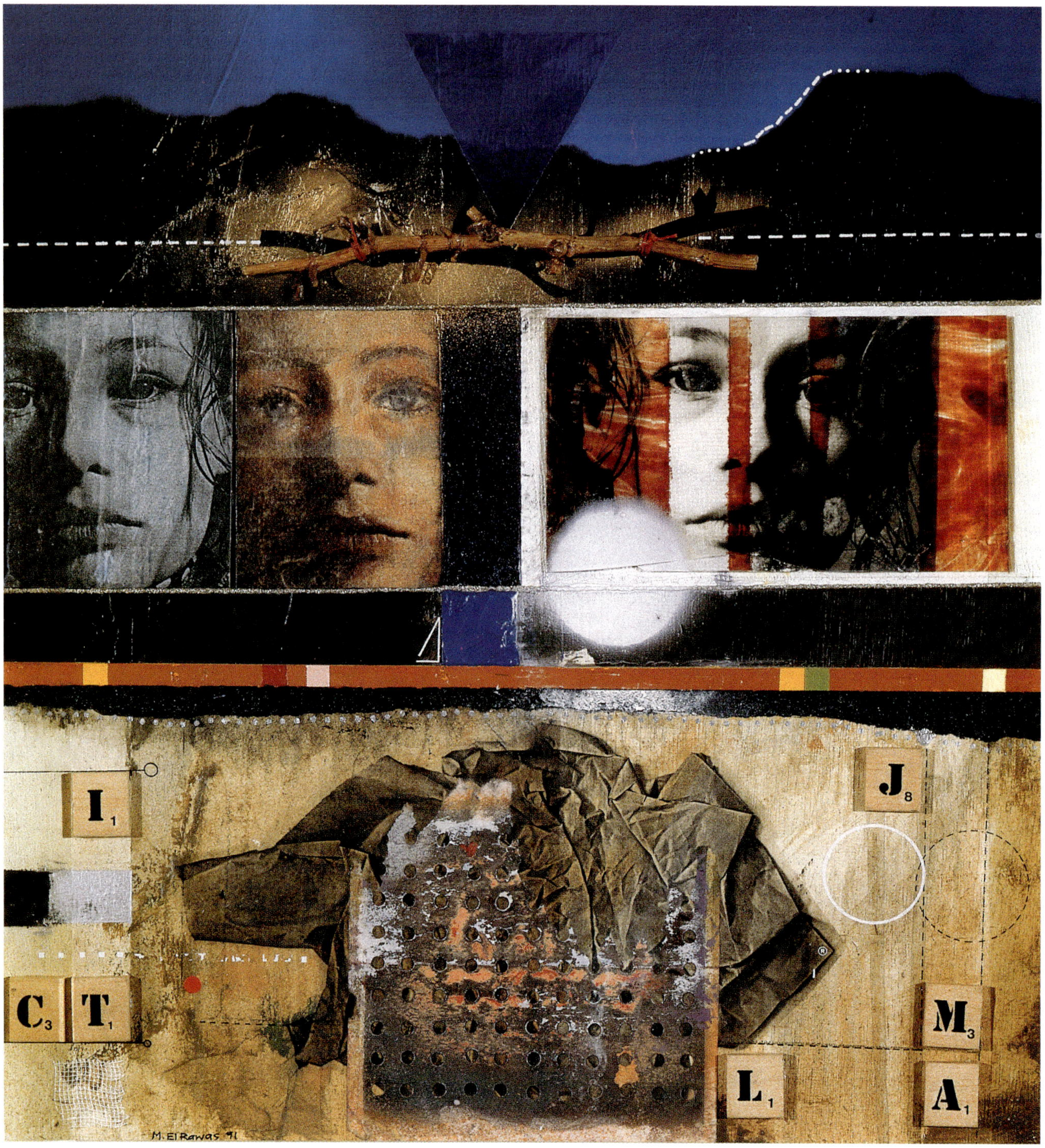

THE SCENT OF AUTUMN, 1991
Mixed media and assemblage on cardboard
47 x 44 x 4.5 cm
Collection Ms. N. Sakkaf

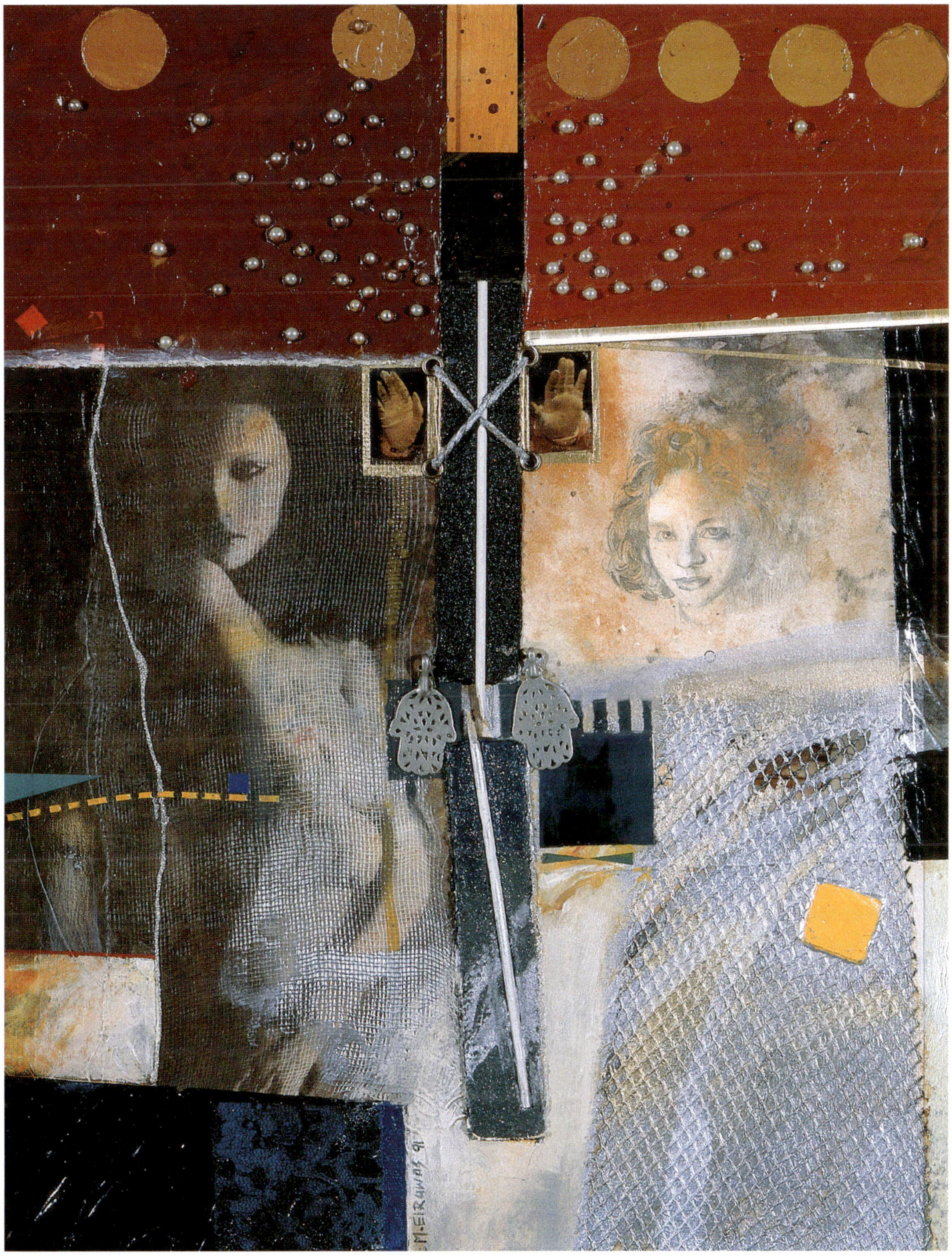

THE WOLF, 1991
Mixed media and assemblage on cardboard
50 x 39 x 3 cm
Collection Ms. N. Sakkaf

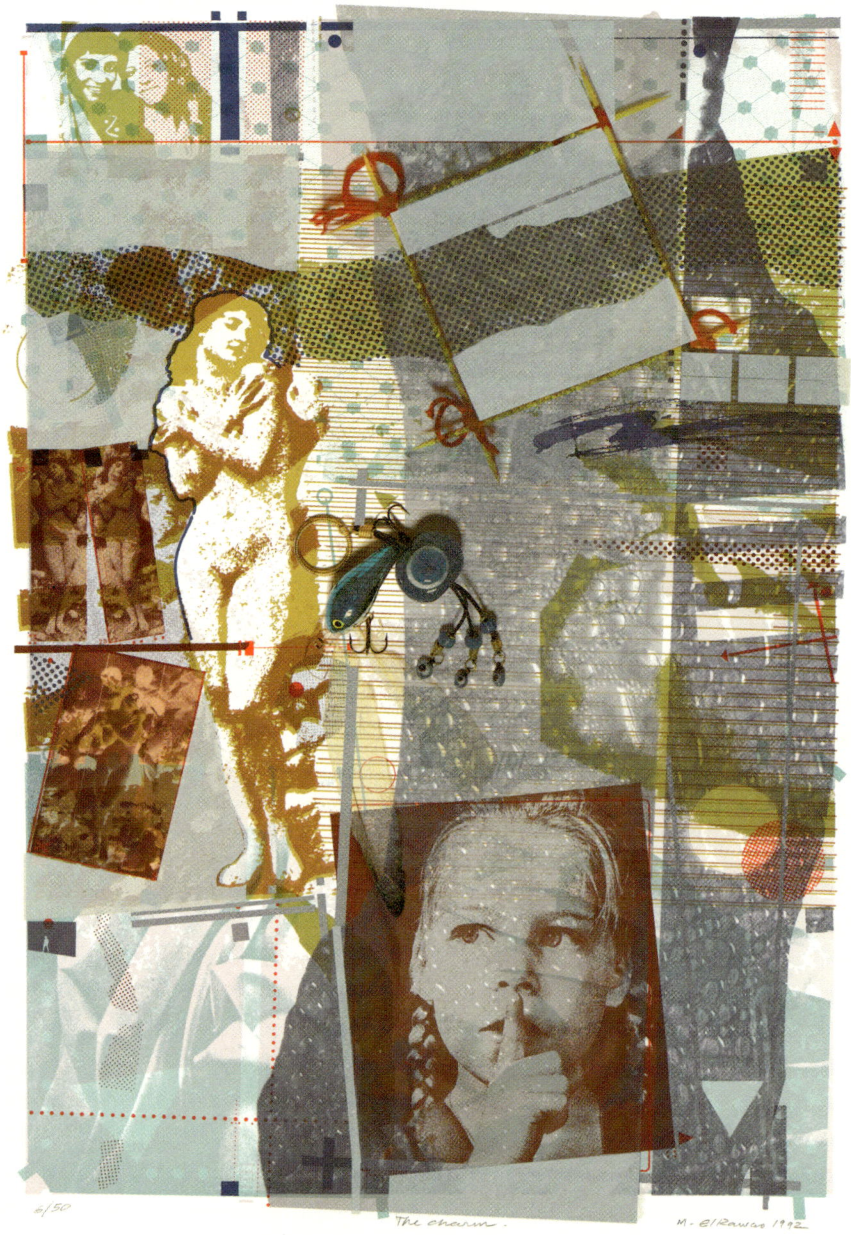

THE CHARM, 1992
Lithography
61 x 42 cm

Exhibited at:
– Tenth Norwegian International Print Triennale - Friedrikstad 1992
– First International Print Biennale, Maastricht, Holland, 1993
– First Egyptian International Print Triennale, 1993
– Alexandria Biennale, 1993–1994

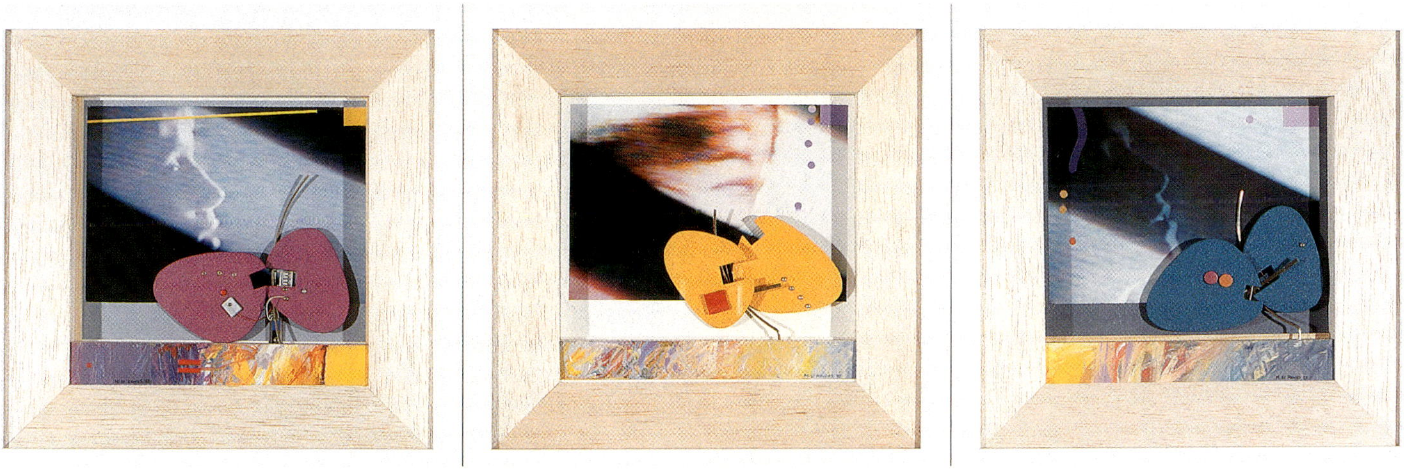

THE MECHANICAL BUTTERFLY, 1993
Mixed media, photography and assemblage on cardboard
21 x 20 x 2.5 cm each
Collection Ms. N. Takla

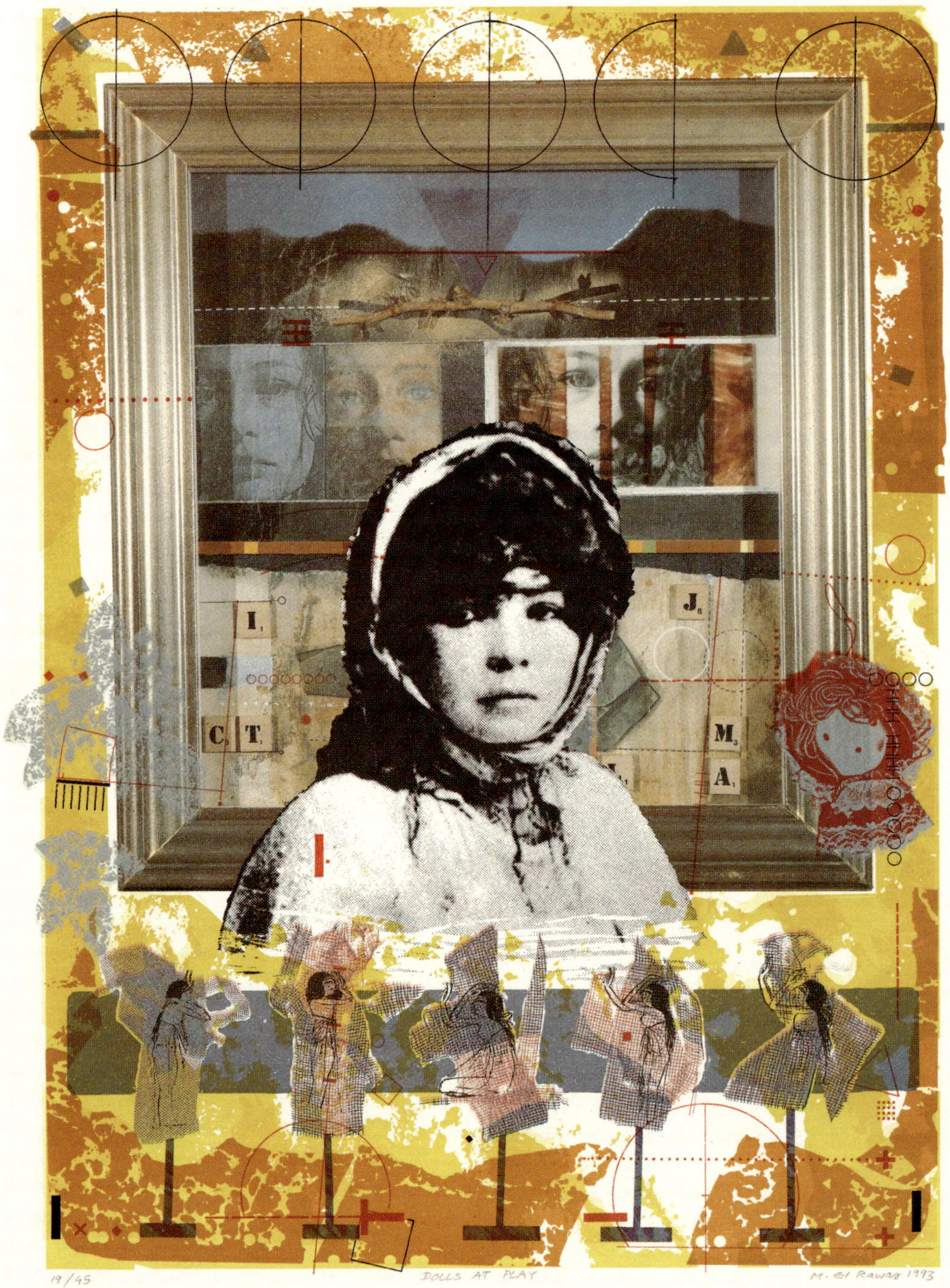

DOLLS AT PLAY, 1993
Lithography
58 x 43 cm

Exhibited at:
– First Egyptian International Print Triennale, 1993
– First International Print Biennale, Maastricht, Holland, 1993
– Alexandria Biennale, 1993–1994
– Eleventh Norwegian International Print Triennale 1995

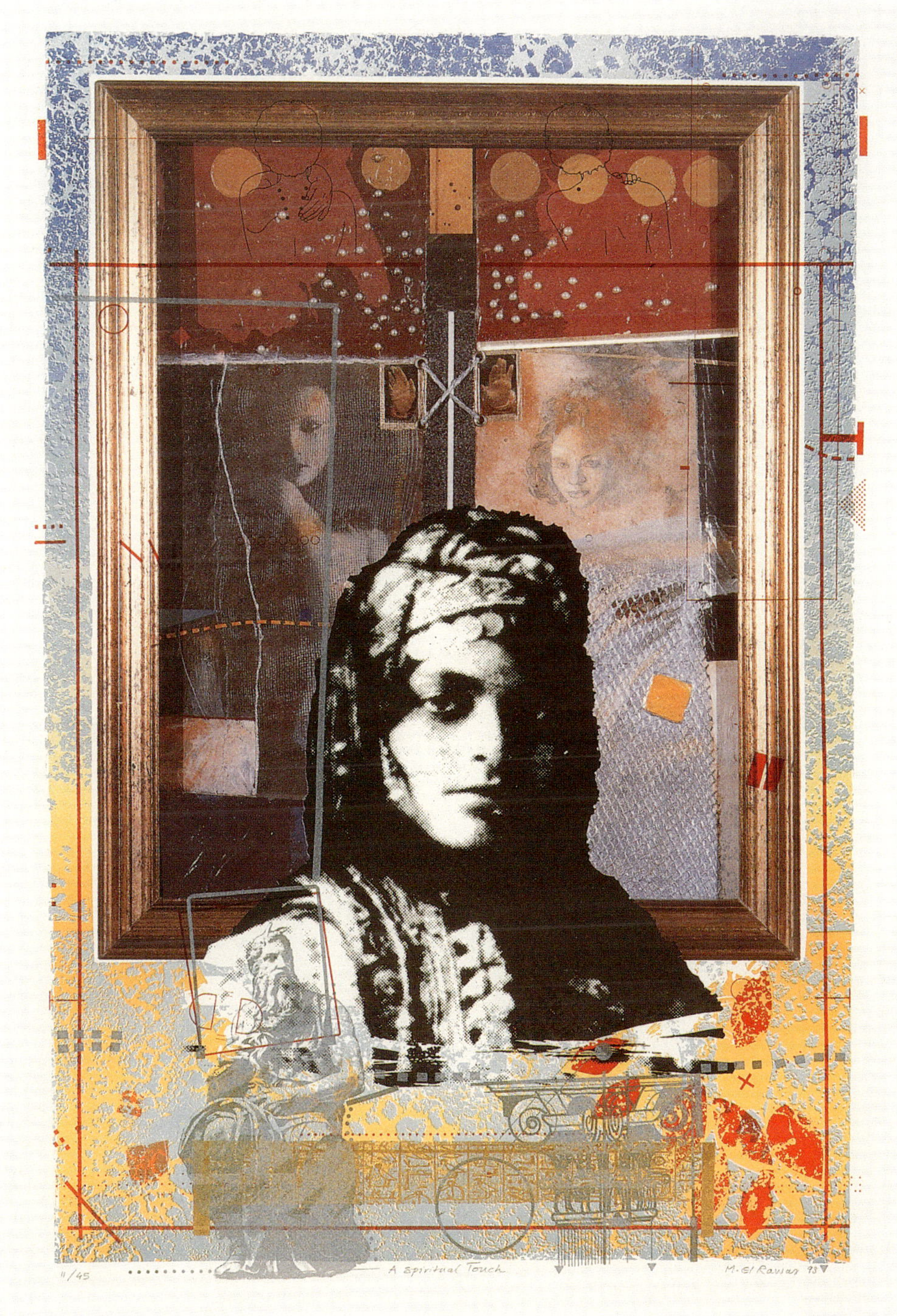

THE SPIRITUAL TOUCH, 1993
Lithography
62 x 41.5 cm

Exhibited at:
- Sursock Museum Salon d'Automne 1993
- First Egyptian International Print Triennale, 1993
- First International Print Biennale, Maastricht, Holland, 1993
- Alexandria Biennale, 1993–1994
- Eleventh Norwegian International Print Triennale 1995
- Krakow International Print Triennale, Poland 1997

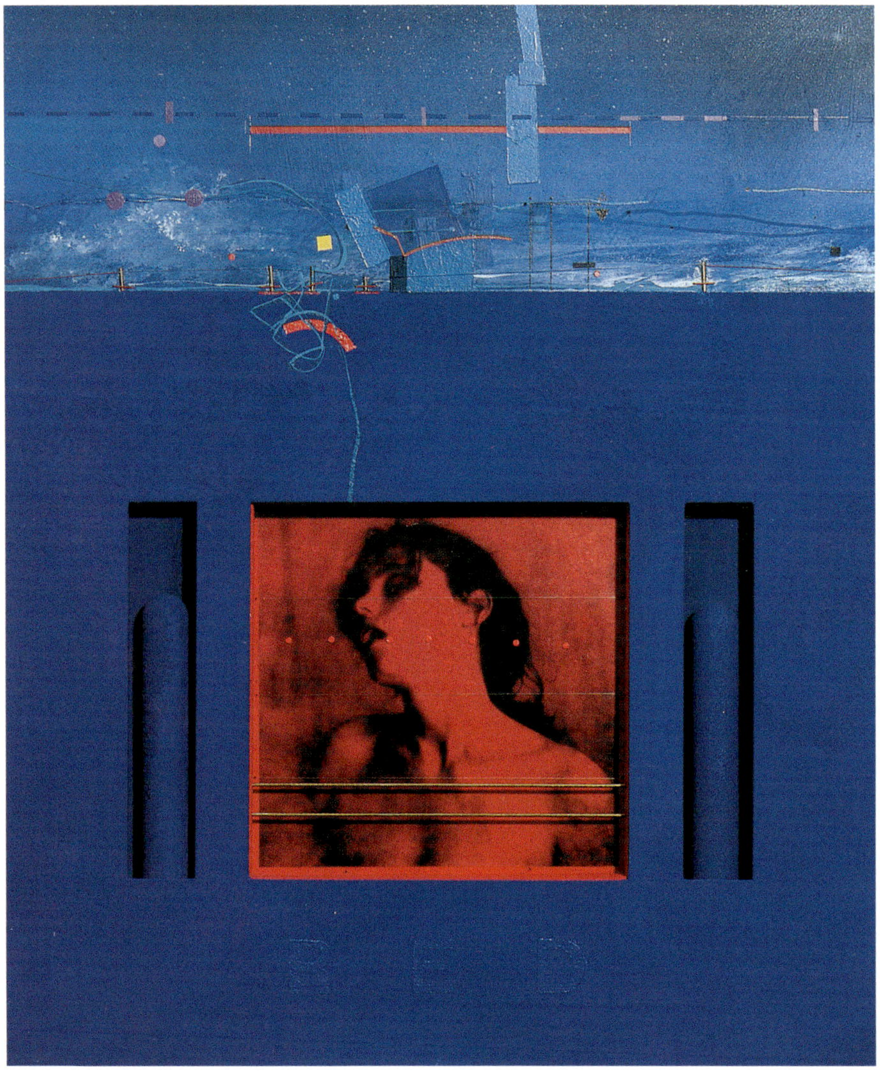

RED, 1993
Mixed media and assemblage on cardboard
50 x 40 x 2.5 cm
Collection Mr. & Mrs. A. Gaspard

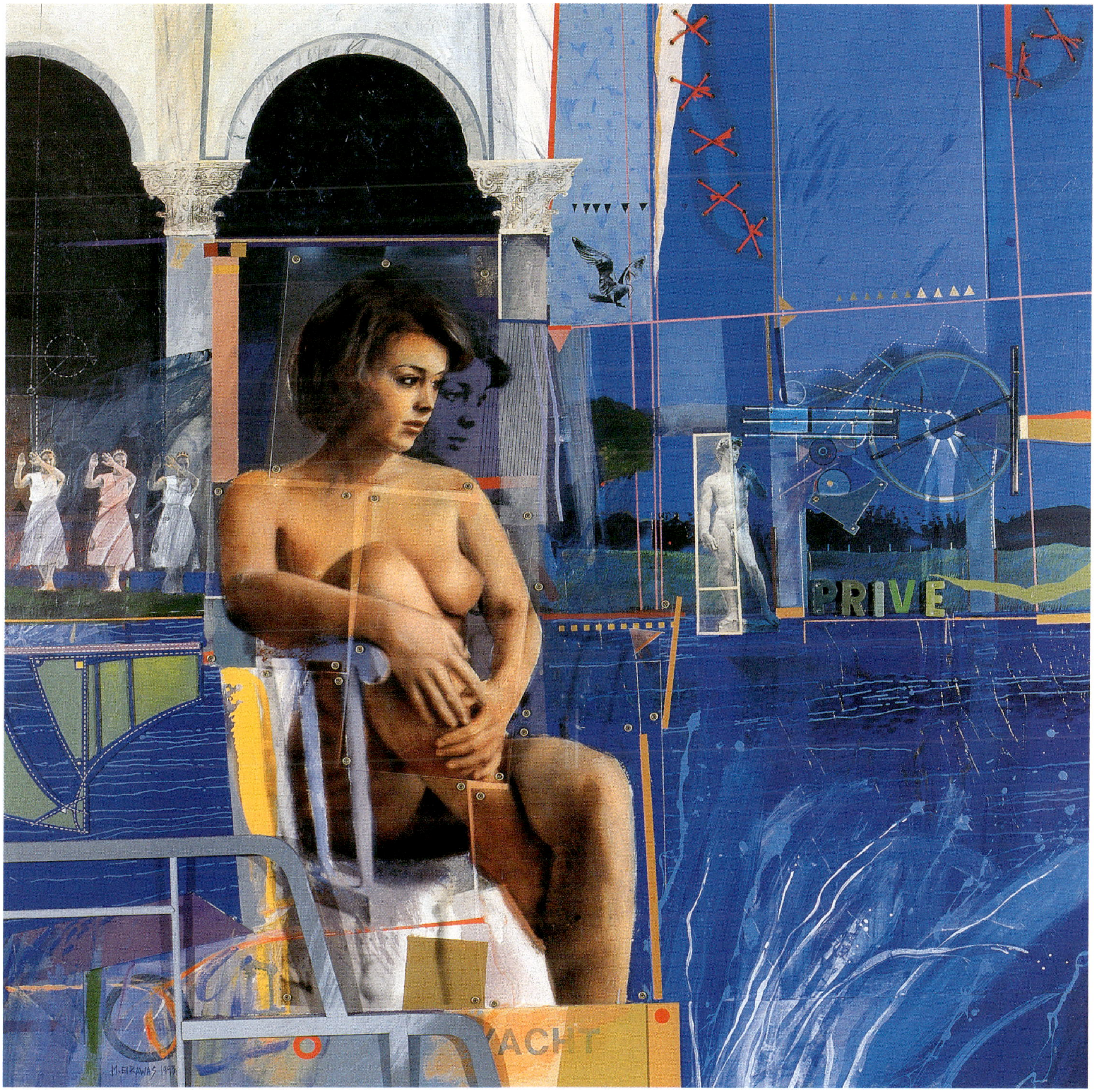

PRIVATE PROPERTY, 1993
Mixed media and assemblage on plywood panel
120 x 120 x 3 cm
Collection Dr. & Mrs. I. Shehadé

Exhibited at the Sursock Museum Salon d'Automne 1994

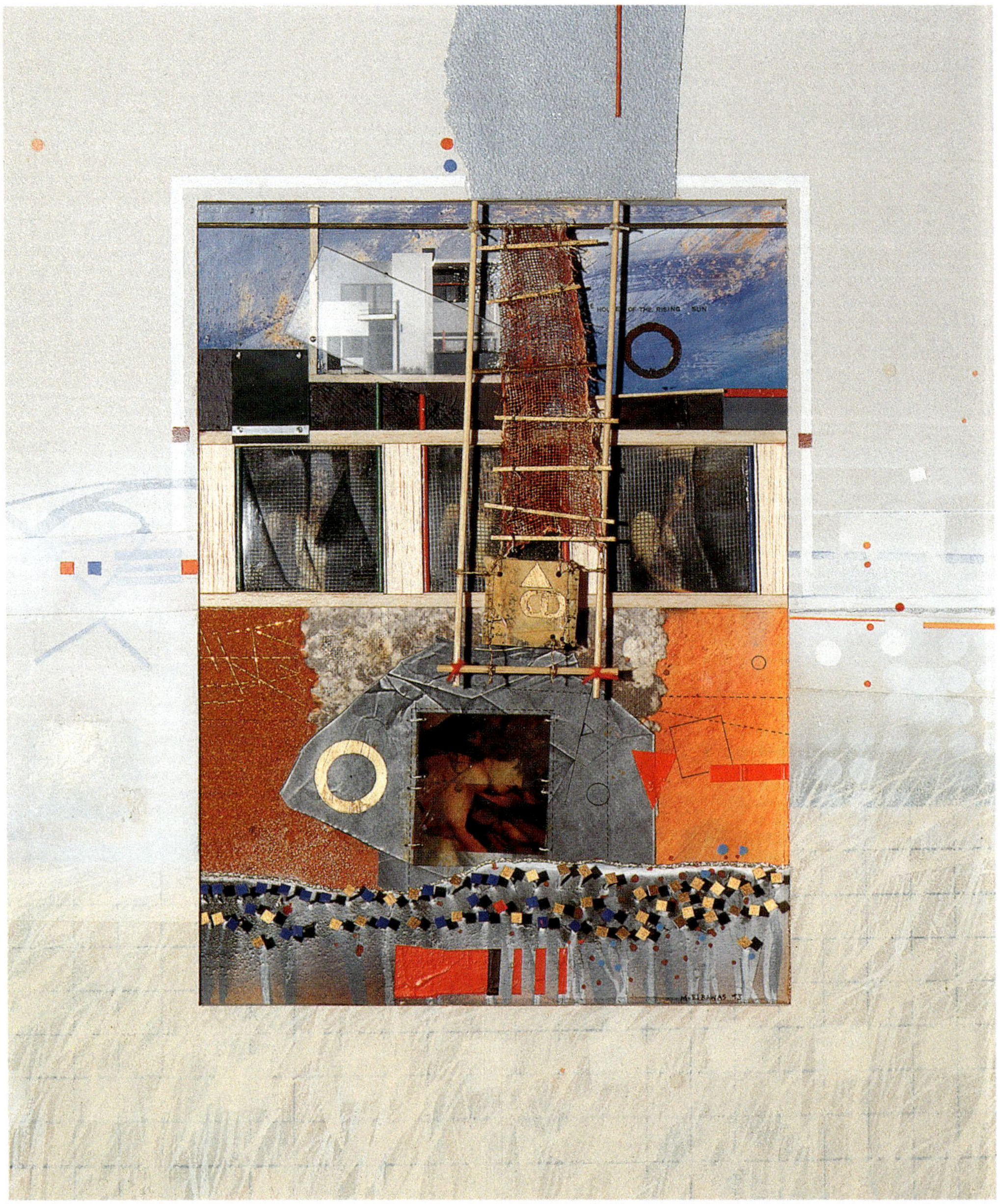

THE HOUSE OF THE RISING SUN, 1993
Mixed media and assemblage on cardboard
55.5 x 46 x 2 cm
Artist's collection

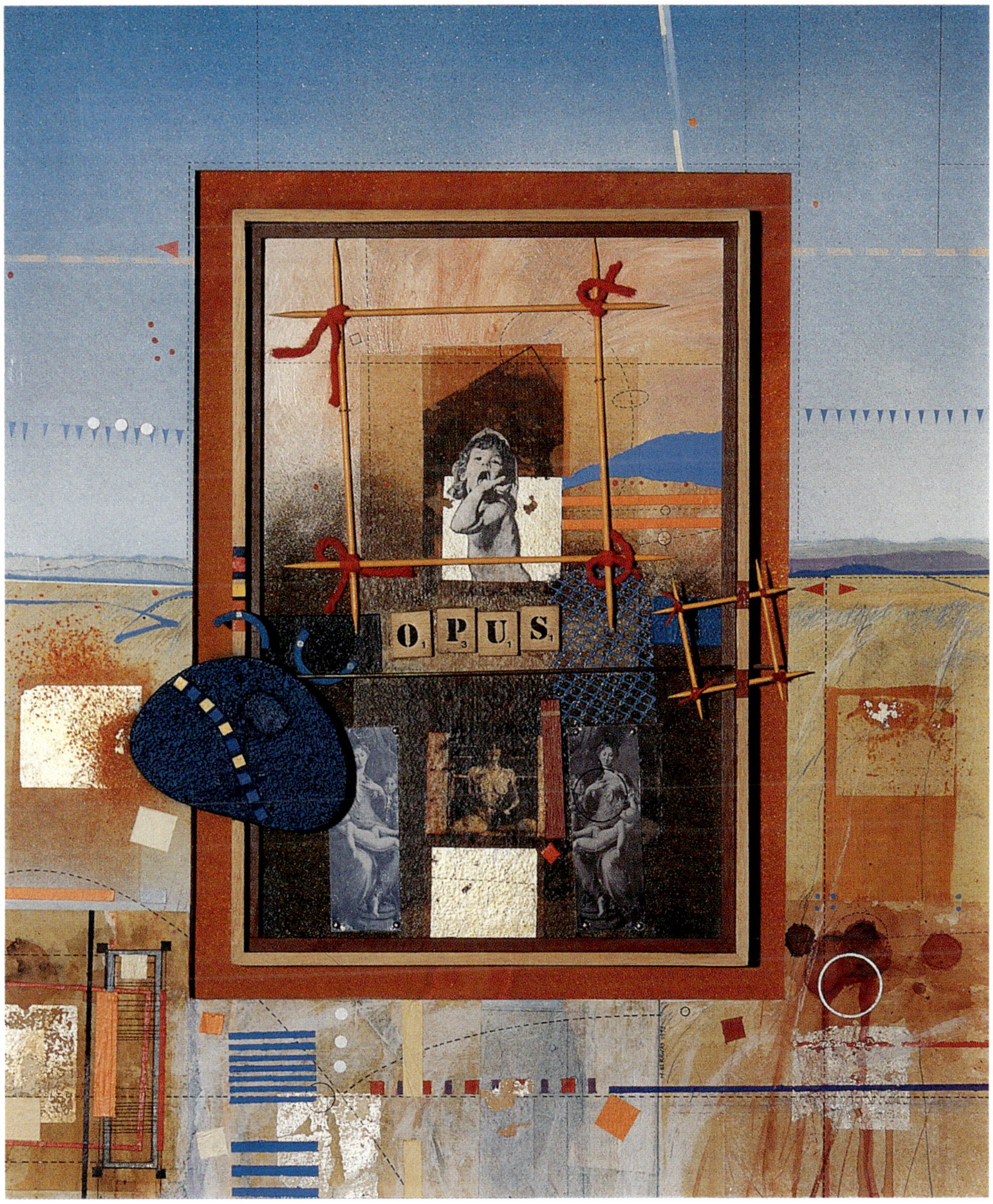

OPUS, 1993
Mixed media and assemblage on cardboard
55 x 46 x 2 cm
Collection Mr. & Mrs. A. Salam

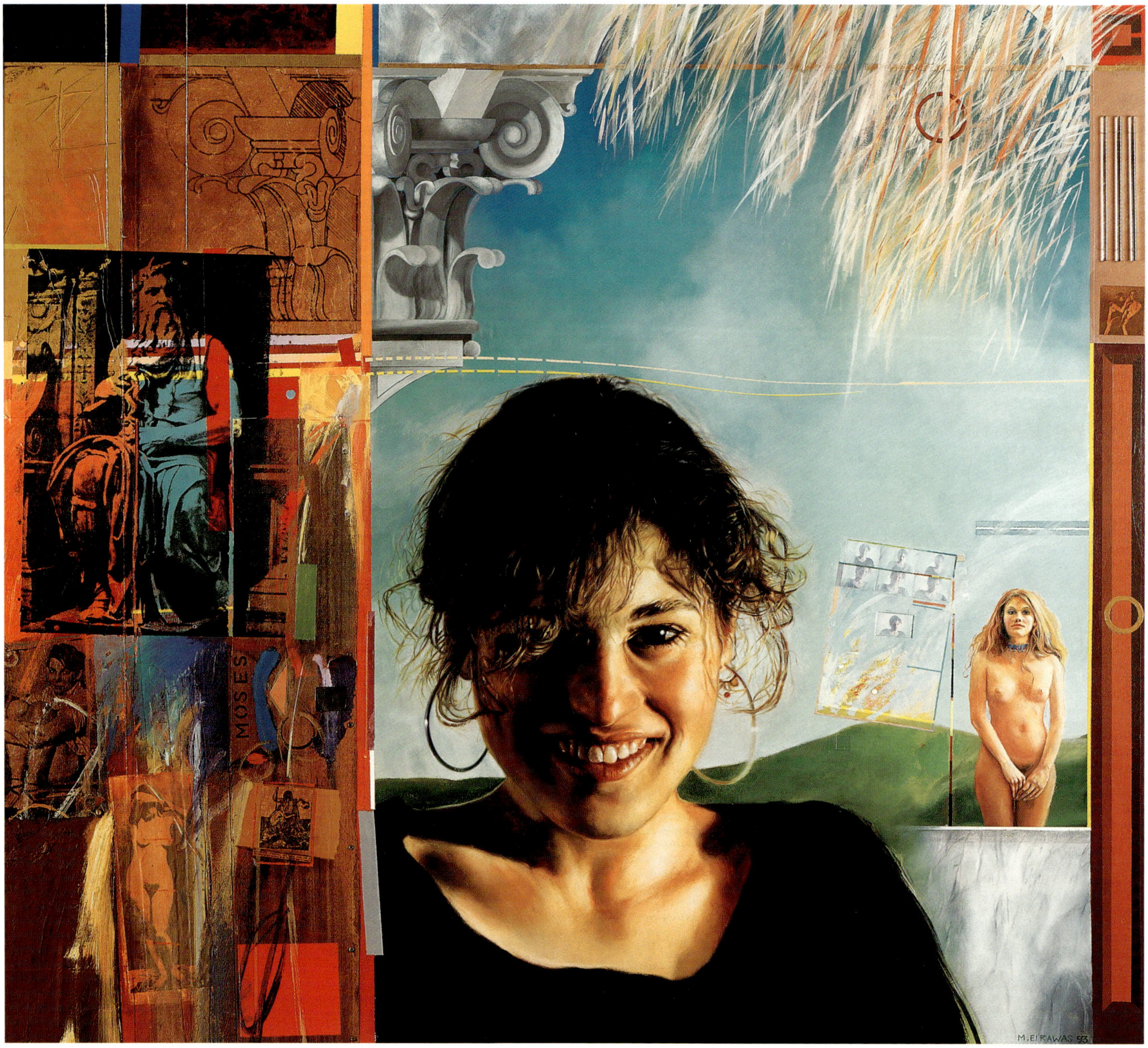
MOSES
M. El RAWAS 93

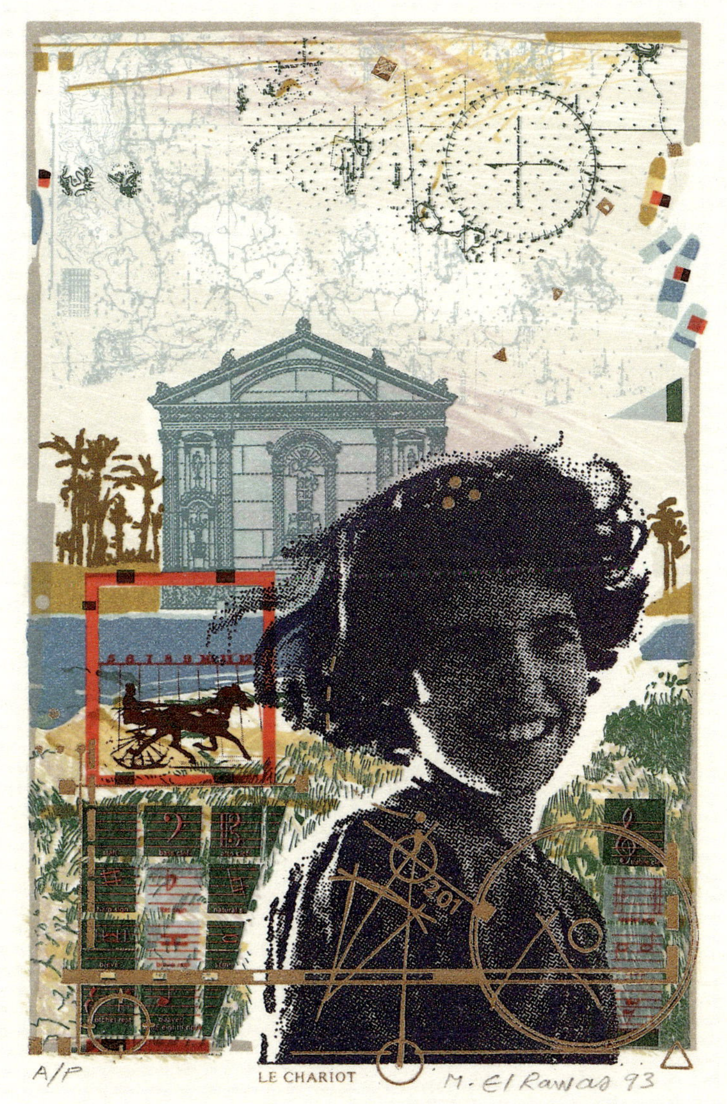

LE CHARIOT, 1993
Lithography and hot press foil
14.5 x 9.5 cm
Commissioned by Janine Rubeiz Gallery, Beirut

Opposite page
THE RETURN OF THE PRODIGAL DAUGHTER, 1993
Oil, mixed media and assemblage on plywood panel
125 x 125 x 1 cm
Artist's collection

Exhibited at the Sursock Museum Salon d'Automne, Beirut, 1993

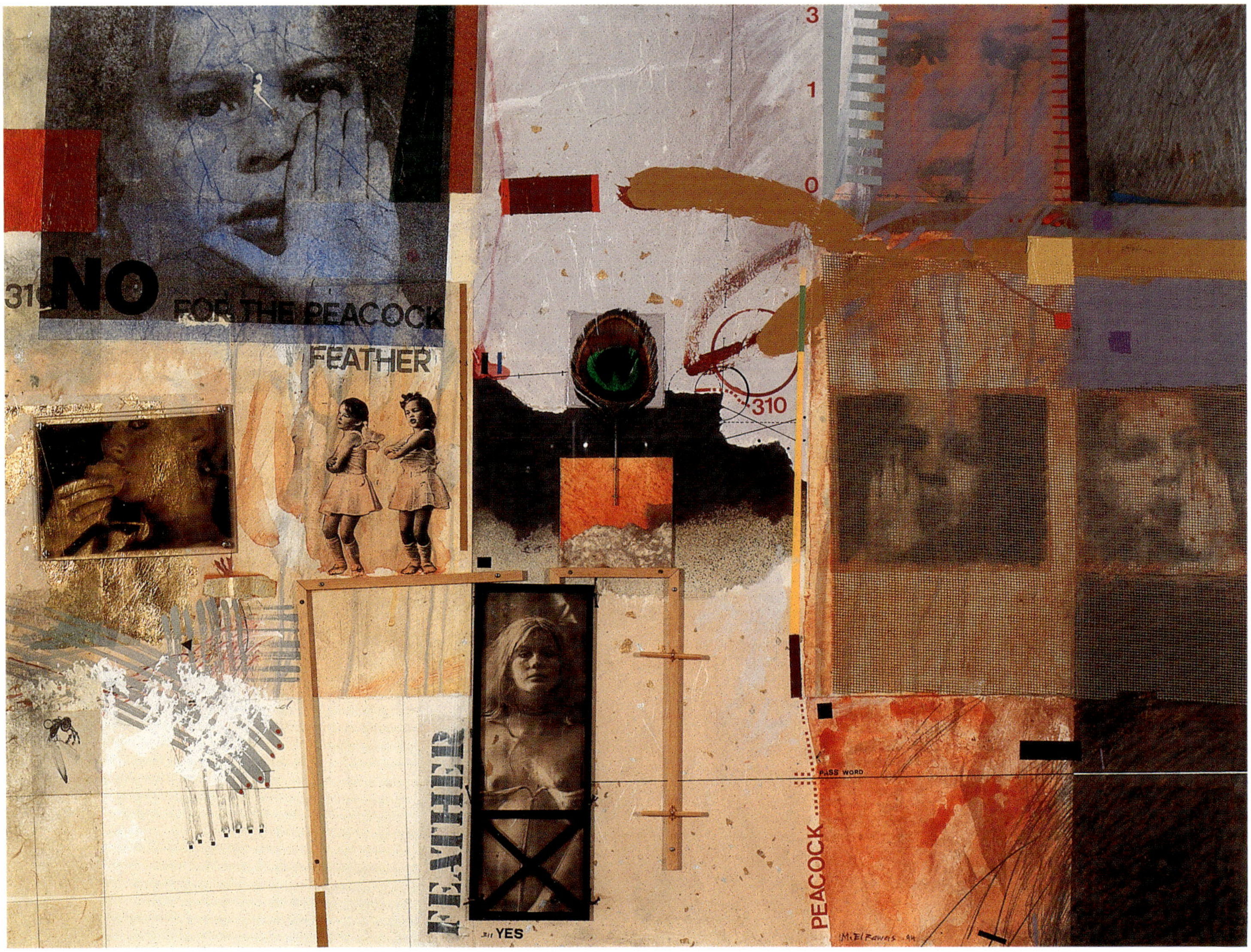

THE PEACOCK FEATHER, 1994
Mixed media and assemblage on cardboard
60 x 79 x 1 cm
Private collection

Opposite page
COLD SILVER, 1994
Mixed media and assemblage on cardboard
60 x 47 x 1 cm
Private collection

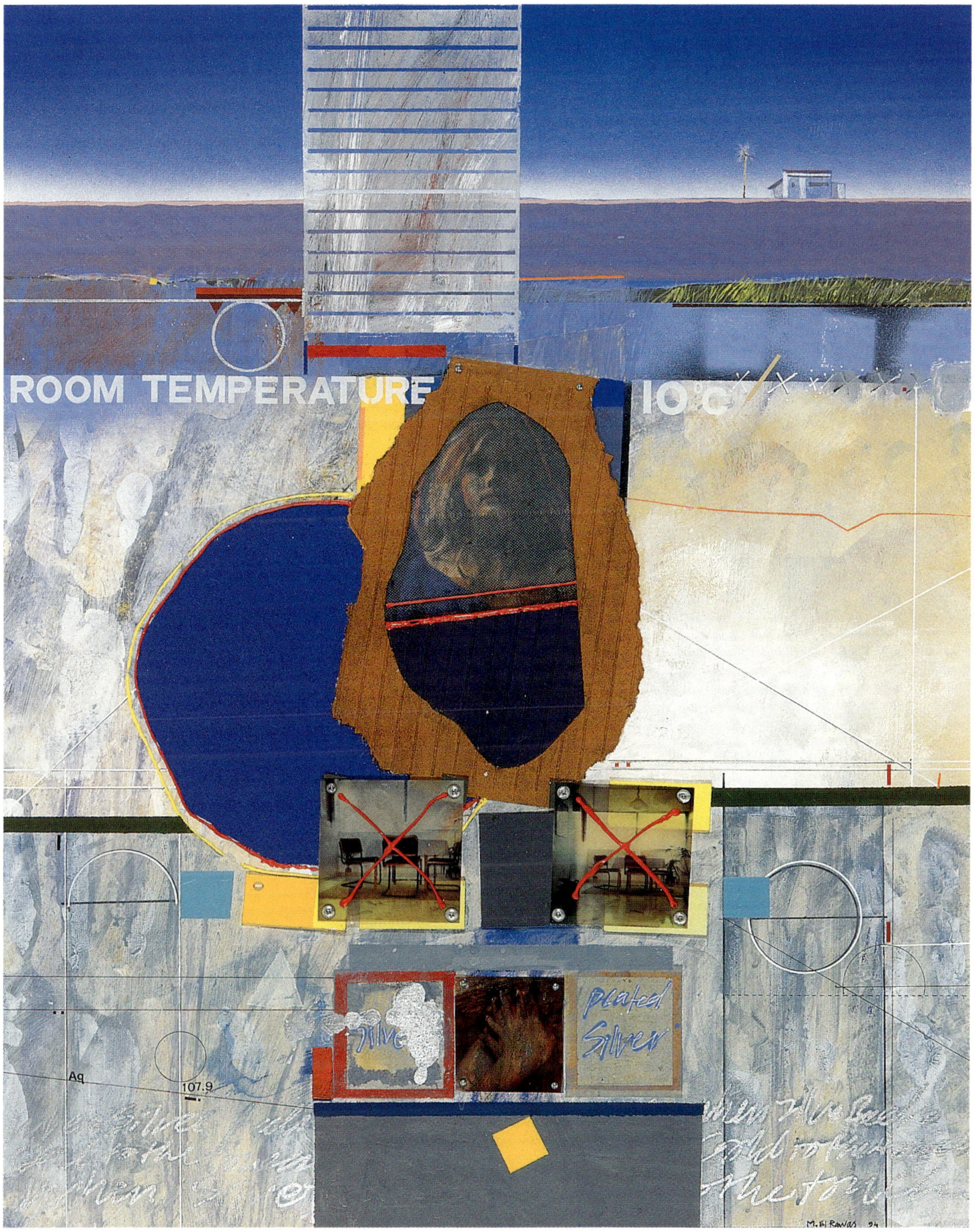
ROOM TEMPERATURE
Plated Silver
Ag
107.9

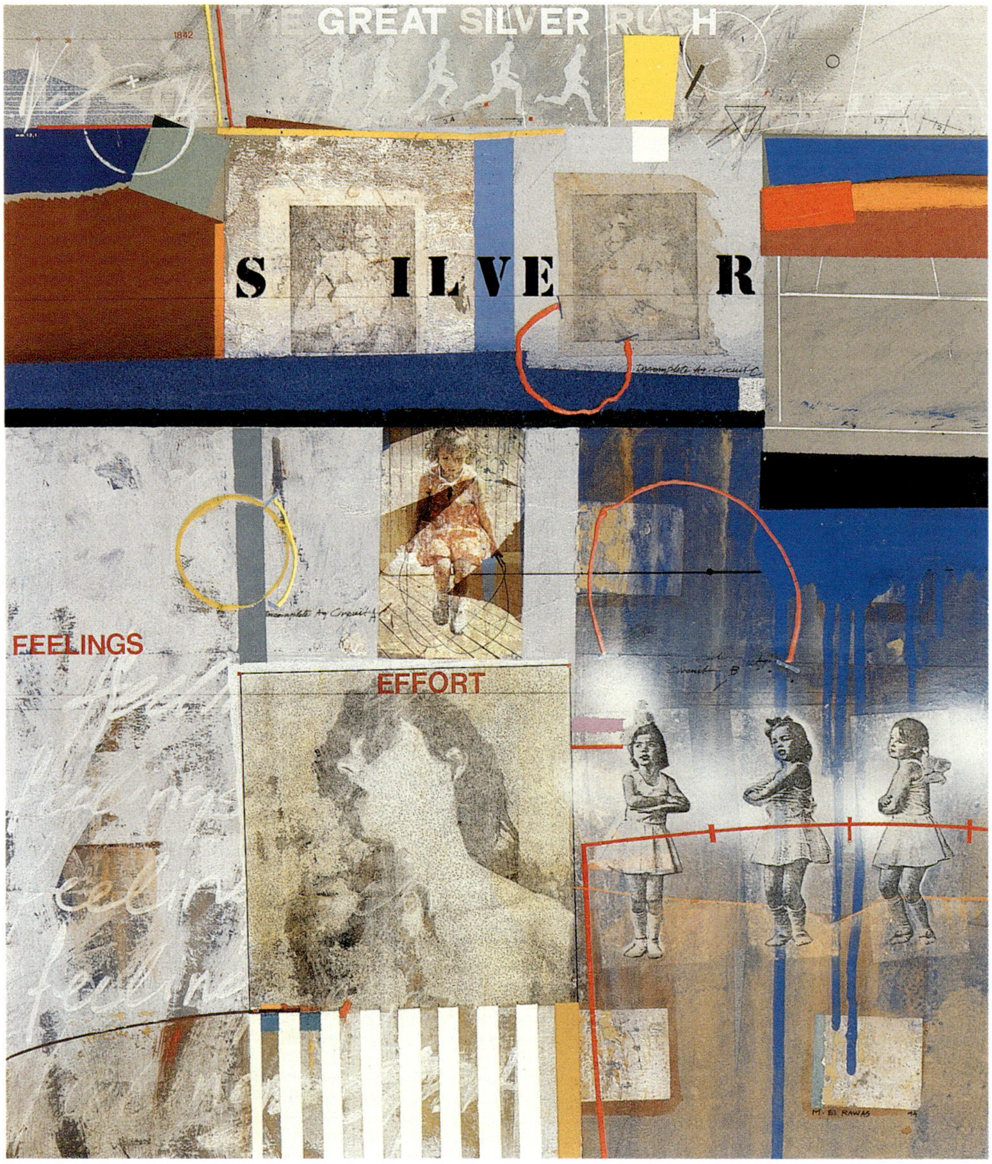

THE GREAT SILVER RUSH, 1994
Mixed media on canvas
59 x 50 cm
Collection Mr. & Mrs. O. Salhab

Opposite page
THE NATURE OF TEMPTATION, 1994
Mixed media and assemblage on plywood panel
140 x 110 x 1 cm
Collection Mr. & Mrs. W. Baydoun

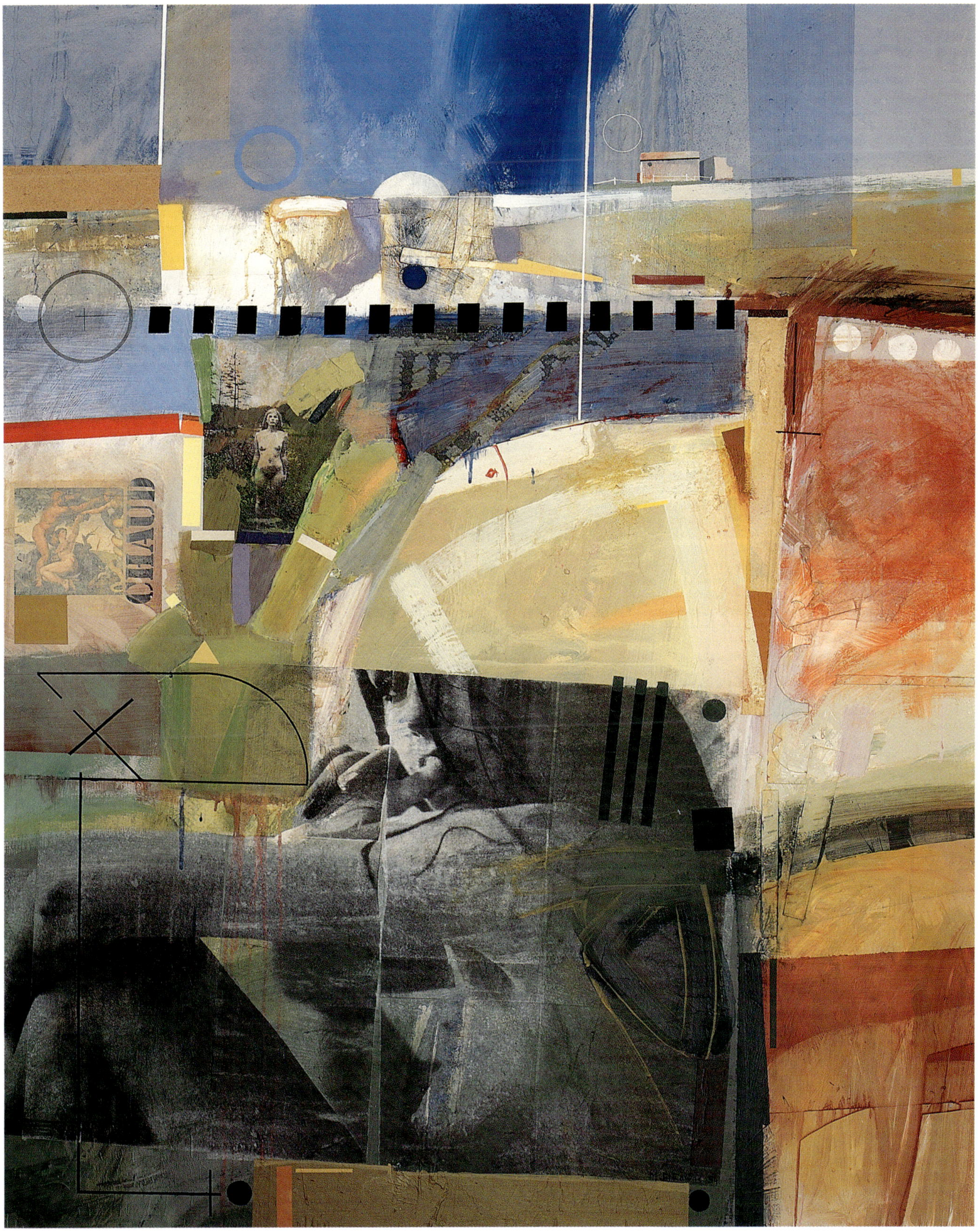
CHAUD

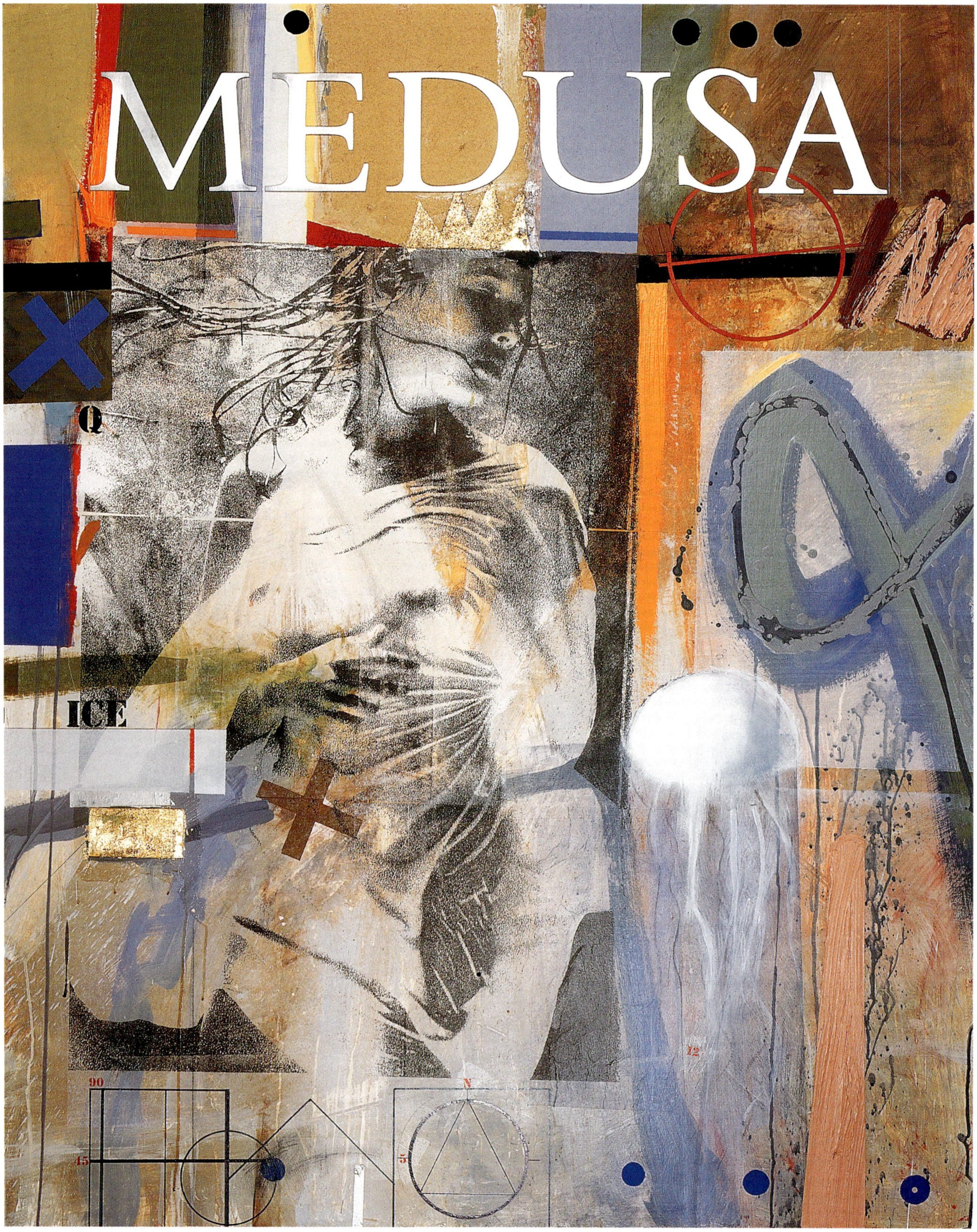
MEDUSA
Q
ICE
90
45
N
5
12

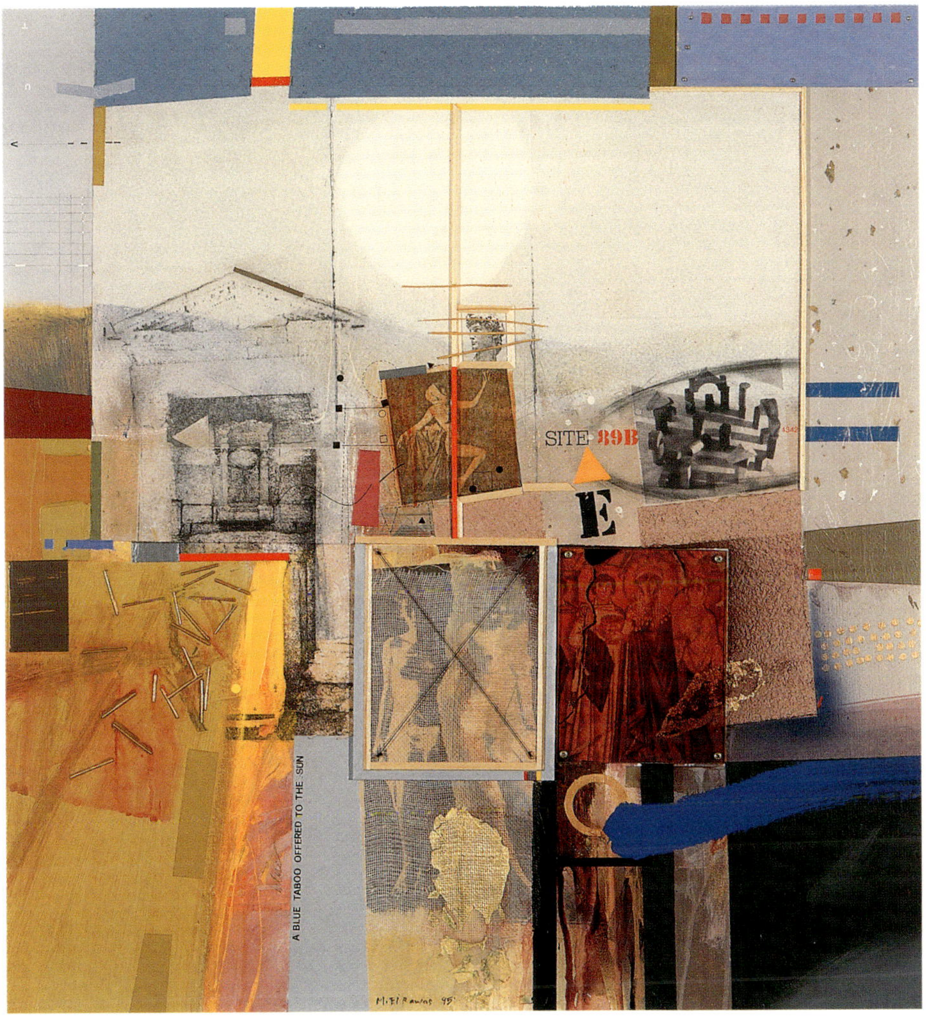

THESE INTENSIVE THINGS, 1995
Mixed media and assemblage on plywood panel
49 x 49 x 1.5 cm
Collection Ms. J. Aswad

Opposite page
MEDUSA, 1994
Mixed media and assemblage on plywood panel
140 x 110 x 2 cm
Collection TIMOTCA (The International Museum of Twentieth Century Art)

Exhibited in the touring exhibition of The International Museum of Twentieth Century Art (TIMOTCA & UNESCO); at UNESCO Headquarters, Paris, France, 1998; MITRA Municipal Gallery, Lisbon, Portugal, 1998; Las Vegas Art Museum, USA, 2000

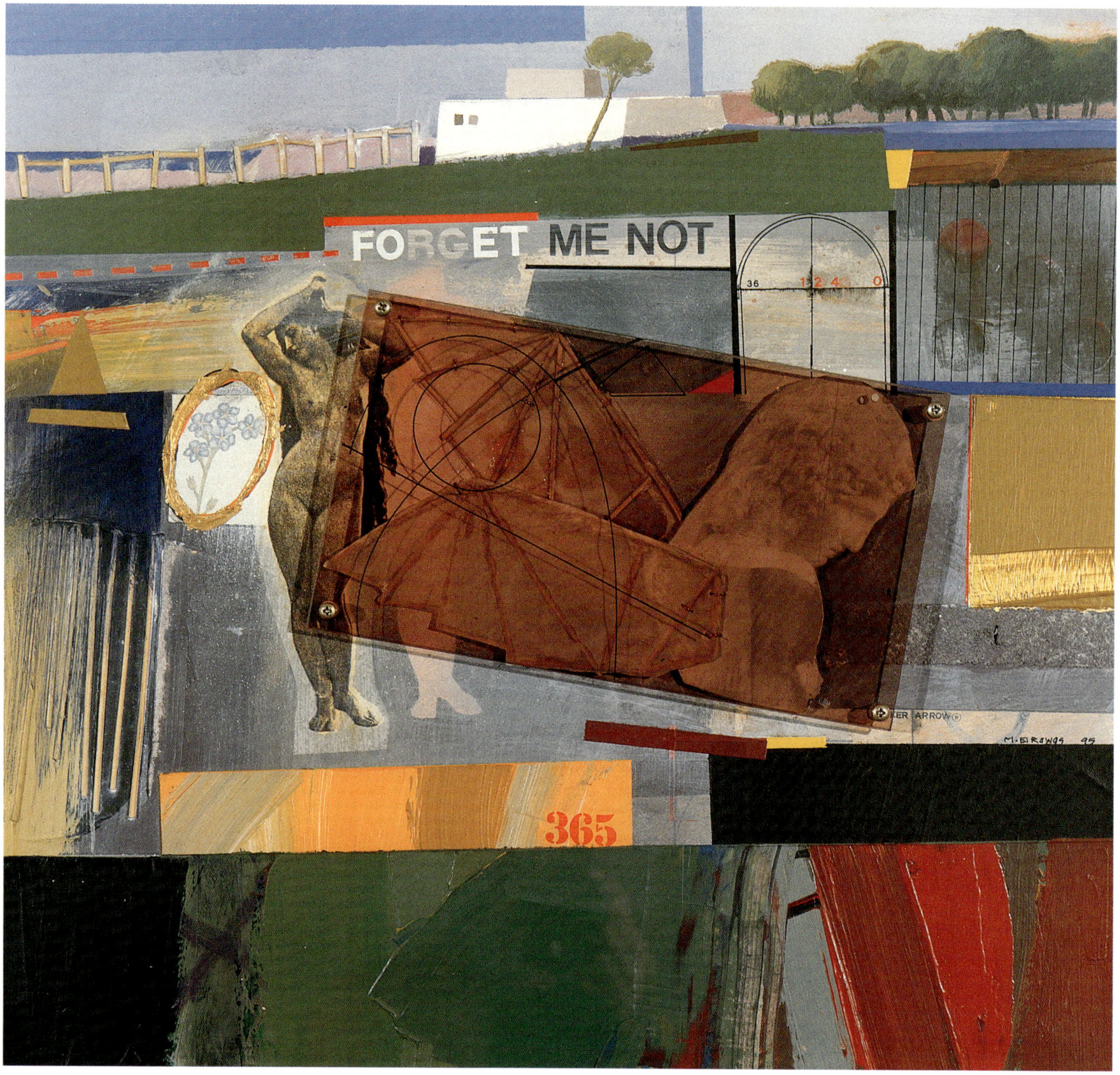

FORGET ME NOT, 1995
Mixed media and assemblage on plywood panel
34 x 36 x 2 cm
Collection Ms. M. Eid

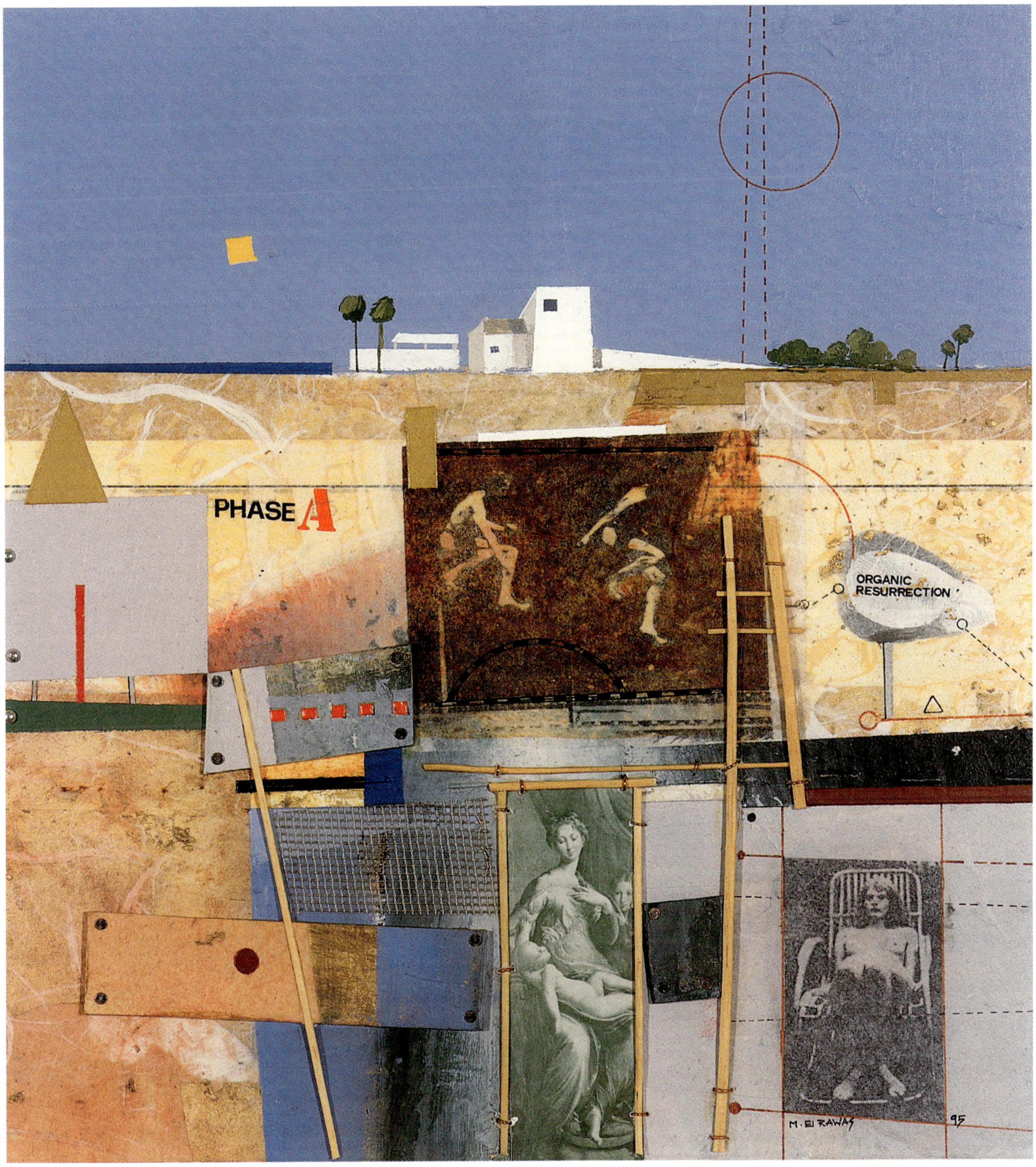

THE RESURRECTION, 1995
Mixed media and assemblage on plywood panel
28 x 25 x 1 cm
Collection Mr. & Mrs. O. Salhab

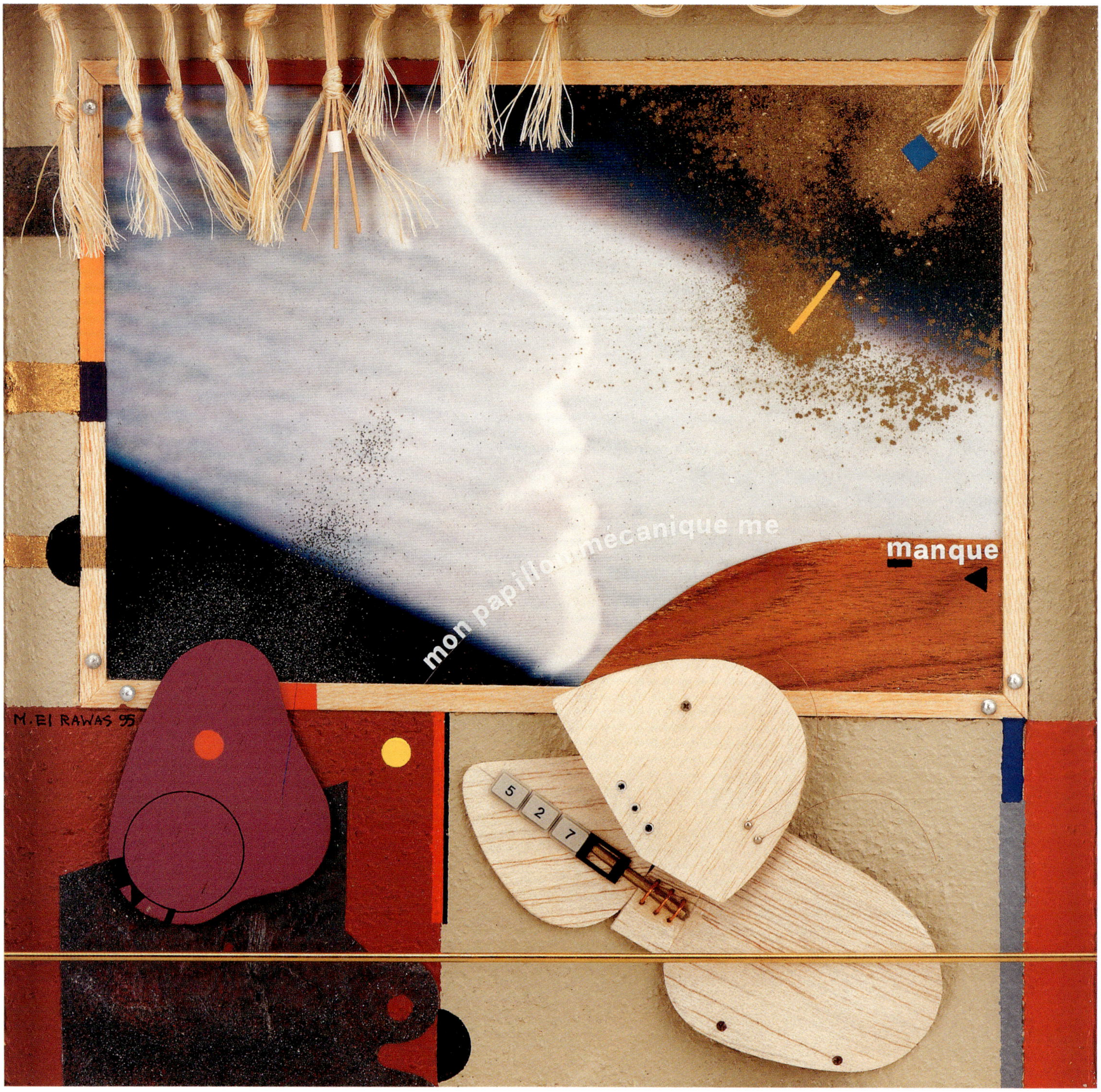
mon papillon mécanique me
manque
M. El RAWAS 95
5
2
7

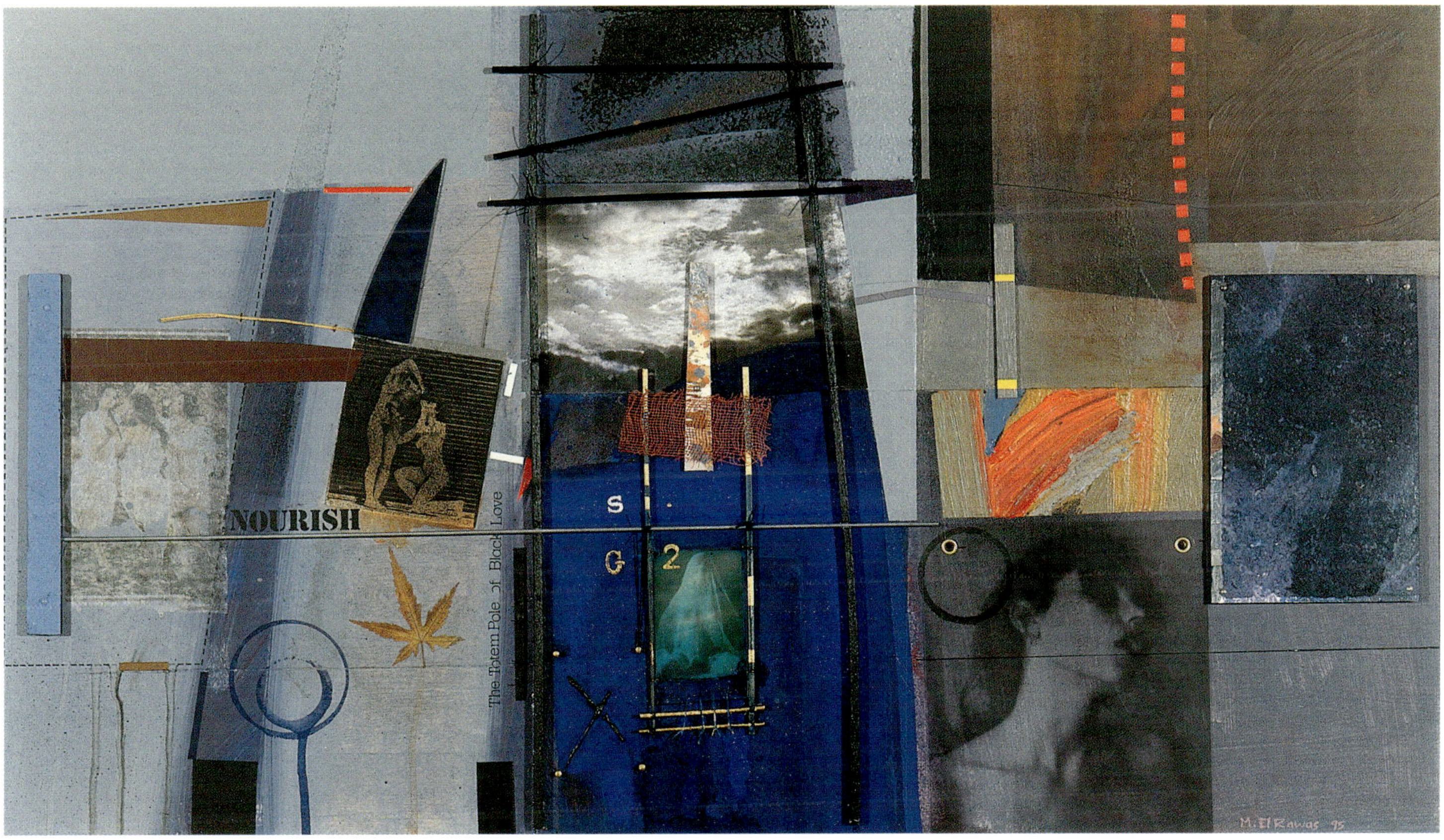

THE TOTEM POLE, 1995
Mixed media and assemblage on cardboard
40 x 70 cm
Collection Mr. & Mrs. A. Sweidan

Opposite page
MON PAPILLON MÉCANIQUE, 1995
Mixed media, photography and assemblage on plywood panel
22 x 22 x 3 cm
Collection Mr. H. Mneimneh

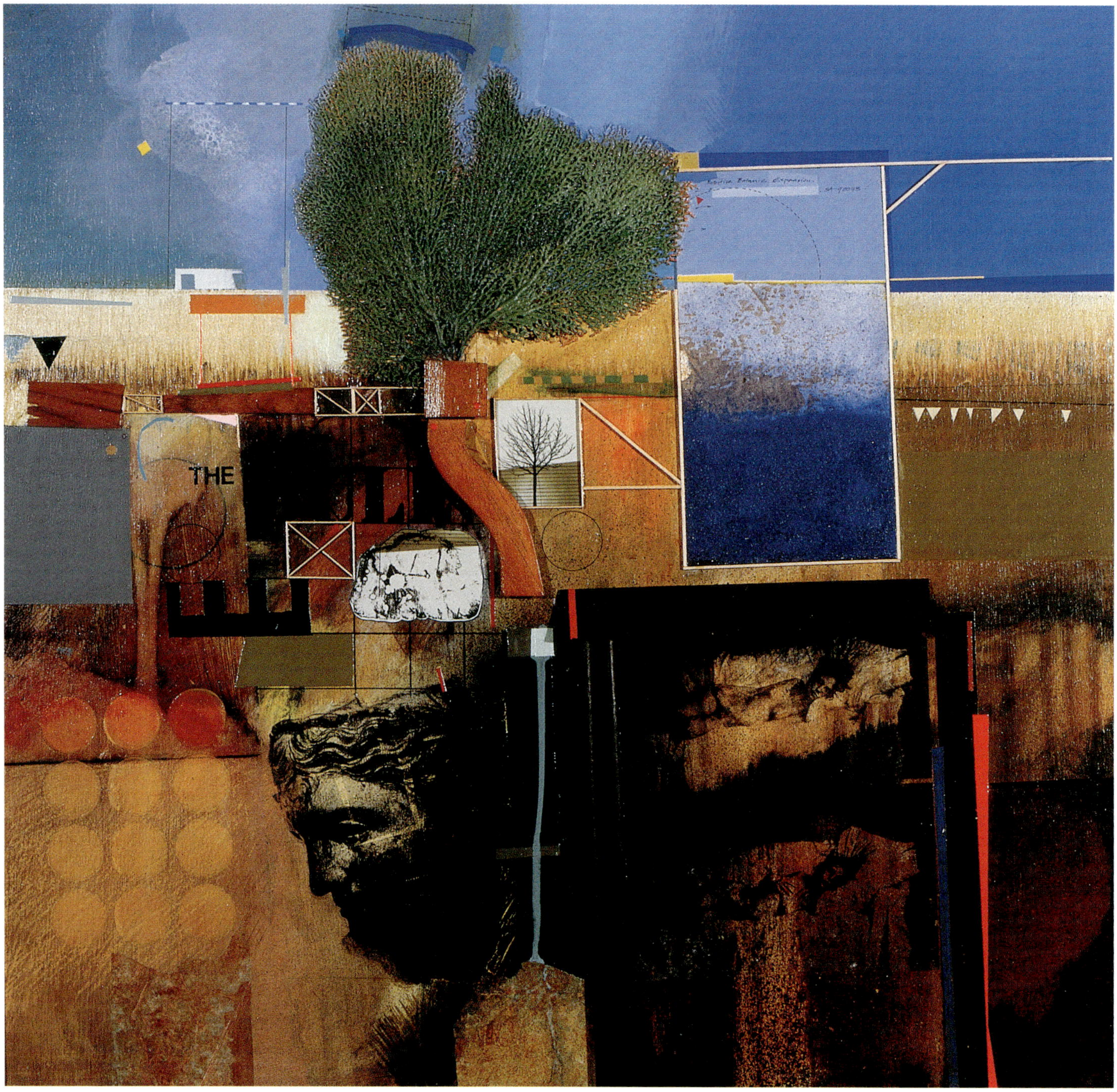

GUARANTEED SATISFACTION, 1996
Mixed media and assemblage on plywood panel
60 x 60 x 2 cm
Private collection

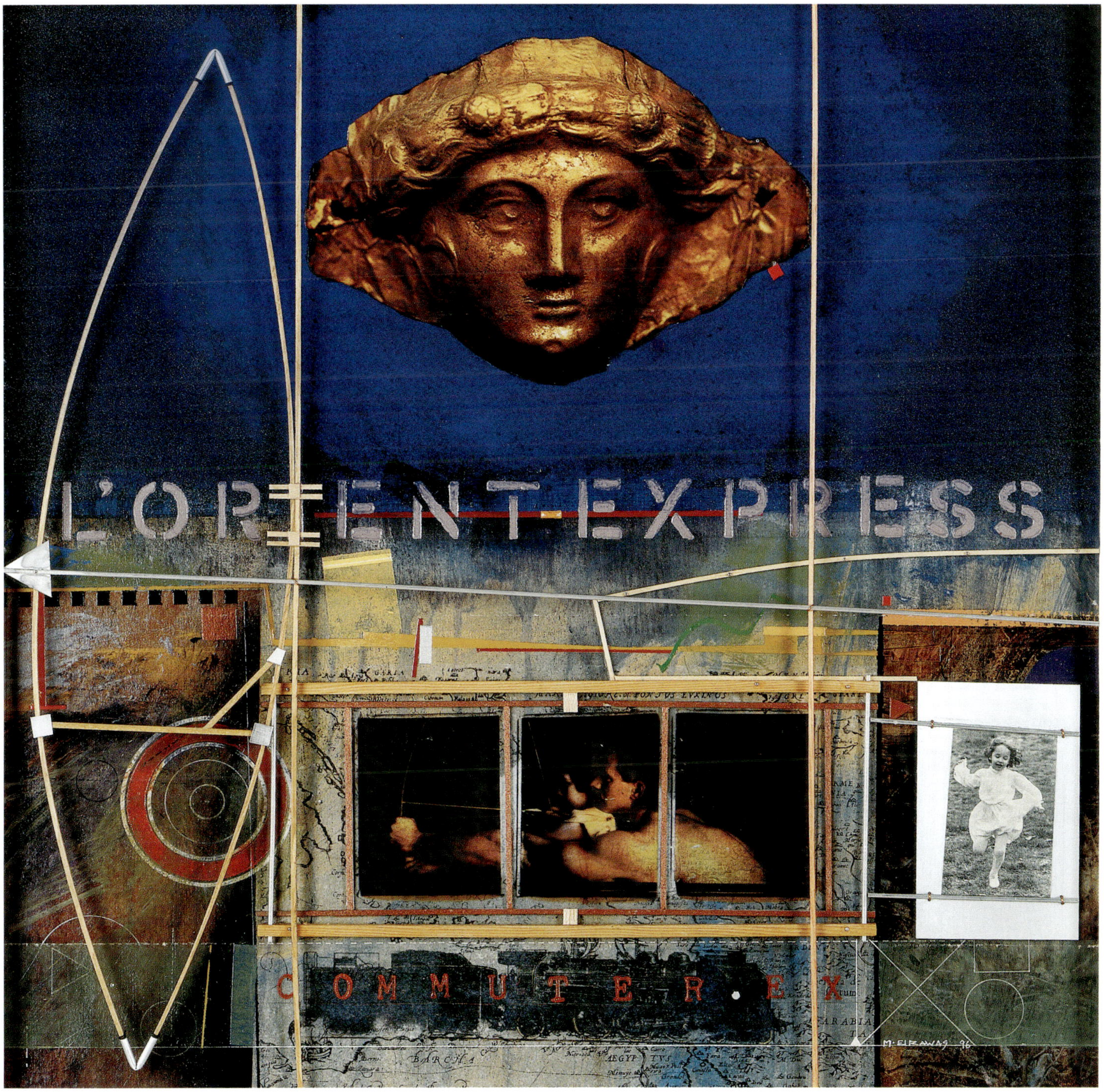

THE COMMUTER, 1996
Mixed media and assemblage on plywood panel
47 x 47 x 2 cm
Collection Mr. & Mrs. A. Takieddine

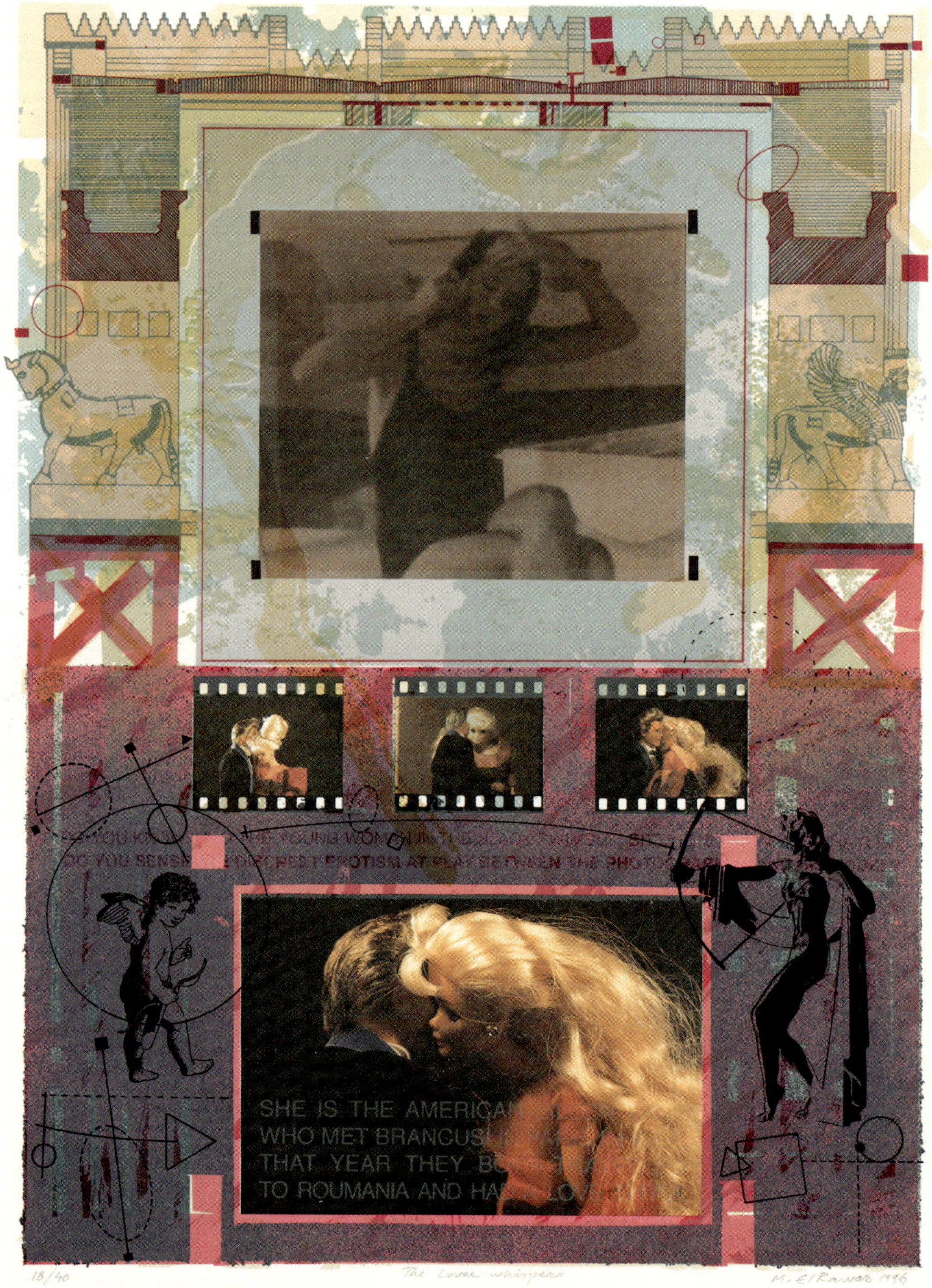

THE LOVER WHISPERS, 1996
Lithography
59 x 43 cm

Exhibited at:
– Krakow International Print Triennale, Poland, 1997
– Nineteenth International Independent Exhibition of Prints in Kanagawa, Japan, 1997

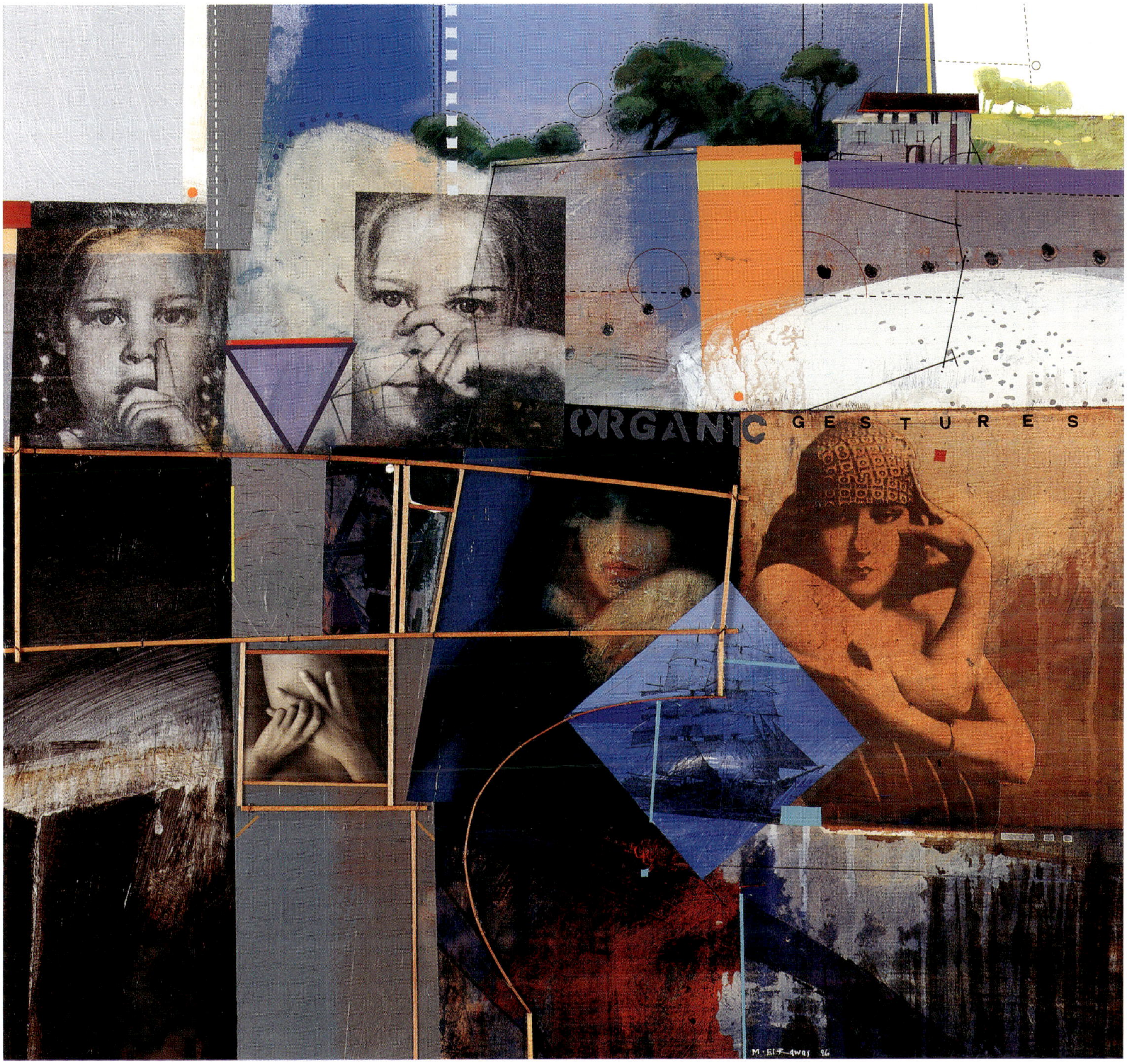

ORGANIC GESTURES, 1996
Mixed media and assemblage on plywood panel
57 x 59 x 2 cm
Collection Ms. R. Faysal

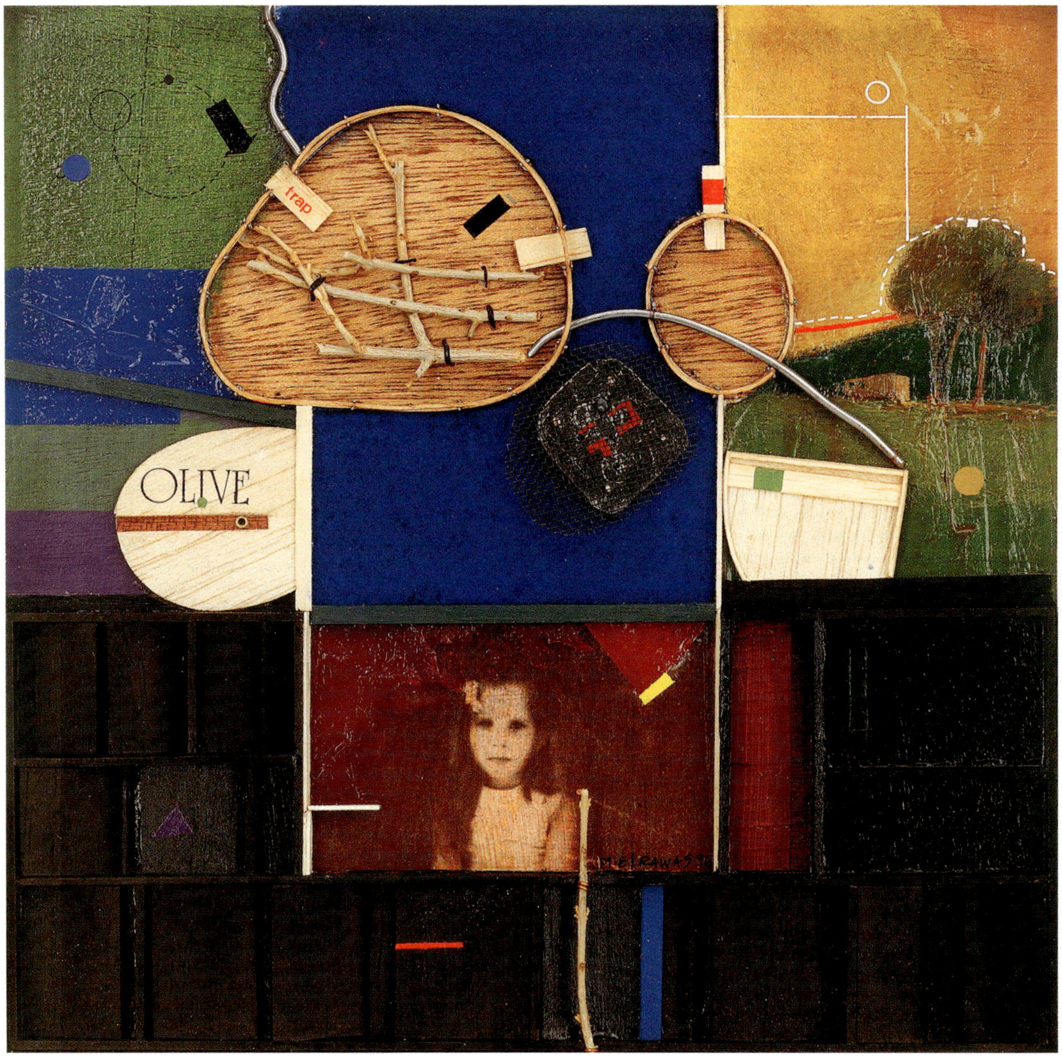

THE TRAP, 1996
Mixed media and assemblage on plywood panel
22 x 22 x 3 cm
Collection Mr. & Mrs. A. Gaspard

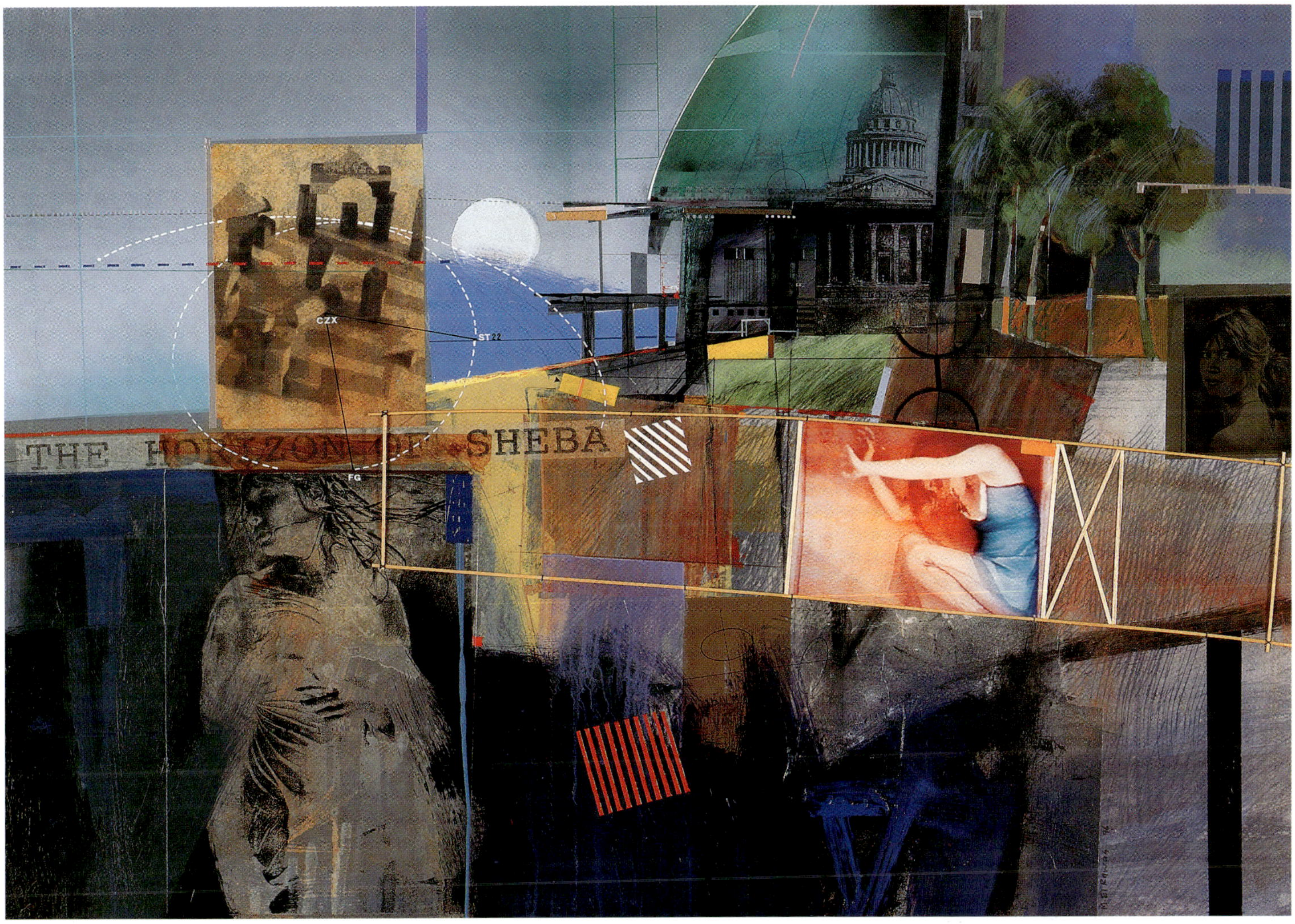

THE HORIZON OF SHEBA, 1996
Mixed media and assemblage on plywood panel
57 x 81 cm
Collection Mr. & Mrs. R. Joreige

Exhibited at the Sursock Museum Salon d'Automne 1996

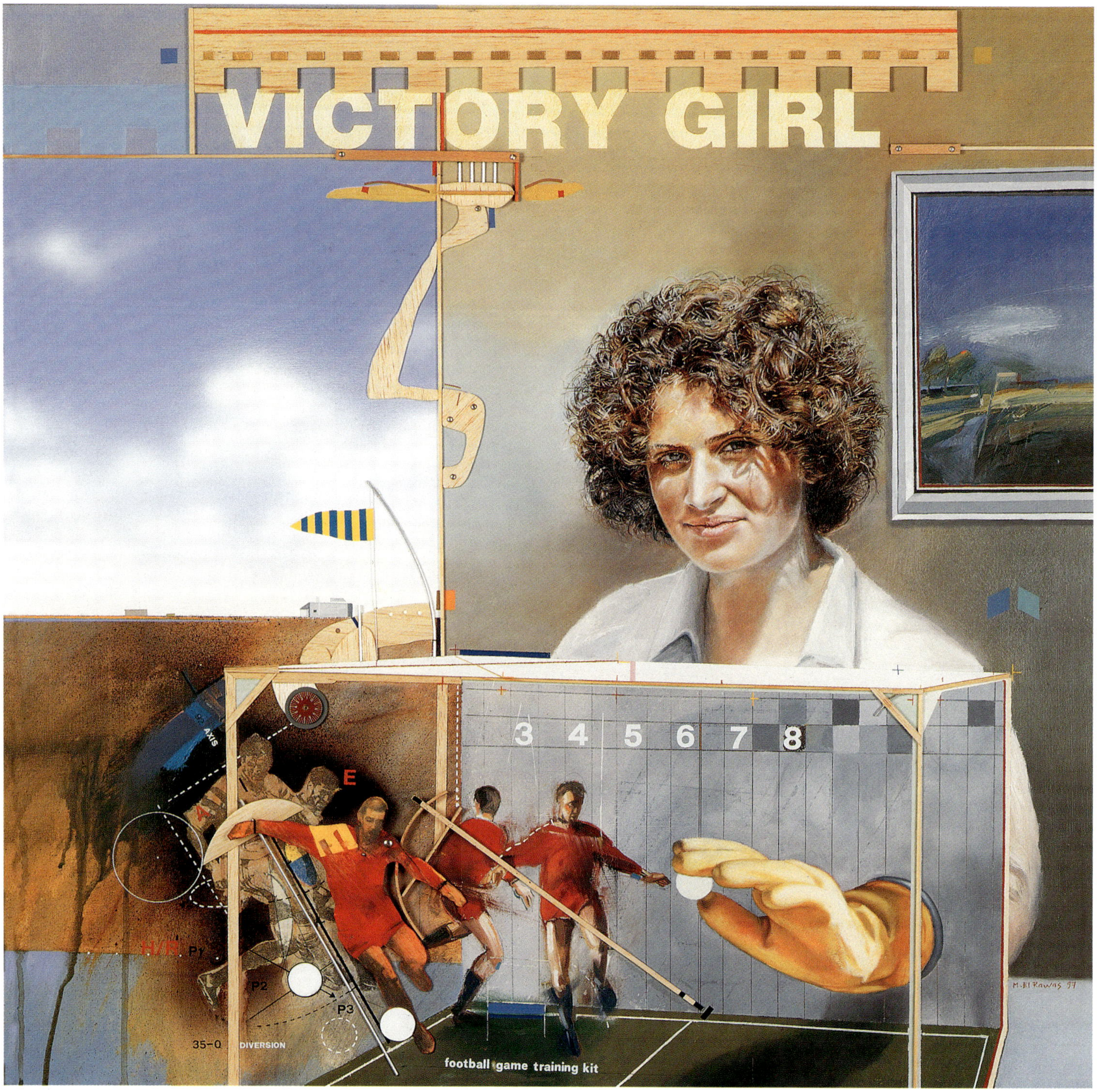

VICTORY GIRL, 1997
Oil, mixed media and assemblage on plywood panel
74 x 74 x 2 cm
Collection Ms. N. Halawi

The Creative Process: Controlling the Spontaneous

Putting things in order is a rule of life for me, because I cannot function in a space that is not tidy. It is only in an ordered environment that I have peace of soul and mind and can live in harmony with my surroundings. And it is only then that I can start to paint.

In contrast to this need for discipline and organization, I hate to plan a work of art beforehand. I never prepare a sketch of my painting prior to starting it because this would kill the excitement of discovery while a work is in progress. A certain element might catch my interest – a picture, a shape or an idea with which to start the work. Then, to expand and develop that initiating element, I allow ideas and thoughts to be projected upon it – or to grow out of it – in terms of themes and visual particularities. Thus, gradually, the whole work is completed. This is the only way I can maintain my interest in what I am doing, remain amused by what I am discovering, fascinated by how this or that idea occured to me, and how particular links were established. For me a painting is, first of all, a combination of visual elements bound together by the principles of design. On one level, it is an endless game of experimenting with the multiple possibilities of combining the visual elements – lines, shapes, textures, values and colors – through the design principles of symmetry, contrast, conflict, unity, balance, dominance, repetition and harmony. It is a complex and truly joyful exercise to build a work of art through the application of these disciplines. Secondly, a painting is a mental and emotional product that addresses our intelligence and feelings. Yet, at both the visual and intellectual levels, I allow for 'accidents', for an unintentional effect or idea to occur. Later, I judge whether to keep it or not. I would say that a work of art I have created is a demonstration of *controlling the spontaneous.*

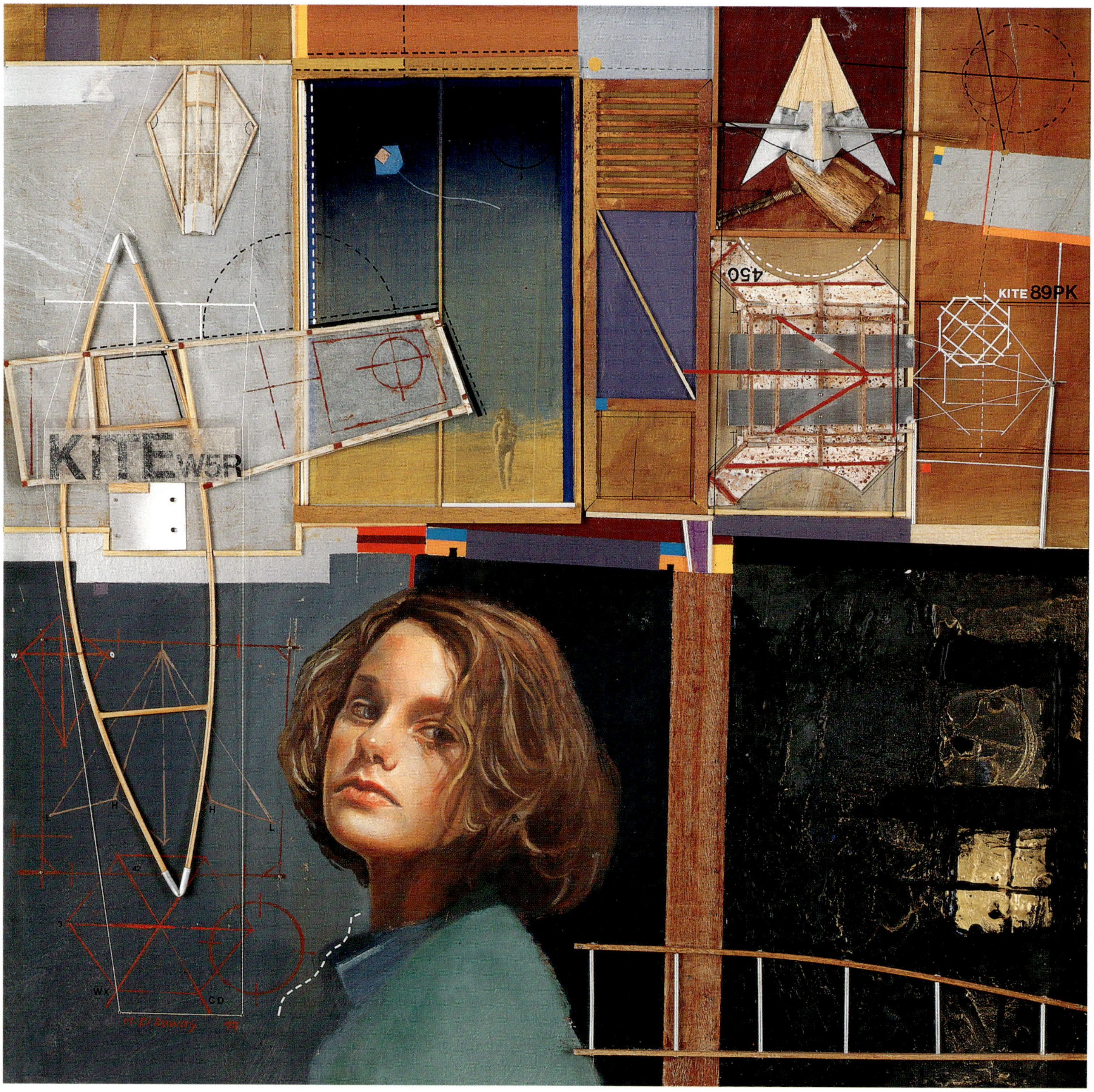

THE KITE MAKER, 1997
Mixed media and assemblage on plywood panel
48 x 48 x 2 cm
Collection Mr. & Mrs. H. Bsat

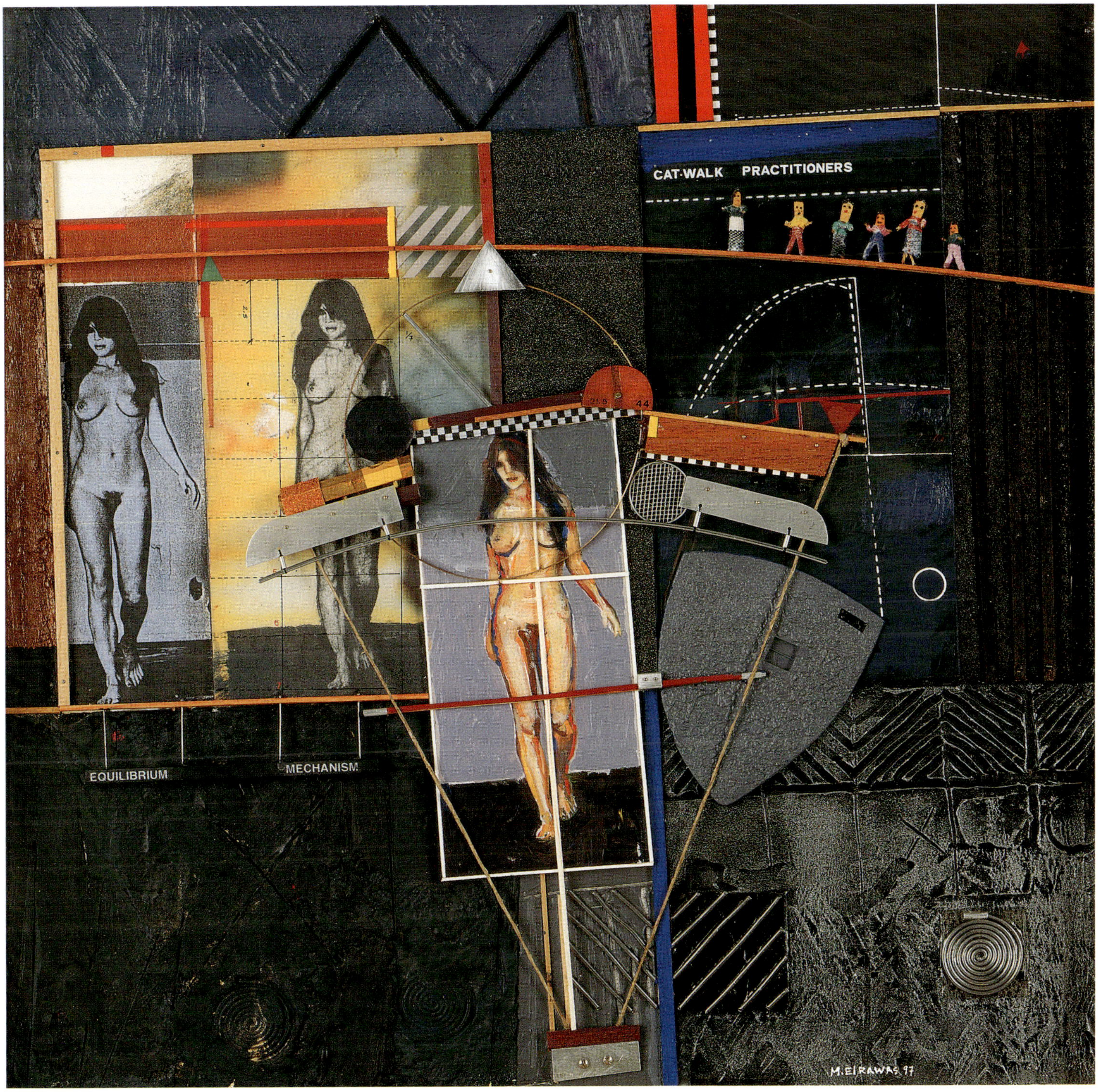

CATWALK PRACTITIONERS, 1997
Mixed media and assemblage on plywood panel
47 x 47 x 2 cm
Collection Dr. R. Selwan

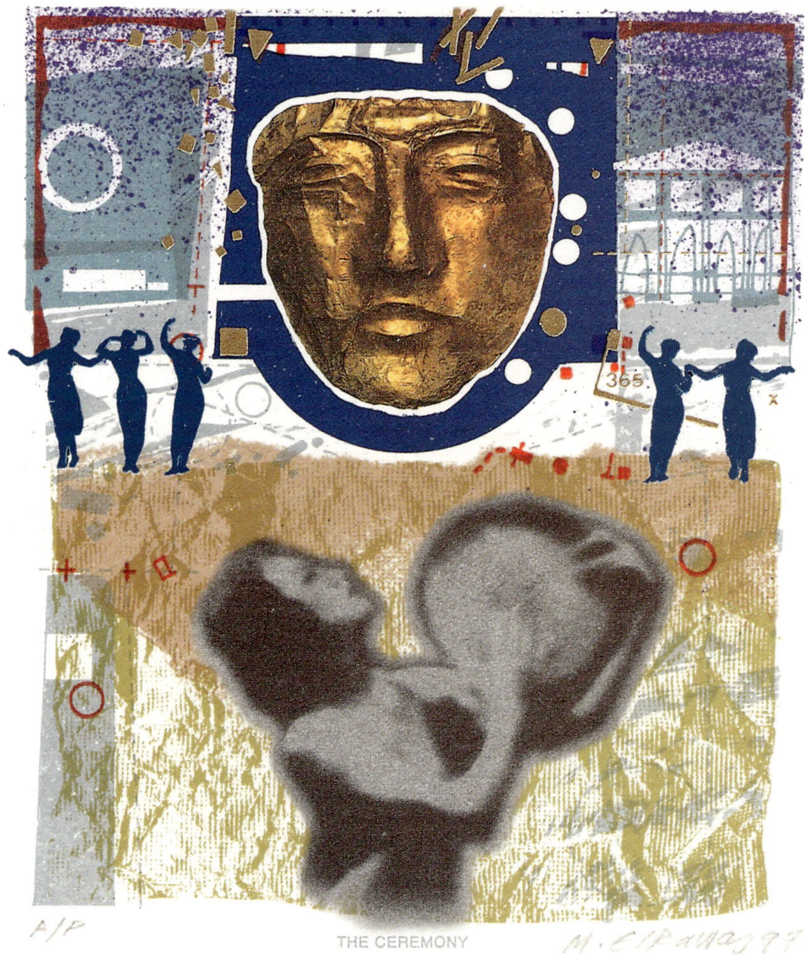

THE CEREMONY, 1997
Lithography and hot press foil
12 x 19 cm

However, even if I do not always know exactly my reasons for making certain specific compositional choices, I like to think I am fully aware of the general process of creating a work of art. I count a lot on the projection and association of ideas. The element that had initially caught my eye and on which I choose to build the painting will have something in it that 'asks for' some particular kind of adjacent element in terms of meaning and content. And thus the mood of the whole work starts to build up.

The expressive mood of my work is, like me, detached and observing rather than involved. Or, at least, this is what it looks like because, on the one hand, I do paint with passion, but on the other hand I try to conceal or tone down its presence. I am a great admirer of the London-born painter Euan Uglow (1932–2000)

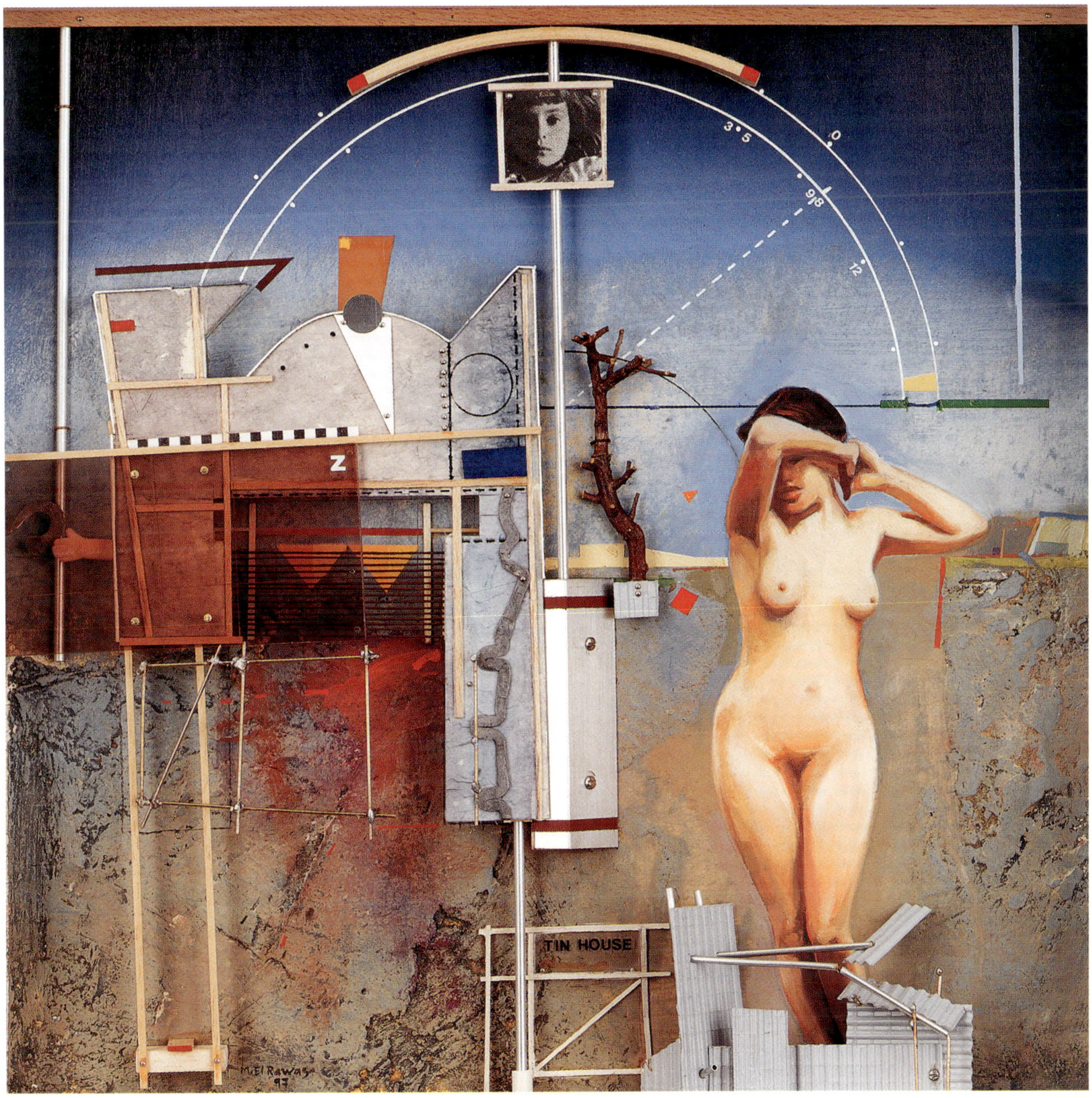

THE BIRTH OF TIN HOUSE VENUS, 1997
Mixed media and assemblage on plywood panel
30.5 x 30.5 x 3 cm
Collection Mr. J. Tarrab

and I have repainted many of his figures, incorporating them into my recent work. I certainly agree with what he has said about the power of a passion that is held in check: 'It's no good unless there is passion ... [but] there is more force in controlled passion than in exuberant passion.' (Quoted in the article 'Are You Sitting Uncomfortably?' by David Ward, *The Guardian*, 7 July 2003.)

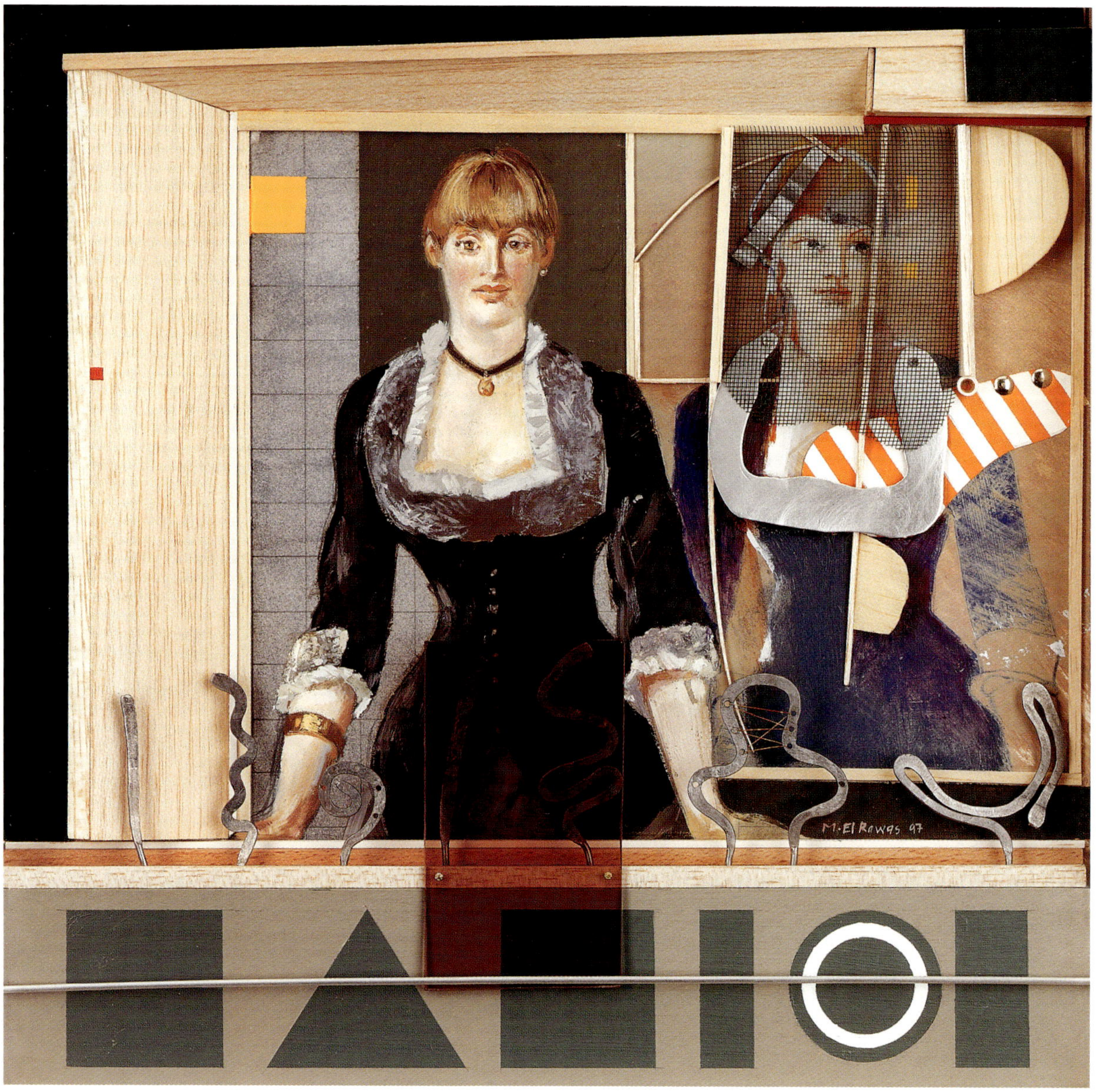

THE ARTIST AND SELF–PORTRAIT, 1997
Mixed media and assemblage on plywood panel
30 x 30 x 3 cm
Collection Mr. & Mrs. H. Bsat

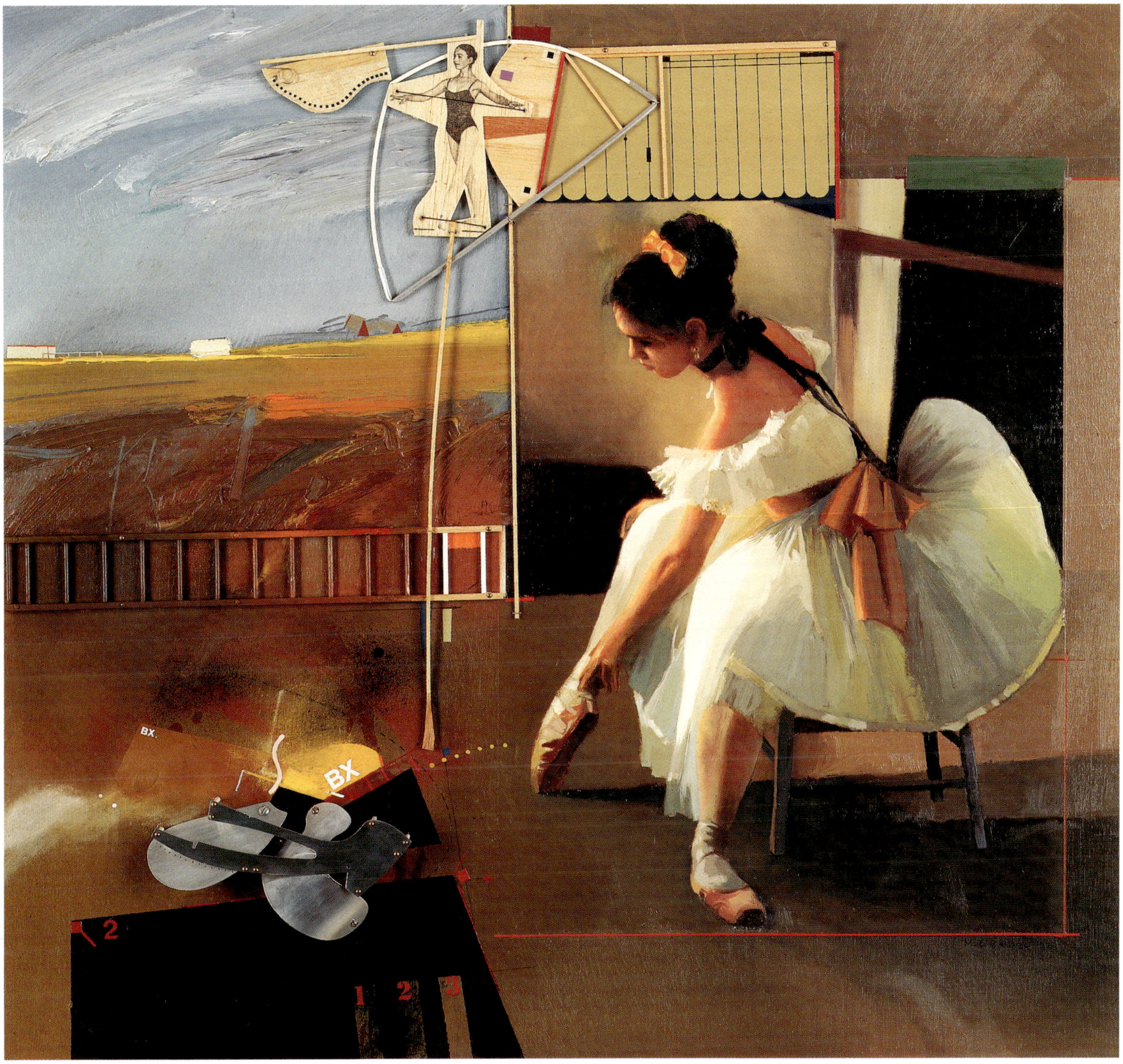

BALLET DANCE MECHANISM, 1998
Mixed media and assemblage on plywood panel
57 x 60 x 4 cm
Collection Mr. & Mrs. M. Assi

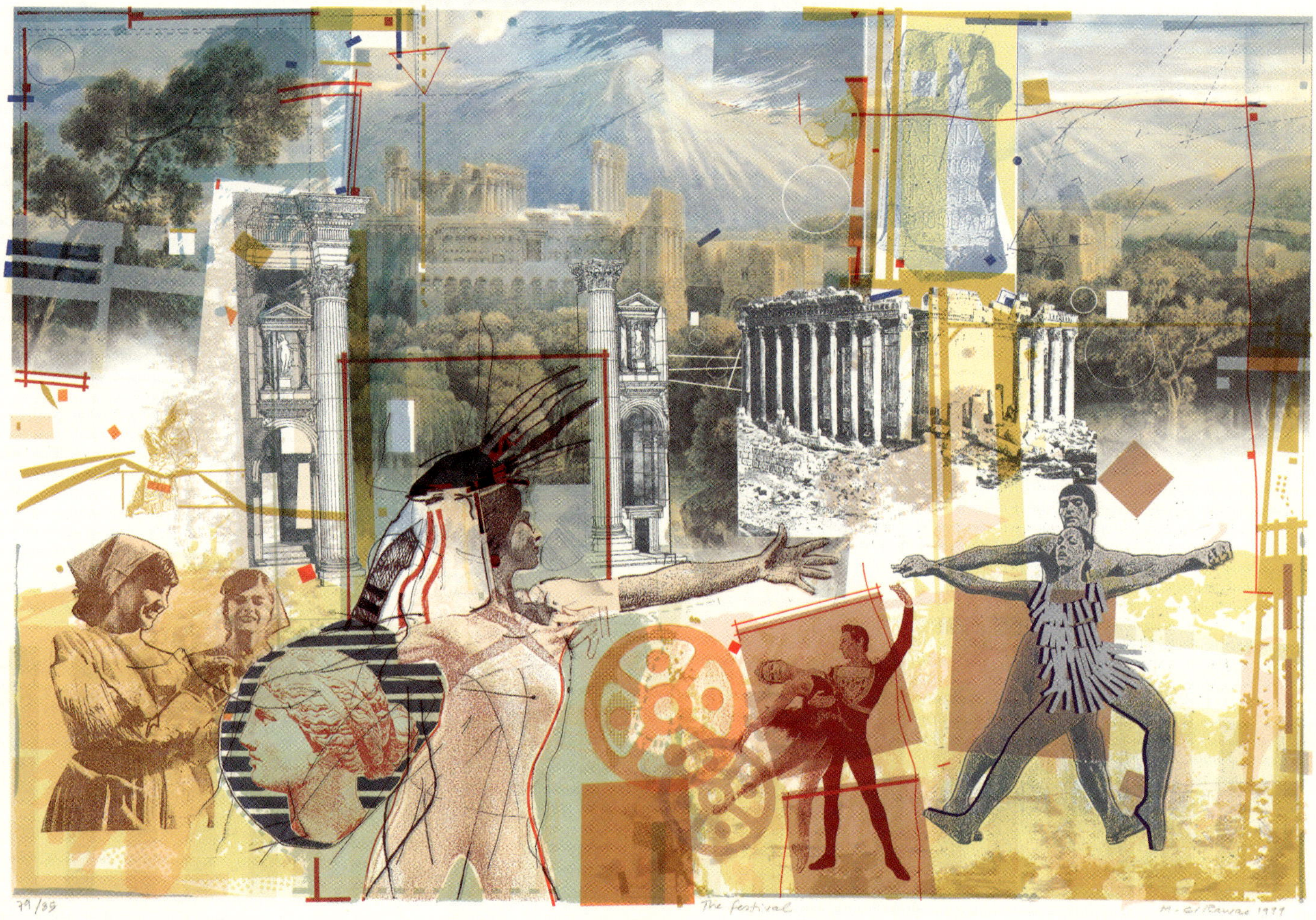

THE FESTIVAL, 1999
Lithography
46 x 66 cm

Commissioned by the Baalbek International Festival, summer 1999

My reasons for admiring Euan Uglow's work in particular, and the Euston Road School in general, are different from those behind my admiration for the work of Peter Blake (which I will say more about). I admire Uglow's dedication, the painstaking and meticulous processes he employs in painting his subjects. The marks and crosses that appear in his work (the result of the measurements he took during the initial observation of his subject) were, I believe, deliberately left in the final work for their intrinsic expression of the cerebral process he had applied. So even if I did not go through the same process of measurement while repainting his images as 'quotations' in my own work, I retained these marks for their own expressive quality – as in *The Golden Section, or Homage to Euan Uglow* (2000) and *The Amusement Park* (2000). In this connection, I was fascinated to read my Slade School tutor Bartolomeo Dos

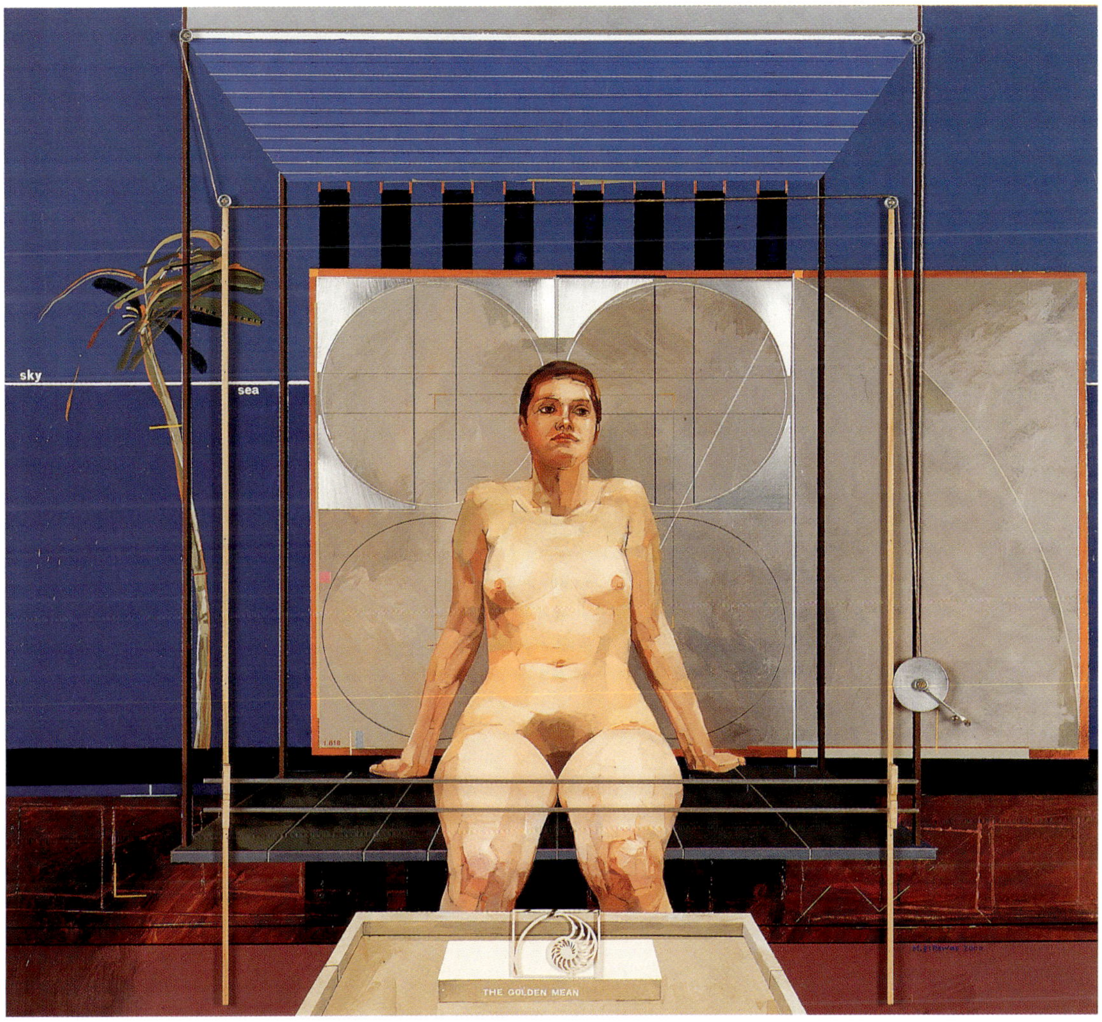

THE GOLDEN SECTION, OR HOMAGE TO EUAN UGLOW, 2000
Oil, acrylic and assemblage on plywood panel
64 x 69 x 3 cm
Collection Mrs. M. Merhej al-Amin

Santos's comment on his early experience as a student at the Slade:

> At the Slade School I was faced with two main currents among the painting students; on the one side a messy, darkish, heavy painting deriving from late Bomberg and on the other a clean cerebral approach that had been initiated by the Euston Road School, of which Coldstream had been one of the founders. I got very confused with that puritan, austere approach to drawing from the model, adding later the appropriate dots and crosses, which in fact should have been part of its initial structure. It was obviously the wrong approach.
> *(Bartolomeo Dos Santos, *45 Years of Printmaking 1956–2001*, Exhibition Catalogue at the London Institute Gallery, London, pp. 4–5.)

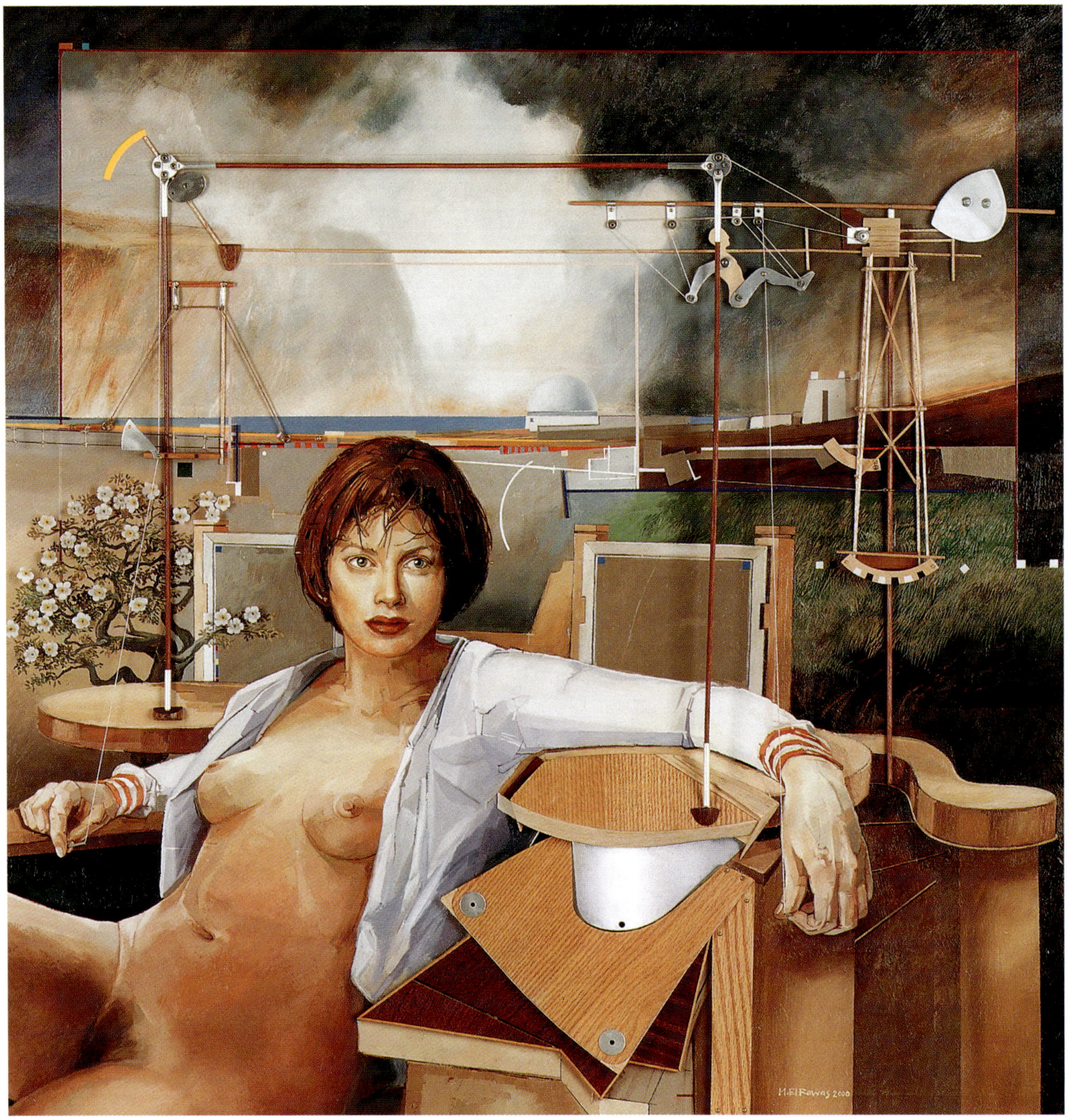

THE AMUSEMENT PARK, 2000
Oil, acrylic and assemblage on plywood panel
89 x 84 x 5 cm
Collection Mr. & Mrs. G. Baalbaki

Opposite page
THE AMUSEMENT PARK, 2000 (detail)

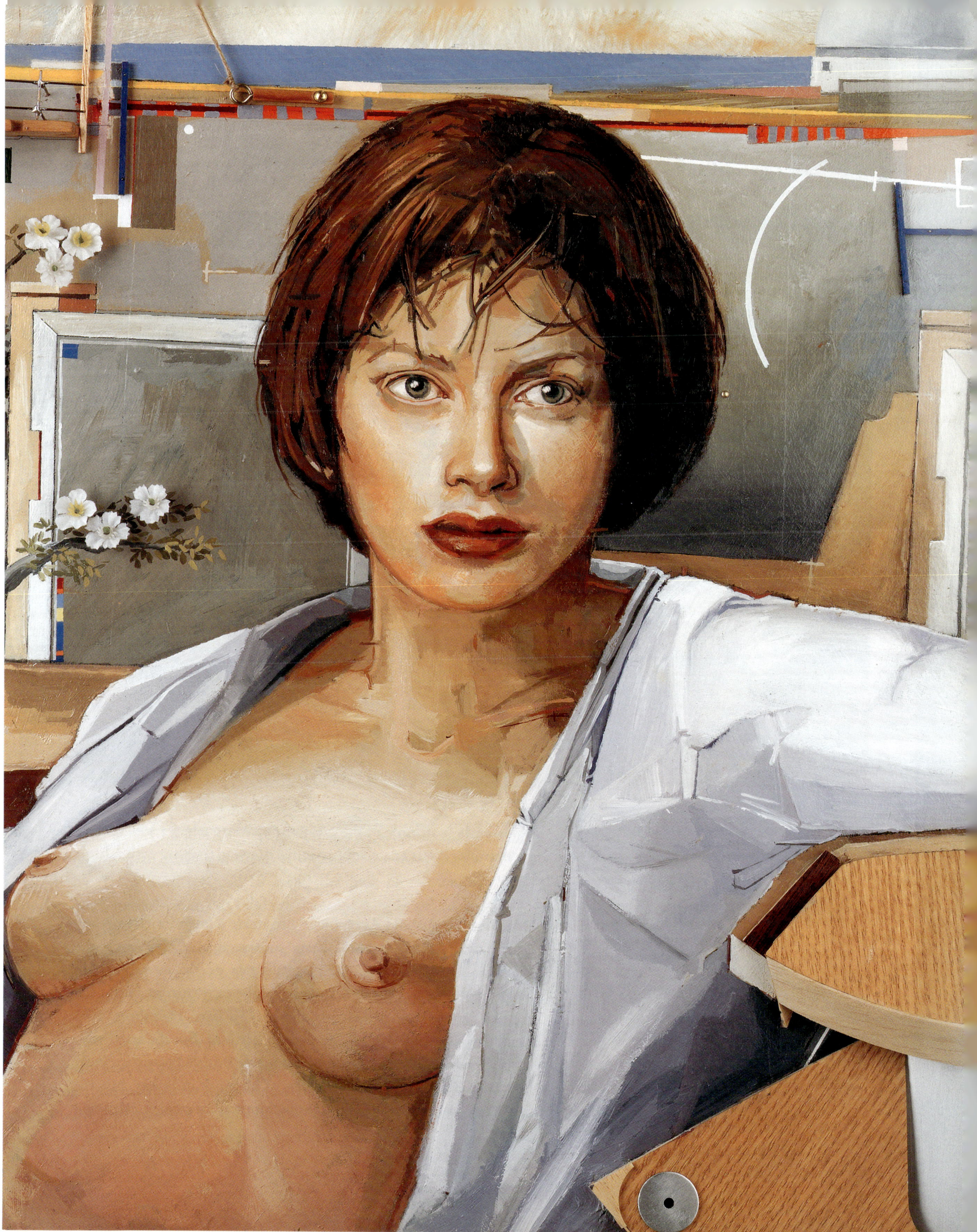

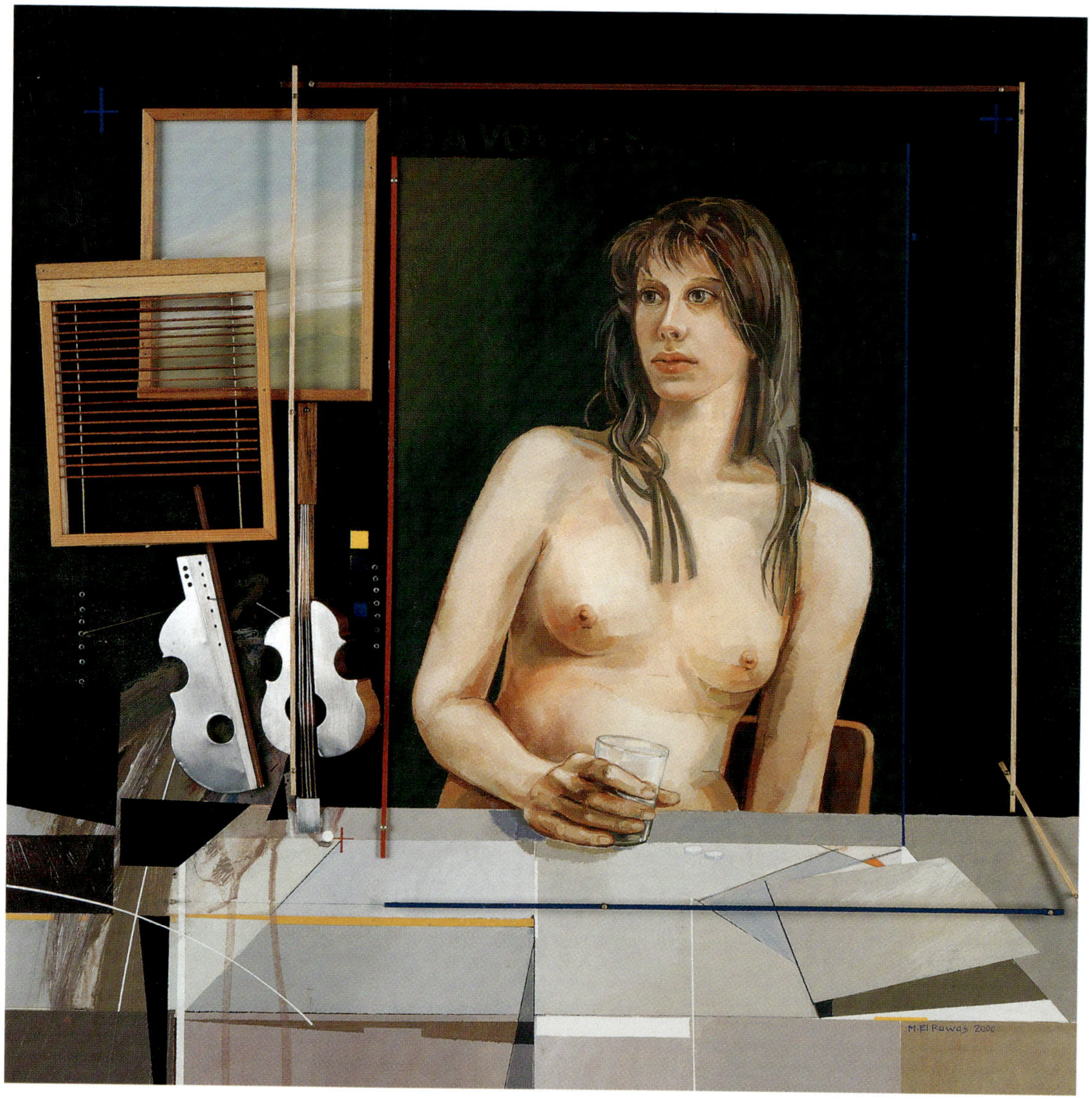

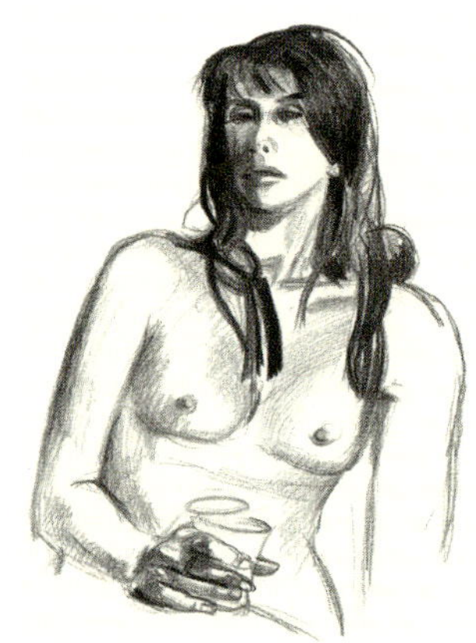

Top left
THE FINALE, 2000
Oil, acrylic and assemblage on plywood panel
49 x 49 x 3 cm
Artist's collection

Top right
A SKETCH FROM A LIVE MODEL, 1995
Charcoal
36 x 25 cm
Artist's collection

The original sketch that triggered THE FINALE

Opposite page
THE FINALE, 2000 (detail)

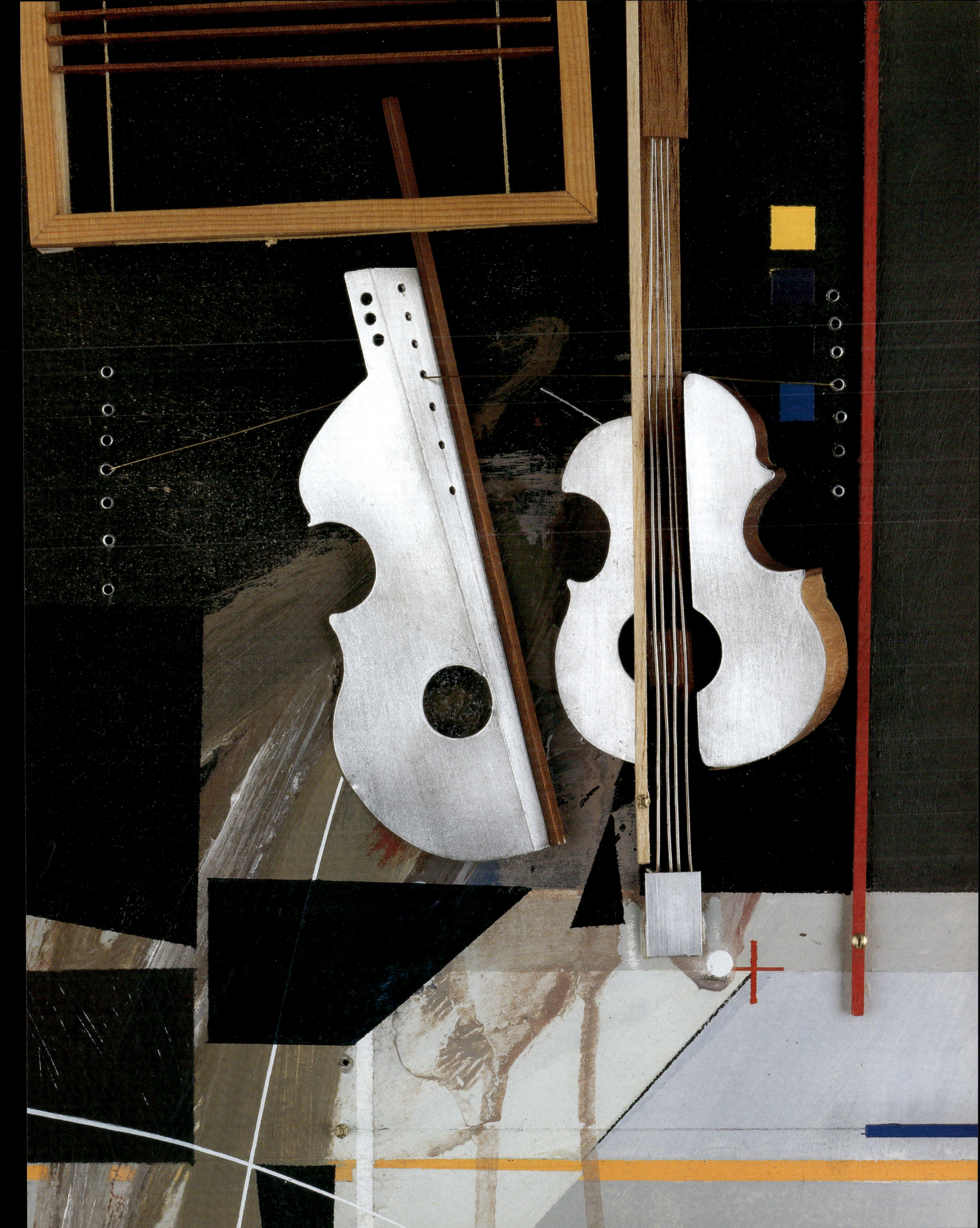

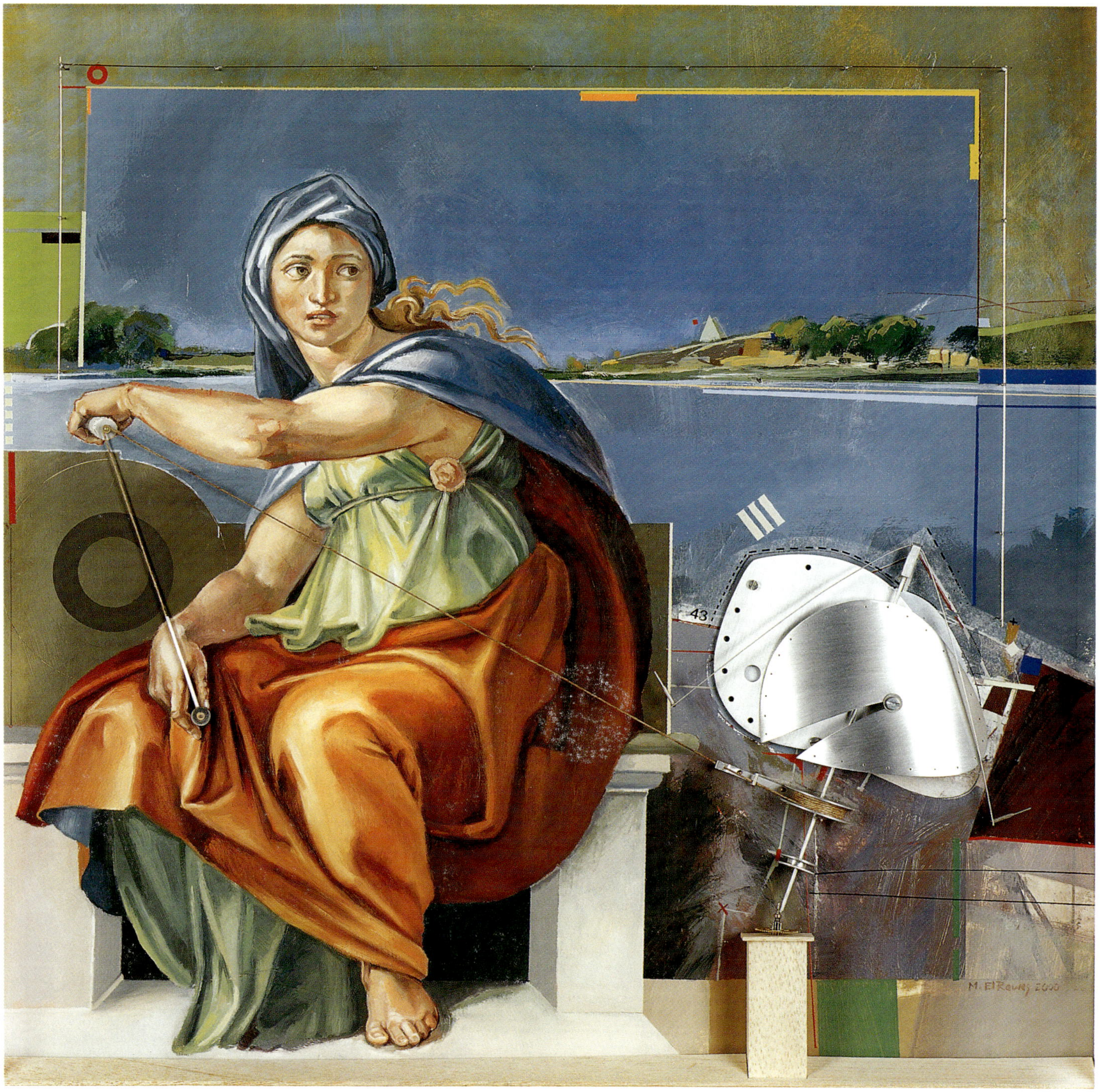

DELPHIC SIBYL AT WORK, 2000
Oil, acrylic and assemblage on plywood panel
57 x 57 x 5 cm
Private collection

Opposite page
DELPHIC SIBYL AT WORK, 2000 (detail)

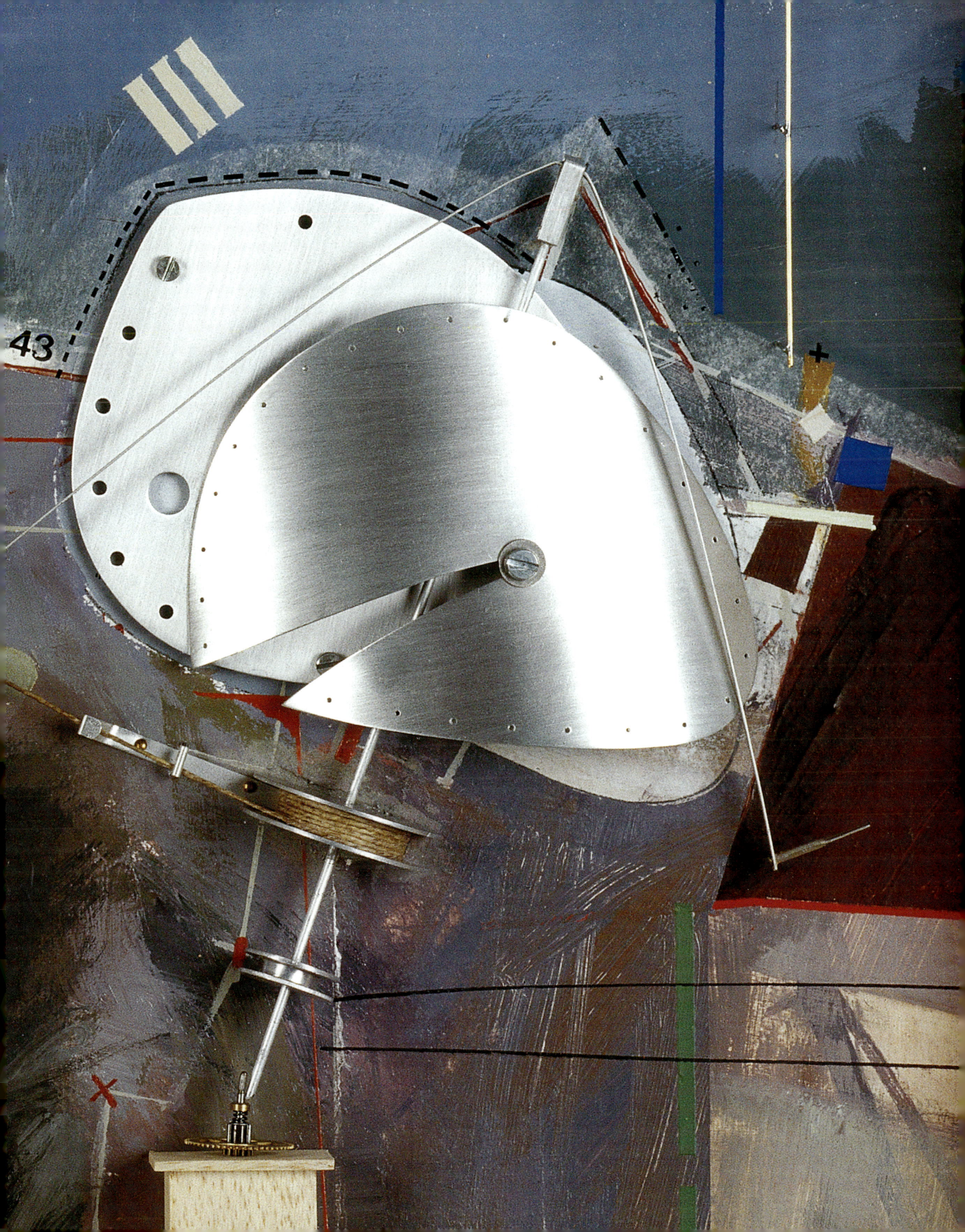
43

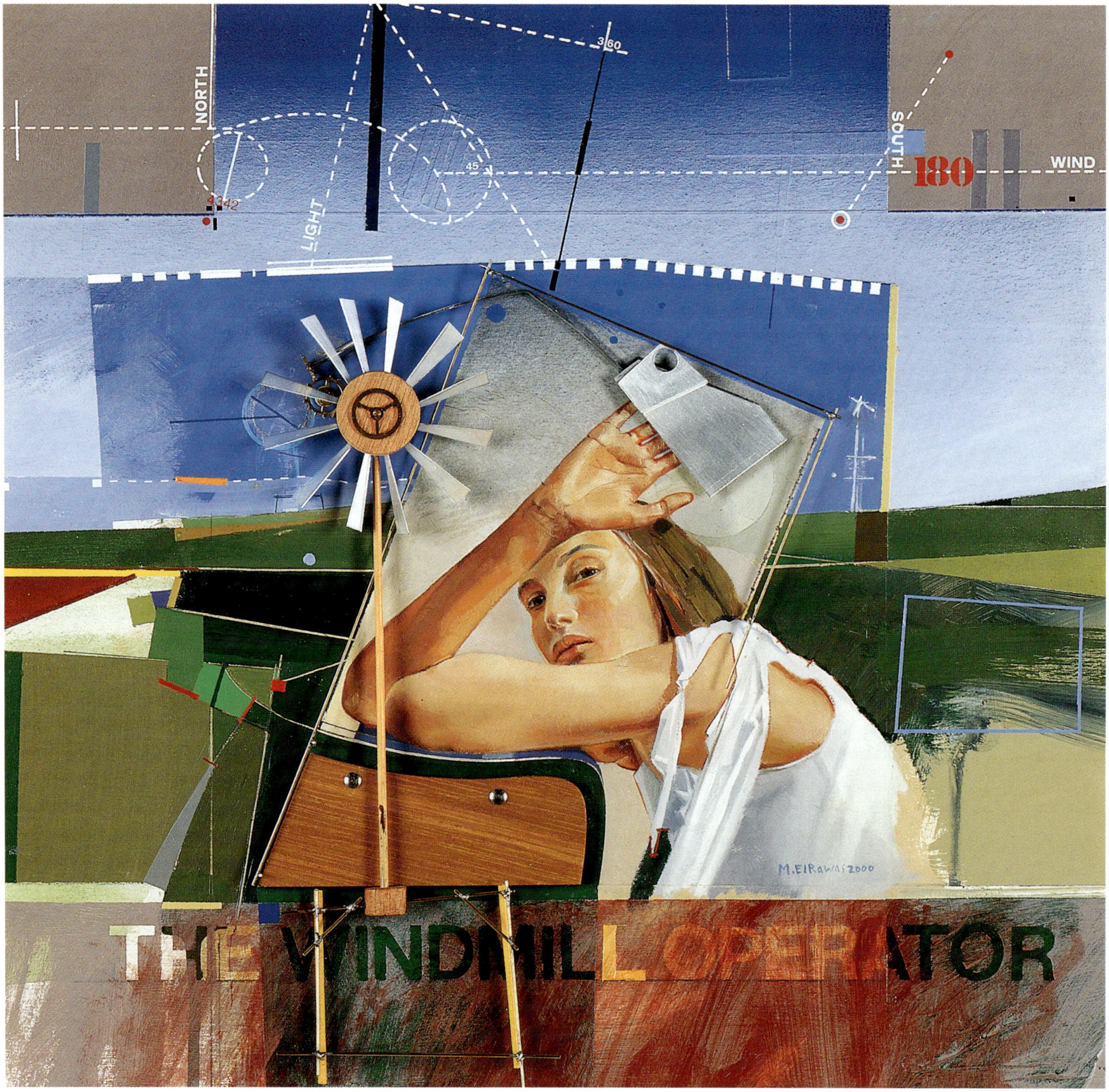

THE WINDMILL OPERATOR, 2000
Mixed media and assemblage on plywood panel
38 x 38 x 3 cm
Collection Mr. & Mrs. M. Baadarani

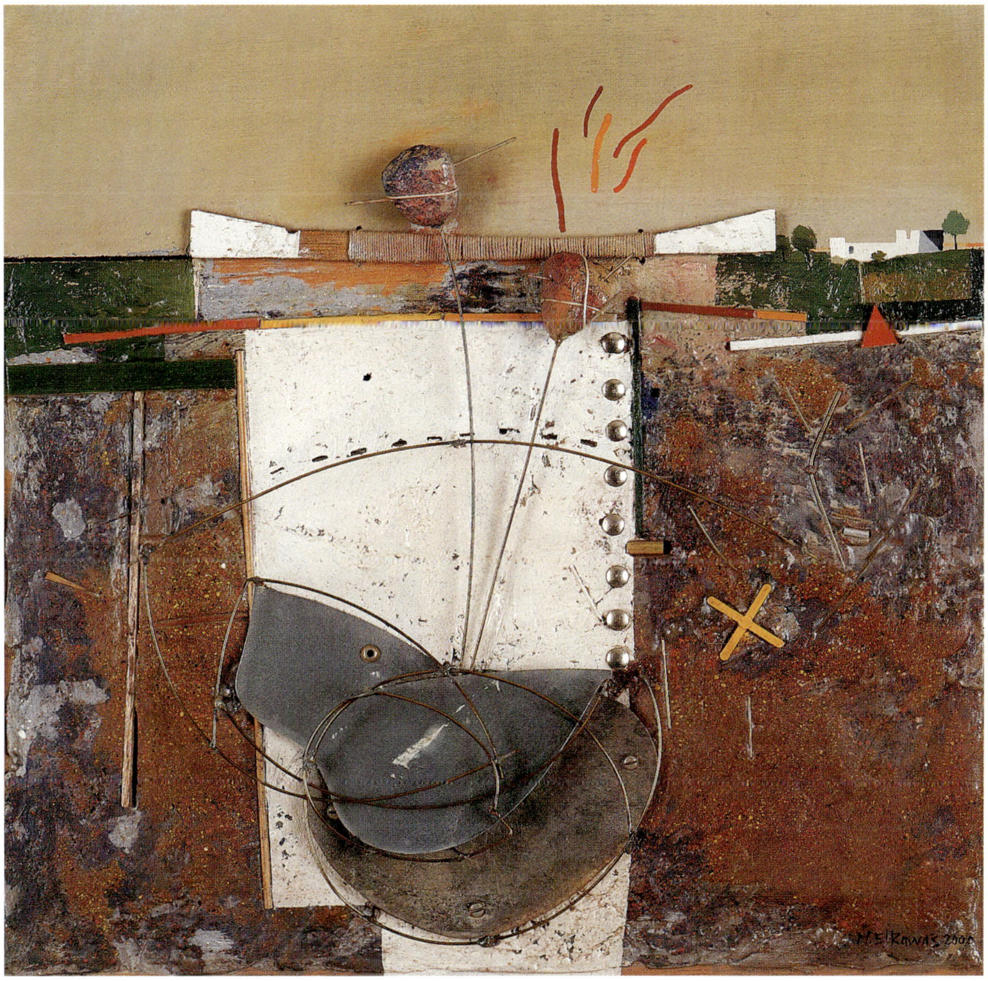

RETROACTIVE POLLINATION, 2000
Mixed media and assemblage on plywood panel
25 x 25 x 3 cm
Collection Ms. N. Andraos

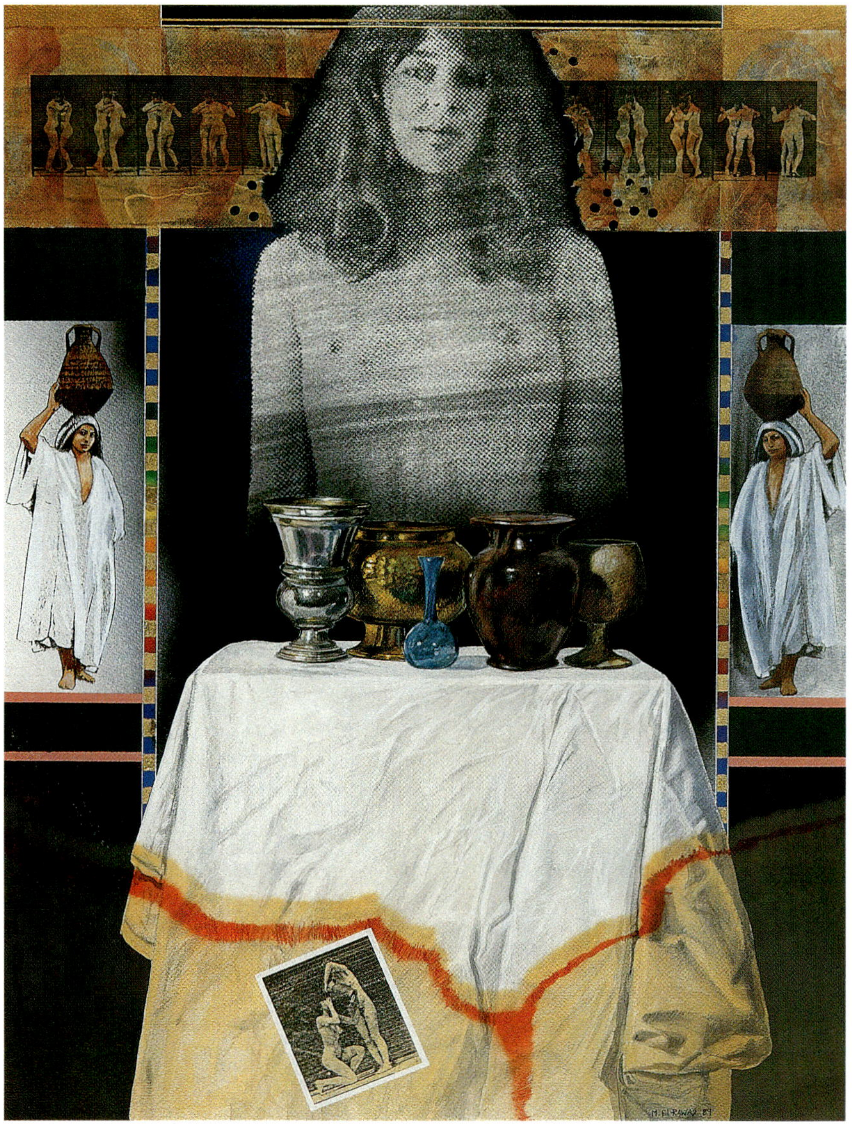

THE OFFERINGS, 1989
Mixed media and transfer on paper
66.5 x 49.5 cm

I mostly work on one painting at a time until I finish it – or rather until I decide to stop working on it, because a painting is never finished. I believe that I have to resolve the problem of one painting before moving on to the next, otherwise I will carry the problem over to the new work. But it is a psychological feeling more than a real fact. I stop when I feel that the work can stand on its own, can survive the way I want it to at that precise moment. At one time I used to rework some of my paintings – and I always feel I could spend my whole life doing just one painting. *The Offerings* (1989/91) and *The Will of God* (1989/91) are two examples of reworked paintings. Nowadays I choose to respect the fact that a painting represents my vision at the time I created it.

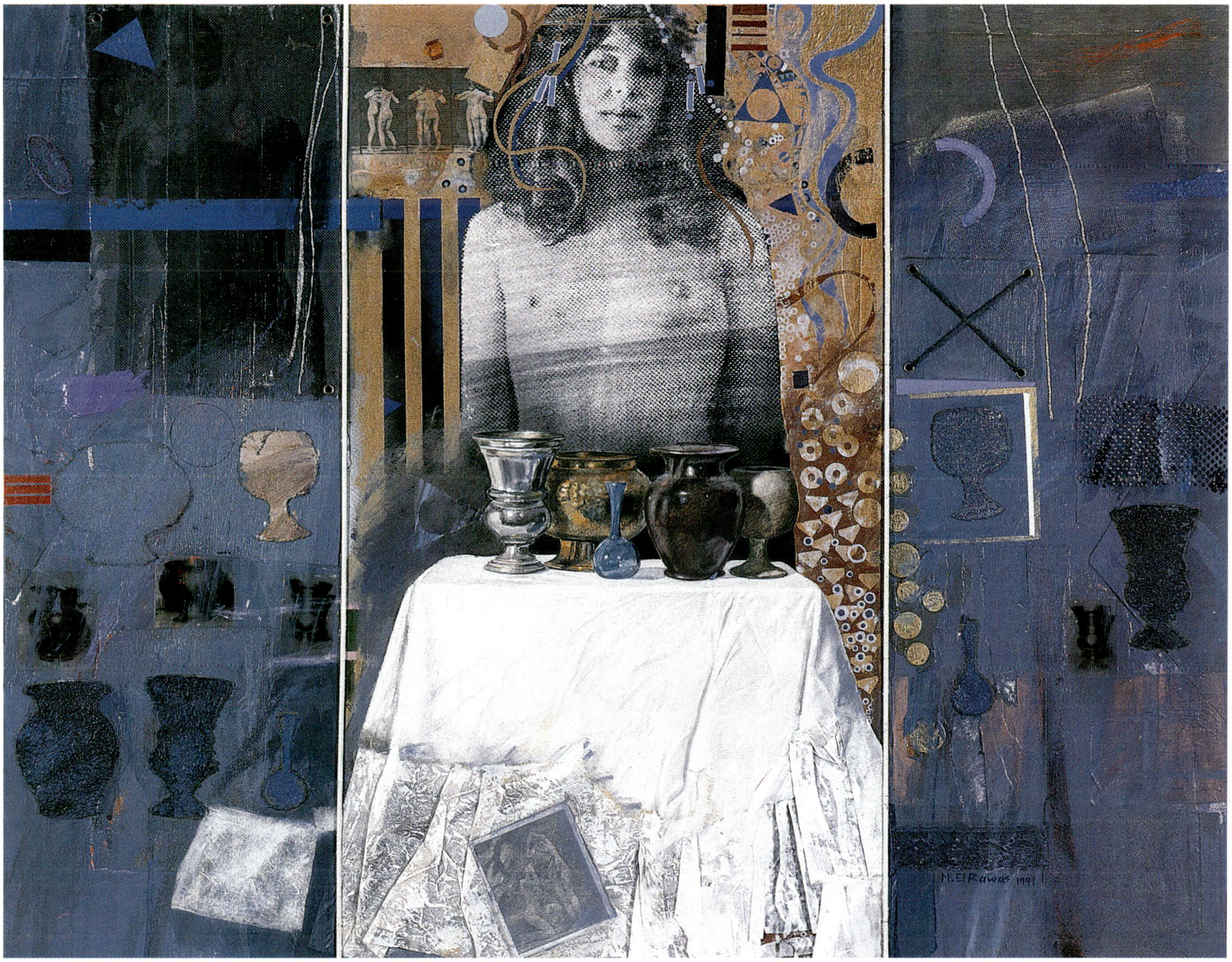

THE OFFERINGS, reworked in 1991
Mixed media, transfer and assemblage on paper mounted on cardboard
66.5 x 90 x 1 cm
Private collection

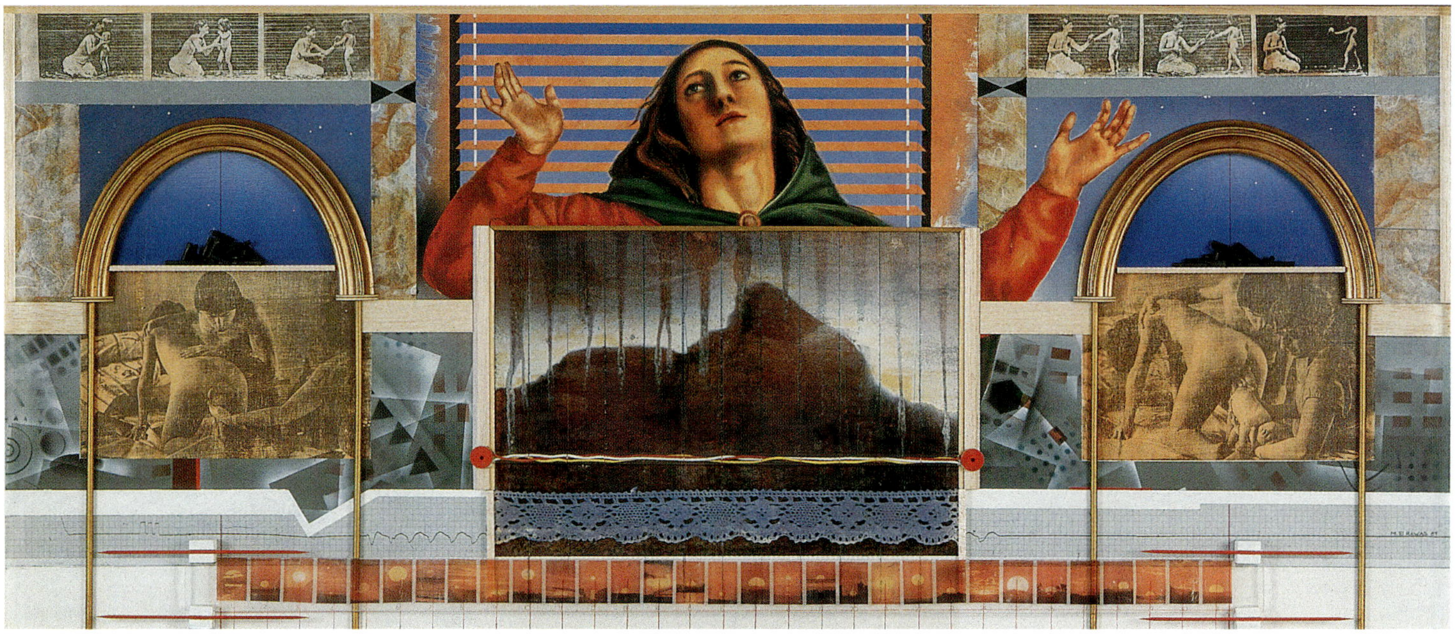

THE WILL OF GOD, 1989
Mixed media and assemblage on plywood panel
66 x 134 x 4 cm

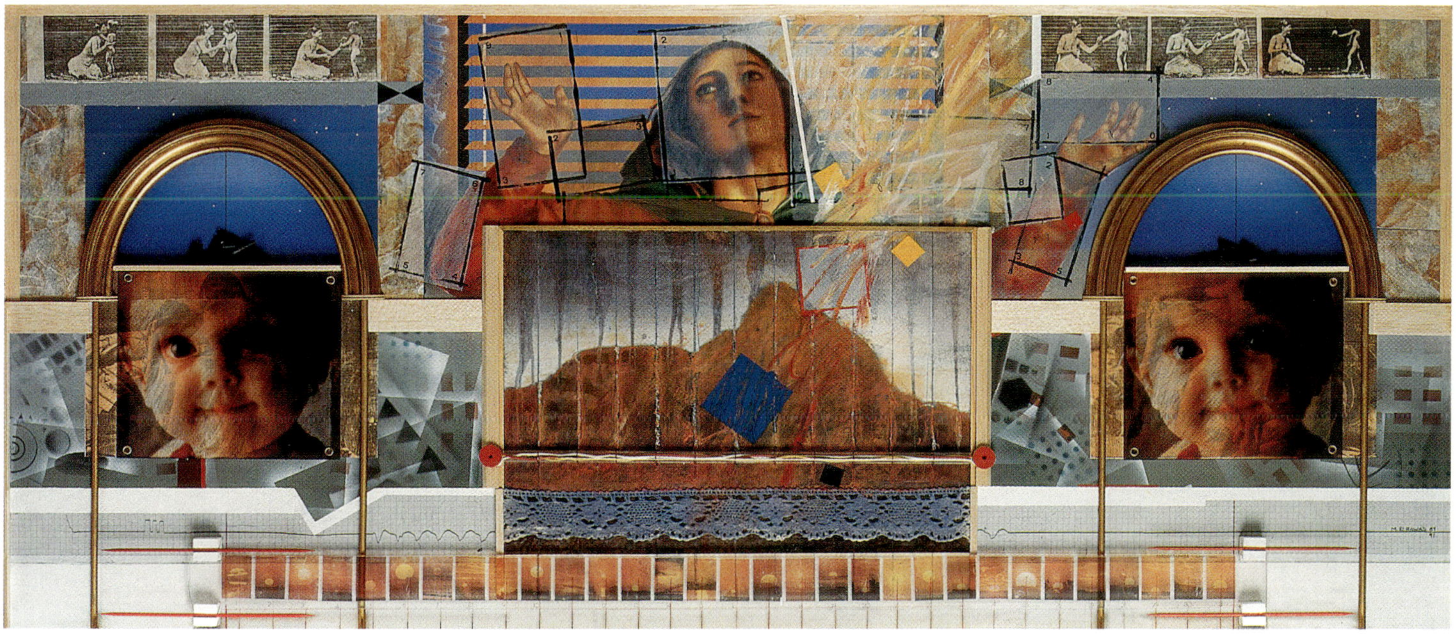

THE WILL OF GOD, reworked 1991
Collection Ms. N. Takla

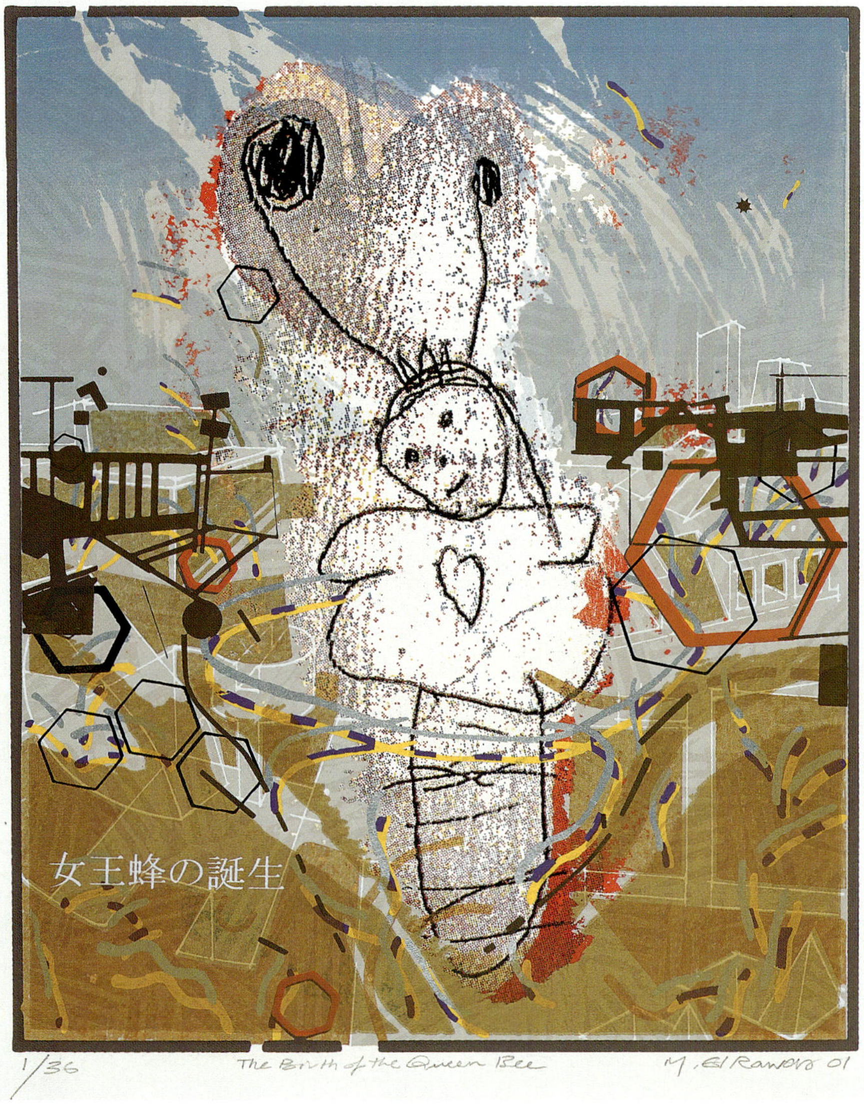

THE BIRTH OF THE QUEEN BEE, 2001
Lithography, relief and silkscreen
20 x 16 cm

Exhibited at the Third Tokyo International Mini Print Triennale, 2002

No precise condition makes me start a new work. Generally it is the interest a certain element arouses in me and that I would like to grasp and use in my work. This element could be merely a color, so in some cases I decide to spread this color over a large area of the painting; or it could be a texture I would like to use. Or it could be a portrait, a certain expression of a figure, so I start the work by painting this figure. It could also be the sensory impact resulting from the proximity of two or more materials placed next to each other: the tension or expression they create, the contrast or dialogue, could be a triggering factor for a painting.

Later the painting just builds up: elements are added based on

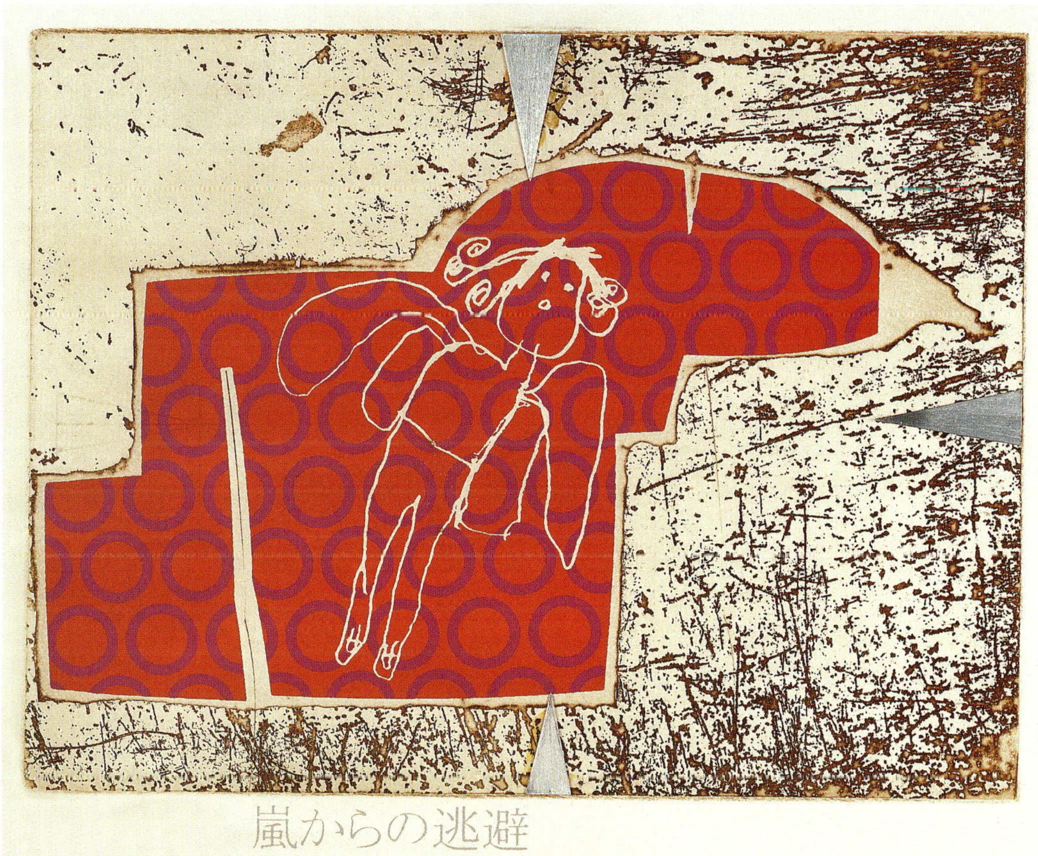

THE SHELTER, 2001
Etching, silkscreen and collage
16.5 x 21.5 cm

ideas, thoughts and visual decisions. When I decide to work with an image, the desire to use this specific element is spontaneous, not planned: it is a spontaneous reaction to that precise element. But when a new element is added, it may or may not be spontaneous. The elements that constitute my paintings may be printed, painted or built in terms of mechanical construction.

When I am faced with what to do next, how to continue, how to add the next element to the previous one, I sometimes get stuck, and it does not always help to reflect intellectually on the problem. The painting might stand for a long time on the easel without my being able to continue. When I have this kind of block, I have to wait for an idea to suddenly strike me, an idea triggered by the mind's ongoing search at the subconscious level. This is no longer cerebral planning. It is, to a certain extent, unguided, uncontrolled – and this is where I discover that chance can play a considerable role in my work. When this 'eureka' happens, I go back to the cerebral planning whereby I compose the visual structure alongside the intellectual and emotional ones.

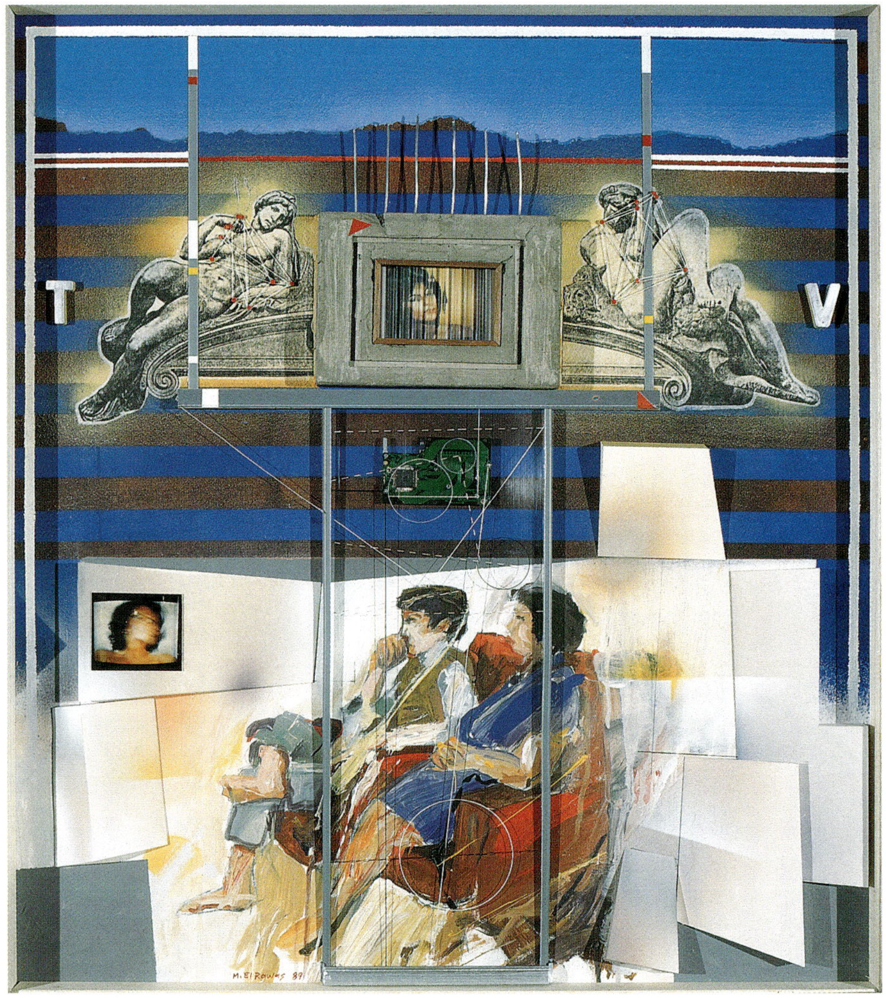

TV, 1989
Mixed media and assemblage on plywood panel
82 x 72 x 5 cm
Collection R. Shhayel

I tend to borrow details from high art, but whenever this occurs the details are always taken out of their original context. Therefore my intention or desire is to create a different context by changing what is expected and juxtaposing things that are not usually seen together. I love to discover a new reading, to open a new context and a different reality with its own personal, internal system of symbols, icons and images, and with a life of its own. This is a kind of recycling process. The list of artists and photographers from whom I have borrowed images, mostly of female figures, is long. The main ones are Michelangelo, Leonardo da Vinci, Guido Reni, Rubens, Ingres, Manet, Balthus, Edward Burne-Jones, Vermeer, Marcel Duchamp, Nadar, Lucian Freud, Karin Szekessy and Eadweard Muybridge. But the artists I have borrowed from most are undoubtedly Peter Blake and, at a later stage, Euan Uglow. A few examples of my use of 'quotations'

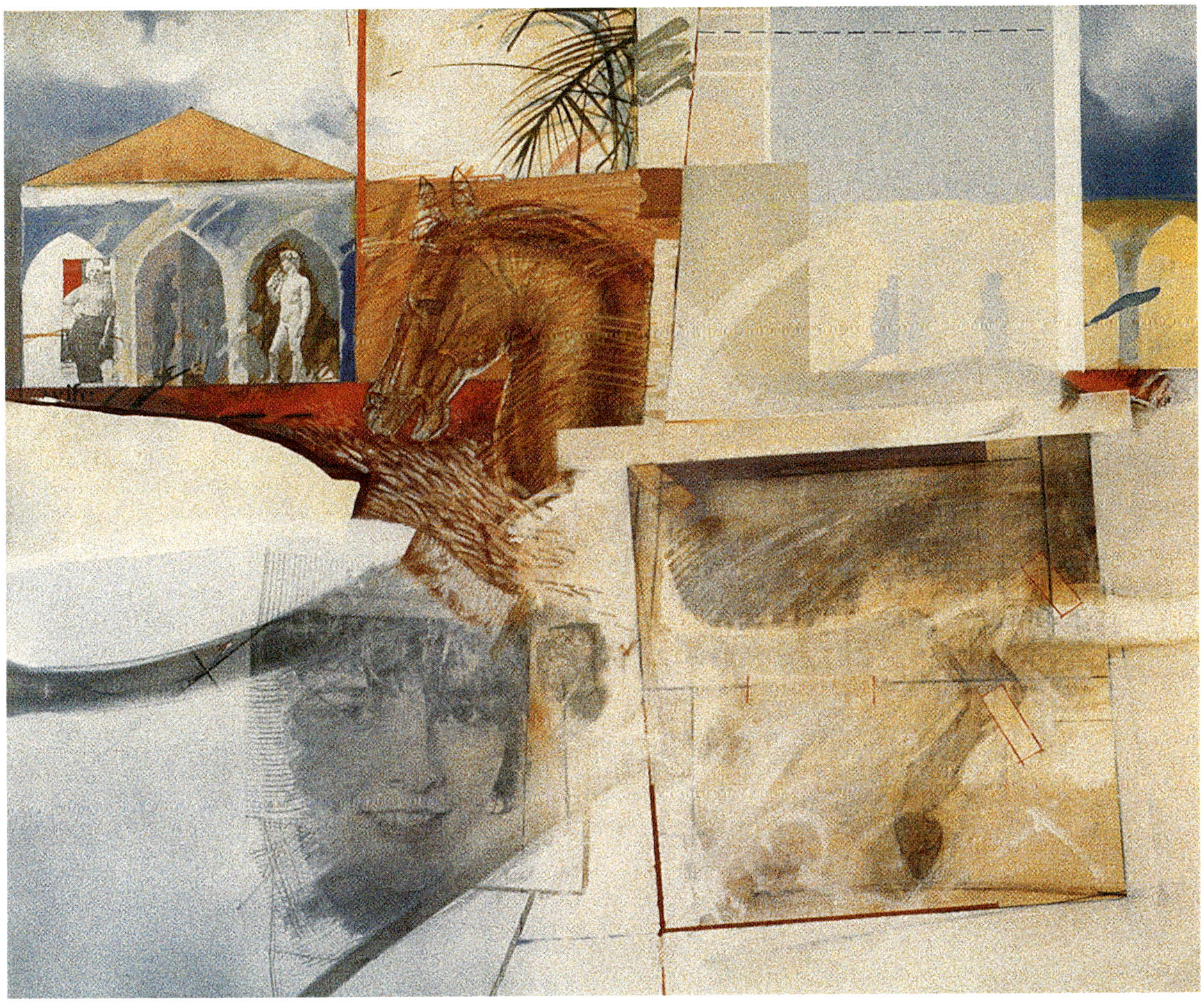

HOPES COMING TRUE, 1985
Oil and transfer on canvas
80 x 96 cm
Private collection

from these and other artists can be found in the following works: Michelangelo in *TV* (1989), da Vinci in *Hope Coming True* (1985), Reni in *The Baby Sitter* (2000) (page 181), Rubens in *Ode to Rubens* (1978), Ingres and Nadar in *Aqua* (1991), Manet and Freud in *Silly Love Song* (2000), Burne-Jones in *When God Created Hunger* (1991), Vermeer in *The House* (1997), Duchamp in *Ode to Marcel Duchamp* (1995), Szekessy in *Husband and Wife* (1995), Blake in *La Bécanicienne* (1997), Uglow in *The Amusement Park* (2000) (page 176), and Muybridge in *The Institution* (2000).

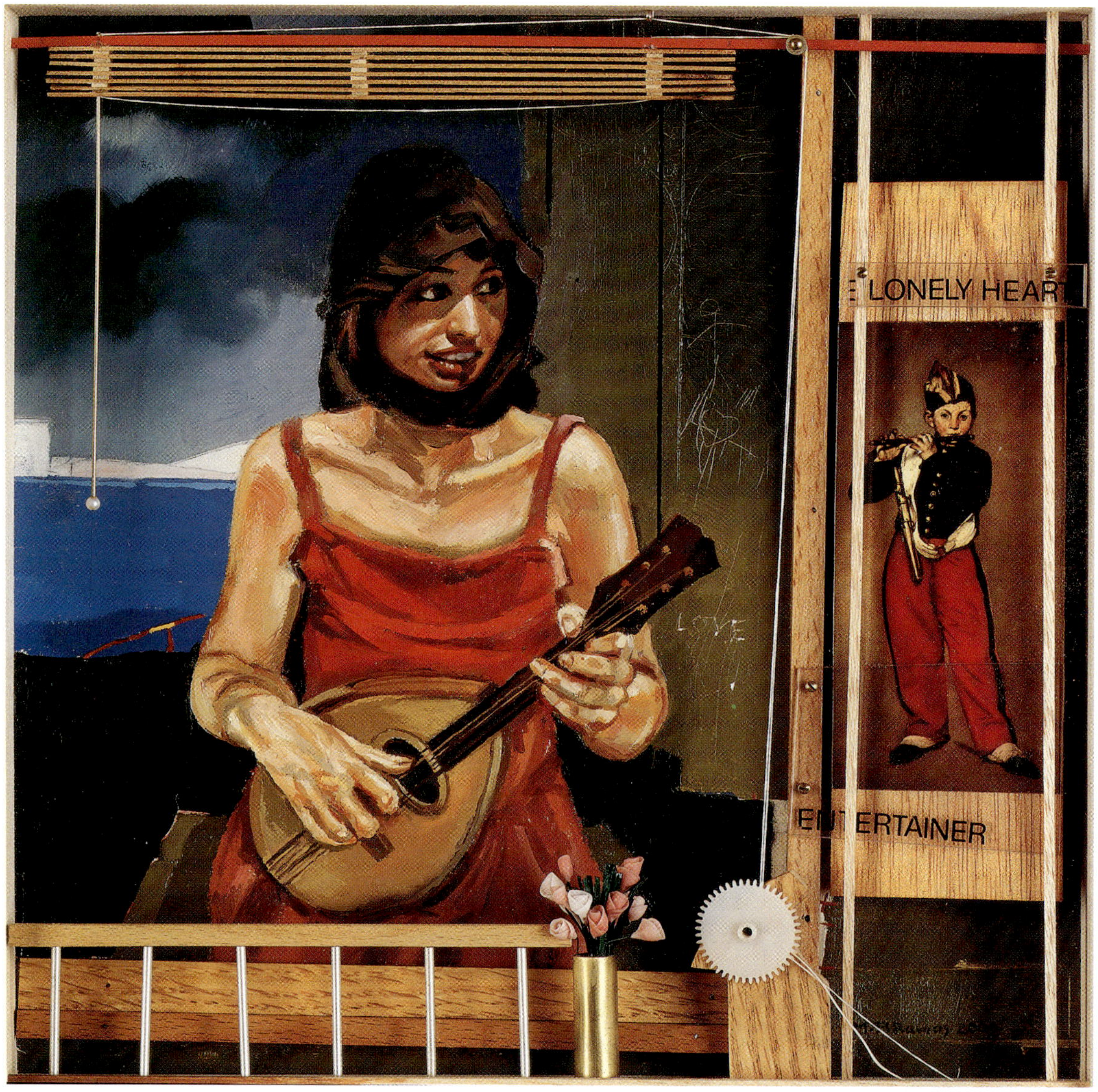

SILLY LOVE SONG, 2000
Mixed media and assemblage on plywood panel
22.5 x 22.5 x 3 cm
Collection Mr. & Mrs. M. Baadarani

Opposite page
WHEN GOD CREATED HUNGER, 1991
Mixed media and assemblage on plywood panel
125 x 125 x 6 cm
Collection H.E. Mr. & Mrs. W. Jumblat

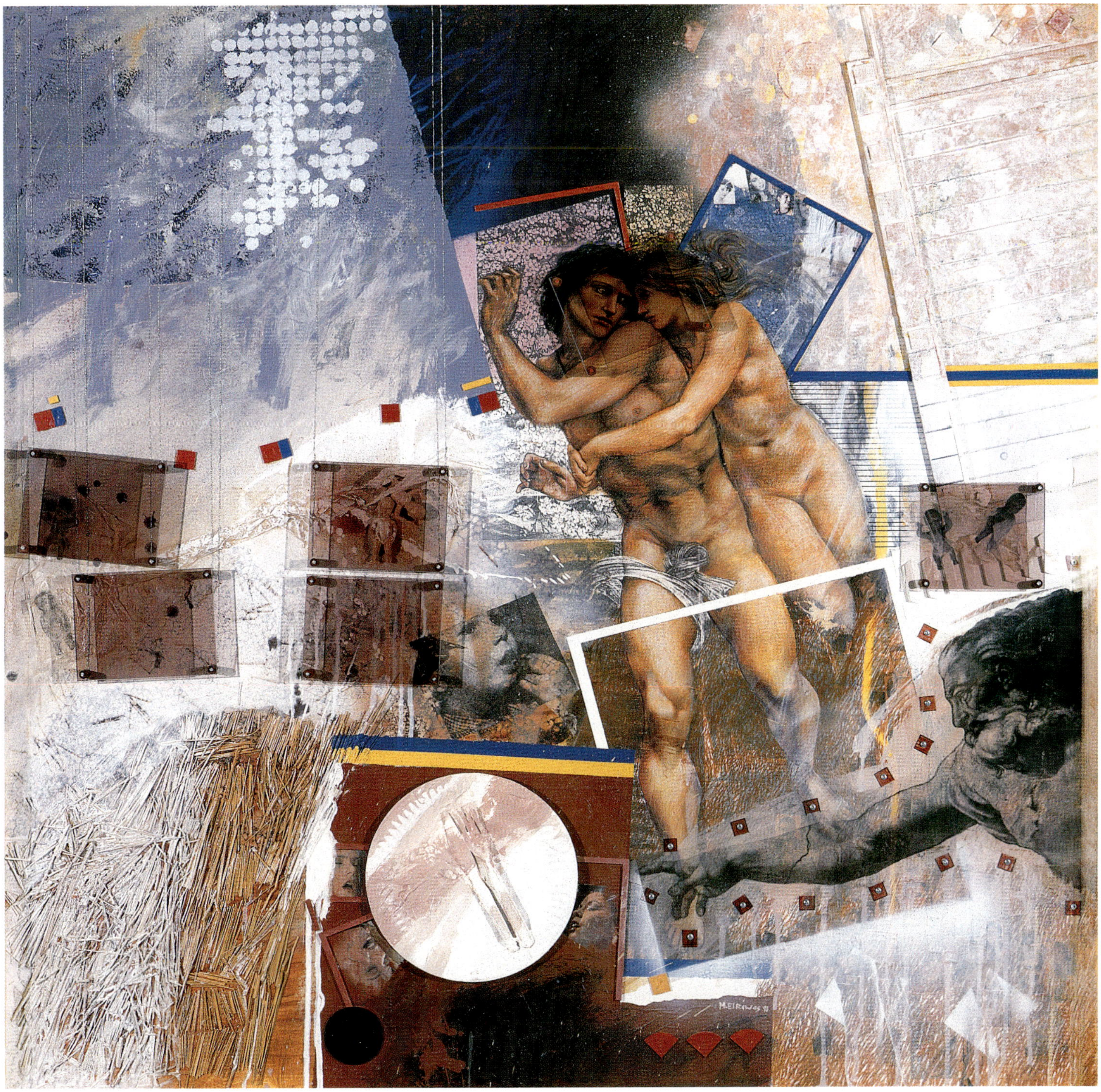

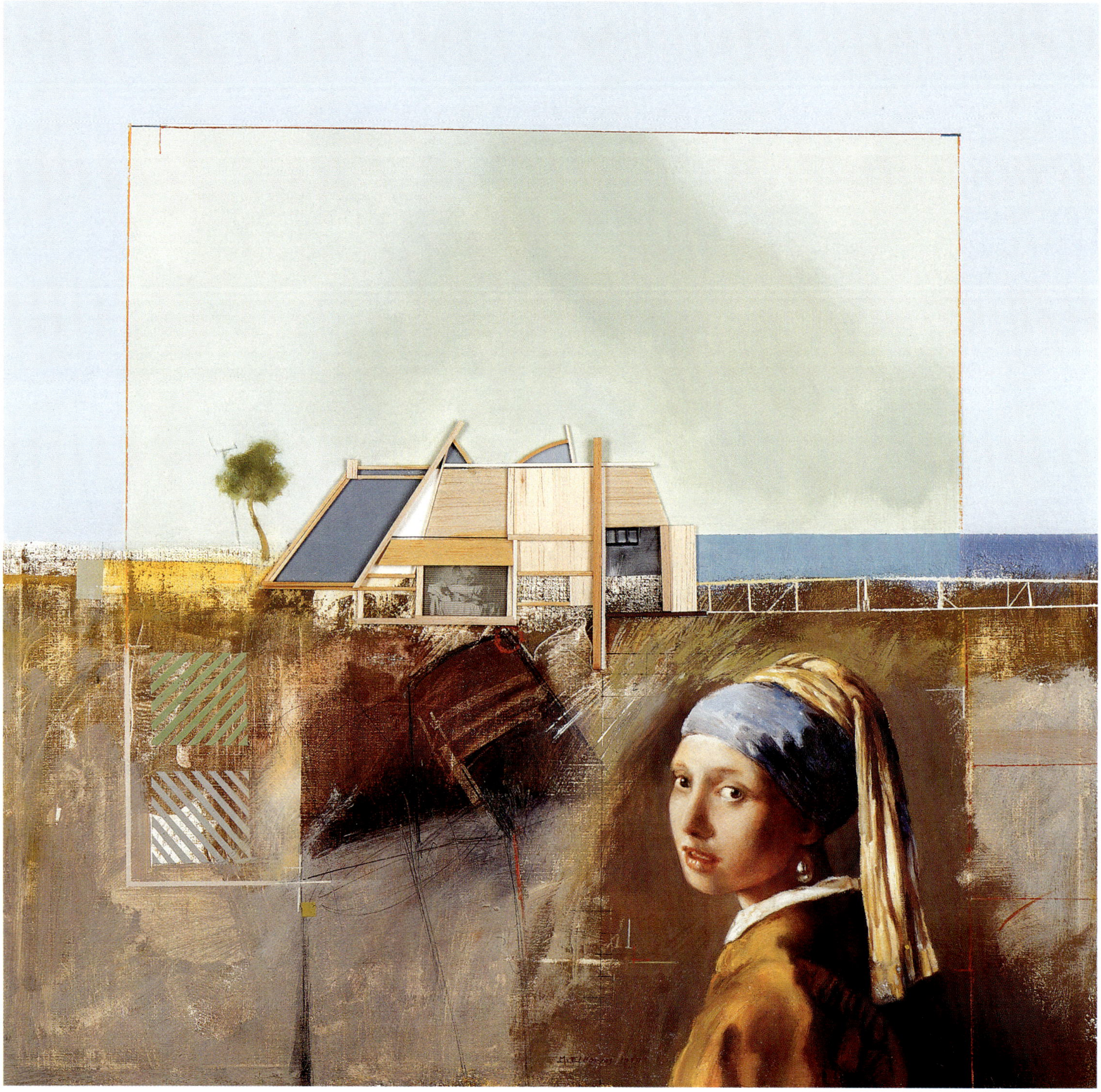

THE HOUSE, 1997
Oil, encaustic and assemblage on plywood panel
65 x 65 x 2 cm
Collection Mr. & Mrs. A. Mneimneh

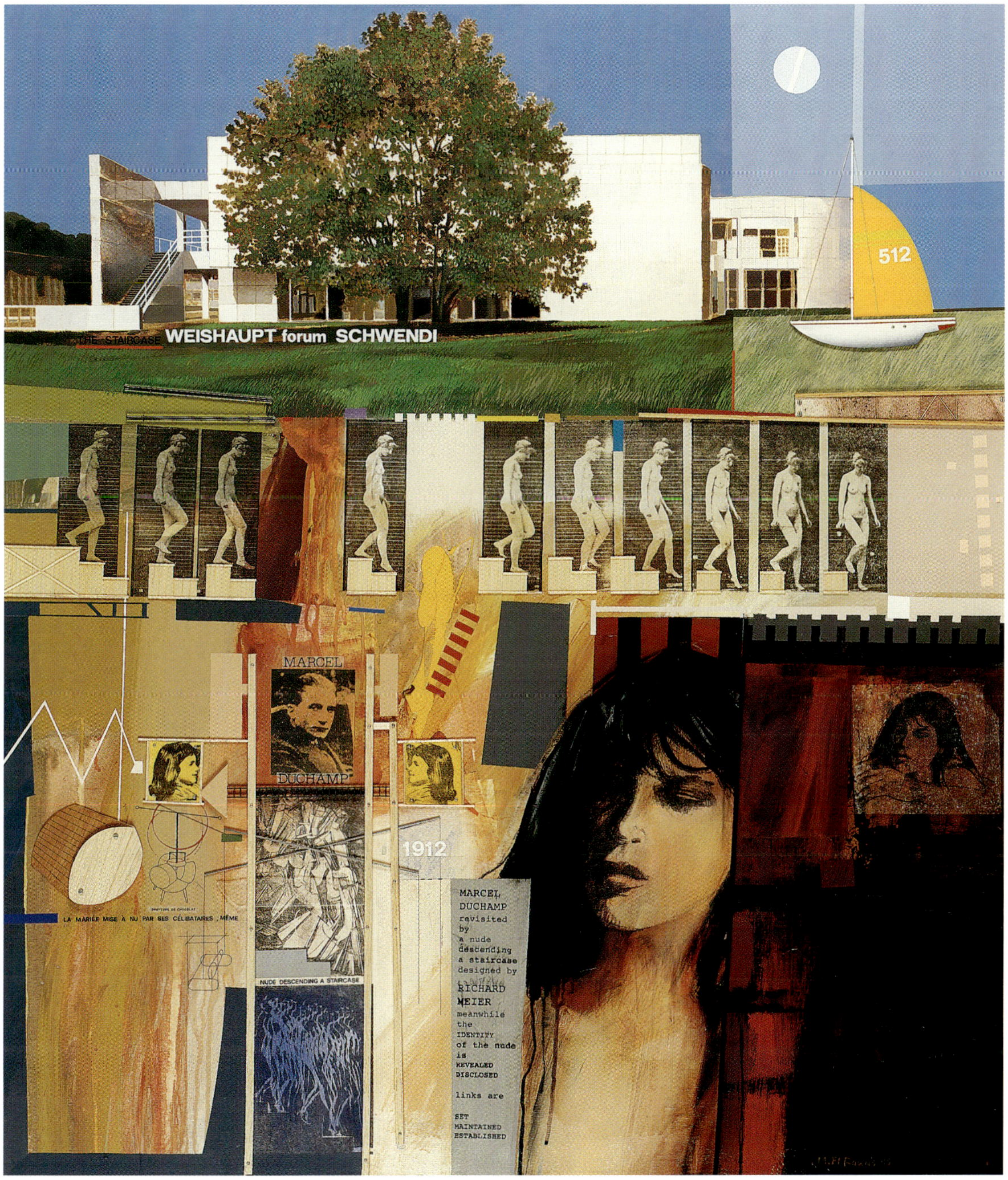

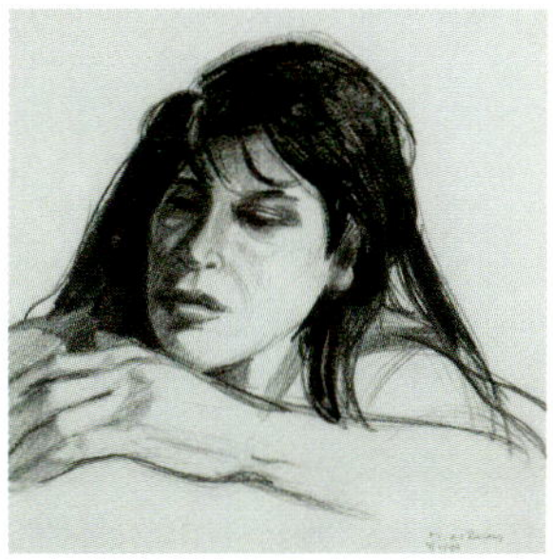

Top left
ODE TO MARCEL DUCHAMP, 1995
Mixed media and assemblage on plywood panel
120 x 102 x 2 cm
Collection Mrs. M. Merhej al-Amin

Top right
HALA, 1995
Charcoal
29 x 29 cm
Artist's collection

The original sketch that was reproduced in ODE TO MARCEL DUCHAMP

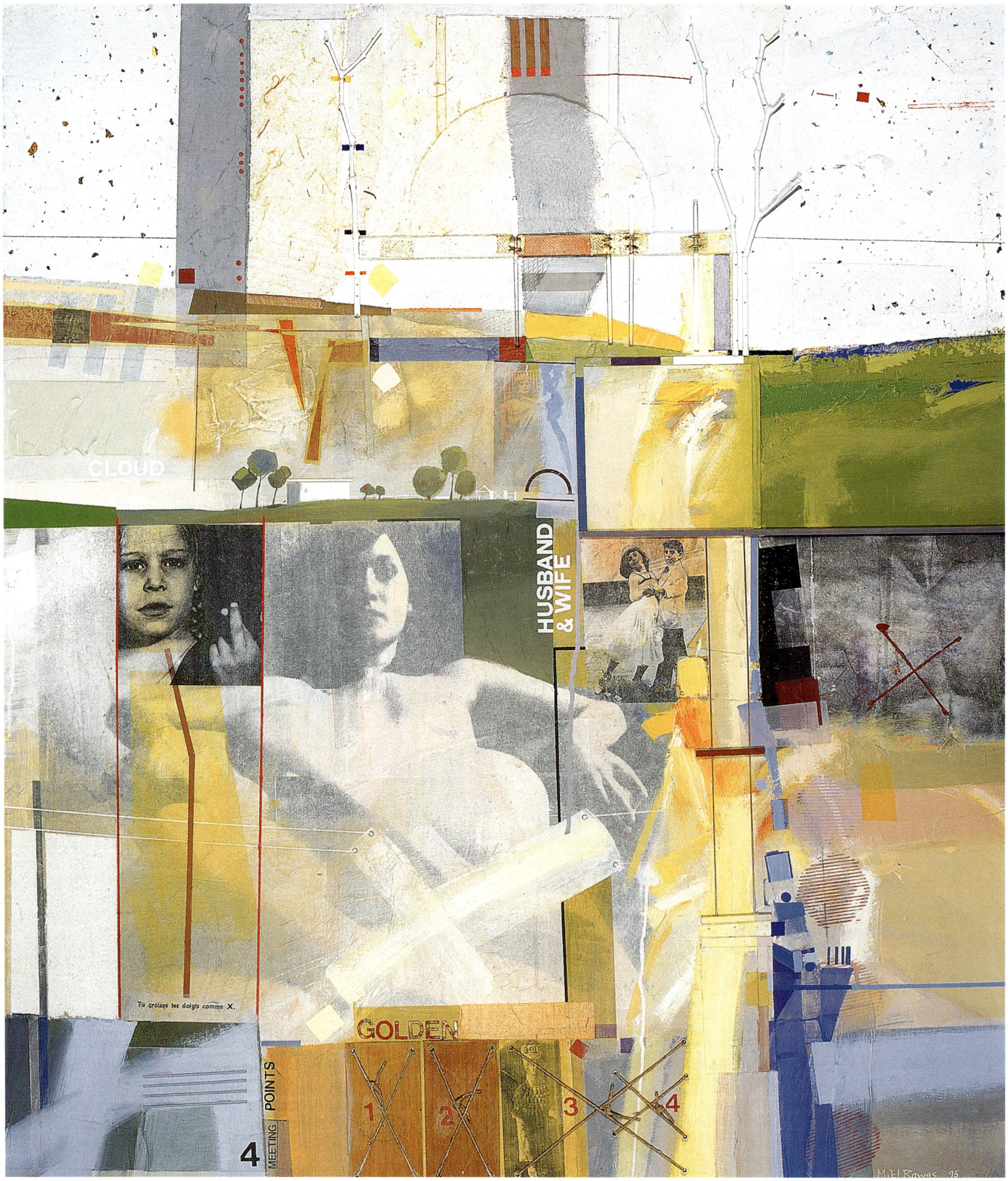
CLOUD
HUSBAND & WIFE
Tu croises tes doigts comme X.
GOLDEN
MEETING POINTS
4
1
2
3
4

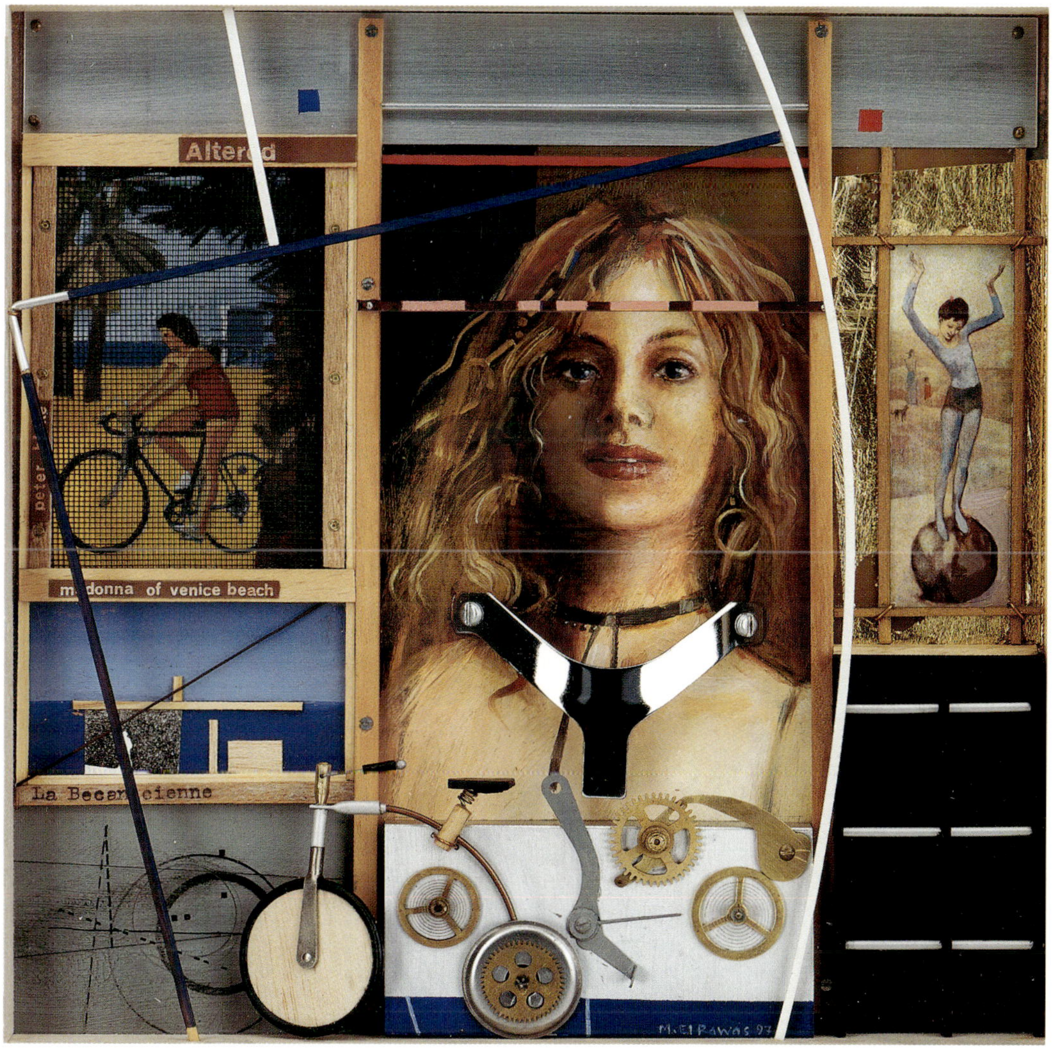

LA BÉCANICIENNE, 1997
Mixed media and assemblage on plywood panel
22 x 22 x 3 cm
Collection Mr. & Mrs. A. Chawraba

Opposite page
HUSBAND AND WIFE, 1995
Mixed media and assemblage on plywood panel
120 x 101 x 1 cm
Collection Mr. & Mrs. S. Bsat

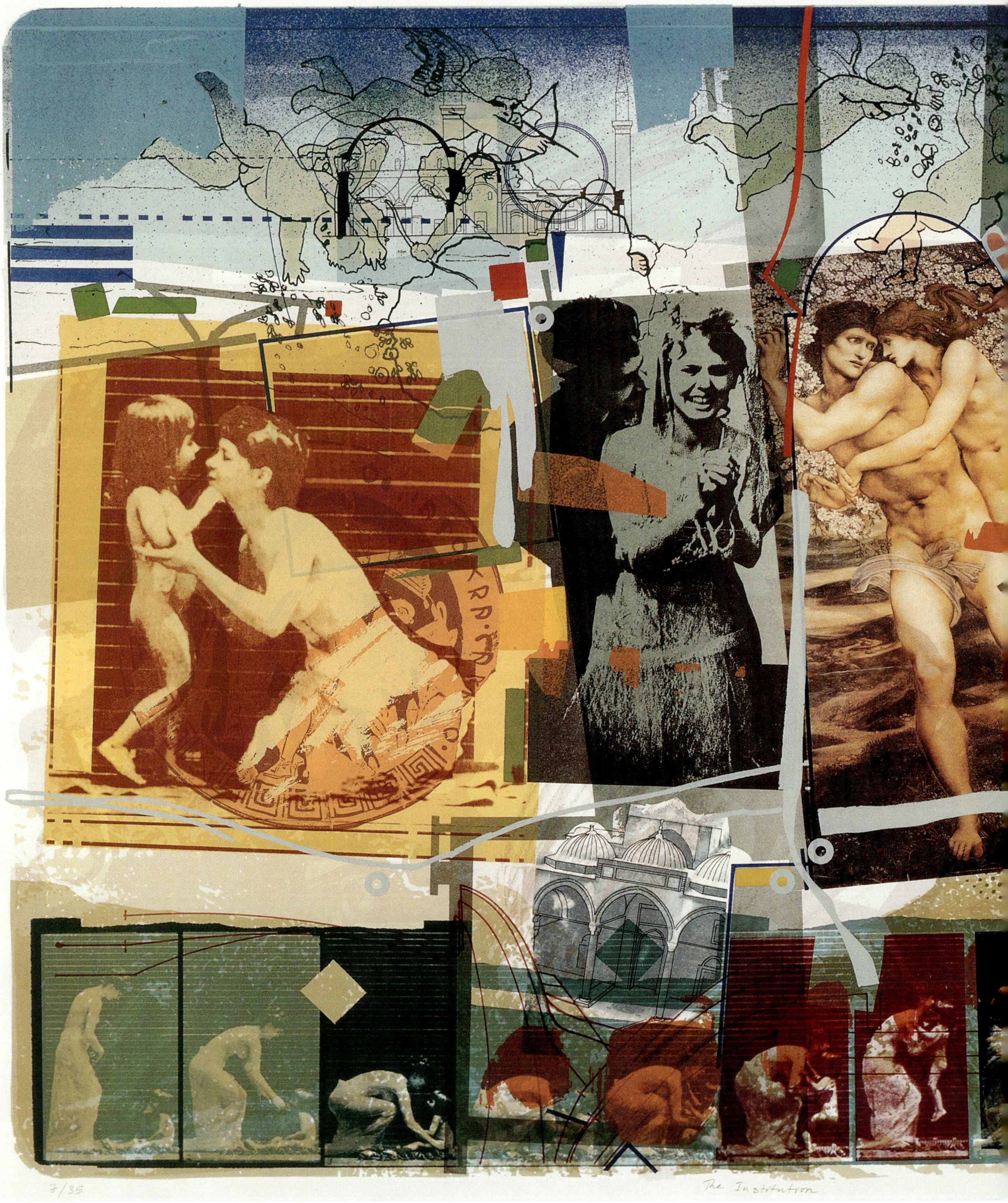
7/35
The Institution

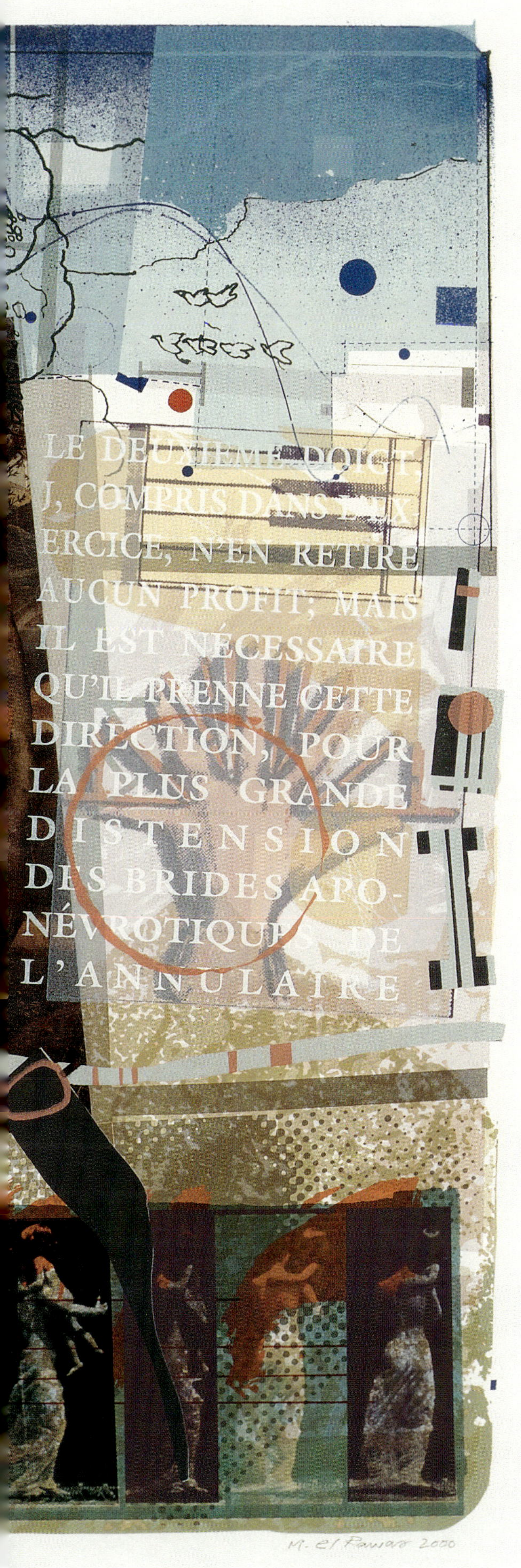

THE INSTITUTION, 2000
Lithography and silkscreen
60 x 74 cm

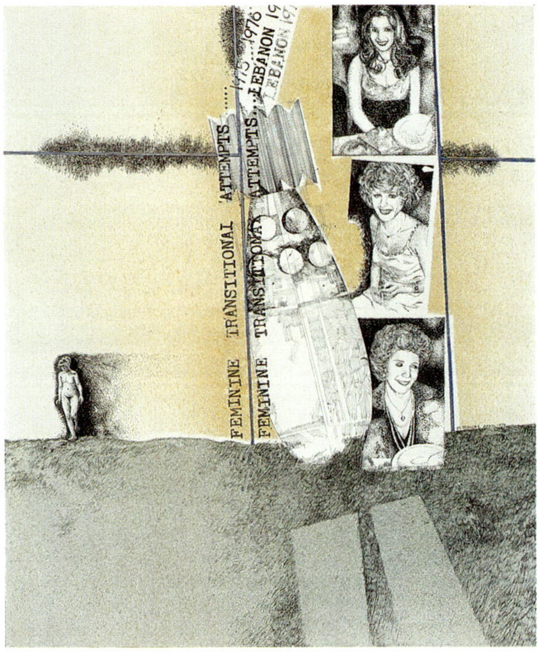

FEMININE TRANSITIONAL ATTEMPTS, 1976
Gouache and china ink on paper
58 x 48 cm
Artist's collection

Eadweard Muybridge's sequential photographs of human figures in motion have always been a great source of inspiration for me. I quoted one of his photos for the first time in 1976 (I refer to this work below), then in several works from 1985 onwards. I came to know Muybridge's work well for the first time when – in the early eighties – I found, by chance, on a dusty shelf in a neglected corner of a Beirut bookshop, an old book: Muybridge's *The Human Figure in Motion* (Dover Publications, New York, 1955). I paid just US $13.50 for this priceless treasure – a book containing around 195 full plates of Muybridge's sequential photographs. Of the many images that I have quoted from this book, the one that fascinated me most was the woman walking downstairs (Plate 121 in the book). I used this – either a single frame or a sequence – in three works: *Feminine Transitional Attempts* (1976 – though at this time, before I acquired the Muybridge book, the image was taken from *Art Without Boundaries* 1950–1970 [op. cit.]), *The Lady Who Descended the Staircase* (1987) (page 217) and *Ode to Marcel Duchamp* (1995) (page 207). I was amazed to realize that the sequence of the nude descending the staircase had inspired several artists: Marcel Duchamp did at least two paintings on this theme (1911 and 1912), while Gerhard Richter painted his own photorealistic-style version of it in 1966. Then, while on a visit to London in 2000, I walked into the England & Co. gallery in Westbourne Grove to discover that the artist Alan Macdonald, whose work I had not previously known, also quoted Muybridge's photographs in some of his pictures, including the nude walking downstairs – in *Three Nudes II* (1999).

My own reasons for finding Muybridge's sequential photographs so interesting have to do with their representation of the idea of 'time', which occupies a central position in the majority of my works. Time fascinates me in being a continuous process of death and rebirth which characterizes the essence of life. With this idea in mind, I have extracted and juxtaposed various symbols and signs to create an amalgam, a hybrid world in which past and present co-exist.

Recycling or borrowing from other artists' work has been practiced by many modern painters. Picasso recycled Velazquez's *Las Meninas* in 1957; Richard Hamilton, by turn, recycled Picasso's *Las Meninas* in 1973; Lucian Freud recycled Antoine Watteau's *Pierrot Content* (c. 1712) in his work *Large Interior* (1981–83); in 1953 Francis Bacon did his own version of Velazquez's *Pope Innocent X*, as well as of Rembrandt's *Slaughtered Ox* in 1946; David Hockney recycled several of Picasso's motifs. Last but not least, I am particularly fascinated by Peter Blake's *The National Gallery*

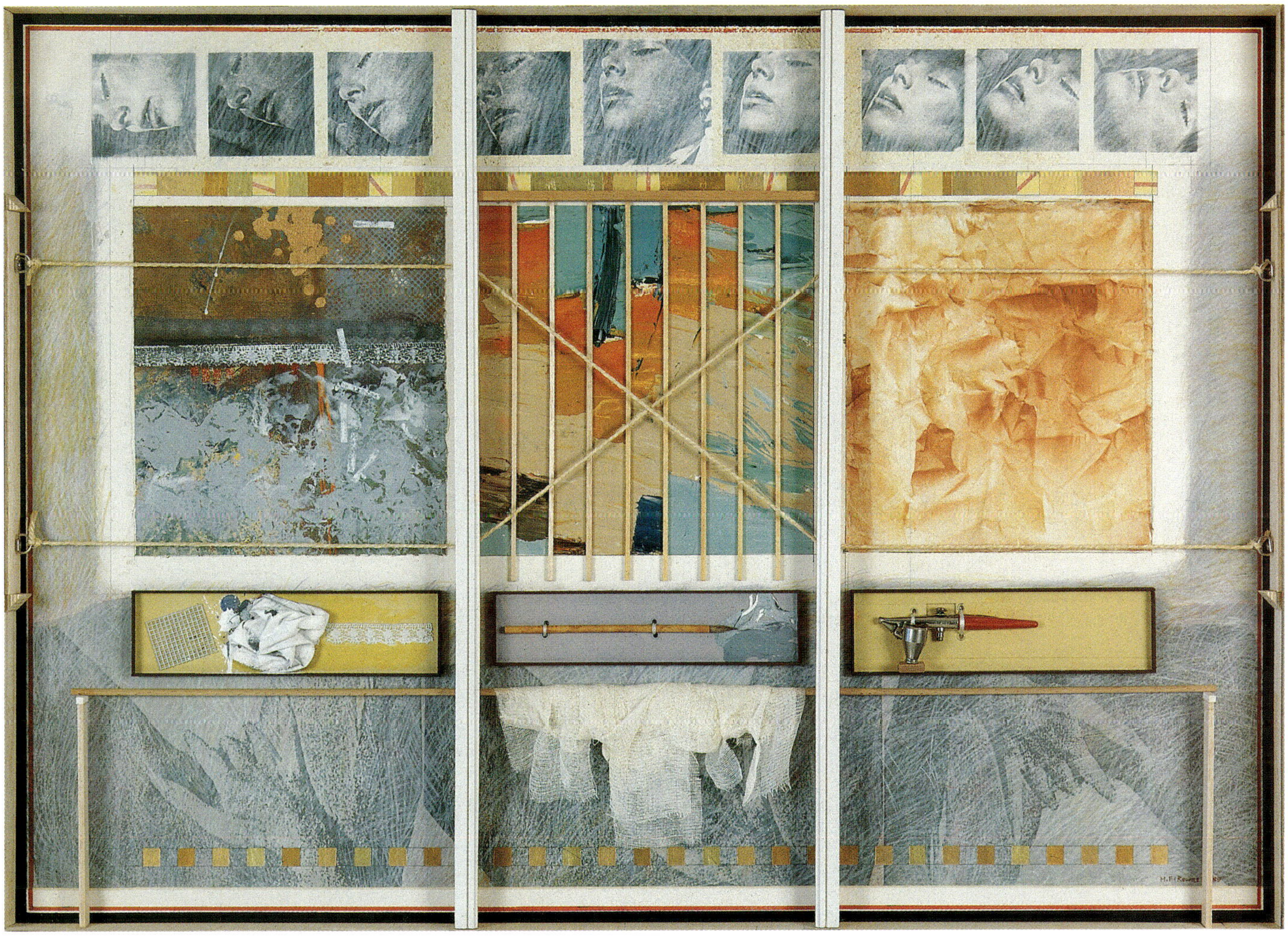

ECSTASY, 1989
Mixed media and assemblage on cardboard
83 x 112 x 6 cm
Collection Mr. & Mrs. J. de Freige

Madonna – 1994–2000, which he based on Bartolomeo Montagna's *The Virgin and Child* (c. 1485–87). As for me, whenever I borrow or repaint an image from another artist's work, I consider it as paying homage to the artist, whether or not it is acknowledged in the title of my painting.

I also love representing the intriguing 'duality' of an object and its image when I have both the object and a picture of it. This has been a topic dealt with previously by many painters and philosophers, such as René Magritte in *The Treachery (or Perfidy) of Images* (1928–29) and Roland Barthes in his book *Camera Lucida* (1980). I particularly hinted at this issue in my work *A Woman on the Shore* (1988) (page 214), where I included real pebbles and their photographed images. Another variation on this same theme appeared in my work *Ecstasy* (1989), where I included, alongside the image I had painted, the actual tools with which I had painted it.

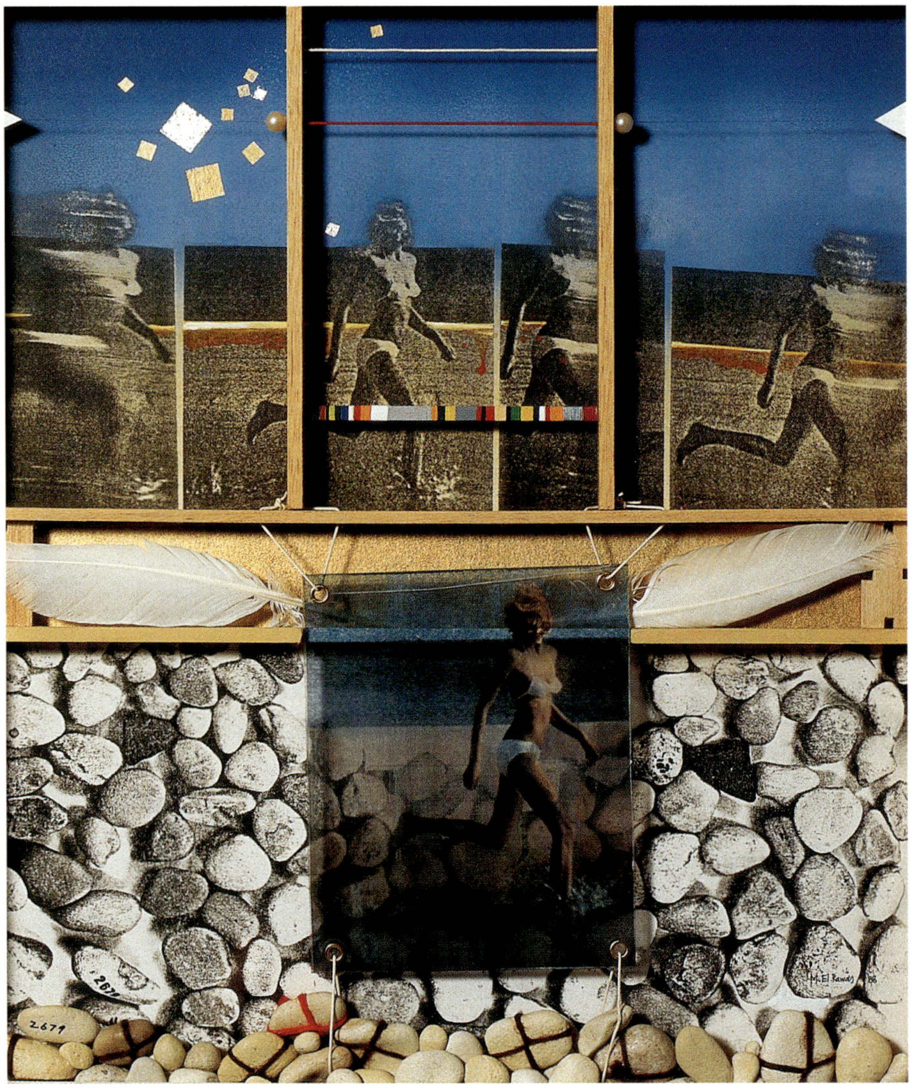

WOMAN ON THE SHORE, 1988
Mixed media and assemblage on plywood panel
48 x 42 x 4 cm
Private collection

Exhibited at the Sursock Museum Salon d'Automne, Beirut, 1988–1989

Opposite page
THE WATER CARRIER, 1990
Mixed media and assemblage on plywood panel
121 x 91 x 5 cm
Collection Ms. N. Sakkaf

In *The Water Carrier* (1990) the main image is 'quoted' from the early British photographer Roger Fenton (1819–69). I was fascinated by his photo of an Egyptian peasant woman with a water jug on her head, taken around 1850. I fell in love with the photo as much as with the woman it depicted.When looking at old photos I am haunted by the possible feelings and thoughts of someone who no longer exists. What was going on in her head when she was looking at the photographer's camera? She had stood for a second in her life to have her photo taken – a photo which she probably never had the chance to see – and her image is registered forever, or as long as the photo will last, after she is no longer there. I find this a fascinating, overwhelming experience. Nowadays we tend to take

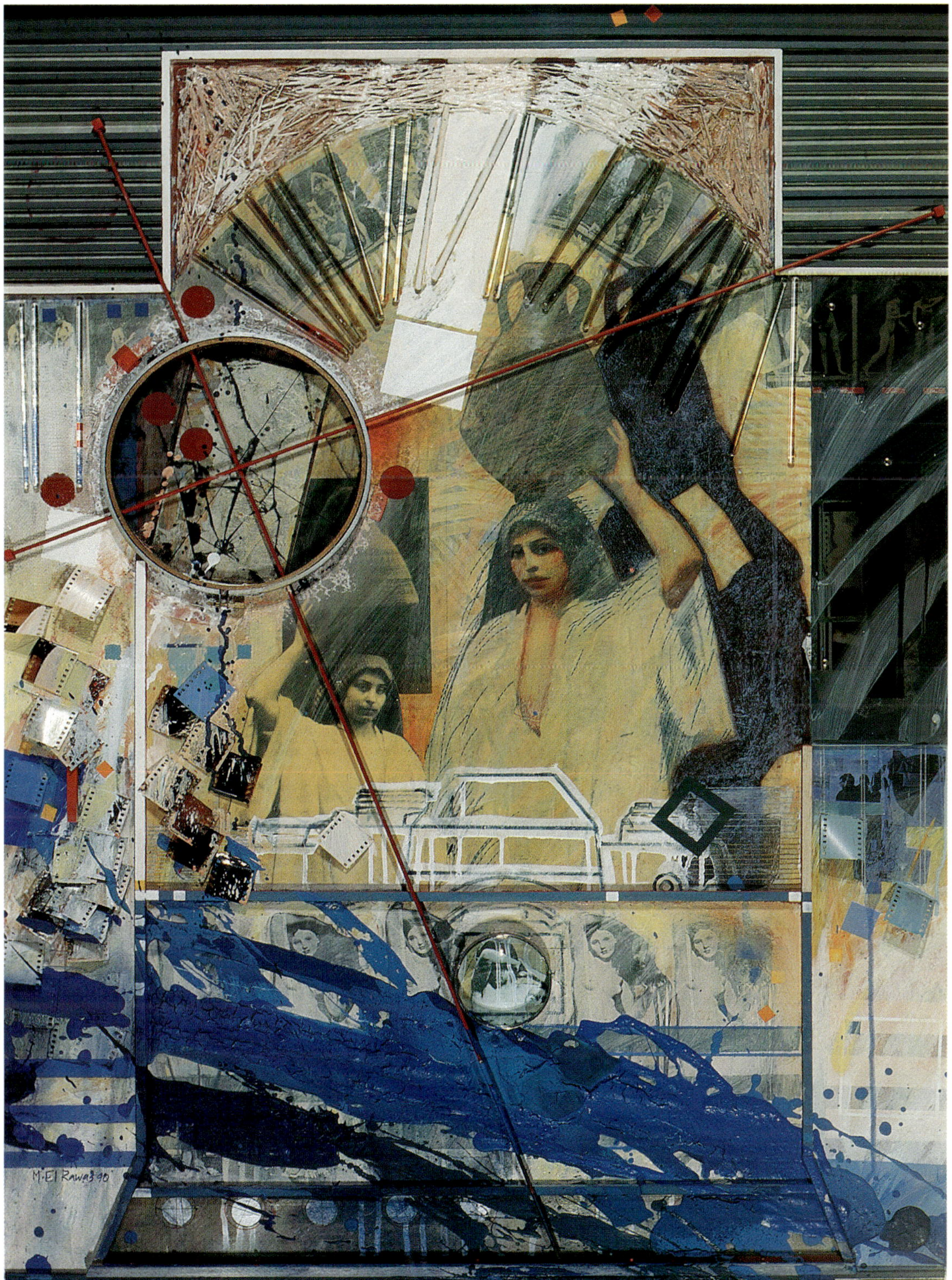
M-El Rawas'90

photography for granted, scarcely considering the huge change in human civilization it introduced by being able to capture reality at a certain moment and freeze it for ever.

I introduced assemblage into my work in 1987 with *The Lady Who Descended the Staircase*, which constituted a major turning point in my art: my first attempt to create a three-dimensional physical space in my paintings. This originated from the need I felt at the time to incorporate into my canvas a paper sculpture I had made of a reclining nude. Assemblage techniques imply raising materials from the level of the flat surface of the painting. Thus the painted and assembled materials further enrich the expressive quality of formal relationships within a work of art. This technique was practiced by artists throughout the thirties and forties, but artists such as Julian Schnabel and Anselm Kiefer are among the many contemporary ones continuing to explore its possibilities. Joseph Cornell, along with Alfonso Ossorio and Robert Rauschenberg, have been major pioneers in the use of assemblage.

The combination of painting and assemblage in a single work is the result of the equal fascination I feel towards both, of my liking the richness and variety of expression they both hold. I find as much joy in rendering in oil paint the subtle nuances of the skin complexion of a nude as in rendering a rough and rugged texture by using encaustic matter (molten beeswax mixed with pigment paint) finished with a vigorous rubbing of oil paint. Such a surface then seems to demand that I take it further and adjoin a three-dimensional structure (meticulously constructed in aluminum, wood and copper wire, for example) by means of soldering, gluing, tying and nailing techniques. I feel like a greedy child who wants it all! What I enjoy most, however, is finding ways to make all these apparently incongruous elements coexist in an interesting state of concord. I believe we need – at all levels – a little bit of everything in order to establish an interesting 'atmosphere of being'. Total harmony and concord bore us as much as a state of total chaos and lack of order perplexes and disturbs us. I strongly agree with the German physiologist Ewald Hering (1834–1918) and with Johannes Itten (1888–1967) in their theories defining the notion of concord and harmony in color. They both proved that true harmony exists in the combining of the unrelated hues yellow, red

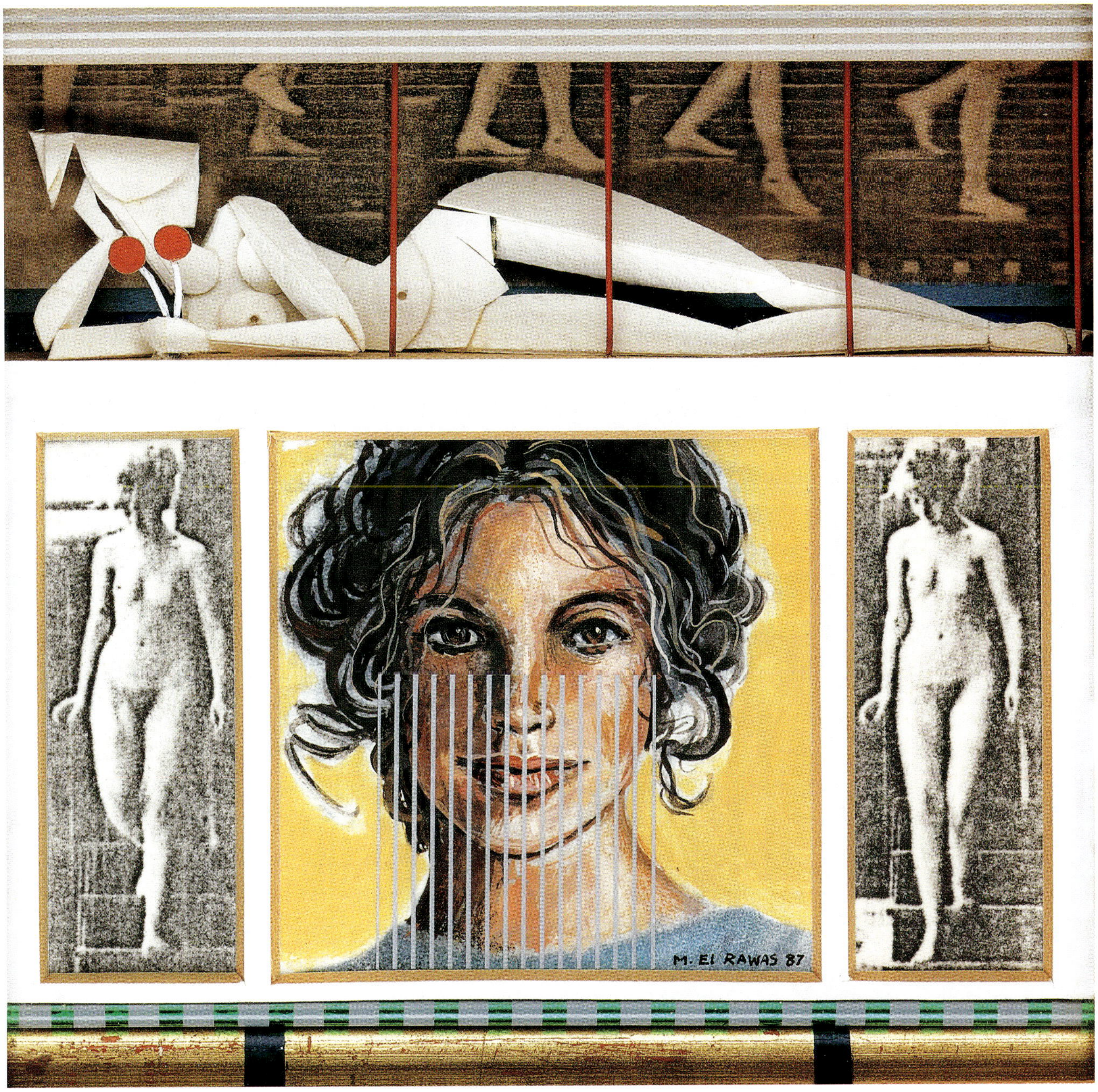

THE LADY WHO DESCENDED THE STAIRCASE, 1987
Mixed media and assemblage on plywood panel
18.5 x 18.5 x 3 cm
Collection Mr. & Mrs. S. Awwad

and blue rather than in bringing together colors of closely similar chromas – such as yellow, yellow-orange and orange – as is generally supposed to be the case.

To give a fairly recent example of my use of mixed media and assemblage, *Narcissism Being Misinterpreted by Marsu* (2002) – my entry for The First Beijing International Art Biennale, China (2003) – is executed in oil, acrylic, wood, aluminum and copper on a plywood panel. It employs figurative, semi-figurative, free brush-stroke and assemblage styles which work together to produce an elaborately textured surface. The combination of the 'real' (the constructions of assembled material) and the painted elements delivers two contrasting esthetic sensations. The painting also juxtaposes symbols, icons and images borrowed from various sources and disciplines, and is a further example of my use of Peter Blake's work: the girl's image is composed from two source paintings by him, the face from *Demolition Squad, Birmingham Drizzle and the Lady Doctor Versus the Nice Girls* (1977) and the body from *Tarzan, Jane, Boy and Cheetah* (1966/75).

In addition to my persistent interest in using a whole range of surface techniques, I continue to use words and written phrases in my work. I have always found it intriguing to combine both cognitive systems of the human brain (the linguistic and the visual), and to set up a play between them. It is amazing how people, when observing a work of art, often feel more comfortable with language than with the purely visual – as if they need the aid of language to understand and hence appreciate the work. As Naum Gabo said:

> More often than not [people] expect a painting to speak to them in terms other than visual, preferably in words, whereas when a painting or a sculpture needs to be supplemented and explained by words it means either that it has not fulfilled its function or that the public is deprived of vision.
> (Quoted in Semir Zeki, *Inner Vision: An Exploration of Art and the Brain*, Oxford University Press, New York, 1999, p. 9. Original source of the quote, Naum Gabo's 1959 lecture 'A Sculptor's View of the Fine Arts', published as *Of Divers Arts: The A. W. Mellon Lectures in the Fine Arts, National Gallery of Art, Washington*, Pantheon Books, Bollingen Foundation, New York.)

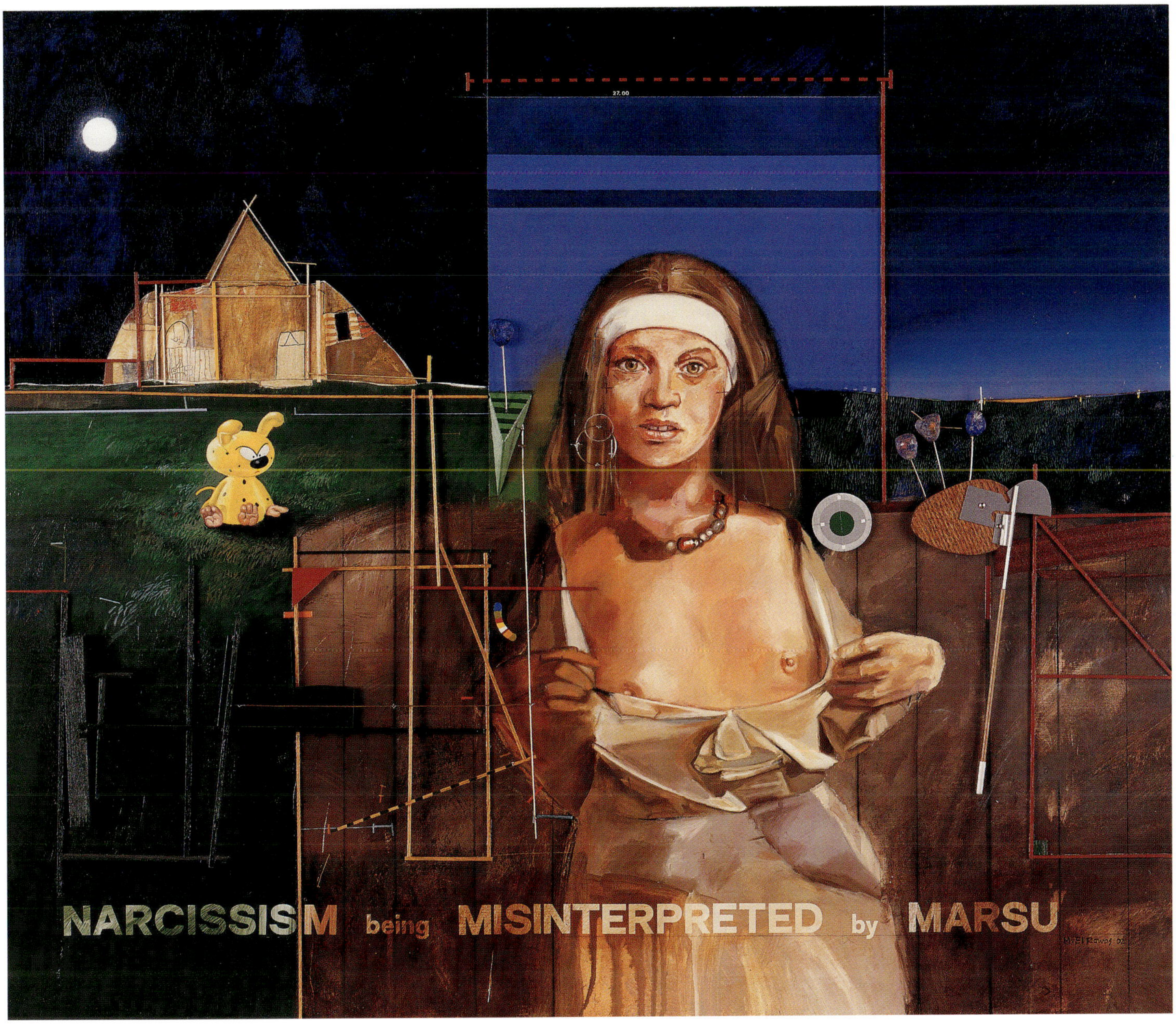

NARCISSISM BEING MISINTERPRETED BY MARSU, 2002
Oil, acrylic and assemblage on plywood panel
68 x 79 x 3 cm
Collection Mrs. M. Merhej al-Amin

Exhibited at the First Beijing International Art Biennale, China, 2003

Semir Zeki draws attention to the 'greater perfection of the visual system, which has evolved over many more millions of years than the linguistic systems.'

> The brain has evolved a quick and highly efficient system of visual recognition. By contrast, language is a relatively recent evolutionary acquisition, and it has yet to catch up with and match the visual system in its capacity to extract essentials so efficiently.
> (Semir Zeki, *Inner Vision*, op. cit., p. 9.)

My own reflections on words and images were expressed in my painting *Art, This is Not a Portrait* (1993–1994), and more elaborately in my lithograph *The Library* (1999) (page 222) into which I incorporated phrases and statements such as the following:

> 'To fix a name to something is the beginning of control over it.'
> 'The erosion of images by words.'
> 'Things for which there are yet to be words.'
> 'Still without language we can signal desire by pointing.'

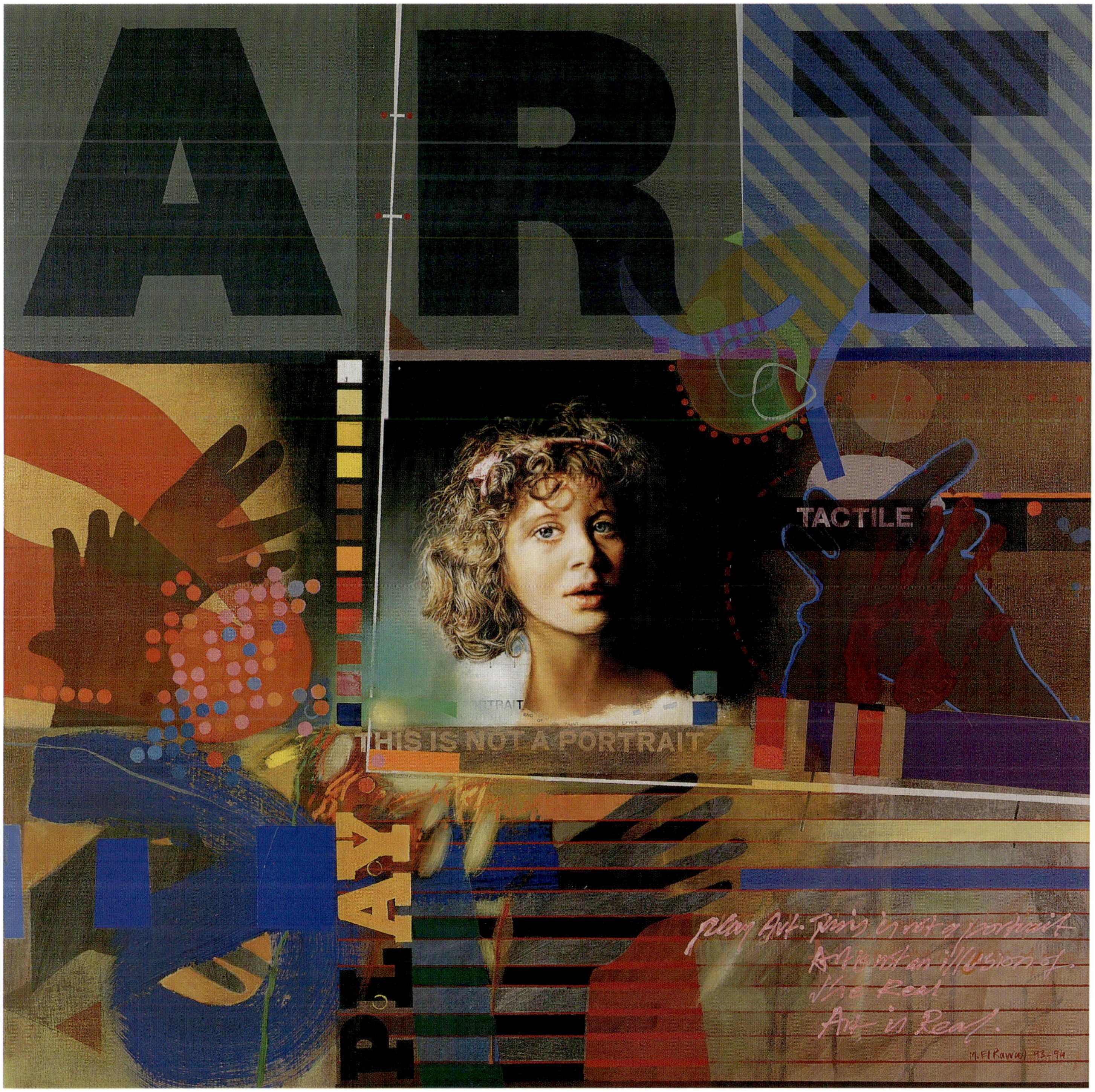

ART, THIS IS NOT A PORTRAIT, 1993–1994
Oil and mixed media on canvas
100 x 100 cm
Collection Ms. N. Halawi

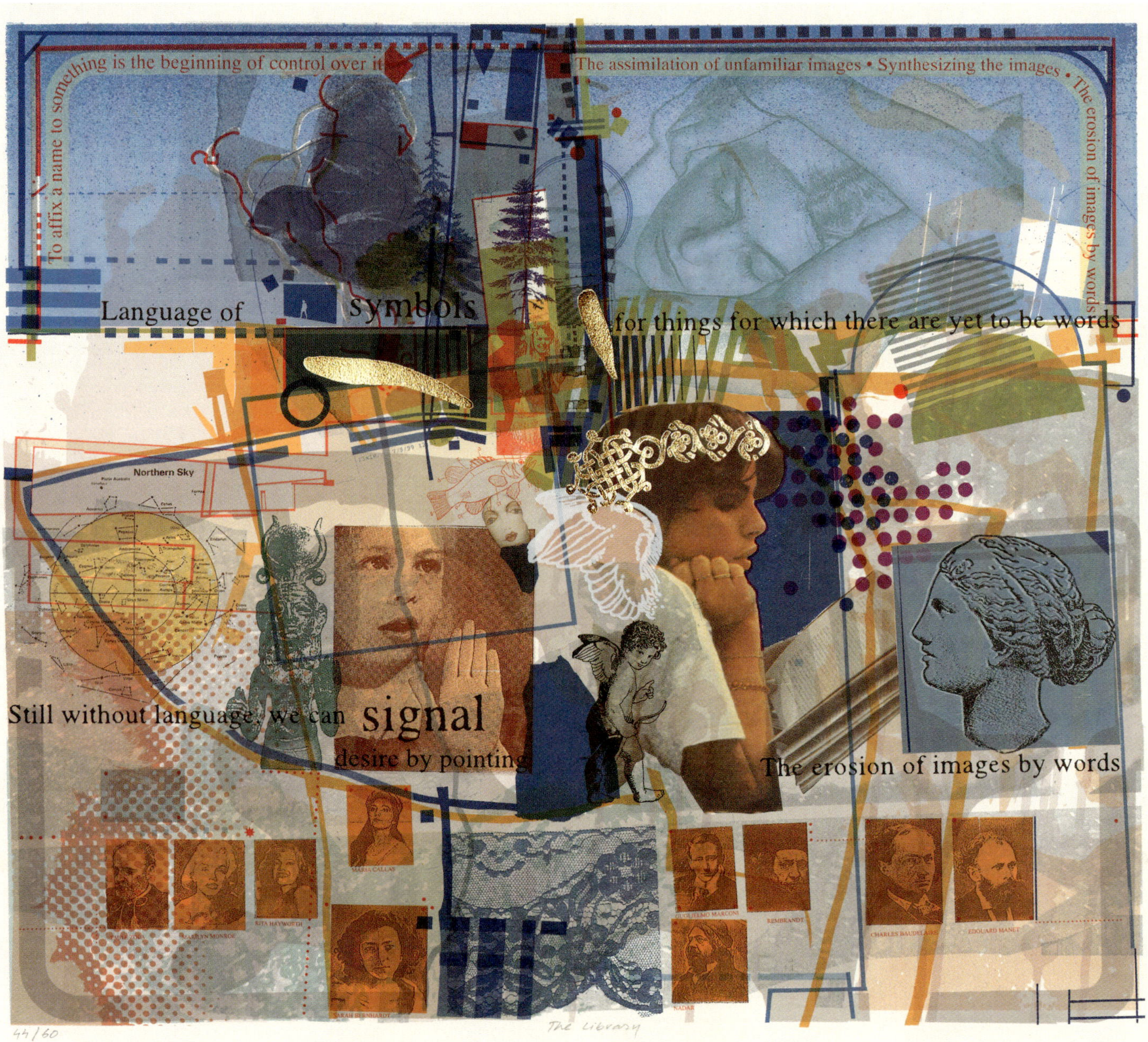

THE LIBRARY, 1999
Lithography and hot press foil
45 x 50 cm

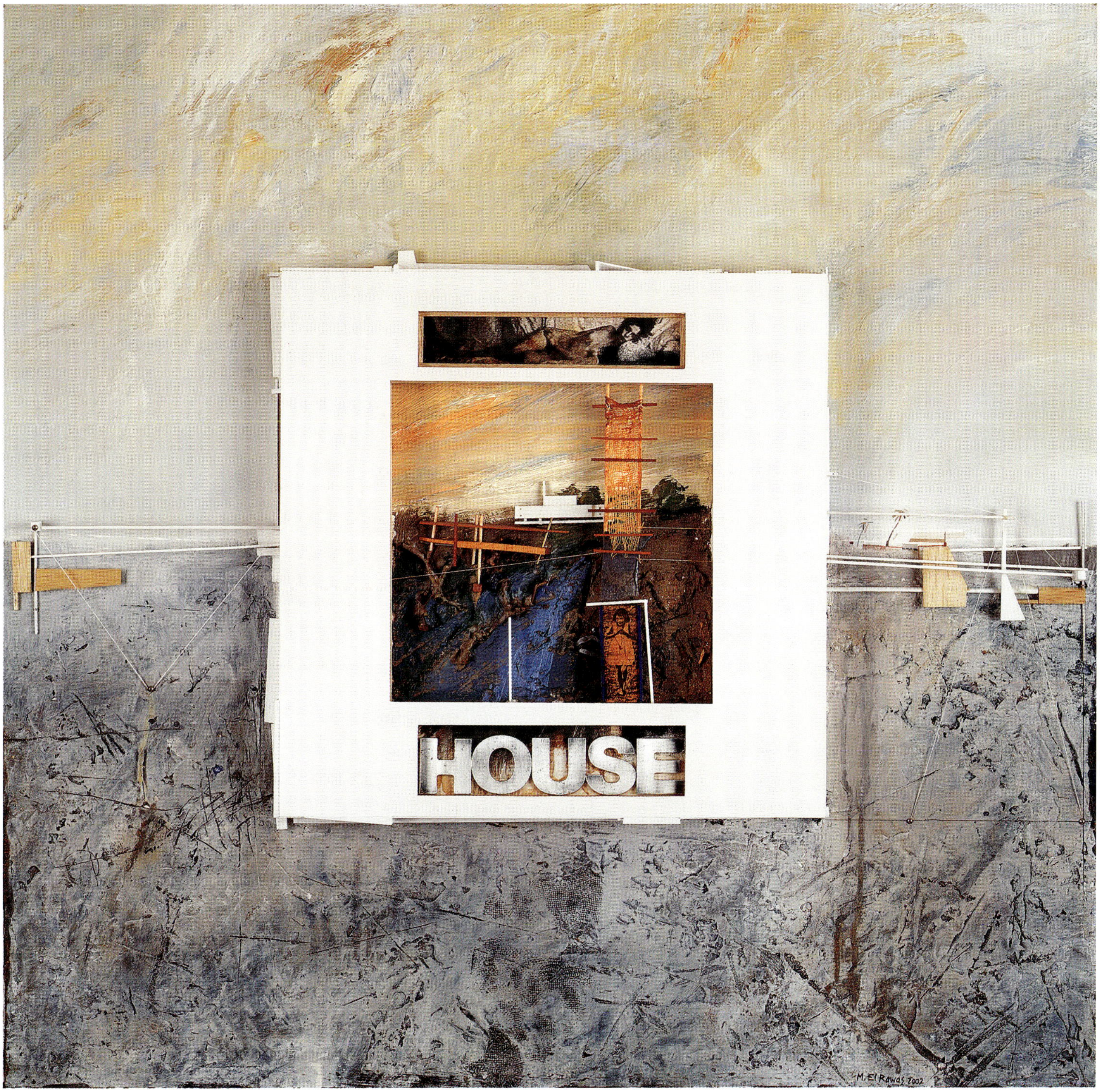

THE OUTFLUX, 2002
Mixed media and assemblage on plywood panel
80 x 80 x 5 cm
Collection Mrs. M. Merhej al-Amin

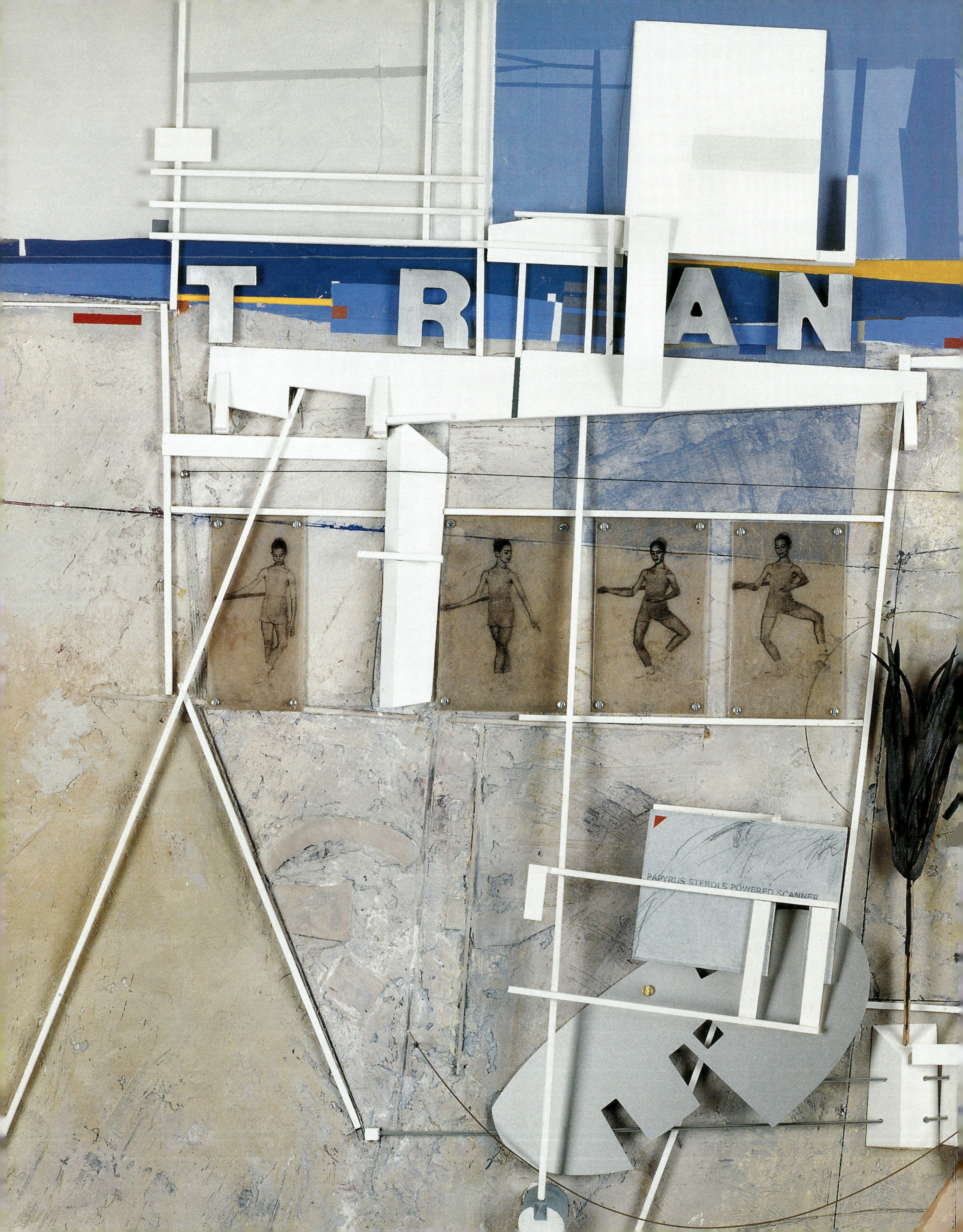
TRAN
PAPYRUS STEROLS POWERED SCANNER

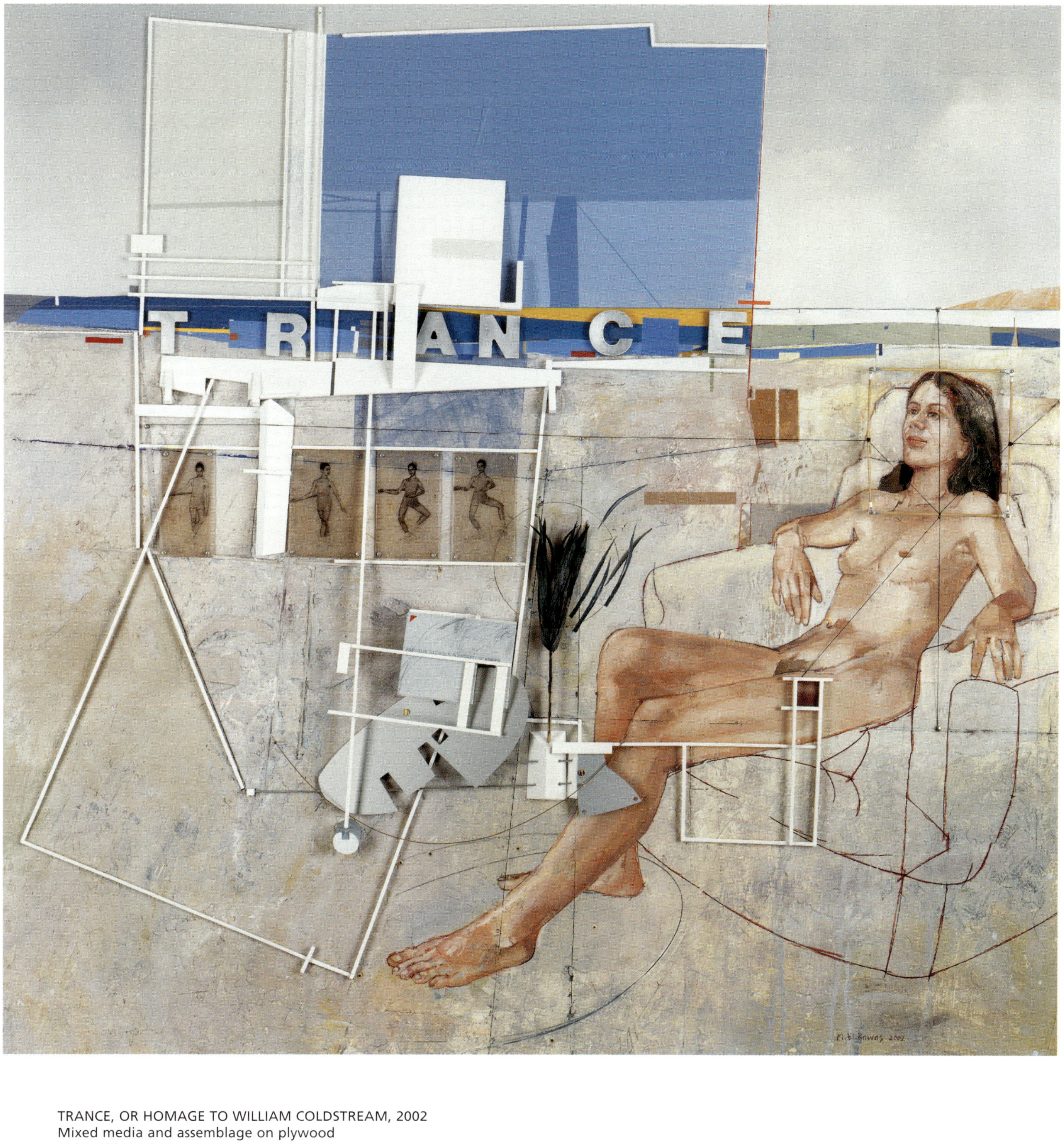

TRANCE, OR HOMAGE TO WILLIAM COLDSTREAM, 2002
Mixed media and assemblage on plywood
100 x 100 x 4.5 cm
Artist's collection

Opposite page
TRANCE, OR HOMAGE TO WILLIAM COLDSTREAM, 2002 (detail)

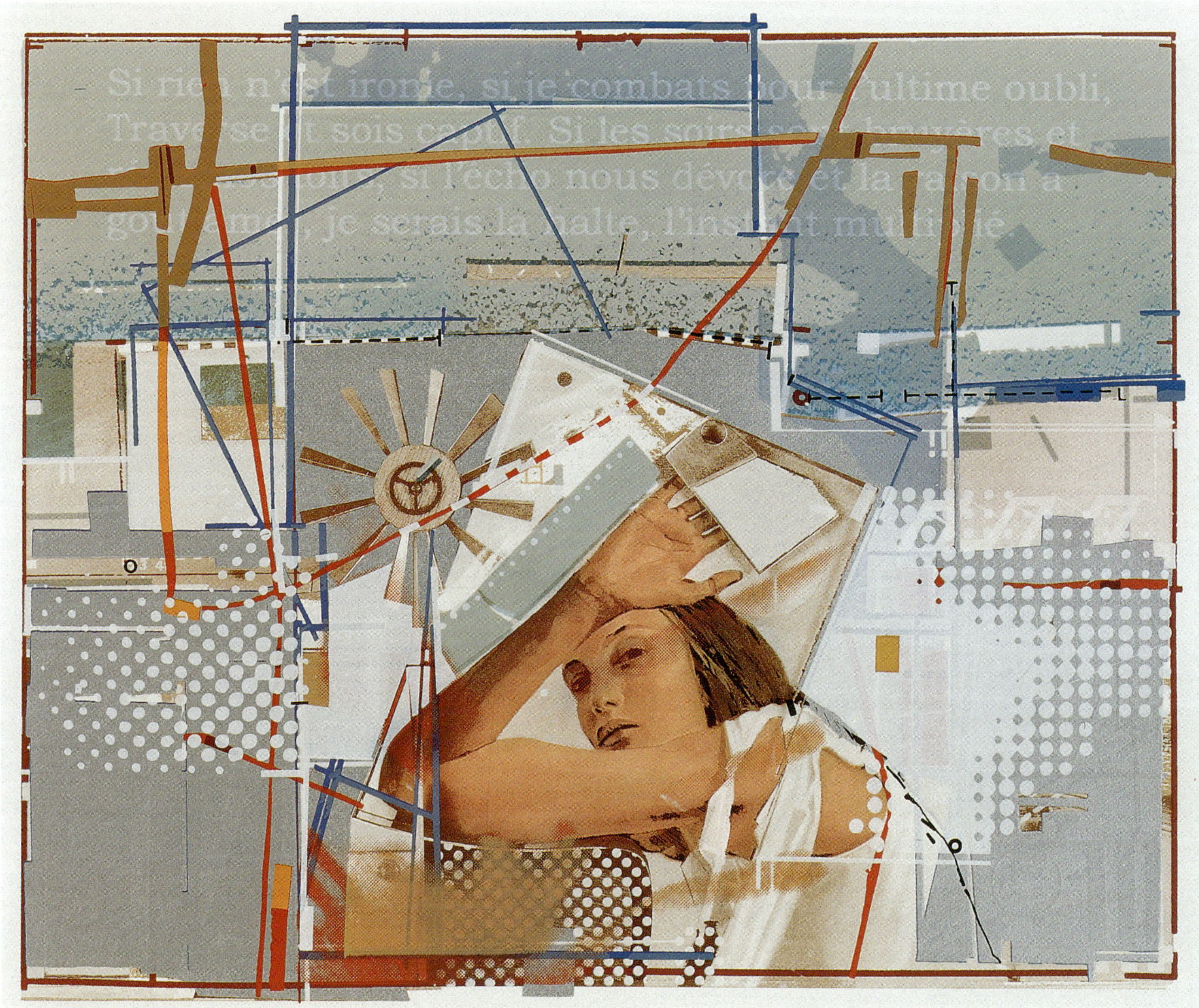

LIMITS, 2003
Lithography and silkscreen
23.5 x 27.5 cm

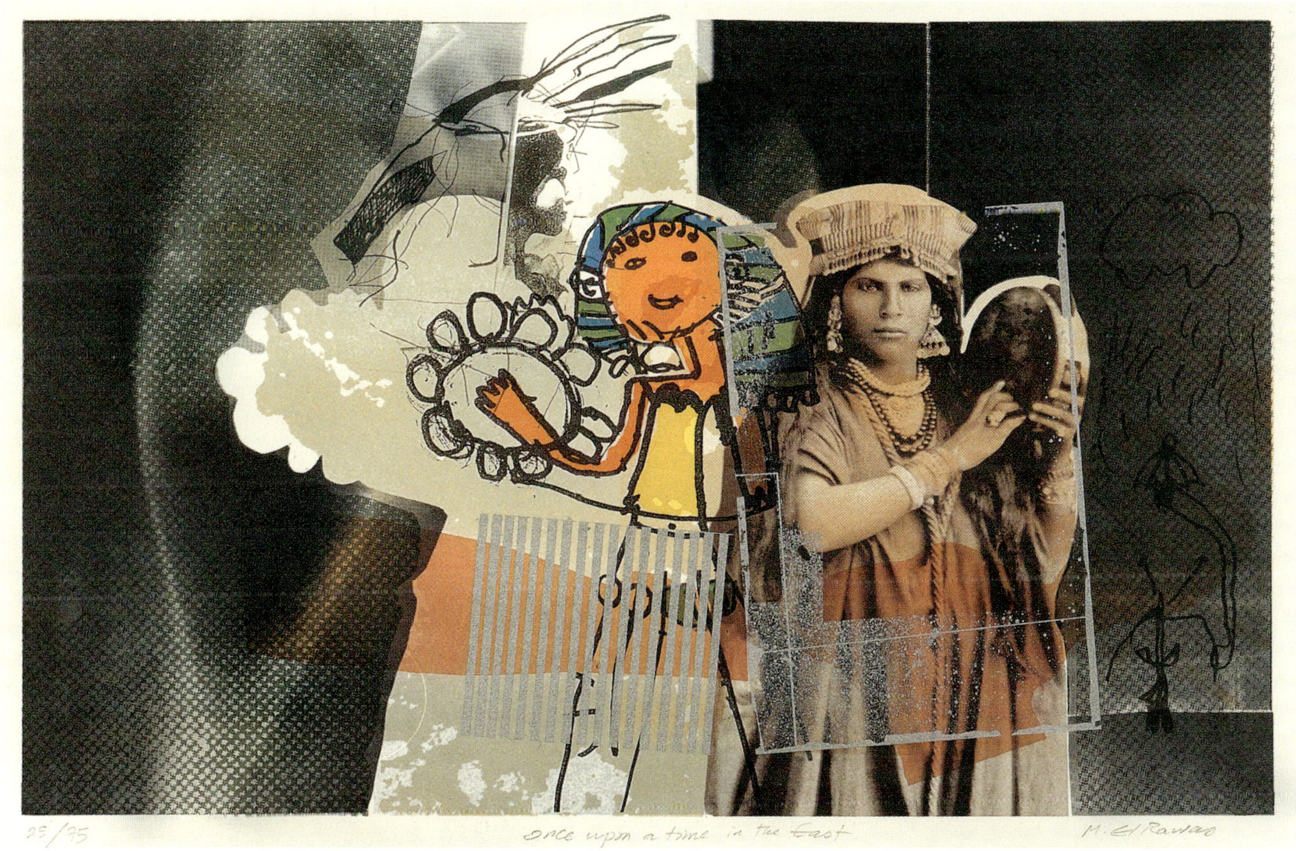

ONCE UPON A TIME IN THE EAST, 2002
Lithography
21.5 x 34 cm

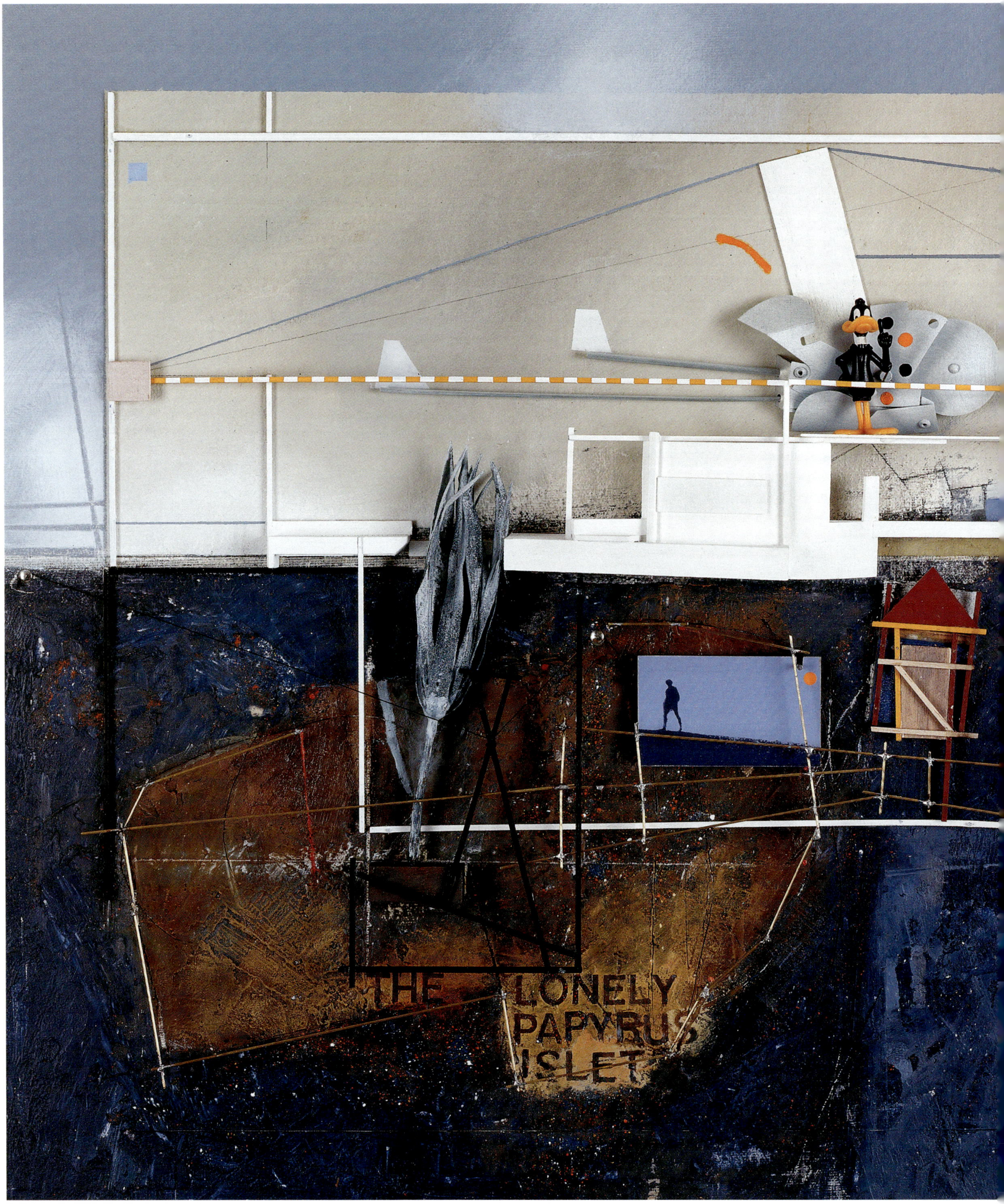
THE LONELY
PAPYRUS
ISLET

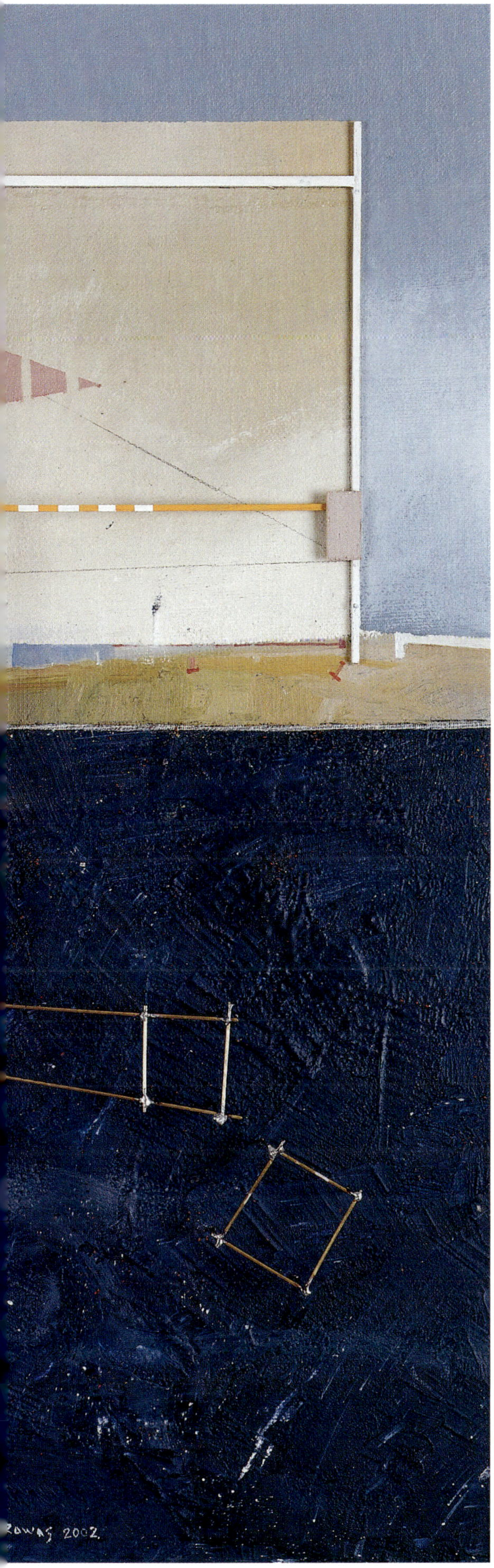

THE LONELY PAPYRUS ISLET, 2002
Mixed media and assemblage on plywood panel
60 x 50 x 4.5 cm
Collection Mr. & Mrs. H. Naser

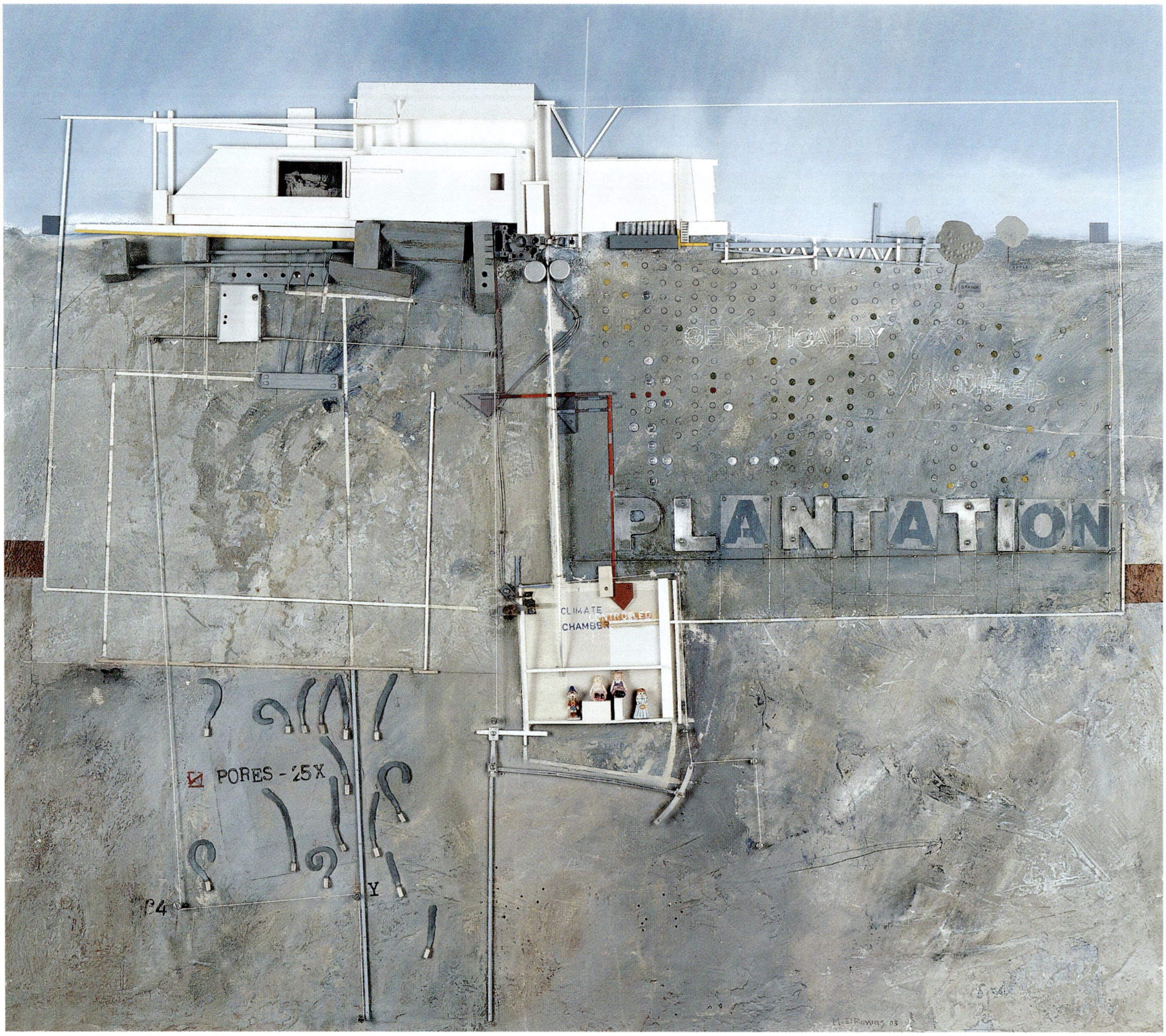

GENETICALLY MODIFIED PLANTATION, 2003
Encaustic, oil and assemblage on plywood panel
79 x 89 x 3 cm
Artist's collection

The View from the Present

Art, for me, is an esthetic visual discipline the rules of which are shared by all other design practices, whether graphics or interior design, architecture or industrial design. As all these practices share the same engagement with the visual reality around us, I am just as interested in designing a poster, a book cover, or anything else related to the field of visual esthetics.

I have learnt – and am still learning – many things in the process of creating works of art. I used to overload my work with visual details, but less so now. I am also becoming more subtle in my conceptual statements and more selective which, in fact, is harder because it means having to look only for the essence of things.

On the behavioral level, I have learnt patience and rule out setting a time limit for finishing or stopping work on a painting because in art, as in everything else in life, I believe one should avoid shortcuts. I give things the time they need to develop and mature, at the pace they need. I have always hated rushed actions. I cannot, for instance, accept having to finish ten paintings in six months in order to meet a deadline for an exhibition.

Looking back now at the work I produced during 1982 and 1983, I judge it with a critical eye, although at the time I was fully convinced of the validity of what I was doing. And, had I not accomplished the volume of work I did during this period, I would possibly not have moved on into new areas. The paintings were easy and somehow superficial; looking back, I feel that what I wanted during this period was to simply produce work for the sake of producing it. Marcel Duchamp was once asked what chess meant to him – why he spent so much time playing it. He answered that it was the only thing that could prevent him from painting. He did not want to duplicate his statement in more than one work, and by playing chess he could fill his time until he had a new vision, a new statement for a work of art which he could then create.

However, the work I produced during the early 1980s, with a few exceptions, appealed to people because of its pleasant images and simple themes – mainly women and flowers. They were pretty with no significant content. From 1984 onwards I became more selective in my painting. My works were, from that point, on the whole, more thoroughly studied, more carefully planned and structured.

Contemporary international trends in art are very much shifting away from the conception of the wall-mounted painting. Installations, happenings, earth and body art, along with computer-related and video art, are becoming the prevailing languages of artistic expression. These trends challenge the original criterion of art as being primarily 'visual' and adopt a new criterion which is that of the 'idea' or 'concept'. It is my belief that 'visual art' and 'conceptual art', while regarded as two different categories, can co-exist, and there is no reason why one should replace the other. Visual art can accommodate 'ideas' while conceptual art usually gives much less attention to the purely visual elements, prioritizing the intellect as the *raison d'être* of creative art. The distinction between form and concept in the visual arts is a hypothesis, since the artist, throughout the making of a piece of art, does not tackle each issue alone, at separate times. The strength of any visual work of art lies in the successful amalgamation of an innovative form and a brilliant conceptual level of expression. Because the principal merit of conceptual art lies in the 'idea', there is a much greater responsibility placed upon the artist to come up with original thoughts – a condition, I guess, that is not always met. Hence art appears to be moving away from architecture and design, and drawing closer to philosophy. In *Behind Appearances* C. H. Waddington writes:

The esthetic experience involves many different levels and

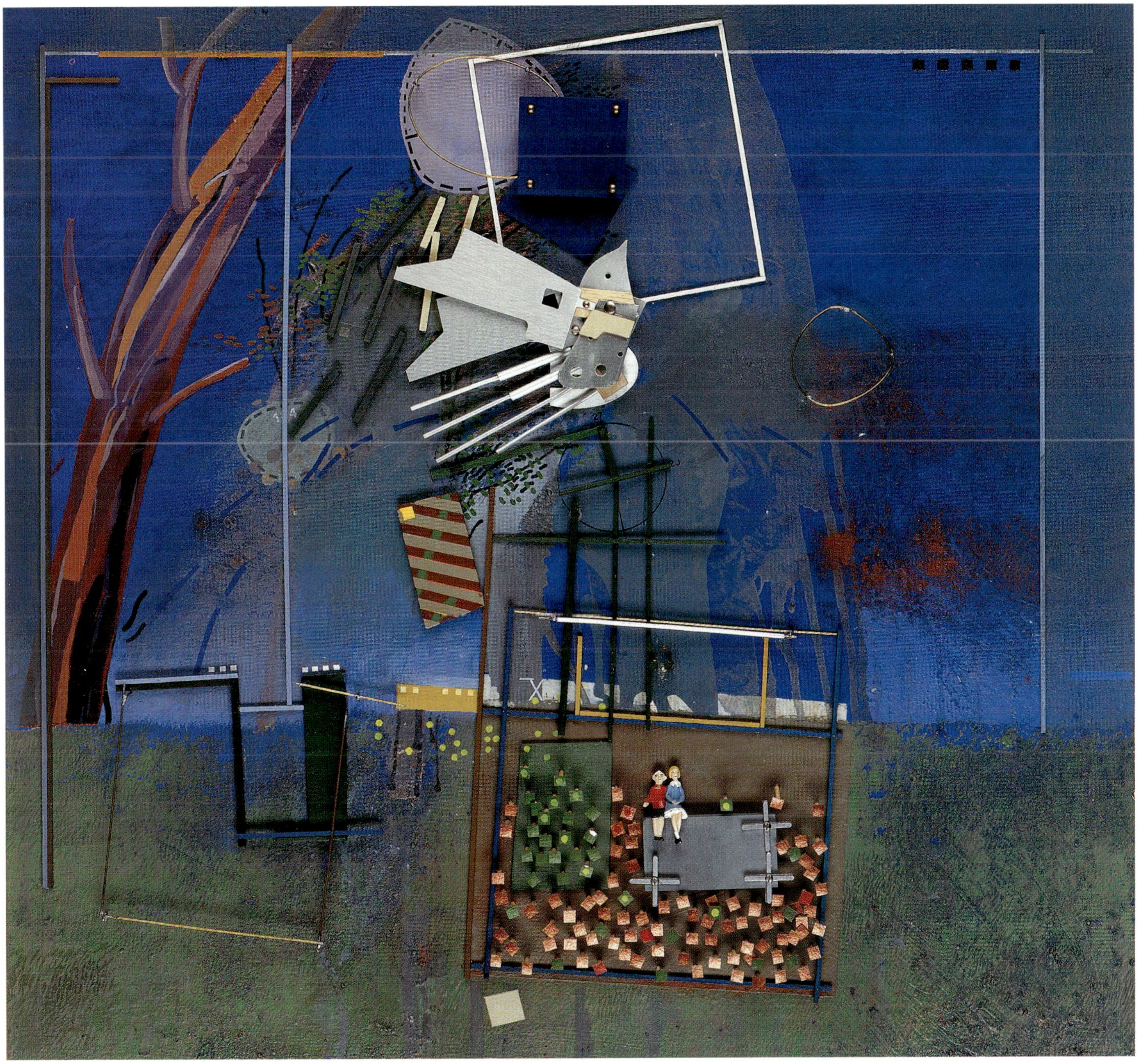

THE REBIRTH OF THE BIRD OF PARADISE, 2003
Mixed media and assemblage on plywood panel
48 x 50 x 3 cm
Collection Mr. & Mrs. M. Baadarani

> kinds of reaction to sensory stimuli, and an intellectual understanding of a work's implications for natural philosophy may be one of them.
> (*Behind Appearances*, Edinburgh University Press, 1969, Preface, p. X.)

It is this level that conceptual art is tackling, although Waddington is here referring to the effect of the science-based environment on visual art – mainly on Cubism, Futurism, the Bauhaus and Surrealism.

When questioned about the status of my art in this 'anti-form' era, my response is that visual art is richer and more comprehensive than conceptual art because it can accommodate the 'idea' whilst maintaining the visual qualities akin to a work of art. The problem is that if the 'idea' is the only criterion for a work of art – and ideas are innumerable and limitless – anything and everything could be defined as a work of art, and the term itself might come to lack any real meaning.

I would like to conclude by pointing out that I am not a mass producer. I cannot paint constantly. My academic duties often hinder me from devoting all my time to my art. If an idea occurs to me, I try to take notes and make sketches, hoping to work on them later – though I admit this is never entirely satisfactory. It is hard to recreate my initial enthusiasm just by looking at a sketch I made or notes I took. The start I make on a work of art needs to be fresh and immediate. So now I am looking forward to the day when I will be able to cut down on my teaching load and devote more time to my art. I admit that teaching, however hard, is an enjoyable experience – yet the substance of one's teaching should spring directly from the artist's personal experience and first-hand discoveries. This condition cannot, of course, be achieved without having more time in my studio to paint and explore. In art there is great fun as well as hard work, and the new and interesting directions yet to be discovered in the visual arts are endless.

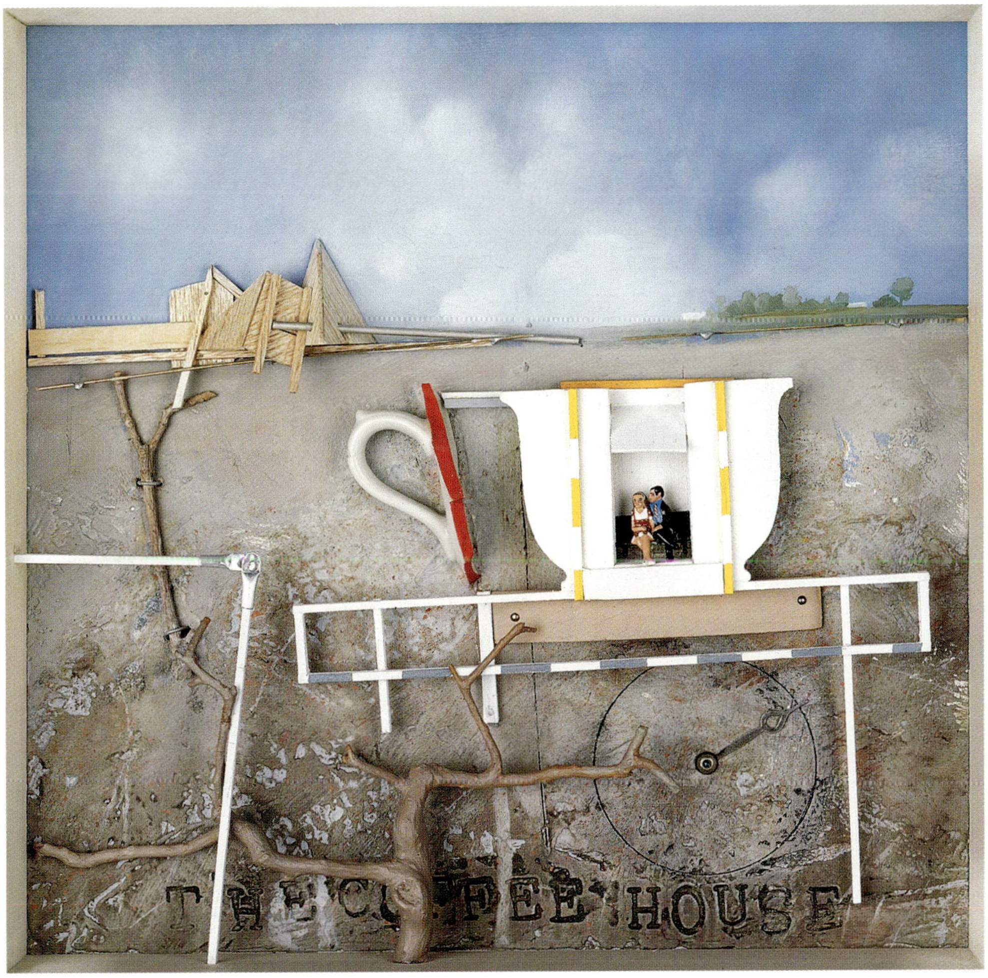

THE COFFEE HOUSE, 2004
Work in progress
Mixed media and assemblage on plywood panel
23 x 23 x 3 cm

Biography

1951	Born 26 May, Beirut, Lebanon
1971–75	Studied at the Lebanese University, Institute of Fine Arts, Beirut, Lebanon. B.A. in Painting.
1977–79	Taught at the Ecole Normale des Institutrices, Rabat, Morocco.
1979–81	Studied at The Slade School of Fine Art, University College London, London, UK. M.A. in Printmaking.
1982	Started teaching at the Lebanese University, Institute of Fine Arts.
1983–92	Served as Secretary General of the Association of Lebanese Artists.
1992–2004	Taught at the American University of Beirut, Department of Architecture and Design.

One-Man Exhibitions

1979	Rencontre Art Gallery, Beirut
1990	Kufa Gallery, London
1991	Platform Gallery, Beirut
1995	Janine Rubeiz Gallery, Beirut
1997	Janine Rubeiz Gallery Beirut
2000	Janine Rubeiz Gallery Beirut

Selected International Group Exhibitions

1980	Third World Biennale of Graphic Art, Iraqi Cultural Center, London, UK (Honorable Mention).
1981	West Surrey College of Art & Design, postgraduate students from Royal College of Art, Slade School of Fine Art and the Royal Academy Schools.
1981	Slade Folio Show, Greenwich Theatre Art Gallery, London, UK.
1982	Contemporary Arab Graphics, Graffiti Gallery, London, UK.
1983	Contemporary Arab Graphics and Works on Paper, Graffiti Gallery, London, UK.
1982 & 84	Sixth and Seventh Norwegian International Print Biennale, Fredrikstad, Norway.
1983	World Print Four, San Francisco Museum of Modern Art, USA.
1984 & 86	Eigth and Ninth British International Print Biennale, Bradford, UK.
1984	The First Contemporary Arab Art Exhibition, Centre d'Art Vivant de la Ville de Tunis, Tunisia (Third Prize).
1985	Cabo Frio International Print Biennale, Brazil (Prize of Honor).
1985 & 97	Eleventh and Nineteenth International Independent Exhibition of Prints, Kanagawa, Japan.
1985	Arab Art Biennale of Kuwait.
1986	Contemporary Arab Art, The Mall Galleries, London, UK.

1988	Contemporary Lebanese Artists, Kufa Gallery, London, UK.
1988	Presence de la Gravure, Centre d'Art Vivant de la Ville de Tunis, Tunisia.
1989	Ninth Norwegian International Print Triennale, Fredrikstad, Norway (Honorable Mention).
1989	Lebanon, The Artist's View, Concourse Gallery, Barbican Center, London, UK.
1989	Liban, Le Regard des Peintres, Institut du Monde Arabe, Paris, France.
1992 & 95	Tenth and Eleventh Norwegian International Print Triennale, Fredriskstad, Norway.
1993	First International Print Biennale, Maastricht, Holland.
1993 & 96	First and Second Egyptian International Print Triennale, Cairo, Egypt.
1993	Eigtheenth Alexandria Biennale, Egypt.
1995	Second Qarin Cultural Festival, Kuwait.
1996	Contemporary Lebanese Artists, Sharjah Art Museum, UAE.
1997	Krakow International Print Triennale, Poland.
1997	Eighth Asian Art Biennale, Dacca, Bangladesh.
1998–2000	Art Beyond Borders, UNESCO and TIMOTCA (The International Museum of Twentieth Century Art).
	– UNESCO Headquarters, Paris, France, 1998.
	– Mitra Municipal Gallery, Lisbon, Portugal, 1998.
	– Las Vegas Art Museum, USA, 2000.
1998	Nine International Graphic Artists, Trondheim Art Center, Trondheim, Norway.
2000	93e Salon de la Société Internationale des Beaux-Arts (SIBA), La Mairie de Paris, France.
2002	Southern Graphic Council Conference, New Orleans, USA.
2002	Tokyo Mini Print Biennale, Japan.
2003	First Beijing International Art Biennale, China.

Public Collections

Sursock Museum, Beirut, Lebanon.
The National Museum of Modern Art, Baghdad, Iraq.
Centre d'Art Vivant de la Ville de Tunis, Tunisia.
The British Museum, London, UK.
Trondheim Kunstmuseum, Norway.
The International Museum of Twentieth Century Art Collection.
Sharjah Museum of Contemporary Arab Art, UAE.
American University of Beirut Art Center Collection, Lebanon.
Darat al-Funun, Amman, Jordan.

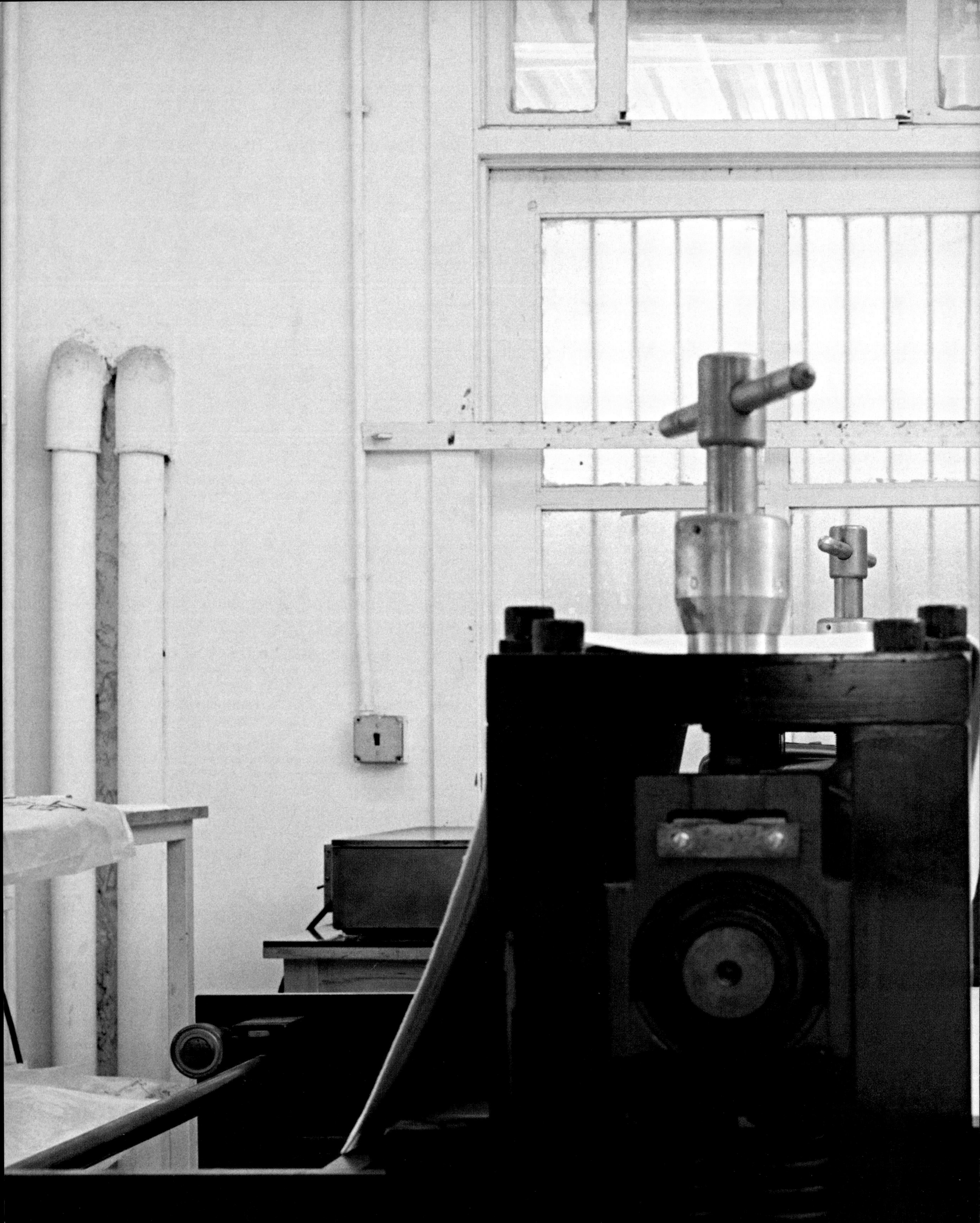

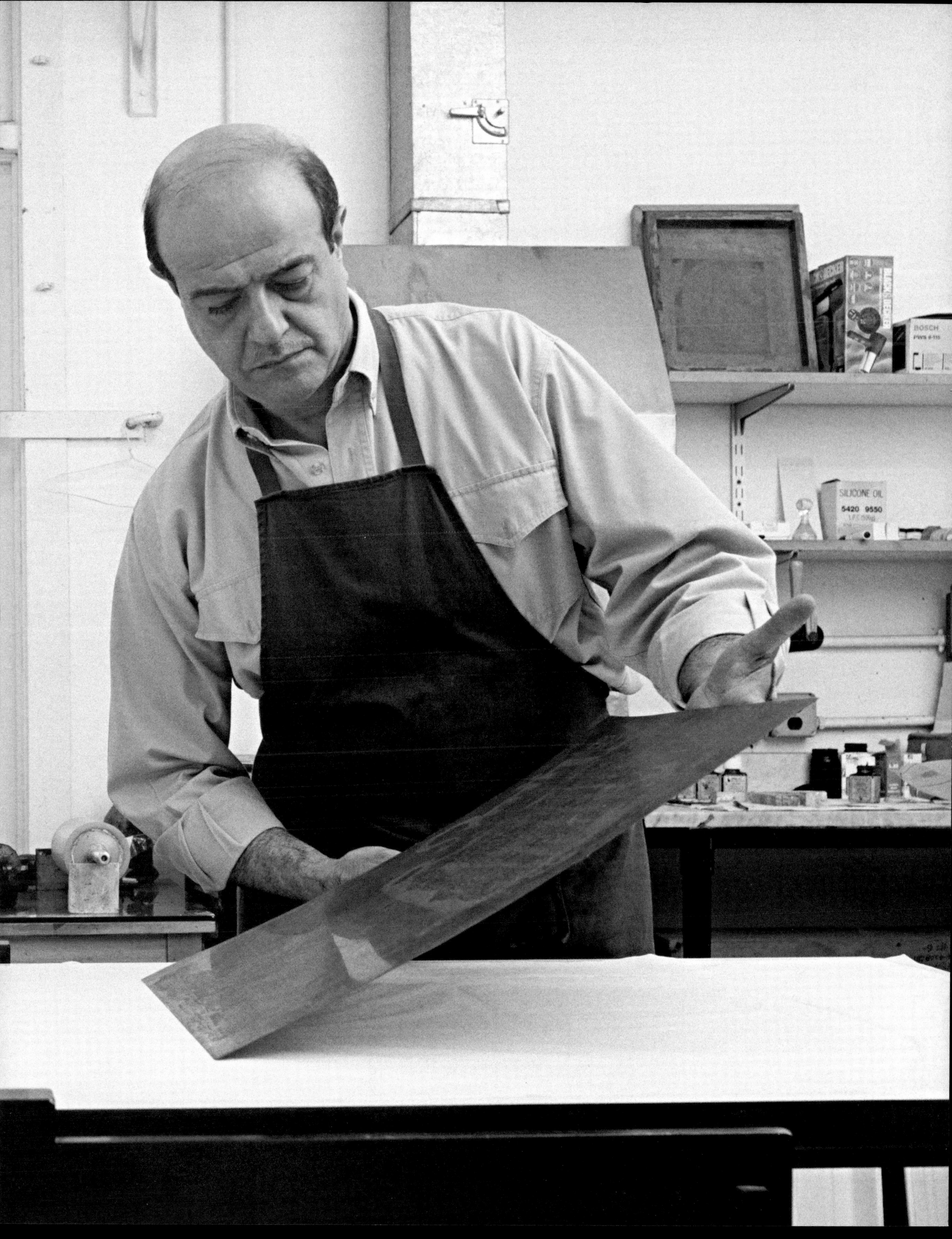
BOSCH
SILICONE OIL
5420 9550